A Concise History of Theatre

JIM PATTERSON
University of South Carolina

TIM DONAHUE

PEARSON

Boston   Columbus   Indianapolis   New York   San Francisco   Upper Saddle River
Amsterdam   Cape Town   Dubai   London   Madrid   Milan   Munich   Paris   Montréal   Toronto
Delhi   Mexico City   São Paulo   Sydney   Hong Kong   Seoul   Singapore   Taipei   Tokyo

Editor-in-Chief, Communication: Karon Bowers

Senior Acquisitions Editor: Melissa Mashburn

Editorial Assistant: Megan Hermida

Senior Marketing Manager: Blair Zoe Tuckman

Managing Editor: Linda Mihatov Behrens

Production/Project Manager: Raegan Keida Heerema

Project Coordination, Text Design, and Electronic Page Makeup: Integra

Senior Cover Design Manager: Jayne Conte

Cover Art: funkyfood London—Paul Williams

Manufacturing Manager: Mary Ann Gloriande

Printer/Binder: R.R. Donnelley/Harrisonburg

Cover Printer: R.R. Donnelley/Harrisonburg

For more information about the Penguin Academics series, please contact us by mail at Pearson Education, attn. Marketing Department, 51 Madison Avenue, 28th Floor, New York, NY 10010, or visit us online at www.pearsonhighered.com/communication.

A Concise History of Theatre is based, in part, on *The Enjoyment of Theatre*, published by Pearson.

Cover photo shows a detail of the Roman theatre at Aspendos, Turkey, built in 155 CE.

Credits and acknowledgments borrowed from other sources and reproduced, with permission, in this textbook appear on the appropriate page within text.

Library of Congress Cataloging-in-Publication Data
Patterson, Jim (Jim Aris)
   A concise history of theatre/Jim Patterson, Tim Donahue.
      p. cm.
   Includes bibliographical references and index.
   ISBN-13: 978-0-205-20982-8
   ISBN-10: 0-205-20982-3
1. Theater—History.   2. Drama—History and criticism.   I. Donahue, Tim,
[date].   II. Title.   III. Title: Concise history of theatre.
   PN2101.P38 2014
   792—dc23

                                         2012031006

36 2022

Student Edition:
ISBN 10:   0-205-20982-3
ISBN 13: 978-0-205-20982-8

Instructor Review Copy:
ISBN 10:   0-205-93004-2
ISBN 13: 978-0-205-93004-3

Contents

Preface   xvii

Introduction: The Theatre of Many Times and Places   1

THE PAST IN THE PRESENT   1

THEATRE: A DEFINITION   4

LANGUAGE AND ITS PROBLEMS   5

THEATRE-LIKE ACTIVITIES   6
Rituals   6
Paratheatrical or Theatre-Like Forms   8

HISTORICAL EVIDENCE, EMPHASIS, AND OMISSIONS   8

ORGANIZATION   9

1   Greek Theatre   11

CONTEXT   11

THEORIES OF THE ORIGINS OF THEATRE   14
Aristotle's Theory   14
The Ritual Theory   14
The Great Man Theory   14
The Storytelling Theory   15
The Dance Theory   15
Uncertainty about Origins   16

TRAITS OF GREEK THEATRE   17
Closely Associated with Greek Religion   17
Performed on Special Occasions—The Festivals   17
Choral   17
All Male   18
Competitive   18
Not a Commercial Activity   19

PLAYS AND PLAYWRIGHTS 19
Thespis 20
Aeschylus 20
Sophocles 21
Euripides 22
Aristophanes and Old Comedy 23

THEATRE BUILDINGS AND PRACTICES 24
Audience 25
Acting 25
Settings and Machinery 26
Costumes and Masks 27

THE HELLENISTIC PERIOD 28
An Altered Greek Drama and Theatres 30
Aristotle's *Poetics* 32
Mime 33

THE SHIFT TO ROME 35

CHAPTER 1 AT A GLANCE 36

HOW WE KNOW Paintings on Greek Vases 13
Menander and *The Grouch* 31
THE PLAY'S THE THING Sophocles's *Oedipus Rex*, 427 BCE 21

2   Roman Theatre, 240 BCE–550 CE   37

CONTEXT 37

ROMAN FESTIVALS AND THEATRE OF THE REPUBLIC 39

TRAGEDY AND COMEDY, MOSTLY COMEDY 39
Plautus 42
Terence 42

THREE IMPORTANT TEXTS 43
Vitruvius 43
Horace 43
Seneca 44

THEATRE BUILDINGS, SCENERY, COSTUMES, AND MASKS 45

PARATHEATRICAL ENTERTAINMENTS 46

CHRISTIAN OPPOSITION TO THEATRE   47

THE BREAKUP OF THE EMPIRE   50

THE EASTERN (BYZANTINE) EMPIRE AND THEATRE   51

CHAPTER 2 AT A GLANCE   53

HOW WE KNOW   Theatre in an Ordinary Roman Town   48

THE PLAY'S THE THING   Plautus's *The Menaechmi*   41

3   Early Theatre of Asia, 200 BCE–1800 CE   54

CONTEXT   54

INDIA   56
The *Natyasastra*   57
Indian Folk Theatre Traditions   58

CHINA   60
Paratheatrical Beginnings   61
Kunqu Opera   61

JAPAN   63
Paratheatrical Beginnings   63
Noh Drama   65
Kabuki   67

CHAPTER 3 AT A GLANCE   70

HOW WE KNOW   *Shakuntala*'s First Translation   60

THE PLAY'S THE THING   *Shakuntala*   59

Li Xingdao's *Chalk Circle*   62

The Peony Pavilion   64

4   The European Middle Ages   71

CONTEXT   71

EARLY MEDIEVAL DRAMA THEATRE: 476–1200   73
Hroswitha in Germany and Bishop Ethelwold in England   74

PRODUCTION INSIDE THE CHURCH   77

LATER MEDIEVAL CULTURE AND THEATRE, C. 1200–1550   77

RELIGIOUS DRAMA OUTSIDE THE CHURCH   79

STAGING RELIGIOUS PLAYS OUTSIDE THE CHURCH   83
Fixed and Movable Staging   84
Costumes   89
Audiences   90

SECULAR DRAMA   90
Production of Secular Plays   91

THE END OF MEDIEVAL RELIGIOUS THEATRE:
THE TRANSFORMATION OF MEDIEVAL
SECULAR THEATRE   92

CHAPTER 4 AT A GLANCE   93

HOW WE KNOW   Bishop Ethelwold's Stage Directions for the *Quem Quareritis* Trope   75

Oberammergau Passion Play through the Years   85

Pageant Wagons   88

THE PLAY'S THE THING   *The Second Shepherd's Play*, Anonymous   81

Everyman, Anonymous, c. 1490   82

5   The Italian Renaissance   94

CONTEXT   94
Humanism   95
Secularism   95
Reformation   95
A Widening World   95
The Fall of Constantinople   96
The Printing Press   97
The Arts and Theatre   97

THEORY: NEOCLASSICISM   97
Verisimilitude   98
Purity of Genres   99
The Three Unities   99

The Five-Act Form   99
A Twofold Purpose: To Teach and to Please   99

PRACTICE: ITALIAN RENAISSANCE DRAMA   100
Erudite Drama   100

ILLUSIONISM   101
Vitruvius in the Renaissance   102
Perspective   102

RENAISSANCE THEATRE STRUCTURES   103
Teatro Olimpico   103
Sabbioneta Theatre   105
Teatro Farnese   105

STAGE SETTINGS FOR ILLUSIONISTIC THEATRE   107
Movable Scenery   109

CONTRADICTION IN MAINSTREAM THEATRE   110

AN ALTERNATIVE THEATRE: COMMEDIA
DELL'ARTE   110
Commedia Characters   112
Commedia's Influence   114
Commedia's Roots   115

ITALY: ECLIPSE   115

CHAPTER 5 AT A GLANCE   116

HOW WE KNOW   Commedia Scenarios   111

6   The Golden Ages of England and Spain   117

CONTEXT   117

ENGLAND AND THE GOLDEN AGE   118
Theatre Architecture   118
Public Theatres   119
Private Theatres   124
Audiences   124
Production Practices   125
Actors and Acting   125
Acting Companies   126
Tudor Plays and Playwrights   127

Stuart Plays and Playwrights   130

Shakespeare's Legacy   131

COURT MASQUES AND NEW CONVENTIONS: INIGO JONES   132

Masque Production Practices   134

Significance   135

THE CLOSING OF ENGLISH THEATRES   135

SPAIN IN THE GOLDEN AGE   135

Women as Audience and as Actors   136

Spanish Public Theatres   136

The *Corral del Principe*   136

Plays and Playwrights   138

CHAPTER 6 AT A GLANCE   141

HOW WE KNOW   The Swan Drawing   120

Four Public Theatres   122

Philip Henslowe's Inventory   126

THE PLAY'S THE THING   Calderón de la Barca's *Life Is a Dream*, 1635   139

7   Neoclassicism: Triumph and Decline in France and England   142

CONTEXT   142

FRENCH THEATRE THROUGH ITS GOLDEN AGE   143

Neoclassicism: Corneille and *Le Cid*   144

Italianate Staging: Public versus Court Theatres   146

The Sun King and the Golden Age   146

Playwrights   147

Theatre Companies   150

Sentimentalism   151

Changes in Production Practices   151

Changes in Performance Practices   152

ENGLISH RESTORATION THEATRE (1660–C. 1750)   154

English Public Theatre   154

Theatre Architecture   154

Restoration Drama   155

Comedy of Manners   156
Comedy of Intrigue   157
Tragedy   157
Audiences   158
Acting Companies and Actors   158

THE RISE OF SENTIMENTALISM: 1700—1750   160
Sentimental Comedy   160
Serious Plays: Domestic Tragedy   161
Minor Forms   161
Changes in Production and Performance Practices   162

CHAPTER 7 AT A GLANCE   164

HOW WE KNOW   A Forgotten Theatre Recovered   153

THE PLAY'S THE THING   Jean Racine's *Phèdre*, 1677   148

Molière's *Tartuffe*, 1669   149

8   Melodrama and the Rise of Commercialism, 1750–1900   165

CONTEXT   165

THEATRE BECOMES COMMERCIAL   166

THEATRE IN FOUR COUNTRIES, C. 1700–C. 1850   167
Germany   167
England and France   168
America   168

COMMERCIAL THEATRE DEVELOPS   169

ACTORS AND ACTOR-MANAGERS   170
David Garrick   170
Edmund Kean   171
Charles Macready   171
Ellen Terry   172

FROM ACTOR-MANAGER TO PRODUCER   173
The Star System   173
Theatrical Syndicate in the United States   175

DRAMA IN THE COMMERCIAL THEATRE   175
Shifts in Western Drama after c. 1750   177

MELODRAMA IN THE COMMERCIAL THEATRE   178
Music   178
A Simplified Moral Universe   179
Spectacle   179
Realistic Melodrama after c. 1850   180
The Most Important Melodrama in English: *Uncle Tom's Cabin*   181
Playwrights of Melodrama   182
Melodrama after 1900   183

COMEDY IN THE COMMERCIAL THEATRE   184
Sheridan and Goldsmith: English Comic Playwrights,   184
France and the Well-Made Play Beginning in 1815   186
Oscar Wilde   186

REACTIONS TO THE COMMERCIAL THEATRE   188

CHAPTER 8 AT A GLANCE   189

HOW WE KNOW   Early Theatre Photography   187

THE PLAY'S THE THING   Augustin Daly's *Under the Gaslight*, 1867   176

9   Romanticism and Realism, 1750–1900   190

CONTEXT   190
A Cluster of Ideas and Impulses   191

ROMANTICISM IN THE THEATRE   193
Romantics Revive Shakespeare   194

ROMANTICISM IN GERMANY, ENGLAND, AND FRANCE   194
Germany   195
England   196
France   196

ROMANTICISM DWINDLES   197

AN AFTERSHOCK: RICHARD WAGNER, A ROMANTIC ARTIST,
FLOURISHING 1842–1882   198
Unity through the Master Artwork   198
The Separated Audience   198

REFORM AFTER ROMANTICISM: REALISM AND
NATURALISM, FROM C. 1850   199

IMPORTANT LEADERS OF REALISM AND
NATURALISM   200

    Georg II, Duke of Saxe-Meiningen   201

    André Antoine and the *Thèâtre-Libre*   203

    The Free Stage in Germany; The Independent
      Stage in Britain   205

    Konstantin Stanislavski and the Moscow
      Art Theatre   205

PLAYS AND PLAYWRIGHTS OF REALISM   207

    Ibsen   207

    Chekhov   207

    Naturalistic Playwrights: Hauptmann
      and Gorky   209

SUCCESS AND REFORM   209

CHAPTER 9 AT A GLANCE   211

THE PLAY'S THE THING   Henrik Ibsen's *A Doll's
      House*, 1879   208

10   Theatre in Africa   212

CONTEXT   212

    Northern Africa   212

    Sub-Saharan Africa   213

    Colonialism in the Country of South Africa   215

THEATRE IN NORTHERN AFRICA   216

THEATRE IN SUB-SAHARAN AFRICA   217

    Yoruba Performance   219

    Nigerian Playwright Wole Soyinka   220

    South African Playwright Athol Fugard   223

    Theatre for Development   224

HOW WE KNOW   Theatre in Ancient Egypt   226

THE PLAY'S THE THING   Wole Soyinka, *Death and the King's
      Horseman*, 1976   221

11 Reactions to Commercialism, 1900–1950   228

CONTEXT   228

REVOLTS AGAINST COMMERCIALISM   229
   Naturalism   231
   Symbolism   231
   Surrealism   231
   Expressionism   232
   Cubism   232
   Constructivism   232
   Epic Theatre   232
   Absurdism   232
   Postmodernism   233

TWO INFLUENTIAL THEORISTS AGAINST COMMERCIALISM   233
   Bertolt Brecht and Epic Theatre   233
   Antonin Artaud and the Theatre of Cruelty   236

IMPORTANT US THEATRE GROUPS   238
   The Theatre Guild   238
   The Group Theatre   238
   The Federal Theatre Project   239

THE ART THEATRE MOVEMENT   241
   Art Theatre Pioneers in Europe   241
   Influential Nonrealistic Stage Designers   243
   The Art Theatre in the United States   243

PLAYWRIGHTS: SOMETIMES COMMERCIAL, SOMETIMES NOT   245
   Eugene O'Neill   245
   Elmer Rice: Expressionism on Broadway   247
   Thornton Wilder   247
   Luigi Pirandello   248
   Federico García Lorca   249
   Comedy in the Commercial Theatre   249
   George S. Kaufman   250
   George Bernard Shaw   250
   Noel Coward   250

THEATRE UNDER OCCUPATION AND TOTALITARIANISM   252

COMMERCIAL THEATRE DECLINES   252

CHAPTER 11 AT A GLANCE   255

THE PLAY'S THE THING   Antonin Artaud's *Jet of Blood*, 1924   235

Eugene O'Neill's *Long Day's Journey into Night*, Produced 1956   246

12   Musical Theatre   256

CONTEXT   256

THE US MUSICAL EMERGES   258

Composers   259
Lyricists   260
The Integrated Musical   262
Gender and Race and the US Musical   264

SONG FORMS   266

MUSICALS SINCE 1950   268

Concept Musicals   269
Stephen Sondheim: Lyricist and Composer   270
Musicals and Popular Songs   271
The Sung-Through Musical   271
Jukebox Musicals   273
Disney Recycles and Musical Revivals   275

CHAPTER 12 AT A GLANCE   277

HOW WE KNOW   Preserving Musicals   267

THE PLAY'S THE THING   *Girl Crazy*, 1930   263

13   Eclecticism: US Theatre from 1950   278

CONTEXT   278

The Age of Anxiety   278
Societal Changes   279
Technology   280
The Rise of Terrorism   280

THEATRE BECOMES ECLECTIC: AN OVERVIEW   281

PROFESSIONAL THEATRE 283
Commercial Theatre 283
Not-for-Profit Theatre 286

PLAYS AND PLAYWRIGHTS SINCE 1950 288
Tennessee Williams 288
Arthur Miller 289
Edward Albee 290
Other US Plays and Playwrights 291
Imported Plays 292
Comedy, Mostly Neil Simon 293
The Decline of the Nonmusical Play on Broadway 294

THE POLITICAL AVANT-GARDE IN THEATRE 294
The Political Avant-Garde in Miniature: The Living Theatre 295

THE ARTISTIC AVANT-GARDE IN THEATRE 297
The Artistic Avant-Garde in Miniature: Joseph Chaikin
and the Open Theatre 297

THE AVANT-GARDE FADES 298

IDENTITY THEATRE EMERGES 299
Identity Theatre for African Americans 300
Identity Theatre for Women 304
Identity Theatre for Gays and Lesbians 307
Identity Theatre for Latinos/Latinas 310
Identity Theatre into the Mainstream: Two Examples 311

ABSURDISM, PERFORMANCE ART, AND POSTMODERNISM 312
Absurdism 312
Performance Art 313
Postmodernism 314

THEATRICAL RESPONSES TO 9/11 AND NEW WARS 315
Metamorphoses: New York 316
Guantánamo: British 316
The Lysistrata Project: International 316
Black Watch: Scotland 317
All My Sons: New York 317

THE CULTURAL DISPLACEMENT OF THEATRE 317

HOW WE KNOW Theatre on Film and Tape Archive 292

THE PLAY'S THE THING   Tennessee Williams's *A Streetcar Named Desire*, 1947   289

August Wilson's Century of African American Life   301

Tyler Perry and the Chitlin' Circuit   303

Paula Vogel's *The Baltimore Waltz*, 1992   308

14   European Theatre after 1950   319

CONTEXT   319

GERMANY   320
   Important German Playwrights   321

GREAT BRITAIN   324
   The Royal Shakespeare Company and the Royal National Theatre   325
   British Playwrights   326

FRANCE   330
   French Playwrights   332

ITALY   334

POLAND   335

EUROPEAN THEATRE AFTER WORLD WAR II HAD WIDE IMPACT   337

THE PLAY'S THE THING   Caryl Churchill's *Top Girls*, 1982   331

15   Theatre in Asia from 1800   338

CONTEXT   338

THEATRE IN INDIA SINCE CA. 1800   340
   Western-Style Theatre Emerges   340

CHINESE THEATRE AFTER 1790   342
   Beijing Opera   342
   Spoken Drama   343
   Theatre in Communist China   343

LATER JAPANESE THEATRE   346
   Butoh: Dance, Theatre, or What?   347
   Kabuki Continues   347

WHY ASIAN THEATRE IS OFTEN WESTERN FOCUSED   347

THE PLAY'S THE THING   Tagore's *The Post Office*, 1912   341

16   Globalization of Theatre   349

CONTEXT   349

MUSICALS IN ASIA   351

OTHER INTERNATIONAL MUSICAL SUCCESSES   353

TECHNIQUES AND STYLES TRAVEL THE WORLD   355

NON-EUROPEAN THEATRE IN WESTERN COUNTRIES   359

GLOBAL SHAKESPEARE   360
   A Safe Way to Dissent   361
   Theme-Park Shakespeare   362

BELARUS FREE THEATRE   363

IS GLOBALIZATION THEATRE'S DESTINY?   364

Glossary   365
Index   375
Photo Credits   381

Preface

A Concise History of Theatre provides a selective, culturally diverse introduction to the world's most in-fluential theatrical and dramatic traditions. The primary focus of this new book is to place theatre in the society that spawned it. Although names and dates are important, these facts are presented as less important than the significance of these names and dates in the culture of a particular society. *A Concise History of Theatre* is designed in full color to help students understand the events, places, and people that have populated theatre during the past three millennia. The book's clear and logical presentation of material, together with the carefully chosen illustrations, will appeal to students. The captions for each image are presented as teaching tools that clarify and enrich the text.

Special Features

Two sidebars supplement most chapters:

`The Play's the Thing` centers on the story of a significant play and why it is important, and offers some biographical information about the playwright. This feature is intended to give students a general sense of a play; it is not intended as a substitute for reading a particular play that the instructor may assign as collateral reading. This feature can, however, introduce a student to the theatre literature of specific eras.

`How We Know` concentrates on original documents and artifacts with commentary to describe how we know—or do *not* know—about theatre history. This will introduce students to the work of theatre his-torians and to the sometimes provisional nature of the conclusions drawn from fragmentary evidence. These sidebars are not intended to teach facts about theatre history as much as to teach that theatre history is a living discipline that has changed through time. The implication is that it will continue to change as new evidence surfaces and new theories are posited and supported by evidence.

A Concise History of Theatre contains five additional teaching features to help students master the material:

- **Learning Objectives** at the beginning of each chapter alert students to what is important for them to take away from reading each chapter.

- **Key Terms** at the conclusion of each chapter alert students to significant, and probably testable, concepts. These terms can also serve as a brief review. For some foreign key terms, pronuncia-tion guides are provided. These are meant to be general US pronunciations, not authentic foreign pronunciations.

- **Glossary** at the end of the text includes definitions of all key terms with notation of the page on which the term first appears.

- **Timelines** for most chapters, titled "Chapter at a Glance," offer a quick view of important events along a vertical continuum to aid understanding of theatre chronology. The left col-umn of the timeline is a context section offering a small number of other historical events of the period covered, which should connect theatre history to other commonly taught historical dates.

- **Illustrations and photographs** help students to visualize important places and events. These carefully chosen illustrations, engravings, and photographs present visual records of theatre over its 2,500-year history. *A Concise History of Theatre* is profusely illustrated.

Teaching Resources for Instructors

Instructors who use *A Concise History of Theatre* will have access to three ancillary features designed to help students master the intricacies of a serious inquiry into theatre's history. First a chapter-by-chapter PowerPoint™ presentation that includes illustrations found in the text plus additional visual material not included in the text. Captions link the new and old images. This feature will help instructors build compelling visual classroom presentations.

A second resource is an *Instructor's Manual* that provides for each chapter suggestions for lectures and questions for classroom discussion.

The *Test Bank* resource presents the instructor with chapter-by-chapter test questions in three formats: True/False, Multiple Choice, and discussion. Correct answers are provided for the first two types of questions.

The three resources are available electronically via Pearson's Instructor's Resource Center at www.pearsonhighered.com/irc. (Instructors should contact their local Pearson representative for access.)

Acknowledgments

We would like to thank reviewers who helped us with the development of this project, including:

Cheryl Black, University of Missouri
Mary English, Montclair State University
Philip G. Hill, Furman University
Christina Gutierrez, University of Texas at Austin

Jane Peterson, Montclair State University
Kathleen Sills, Merrimack College
Stephen Taft, University of Northern Iowa
E.J. Westlake, University of Michigan

Introduction: The Theatre of Many Times and Places

A Concise History of Theatre offers a broad but compact sweep of the global history of theatre. Lovers of theatre—like all lovers—want deeper, more meaningful engagement with what they love. Studying theatre history is one approach to an enhanced relationship with the art of theatre. This book is a kind of backstage tour, moving through time and geography. It cannot recreate the performances of the past, but it describes the techniques, the forms, the participants, the sponsors, and some of the cultural influences.

The Past in the Present

In the summer of 2009, the Royal National Theatre (NT), a highly regarded government-supported theatre, presented Jean Racine's *Phèdre* at its theatre complex in London. The script for this production was a recent English language adaptation of the French verse play written by Jean Racine in 1677. Based on ancient Greek mythology, the story of the play in its bare bones is racy enough for a contemporary television soap opera or a confessional daytime

1

THE ROYAL NATIONAL THEATRE

Helen Mirren and Dominic Cooper as Phèdre and Hippolytus in the Royal National Theatre's production, in English, of Racine's *Phèdre*. Here both characters have a distinctly current look: Cooper wears a sleeveless undershirt and fatigue boots and sports a fashionable five o'clock shadow whereas Mirren seems to wear a "no-period" gown. The difference in the characters' ages is clear through casting.

talk show: While her royal husband is gone, Phèdre confesses that she feels a passionate love for her stepson, Hippolyte. When the husband returns, Phèdre, afraid of exposure, tells him that Hippolyte raped her. The aftermath is deadly for almost all involved.

The Greek playwright Euripides wrote a play titled *Hippolytus* in 428 BCE that was based on the Greek myth. The Roman playwright Seneca adapted Euripides's play into a longer, literary tragedy sometime in the first century CE, titled *Phaedra*. Racine's *Phèdre* comes from the period of French neoclassicism; he was one of its foremost practitioners. The twentieth-century US playwright Eugene O'Neill used the story of Phaedra for his play *Desire under the Elms* (1925), which he set in New England before the Civil War. Long before the NT staged its adaptation of Racine's version then, the story of Phaedra repeatedly interested theatre artists.

The title character at the NT was played by Helen Mirren, an internationally acclaimed actor. In addition to a lifetime of stage work, Mirren has appeared in film and on television. She has won an Academy Award, four Screen Actors Guild Awards, four British Academy of Film and Television Arts awards, three Golden Globes, and four Emmy Awards. The role of Phèdre requires an actress of such stature and proven magnetism.

Phèdre was directed by Nicholas Hytner, an English director of stage and film productions who is also NT's artistic director. His productions of the musicals *Miss Saigon* and *Carousel* had long commercial runs in London, New York, and many other places throughout the world. His worldwide success with two plays he directed on the NT stages led to his directing the stories on film to similar acclaim, namely *The Madness of King George* and *The History Boys*.

The NT production of *Phèdre* with Mirren was later presented for two performances at the outdoor theatre in Epidaurus, Greece, as part of the Athens and Epidaurus Festival, also a government-supported cultural activity. The Epidaurus theatre structure dates from the fourth century BCE and in its current configuration seats about fifteen thousand people.

This revival of *Phèdre* is compelling evidence of the lasting power of theatre through millennia. A French play from the late 1600s based on ancient Greek mythology, interpreted through Euripides and Seneca, becomes a much-admired international theatre event. This anecdote from recent theatre history exemplifies several basic truths of theatre art as we understand it. Theatre involves the seemingly eternal appeal of live actors in front of a live audience; not-for-profit and government-supported theatres are crucial to the cultural life of the West today; theatre stories provoke interest the world over; and plays and stories from other eras and languages return again and again to thrill and chill audiences today, not as museum pieces but as living drama. But there is one more pertinent detail about this single production and the power of theatre.

The NT expanded the reach of *Phèdre* beyond London and Greece. On June 25, 2009, with an audience present, *Phèdre* was broadcast live, from the NT stage, unedited, through high-definition satellite transmission to eighty theatres around the world. Over the next few days, an additional two hundred locations showed the unedited production. The project was a huge success, seen by twenty-eight thousand people in the first twenty-four hours and ultimately by forty-eight thousand people worldwide.

Liz Lauren

DESIRE UNDER THE ELMS
Eugene O'Neil based his play *Desire under the Elms* on the Phaedra myth. Here, a moment from the 2009 Broadway production, first mounted in Chicago by the Goodman Theatre, featuring Carla Gugino as the Phaedra character and Pablo Schreiber as the Hippolytus character.

The broadcast version of *Phèdre* is an unusual kind of theatre; although mediated by technology, it still has almost all of the elements of theatre as theatre will be defined shortly. This worldwide event demonstrates the appeal of lasting plays, great acting, and contemporary stage productions.

The account of one extraordinary production sets the stage for a look at the many reasons to study theatre history. In part, it's important to understand how theatre relates to the larger culture—how forces for change work in theatre and beyond it. The history of theatre reveals how people and theatre practices today differ from—and how they resemble—the peoples and practices of other times and places. Finally, knowing theatre history enhances the experience of today's theatre, both for audience members and for theatre practitioners.

Theatre: A Definition

Theatre is entertainment and art. In this era it can also be a business, either a commercial profit-making business or a not-for-profit business serving the public interest. There is amateur theatre, too, which is organized for the love of it. Theatre is one medium of many media, one of several performing arts, and one approach to storytelling. Because there are other events that share some of the properties of theatre, a definition is *essential*.

First the term *theatre* is the art itself, a branch of the performing arts that also include music and dance. Additionally, the word *theatre* denotes the playscript performed, (*Phèdre*), the building or space where the art is performed (Royal National Theatre), and even the economic organization of its presenters (Athens and Epidaurus Festival). Although *A Concise History of Theatre* will consider theatre buildings, plays, musicals, and the organization of theatre companies, the focus will be on the history of theatre as a performing art. Theatre can be distinguished from other theatre-like—or paratheatrical—activities by these qualities:

- Theatre has performers, often called *actors*, who impersonate characters who are different than themselves.
- Theatre has a structure, which usually means a theatre performance tells a story. Storytelling is part of the heritage of every world culture. Storytelling is generally a third-person account and theatre is generally first person.
- Theatre is ephemeral. It is performed by live actors in front of a live audience whose members have gathered for the performance. No performance is exactly identical to the one that preceded it or follows it, even if the same play has been performing in the same theatre for years.
- Theatre is immediate for the same reason that it is ephemeral. It is always in the present. Actors and audiences share both space and time.
- Theatre is usually collaborative. It usually takes many individuals—visual artists, actors, dancers, and musicians—to make theatre happen, usually in a special space made for theatre performances.

Although this definition could include opera and some ballet, these performing arts are not covered in *A Concise History of Theatre*. In Western culture, opera and ballet have their own histories and their own books tell them.

Some theatre scholars will find the definition presented here too limited, and they may be right. In fact, there remains much professorial discussion about problems in defining theatre, as there is discussion about defining many cultural terms. Those rich discussions and the many broader definitions of theatre are for more advanced, more encyclopedic books on theatre history and theory than this concise textbook designed for undergraduates.

Language and Its Problems

The history of the word *theatre* presents some problems when considering forms of performance that do not spring from Europe. *Theatre* is from the Greek *theatron*, meaning "a place to see." From the Greeks, the word moved to many European languages, often sounding much the same: *teatro*, *teater*, *teatteri*, and *teātris*. Ancient Greek is also the source for the related English words *drama*, *tragedy*, and *comedy*. When the word *theatre* is applied to cultures other than Western cultures, those cultures' indigenous practices are overlaid with a clearly Western term that has had an interrupted but fairly consistent use and meaning in Europe and the rest of the West for millennia. Often, the word *theatre* is not a perfect fit when applied to some performing arts that are not inheritors of the ancient Greeks.

An alternative is to declare that these cultures did not have theatre, for the most part, until contact with the West. Such a fiat ignores too much in too much art. Thus, *A Concise History of Theatre* applies the Western definition of theatre to Western culture fairly rigorously but loosens the definition when applied to other cultures, understanding that there is much to learn from other cultures' theatre and theatre-like practices

Were this account of theatre history written by a scholar of Asia or Africa, this problem of definition would likely be reversed. Western distinctions among theatre, dance, and opera might be seen as arbitrary and limiting, restricting the development and understanding of complex artistic forms.

The distinction between Western theatre and global theatre has become less acute during the late twentieth and the twenty-first centuries. Asian and African theatre has been reshaped by a tsunami of Western culture of all sorts—mostly film and television, but also theatre. Asian and African cultures have, to varying extents, experimented with or adopted and adapted Western **theatrical**

CHURCH SERVICES ARE NOT THEATRE

Church services resemble theatre with a congregation like an audience, celebrants like actors, and the dias like a stage, but church services are more appropriately called ritual.

styles. The musical in particular, generally regarded as a genre that originated in the United States, is cropping up in every culture that has enough wealth to support its significant financial costs. Western theatre is adopting some genres and techniques of Asian and African theatre. The last chapter on globalization focuses on this phenomenon.

Theatre-Like Activities

Christian church services can resemble theatre, with the congregation in pews replacing the audience, the raised dais a kind of stage, the minister with attendants and choir as the performing company, and an altar and religious art for scenery. But church services are not theatre nor are other religious rituals. A football game is an entertainment with an audience and it is sometimes a big-money business, but it is not theatre-in-the-round. Football players may project somewhat manufactured personas for the camera and microphone, but they do not impersonate different characters.

Rituals

In many cultures, various **rituals**, ceremonies, and performances share elements that we now associate with theatre: masks, costumes, dance and music, and some sort of text. Rituals also have major recurring elements that are not generally shared with those of theatre. They include:

- **Communal bonding of all those present.** In ritual, the identifying element is "community." In Western theatre, the identifying element is "art."

- **No clear separation of audience and performer.** In ritual, those in attendance sometimes participate in the activities. In Western theatre, audiences typically watch and listen to activities performed by others.

- **Diffused focus.** Rituals may take place over several miles of countryside, without an audience and with some people able to catch only occasional glimpses of the activities. Western theatre typically takes place in one place arranged so that the audience's attention is focused on the event.

- **Little or no "scenery" (visual clues to location).** Rituals often make no attempt to recreate a location different than the worship location of the event. Western theatre typically strives to represent and identify some place other than the theatre itself.

- **Purposes that are functional and cultural.** Most importantly, ritual aims to do things like heal, honor, or mourn. Some rituals perform specific acts within the belief system. Western theatre typically aims to do things of a very different sort, such as teach, entertain, or make money.

Note that theatre sometimes has a purpose but is not functional. That is, theatre may want to teach or proselytize, change attitudes, or move people to action. Though theatre may wish to do these things, performance only rarely accomplishes this aim. In fact, when theatre attendance is voluntary and costly, it rarely does these things. Often only people already sharing the purposes of a given playwright or production will actually attend the show.

By contrast, ritual is often functional. Christian baptism, for example, is a prerequisite for entering heaven after death for many sects. In many cultures, burial rites prepare the deceased for a better life after death. Ritual doesn't just desire and persuade when it is functional, the ritual actually accomplishes something. For nonbelievers, the rites can seem more expressive than functional, but for believers the rituals do things.

THEATRE? THEATRICAL? PARATHEATRICAL?
Actors? Perhaps. *Costumes?* Yes. *Makeup?* Yes. *Theatrical?* Yes. *Paratheatrical?* Yes. But is it "theatre" as defined in this introduction? Probably not. In Chicago, a street performer in a strange costume holding an umbrella lets his audience know that he charges two dollars if his picture is taken. The seated couple covered in adobe-like mud slowly change positions when they hear coins dropping in their metal pot. Although each of these figures may have a hidden story, they do not seem to operate in some kind of play-like structure.

Paratheatrical or Theatre-Like Forms

Indigenous forms that are clearly related to theatre have received much attention from scholars. Important and representative among such forms include the following:

- **Storytelling:** Often with music and mime.
- **Cultural transmission:** The passing on of knowledge in cultures without writing. This varies enormously, from simple but expert pantomime of birds and animals to elaborate instruction in traditions through pantomime, song, and dance.
- **Dance.**
- **Puppet theatre**.

(Some commentators would add film and television to this list, but in those two media the audience and the performers are removed in space and time.)

In some instances, these paratheatrical forms are important antecedents in the history of theatre in Western, Asian, and African cultures, so *A Concise History of Theatre* presents some of them, but identifies them as theatre-like, or **paratheatrical**, practices.

Historical Evidence, Emphasis, and Omissions

We pay special attention to noting where the evidence of the historical record is strong and where is it weak. Note throughout this concise history the use of qualifying phrases:

- is said to be
- scholars suppose
- legend has it
- we imagine

Those phrases and other qualifiers signal that there is not enough evidence to make a definitive statement. Where history is just supposition, we mention it and move on. But note the qualifiers. There is nothing wrong with supposition, particularly when a scholar turns supposition into hypothesis and organizes the evidence for and against the question at hand. That's how history or any field moves ahead. But by itself, a supposition is not evidence.

Fads, hidden agendas, and unstated assumptions affect any history, including theatre history. As you read what follows, you should notice where and why emphases have been put and where and why omissions have occurred, remembering that in history of all sorts, a lack of evidence in one area and an oversupply in another greatly affects how much appears on the page. Remember, too, that time is an eccentric editor—through accident, war, intentional erasure, and neglect, information is lost that would be vital if it were available. For example, the names of more than one hundred playwrights of ancient Greek comedy are known. Some fragments exist here and there but only eleven complete ancient Greek comedies are extant, all by Aristophanes, out of the forty he is thought to have written. As a result, in discussing ancient Greek comedy there is little to say about any plays other than those of Aristophanes. That's what the vagaries of time have left of all of ancient Greek comedy. A different example of omissions in the historical record: The indigenous peoples of sub-Saharan Africa and North America had in essence no alphabet, no written language before the advent of Europeans. What remains is oral tradition—stories passed from mouth-to-ear down the line of generations—to suggest whether theatre or theatre-like performances existed in these areas in earlier times.

There is an old adage of historians: It is the winners who write history. Moreover, until quite recently *most* people went unrepresented in history, including theatre history, which took as its subject people very like the ones who wrote the history: educated, male, white, European, often affluent, and close to the center of power. The winners not only write history but until recent times only people with a good deal of wealth and power—mostly white men—had the means to leave any record for history to recount and analyze.

Many historians maintain that art validates the center of power. No more important understanding can come from the study of theatre's past than to learn how theatre art and sociopolitical power come together and drift apart, validating, amplifying, in a few cases skirmishing, and then becoming invisible to each other. To understand that relationship is to understand how theatre history is *history*.

Organization

Because this is a concise theatre history intended as an introduction to the subject, we have had to make choices to omit details and, sometimes, entire areas that would be worthy of further attention if this were a much longer, more encyclopedic book. Our goal has been to transmit a sturdy central structure of theatre history that will inform a student's later experience of theatre, as a reader, student, and audience member. Each conscious omission has been the subject of research, argument, and discussion. Finally, we concede that there is no perfect synopsis of theatre history. Here is ours.

This concise history overlays both temporal and geographic organization. Still, inevitably, the neat divisions that would make the study of history so simple are not to be found in reality. For an example, the Renaissance in Europe occurred in different times and in different places, perhaps for more than a century. Similarly, non-European theatre developed on its own timetable that is irreconcilable with Western theatre's timetable. Thus, there are in this account of theatre history some overlaps in time, backtracking in styles, and so on. We believe that to be more meticulous in a time-and-space organization of the historical story would make the subject harder to follow and understand. For example, the second chapter on Asian theatre starts at 1800 and runs to about the present. Because in the twentieth century, the theatre of Asia took up some of the dominant styles of Western theatre, such as, epic theatre and absurdism, to order this chapter before the chapters on twentieth-century theatre in the West would be confusing. On the other hand, jumping back to 1800 isn't ideal either. A third alternative is to scatter very short chapters about Asian theatre throughout the later part of the text. We chose two chapters on Asian theatre and placed them in the text not strictly chronologically. So this concise theatre history is *generally* organized temporally and geographically, but not purely so.

With this introduction as overture, *A Concise History of Theatre* begins where the historical record of theatre begins, in Ancient Athens, fifth century BCE.

KEY TERMS

Key terms are boldface type in the text. Check your understanding against this list. Persons are page-referenced in the Index.

paratheatrical, p. 8	theatre, p. 4
ritual, p. 6	theatrical, p. 5

Greek Theatre

Context

The very first records of drama (play scripts) and theatre (performance) come from Athens, Greece, and date from the sixth century BCE. Within a hundred years, Athenian drama reached a peak of excellence seldom equaled since. The result is that when people speak of Greek theatre today, they are almost certainly referring to the plays and productions of the fifth century BCE in Athens.

Why drama and theatre should have arisen there and not in other civilizations of the time remains a mystery, but the position of Athens in the ancient world offered some advantages.

Greece, a peninsula about half the size of the state of New York, with numerous bays, harbors, inlets, and adjacent islands, has one of the longest coastlines in the world. Its geography made it, during the sixth century BCE (500s), the leading merchant of the Mediterranean, a role it took over from the Phoenicians. Exporting pottery, olive oil, wine, and slaves, Greece brought in a variety of items from North Africa and the East, where advanced civilizations were already flourishing in Egypt, China, India, and Persia (today's Iran). In fact, Greece formed the western edge of the then-civilized world and served as a crossroad for trade.

To speak of "Greece," however, is misleading because there was no unified nation. Rather, on the peninsula were organized individual city-states, each called a polis (pl. poleis) and each consisting of a town and its surrounding countryside, the residents of which spoke dialects of the same language and mostly worshiped the same gods. Each polis issued its own coinage, raised its own armies, mined silver, built ships, and the like. Several were important city-states, including Corinth, Sparta, and Thebes. But by the fifth century BCE (400s), Athens had emerged as both cultural leader and trading giant, with its own outposts in Italy, Sicily, France, and Spain. As the word *outposts* suggests, western Europe was at the time a cultural backwater. And Athens itself was a small city by modern standards—100,000 people, about the size of Utica, New York.

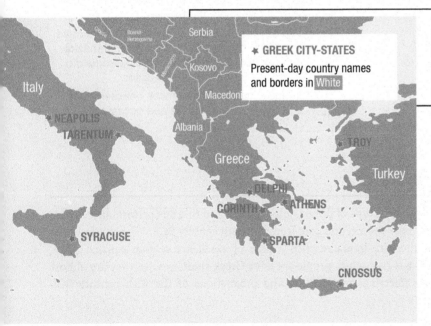

★ GREEK CITY-STATES

Present-day country names and borders in White

THE CIVILIZED WORLD

By the fifth century BCE (400s) Greek city-states influenced much of the Mediterranean, including some outposts on the Italian peninsula.

HOW WE KNOW

Paintings on Greek Vases

Scholars discovered this vase in 1836 in Italy, some calling it the most single important piece of pictorial evidence of ancient theatre to have survived from Greece. The vase, in a form called a *krater*, dates from about 400 BCE, close to the time Euripides's *The Bacchae* was first performed in Athens. The paintings depict what has been termed a "backstage" celebration after the successful performance of a satyr play. Seen are an entire chorus and cast along with a celebrated musician, Pronomos. The container is thus called the Pronomos Vase. Also pictured are Dionysus and two actors. The chorus of satyrs is depicted wearing woolly loincloths, horse tails, artificial phalluses, and bearded snub-nosed masks. Also pic-

tured in the close view of a portion of the vase are two actors, the one on the right clearly Heracles with the traditional lion skin and club. The actors hold their masks.

The masks are not the oversized, distorted masks of the Hellenistic era. Instead they appear to be made of light materials such as stiffened linen or thin, shaped leather. The masks depicted seem to cover the entire head with openings for the eyes and mouth. Other evidence from excavations near the Acropolis by the American School of Classical Studies has corroborated this understanding of Greek masks in the classical era.

By the fifth century BCE, the golden age of Athenian theatre and drama, Athens had already established the world's first democracy, providing a model for the participation of citizens in the decisions and policies of government. However, women had no say in government and something like one-third of Athens' residents were slaves. Under Pericles, its great fifth-century BCE ruler, Athens created statues and buildings, arts, and philosophies whose excellence made them important in European culture for more than two thousand years. By then as well, Athens had developed an alphabet that included both vowels and consonants, becoming the first in history to represent speech both systematically and consistently. (Earlier there are languages with alphabets but not ones with both consonants and vowels.) An alphabet is essential for the consistent communication and continued development of culture that relies on words, theatre included.

Athenians took great pride in their civic accomplishments. To celebrate its culture, facilitate the exchange of goods, and pay tribute to various gods,

Athens sponsored a number of public festivals each year. At three of these festivals, each devoted to the god Dionysus, the earliest recorded theatre and drama appeared. Why did this new art arise? Why did it take the form it did? Why was Athens, rather than Egypt, Persia, China, or India, the birthplace of drama? We do not know although there are several theories.

Theories of the Origins of Theatre

There is almost no written evidence from which to draw information about the origins of Greek drama. The exception is Aristotle's *Poetics*, one questionable source of ancient evidence about the origins.

Aristotle's Theory

The earliest account is Aristotle's *Poetics*, written in 355 BCE. He claimed that "tragedy was produced by the authors of the dithyrambs, and comedy from [the authors] of the phallic songs." Dithyrambs were choral odes, po-ems performed by a chorus. Phallic songs were rites celebrating male sexual potency, but their precise nature is unknown because only fragments sur-vive. Although tantalizing, Aristotle's account is not helpful; we cannot tell from his account which kind of dithyrambs or phallic songs he had in mind, nor can we discern *how* or *why* the authors changed the one to tragedy and the other to comedy. Moreover, Aristotle was writing about two hundred years *after* the first recorded theatre performance and we have no idea where he got his information.

The Ritual Theory

Probably the most fashionable, but not necessarily the most correct, view of the origin of theatre is the ritual theory, which proposes that Greek drama evolved from early religious rituals devoted to the god Dionysus. The the-ory has strengths: drama first appeared in Greece only at great religious festivals and only at festivals devoted to the god Dionysus, who in Greece was associated with wine and sexuality. But it also has weaknesses: virtually no extant Greek tragedy features Dionysus as a central figure or displays the sort of orgiastic worship associated with Dionysus. On the contrary, Greek tragedy is serious and stately. Few reputable scholars still accept the idea that drama "evolved" in some organic, necessary way from religious ritual, al-though most acknowledge that ritual elements can often be found in tragedy.

The Great Man Theory

Some scholars propose that tragedy and comedy arose as creative acts of human genius. Such scholars search for the birth of drama by a revolu-tionary invention of a gifted human being, arguing that art neither evolves

AESCHYLUS'S *THE AGAMEMNON*
In 1968, the Guthrie Theatre produced a somewhat condensed *Oresteia* trilogy as *The House of Atreus*. The masks, designed by Tanya Moiseiwitch, left the mouth uncovered so the actor's articulation was not muffled. Directed by Tyrone Guthrie, the production toured Los Angeles and New York, among other cities.

like a biological organism nor happens by chance. According to this view, an artist purposefully synthesized elements that already existed in Athenian society into a new form, the drama. The theory has strengths: storytelling, music, and dance *did* already exist in Greek society and so were readily available for use. But this theory also has weaknesses: human genius is itself mysterious, and so the theory leaves much unexplained about the origins of theatre and drama.

The Storytelling Theory

Some scholars propose that Greek drama developed from storytelling. It is supposed that storytellers would naturally tend to elaborate parts of the telling by impersonating the various characters, using appropriate voice and movement. From here, it seems a short step to having several people become involved in telling the story; from this "telling," it is thought, drama and theatre arose. This theory, which clearly emphasizes the role of actors and acting in drama, has strengths: Athenians had a rich and long tradition of epic singers—storytellers who gave public performances of works such as Homer's *Iliad* and *Odyssey*, for example. The theory has a major weakness, however: it fails to account for the prominent position played by the chorus in Greek drama.

The Dance Theory

Other theorists suggest that movement rather than speech was at the core of drama. The idea here is that dancers first imitated the physical behavior of animals and humans. When dancers costumed themselves in appropriate skins and garments, they came to impersonate the animals and humans. When several dancers joined together in impersonation and then embroidered this performance with sounds and words, drama was born. Again, this theory has strengths: it accounts well for the dancing chorus present in all Greek drama, and it explains the animal choruses of several comedies (e.g., *The Birds*, *The Frogs*). But it, too, has weaknesses: it suggests the chorus would be the primary part of the production and Greek drama does not display a great emphasis on the chorus's role for the most part. Also, it fails to account for the separation between actor and chorus that began with the first Greek drama that we know anything about.

Uncertainty about Origins

In fact, no one knows the origin of Greek drama. The argument over origins is often an argument over the nature of theatre itself. To anthropologists, the essence of theatre is ritual, and so they tend to favor the ritual theory. Anthropologists cite rituals such as

- the Buffalo Dance of the Mandan American Indian tribes in which a group of men don buffalo skins and dance with rattles and rods, imitating buffalo and magically inciting the return of the important beasts.
- the False Face Society of the Iroquois, a group of medicine men who wear elaborate masks to impersonate a mythical hunchback man who aids in healing.
- and the Egyptian Osiris ritual, which reenacted the death and resurrection of Osiris, with mock battles that sometimes turned bloody at least according to a later account of a Hellenistic traveler to Egypt.

To artists who look at world theatre and see a form rich in human meaning, only an artist's creation can explain its beginnings, and so they favor the great man theory. For those who believe drama began with the actor, the storyteller theory works best; for those who find the essence of Greek drama in its chorus, the dance theory seems most persuasive.

The theory that is accepted often has real-world consequences in adaptations and stagings of Greek drama today. A director who prefers the ritual

A BUFFALO DANCE
The Mandan, a Native American people living in North Dakota, performed a dance each year to ask the gods for good luck in next year's hunting. The ritual, performed to drumming, includes a costume of buffalo skins with the heads forming a kind of mask.

theory, for example, might choose to insert ritual elements such as incense burning and incantation into a tragedy, whereas one who prefers the great man theory may stress instead the individuality of character. A director who prefers the dance theory may emphasize the centrality of the chorus, extending its opportunities for singing and dancing, and a director who favors the storytelling theory might shrink the choral odes and even the size of the chorus, throwing added emphasis to the actors.

Traits of Greek Theatre

During the preceding discussion, we have encountered three important traits of Greek theatre, traits that may seem odd when compared to current Western theatrical conventions. Greek theatre was different from contemporary theatre.

Closely Associated with Greek Religion

A form of polytheism ("many gods"), Greek religion was both private (a part of daily life and centered in the home) and public, expressing itself at a number of major festivals, each devoted to a specific god. Unlike Christianity, Judaism, or Islam, Greek religion was not built around a canonical book such as the Bible or the Quran so religious expression took many forms. Although Greek theatre was performed on religious occasions, it did not have the metaphysical purposes of ritual.

Performed on Special Occasions—The Festivals

During its golden age, drama appeared only in Athens and so far as we know only at three festivals of Dionysus: the City (or Great) Dionysia, the Rural Dionysia, and the Lenaia.

Choral

In addition to actors, the performance of Greek drama required a **chorus**, a group of men who dressed alike, who were masked alike, and who moved, sang, and spoke together most of the time. The chorus affected Greek drama in important ways. Its costumes, songs, and dances added much spectacle to the performance. Because the chorus danced as it spoke, chanted, and sang, its rhythms presumably indicated, both visually and orally, the changing moods within the play. Perhaps most important of all, the chorus in some plays—like the actors—participated directly in the action, providing information, making discoveries, deciding, and doing.

The chorus also influenced a number of theatrical practices. Because the chorus usually came into the performing space soon after the play opened and remained there until the end, its presence had to be considered in both the physical layout of the theatre and the action of the drama. It required a space large enough to move about in. Its presence had to be justified and its loyalties made clear whenever characters shared secrets. Because the vocal and visual power of the chorus was great, the actors presumably adjusted their style of performance so as not to be overwhelmed by the impact of the chorus.

All Male

All actors, playwrights, and civic sponsors were male.

Competitive

Dramatists competed for awards in writing, and actors competed for awards in performing. To ensure fairness in the competition, various rules governed who competed, who judged, and who won.

Plays were produced by the city-state in cooperation with selected wealthy citizens. (Women were not considered citizens.) At the **Great Dionysia**, three tragic writers competed each year for the prize. Each submitted three tragedies—not necessarily a trilogy of *related* stories—and one **satyr play**, a short comic piece that followed the tragedies and occasionally burlesqued them. One day was set aside for the work of each tragic author; therefore, nine tragedies and three satyr plays were presented at the Great Dionysia each year. At the Lenaia, only four tragedies competed each year, each by a different playwright. At both festivals, five comic playwrights competed for a prize in a single day of competition.

ARISTOPHANES'S
LYSISTRATA

"The Lysistrata Project: The First-Ever Worldwide Theatrical Act of Dissent," a global peace action to urge an end to the wars in Iraq and Afghanistan, was performed more than a thousand times in nearly sixty countries around the world on the same day, March 3, 2003. Here, an undergraduate production at the University of South Carolina.

Not a Commercial Activity

How the competitors were selected is unknown, but once chosen, each author was matched with a wealthy citizen-sponsor, who was then responsible for meeting the costs incurred by the chorus. These citizen-sponsors could have a major effect on the outcome of the contests. Legends tell us that Sophocles's *Oedipus Rex* lost its competition because of a sponsor too stingy to fund a suitable production, but that Aeschylus's *Eumenides* had costumes and masks so spectacular and frightening that pregnant women miscarried when they first saw the chorus—legend, remember—the result of the lavish support of its sponsor. In modern times, *Oedipus Rex* is generally acknowledged as one of the greatest written works of Western art of all time.

Most sponsors took their responsibilities seriously, although there were both carrots and sticks to encourage them to do so. Carrot: Support of a chorus was one of the civic duties of a wealthy citizen; those not tapped to fund dramas might be asked to outfit a warship or fund some other equally important project. Considerable acclaim flowed to those who mounted successful productions. Stick: Any wealthy citizen pleading insufficient funds to sponsor a chorus could be challenged by any other citizen. Should the challenger win, he and the would-be sponsor exchanged assets.

The method of selecting judges was ingenious and complicated, devised to assure that all major units of the polis were represented and that the gods had some say in the final decision. First, the names of all eligible citizens were collected within each political unit, and one name drawn from each of the ten units. The votes of only five of these ten citizens actually counted, however, allowing the gods to determine which five votes determined the winner. To serve as judge was both a civic duty and an honor.

Audience members who attended performances, then, not only heard and saw the plays, but they also learned who won the contests. For this reason, attending Greek theatre probably had some of the elements of a long-standing sports rivalry, as well as those of theatre and drama.

Plays and Playwrights

Of the thousands of plays written for the Greek theatre, only forty-six survive complete, although many fragments have also become known to us. Most extant plays come from Athens in the fifth century BCE and from four authors: Aeschylus (seven), Sophocles (seven), Euripides (eighteen), and Aristophanes (eleven). From these four authors came some of the world's greatest plays: plays that are still performed for their powerful effects on audiences, plays that have provided other playwrights from William Shakespeare and Jean Racine to Eugene O'Neill and Wole Soyinka with stories, and plays that have given their names to underlying patterns of human behavior ("Oedipus complex," "Promethean struggle").

AN ALL-MALE PRODUCTION
The Guthrie Theatre's production of *The House of Atreus* cast all female roles with male actors. Here Clytemnestra appears before the doors of the palace. The actor is wearing elevated shoes, body padding, oversized gloves, and a headdress to add stature to his appearance. The effect is highly theatrical even though the costume does not accurately reflect the practices of classical Athens.

Thespis

A fifth name—the playwright and actor, Thespis—is important, although such a person may never have existed. The semilegendary Thespis supposedly wrote tragedies using only one actor and a chorus. Thespis is called semilegendary because the references to his life and work are fragmentary and at best were recorded about two centuries *after* the time he is stated to have lived. None of Thespis's works survived. If they had, the questions regarding his existence would be more or less resolved. Some scholars presume the Thespis works were a series of monologues. With only one actor and a chorus, the opportunity to introduce new information into a scene and thus introduce change into a situation was severely limited. As such, it is difficult to have action on stage, that is, to have two characters acting on each other.

Aeschylus

Aeschylus (525?–456 BCE) probably introduced a second actor, thereby permitting change to occur within the play. Although a second actor would also allow conflict between two characters, Aeschylus still tended to depict a solitary hero, one isolated and facing a cosmic horror brought about by forces beyond his control. With such a grand tragic conception, Aeschylus required great scope, and so he often wrote trilogies, three plays on a single subject that were intended for performance on the same day. One of his trilogies, the *Oresteia* (458 BCE)—comprising the *Agamemnon*, the *Choëphoroe*, and the *Eumenides*—has survived intact along with several single plays: *The Persians*, *Seven against Thebes*, *The Suppliants*, and perhaps *Prometheus*. There is scholarly debate about whether to attribute *Prometheus* to Aeschylus or another unknown poet.

All of the surviving scripts display characteristics for which Aeschylus is admired: heroic and austere characters, simple but powerful plots, and lofty diction. His general tone is well summarized by an ancient commentator: "While one finds many different types of artistic treatment in Aeschylus, one looks in vain for those sentiments that draw tears."

Sophocles

Sophocles (496?–406 BCE) was credited with adding a third actor and with changing practices in scenic painting and costuming. Less interested than Aeschylus in portraying solitary heroes confronting the universal order, Sophocles wrote plays that explored the place of humans within that order. The tragedy of Sophocles's heroes typically erupts from decisions made and actions taken based on imperfect knowledge or conflicting claims. Various aspects of the hero's character combine with unusual circumstances to bring about a disaster caused not by wickedness or foolishness but merely by humanness.

The role of the chorus in Sophocles's plays remained important but not as central as in Aeschylus's. Conversely, the individual characters in Sophocles tended to be more complex, to display more individual traits, and to make more decisions. The result is that in Sophoclean tragedy, the actors, not the chorus, control the rhythm of the plays. Unlike Aeschylus, Sophocles did not

THE PLAY'S THE THING

Sophocles's *Oedipus Rex*, 427 BCE

Part of a group of three plays often referred to as the "Theban plays," *Oedipus the King* is considered one of the greatest dramas ever written. The other two plays in this Theban cycle are *Antigone* and *Oedipus at Colonus*. (The three were not written as a trilogy). Sophocles is believed to have written more than one hundred plays, but only seven have survived.

The Story of the Play Oedipus, king of Thebes, is appealed to by the people (the chorus) to save them from the plague that grips the city. Oedipus has already sent his brother-in-law, Creon, to the oracle at Delphi for a solution; Creon returns and announces that the oracle says that the city must banish the murderer of the former king, Laius. Oedipus vows to "reveal the truth" and save the city.

He calls the blind seer Tiresias to asks his advice. Tiresias is evasive and then, pressured, says, "It is you." Angered, Oedipus turns on Tiresias, saying that he and Creon are plotting against him. The old seer warns Oedipus of one who is "his children's brother and father, his wife's son, his mother's husband."

Oedipus rages again against Creon. His wife, Jocasta, widow of the former king, Laius, tells him of another old prophecy: Laius would be murdered by his own child. When she describes Laius, Oedipus is shaken. He tells of his own long-ago visit to Delphi and a prophecy that he would kill his father and sleep with his mother, which caused him to flee Corinth, his childhood home. He recounts the later killing of a stranger at a crossroads.

A messenger from Corinth comes with news that Polybus, the king of Corinth and Oedipus's supposed father, is dead. Oedipus is not to grieve, however — Polybus was not, the messenger says, Oedipus's real father; rather, the messenger as a young man got the infant Oedipus from a shepherd; the baby's ankles were pierced — hence the name Oedipus, "swollenfoot."

Jocasta begs Oedipus to give up his quest for the truth. An old man, the survivor of the attack on Laius, is dragged in. He was the shepherd who gave the infant Oedipus to the messenger; now, hounded by Oedipus, he says that the infant was to have been abandoned in the wild because he was the child of Laius and Jocasta, and there was a prophecy that he would kill his own father, but the shepherd gave him away, instead.

Oedipus sees the truth: He is the source of the plague, the murderer of his father, later the husband of his mother. Jocasta kills herself.

Oedipus blinds himself with the pins in Jocasta's jewels. He begs to be driven from the city.

need a trilogy to contain his tragedies; his plays stood alone. Of the more than one hundred attributed to him, one, *Oedipus Rex* (c. 427 BCE), is recognized by most critics as among the finest tragedies ever written. The other six remaining tragedies are *Ajax, Electra, Trachiniae, Philoctetes, Antigone,* and *Oedipus at Colonus. Oedipus Rex, Electra,* and *Antigone* are all regularly performed in translation today throughout Western cultures.

Euripides

Euripides (480–407 BCE) was controversial during his lifetime but came to be highly regarded after his death. Growing up at a time when Athens was embarking on policies of imperialism and expansionism, Euripides became a pacifist and a political gadfly, a person who asked unusual or upsetting questions. The intellectual elite apparently admired him. It is reported, for example, that Socrates, one of the wisest men of the age, came to the theatre only to see the tragedies of Euripides and that Sophocles dressed his chorus in black on learning of the death of Euripides.

In comparison with the plays of Aeschylus and Sophocles, those of Euripides are less exalted and more realistic. His characters seem less grand and more human; their problems are less cosmic and more mundane. Euripides tended to examine human relationships and to question the wisdom of social actions: the purpose of war, the status of women, and the reasons for human cruelty. *Trojan Women* (415 BCE) is an example. The play takes place after the Trojan War is decided. The surviving women of Troy learn that their male children have been killed. Each awaits her fate at the hands of the conquering Greeks, learning whether they will be slaves or concubines and to which man. Helen and Menelaus are reunited, and despite his vow to slay her, Menelaus is again enraptured by Helen's beauty and takes back his wandering wife, whose abduction was the cause of the war

Matt Orton

EURIPIDES'S *THE BACCHAE*

Pentheus, a central character in *The Bacchae*, dressed as a woman at the urging of Dionysus. As shown here, he faced a chorus of maenads, the most important members of Dionysus's retinue. Later, the maenads ripped Pentheus's body apart piece by piece. Here, a production from Montavalo University.

and all the loss on both sides. *Trojan Women* is frequently revived today to express the profound human cost of war on women and children.

Euripides's iconoclastic outlook led to changes in dramatic technique. Replacing the philosophical probing common in the plays of Aeschylus and Sophocles, Euripides substituted rapid reversals, intrigues, and romantic and sentimental incidents of the sort much later associated with plays called *melodramas*. Euripides is said by some to be the father of melodrama. (More about melodramas in Chapter 8.) He further reduced the role of the chorus until sometimes it was little more than an interruption of the play's action. As the role of the chorus declined and the subjects became more personal, the language became less poetic and more conversational. Many of the changes that Euripides introduced into Greek tragedy, although denounced in his own time, became standard dramatic practice later during the Hellenistic period.

Although Euripides wrote about ninety plays, only seventeen tragedies and one satyr play survive. The plays most often revived in the last hundred or so years include *Medea* as well as *Hippolytus*, *The Suppliants*, *Electra*, *The Trojan Women*, and *The Bacchae*.

Aristophanes and Old Comedy

Comedy was introduced into the Great Dionysia in 486 BCE, fifty years after tragedy. It seems never to have been comfortable there, perhaps because the festival was an international showcase for Athenian culture and thus often visited by foreign dignitaries. The real home of comedy was the winter festival, the Lenaia, which only Athenians could attend, where a contest for comedy was established in 442 BCE. At both festivals, an entire day was set aside for competition among the comic playwrights, five of whom competed.

All of the eleven extant ancient Greek comedies are by Aristophanes (448?–380 BCE). No comedies from the classical era other than Aristophanes's survive. (There is one comedy extant from the era following classical Athens, a Hellenistic comedy by Menander.) Thus, information about comedy during the classical period necessarily comes from these plays. It is possible, of course, that Aristophanes was atypical, and so the conclusions drawn from his works may not be generally applicable to all ancient Greek comedy.

Although no two plays are exactly alike, surviving examples suggest a set structure for **old comedy**, the political comedy of the classical period of Athens:

- A first part consisting of a prologue, during which an outrageous idea is introduced and then a debate as to whether the idea should be adopted, ending with a decision to put this "happy idea" into action. (In Aristophanes's *The Birds* [414 BCE], for example, the happy idea is to build a city in the sky.)

- Direct address by the chorus or choral leader to the audience, breaking the dramatic illusion.

- A second part made up of funny episodes and choral songs showing the happy idea at work.

The happy idea is the heart of old comedy: It is outrageous and usually fantastic, and it contains social or political satire. Old comedy was scabrous, impolite, even profane, and could identify and lampoon living individuals. In *The Birds*, building the city in the sky is an attempt to get away from the mess on earth. The happy idea also enables the spectacular costuming and behavior of the chorus, which often gives the play its name. Aristophanes is believed to have written about forty plays. The eleven that survive include the often produced *Lysistrata* as well as *The Frogs*, *The Knights*, and *The Thesmophoriazusae* (*The Woman's Festival*). It is *Lysistrata* that receives the most revivals in the modern era. It is seen as an antiwar play whose happy idea is that women should withhold sex until the men give up war.

Theatre Buildings and Practices

Although almost all extant Greek plays date from the fifth century BCE (400s), the extant Greek theatre buildings date from later periods, sometimes much later periods. The result is unsettling: For the time when we know about theatre buildings and production practices, we know almost nothing about plays; conversely, for the time when we know a good deal about the plays, we know almost nothing about the theatre buildings. Theatres after the fifth century were made of stone, they were semipermanent, and so architectural examples of this later theatre have come down to us. The reason later play scripts do not survive is believed to be just historical bad luck.

In Greek, *theatron* meant "seeing-place" or "spectacle-place." Athens's first theatre was apparently in the market, but it soon moved to the outskirts of town. There, the Theatre of Dionysus, Athens' first important theatre, was situated on a hillside at the foot of the Acropolis, where the audience sat, with a circular playing area (the **orchestra**) at its base; a path or road separated audience and playing area and provided entrances (*parodoi*). (The word *orchestra* today refers to the ground floor seating in an auditorium, a reflection of the Greek meaning.) This arrangement—hillside, orchestra, parodoi—was fundamental to all Greek theatres. In theatres of the time, some orchestras were circular and some rectangular.

By the middle of the fifth century, a scene house (**skene**, "tent" or "booth") had been added at the edge of the orchestra opposite the audience. The existence of a skene is inferred from the staging requirements of some of

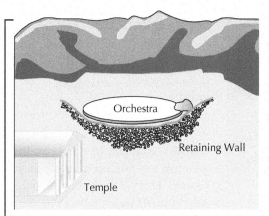

THEATRE OF THE 400S BCE
This conjectural reconstruction of the early Theatre of Dionysus (*left*) shows audience area, orchestra, rock outcropping, and temple. The theatre as it appears today (*right*) at the foot of the Acropolis after hundreds of years of "improvements."

the extant plays. Its original layout is unknown. It may first have been cloth, in essence a tent, but may have later been constructed of wood, becoming stone only centuries later. Whether wood or stone, it provided background and acoustical support and allows us to call the Athenian theatre a **facade stage**—a conventional form in which actors perform in front of a nonrepresentational, often architectural, facade, with the audience arcing to three or fewer sides. The facade, then, does not change as the scene changes; it serves all plays performed in the space.

Audience

The outdoor theatre put the audience at the mercy of the weather. Individuals may have used cushions, sunshades, umbrellas, and so forth. The Athenian hillside, some scholars estimate, could hold about fourteen thousand, and the audience was as visible as the actors in the natural sunlight. Theatre was apparently open to all, including women and slaves, but the exact social makeup of the audience is unknown. Records suggest that it could be unruly at times.

Acting

The first victor in the Athenian tragic contest is supposed to have been Thespis, who also acted in his play (c. 534 BCE)—hence *thespian* is a term still used for an actor. Acting, like playwriting, remained a competitive activity during the classical period, and rules governed its practice. For example, all actors were male. Apparently no more than three *speaking* actors were allowed in the

HELLENISTIC THEATRE BUILDINGS
Stone remains of several Hellenistic theatres have led scholars to speculate that a typical Hellenistic theatre looked something like the reconstruction shown here.

tragedies and five in the comedies, although any number of extras might be used. Because the leading actor, or **protagonist**, was the only one competing for the prize, he was assigned to the playwright by lot, so that chance rather than politics decided who got the best roles or which playwright would get the best actor. The second and third actors were probably chosen by the playwright and the protagonist in consultation. With only three actors, doubling of roles is assumed to have been required because the plays themselves often had eight or more characters. If the protagonist had an exceedingly demanding role he might play only one character but the second and third actors were expected to play two or more secondary roles. Doubling, the use of masks, and the use of only male actors suggest that the style of Greek acting was more formal than realistic; that is, although the acting was true and believable *on its own terms*, its resemblance to real life was of considerably less importance than its fidelity to the dramatic action. Given the size of the audience and the physical arrangement of the theatre, it is believed that vocal power and vocal agility were the actor's most prized assets. Actors, like sponsors and chorus members, performed as part of their civic duties. They were not paid professionals, although chorus members were reimbursed some amount for the time they spent away from business.

Settings and Machinery

The skene was the essential setting. We do not know whether its appearance was changed to suggest different locations; that is, we do not know whether there was scenery in our sense of that word. We do know that some sort of a modern-day flat, a two-dimensional surface for the painting of scenic elements, called a **pinake** existed, but we do not know how or where it was used.

We do *know* that two machines provided special effects:

- The *eccyclema* was a movable platform capable of being rolled or rotated out of the skene to reveal the result of an offstage action. In Aeschylus's *Agamemnon*, for example, the body of the murdered Agamemnon

HELLENISTIC MASKS AND COSTUMES

By the 300s BCE, tragic masks and costumes had become more exaggerated with high headdresses and enlarged eyes and mouths on the masks and perhaps elevated shoes on the actors, all of which served to enlarge the actors's physical presence. Comedic masks and costumes, on the other hand, seem to have moved in the opposite direction, becoming more natural looking.

is "revealed," and in the *Eumenides*, the Furies, the avenging goddesses, seem to have entered first while asleep so they may have been rolled into view.

- The **mechane** ("machine") was some sort of crane that allowed people and things to "fly" in and out. In Aristophanes's *The Clouds*, the character Socrates hangs over the performing space during some of his dialogue, and in Euripides's *Medea*, Medea flies away to escape her pursuers. In fact, Euripides often has gods fly down to sort out the characters's problems at the end of his tragedies. Much later a Roman critic called a too-obviously-contrived ending of a play (in Latin) a *deus ex machina* or "god from the machine." The phrase is used still today to refer to any arbitrary, contrived plot turn in a play, movie, or novel.

Properties were numerous, and play scripts suggest altars, tombs, biers, chariots, staffs, and swords being used in tragedy. Comedies often required furniture, food, clubs, and so on.

Costumes and Masks

Because in Greek theatre one actor played several roles, costumes and masks were exceedingly important; they enabled audiences to identify quickly and certainly which character in the play the actor was impersonating. The mask and the costume, in a sense, were the signs of character. A different principle governed the chorus, whose goal was to make its individual members appear to be a group, and so choral costumes and masks were similar. Although historians once argued for a typically tragic costume for tragic characters, most now agree that some version of normal Athenian dress seems likelier. In tragedy, such dress was perhaps more elegant than normal, and in comedy it was certainly altered to make it laughable—ill-fitting, exaggerated, and so on—but the basic look was recognizable.

GREEK PERFORMERS

These are among the earliest known statuettes of actors, dating from the late fifth to early fourth century BCE. Fourteen of these were found in a burial in Attica, the area of Greece that includes Athens. Originally they were brightly painted.

From references in plays, we know that a costume's appearance allowed audience members to know a character's traits:

- Ethnicity: references are made to some dressed as Greeks and to others dressed as foreigners.
- Gender: males and females are identified as such at a distance.
- Social role: military heroes, servants, shepherds, and so on were visually identifiable.

In the case of comedy, the costume for certain male characters featured a stuffed, oversized penis, or phallus. The color of costumes was also a sign: Reference is made to black for characters in mourning and yellow for an especially effeminate male character, to cite only two examples.

All performers, both actors and chorus members, wore masks. They were full-faced masks, and they carried their own hairstyle, and of course, their own set facial expression. During the fifth century BCE, the masks looked natural in tragedy, although in comedy they could distort features to provoke laughter. Again, masks for actors aimed for individuality and quick recognition of character, whereas choral masks stressed resemblance, membership in a group. Occasionally, comic masks resembled the faces of living people, a fact we glean from an account of Socrates, who, from his seat in the audience, stood up and turned so that others could see that the mask worn by the actor in a comedy mimicked his own face.

The Hellenistic Period

At the end of the fifth century BCE, Athens lost its premiere position among the Greek poleis. At least part of the reason for Athens's decline was a series of devastating plagues. We now know that as a trading power Athens was vulnerable to plagues, brought by fleas that lived on rats that came into port with the cargo. Athens was defeated by Sparta, a militaristic state with few aspirations to high

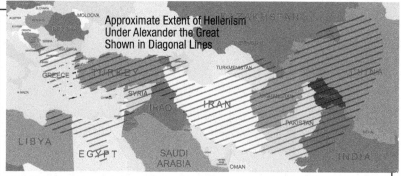

Approximate Extent of Hellenism Under Alexander the Great Shown in Diagonal Lines

HELLENISTIC GREECE

The conquests of Alexander the Great in the 300s extended Greek influence but led to a shift of power away from Athens. Theatres began to be built throughout Greek lands, and acting became professionalized.

culture. With Spartan influence came some sort of censorship, which had the immediate effect of toning down the political satire of Greek old comedies and substituting comedy with a less biting tone called **middle comedy**. Then, near the end of the fourth century BCE (300s), Philip II of Macedon and his son who eventually became known as Alexander the Great (356–323 BCE) overran all the Greek poleis except Sparta and folded them into a single, centralized government.

Alexander then conquered many of the advanced civilizations that abutted this greater Greece, south through Egypt and east as far as India and modern Afghanistan and Pakistan. Founding Alexandria, Egypt, as his capital, he ruled one of the world's great empires in a brief age now called the **Hellenistic period**. ("Greek" is from the Latin term for the people of the peninsula. They called themselves and their language Ἑλληνες, pronounced by non-Greek-speakers as "Hellenes," hence the period being called Hellenistic.) As Alexander and his armies conquered lands, they exported Greek culture to them. Original editions of Greek dramas were transferred to Alexander's library in Alexandria. The library purchased Aristotle's collection of books after his death. Sadly for future scholars, the library burned in 48 BCE.

The culture of Hellenistic Greece, however, differed from that of Athens. The individuality of the various poleis declined, replaced by a cosmopolitan culture centered in Egypt. Gone were Athenian democracy, its great drama, and the centrality of its gods. The trend was toward a common government, common civilization, and common religion. The empire's center of gravity shifted away from the Greek peninsula, which now rested on the westernmost edge of Alexander's holdings, and toward the east, where different religious and philosophical systems were already highly developed. Towns and then cities grew up, as trade competed with agriculture for attention. Within a hundred years, the Hellenistic world had more than four hundred cities with populations more than 200,000, that is, twice the size of Athens during its golden age, the fifth century BCE.

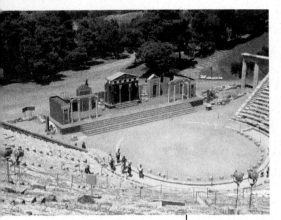

THE THEATRE AT EPIDAURUS

By the beginning of the fourth century, the seating was connected to the skene by two portals, seen here. Some scholars believe that the audience as well as the chorus at the play's beginning entered through these archways. A well-preserved example of a Greek theatre of this era is the one at Epidaurus, seen here with a setting for Aristophanes's *The Knights*.

An Altered Greek Drama and Theatres

Plays began to be performed throughout Greek lands—which is to say, the Hellenistic lands—not merely at Athens, and they were now performed on special military and civic occasions as well as during Dionysian festivals. Satyr plays disappeared. Tragedy declined in popularity; such tragedies as were written apparently modeled themselves on Euripides's plays, with a reduced emphasis on the chorus and an increased emphasis on sensation, realism, and melodrama. Only fragments of such tragedies exist today. Tragedies from the fifth century BCE continued to be revived, however, attesting to their power to move audiences. Comedy remained popular, but it abandoned both its political bite and its formal structure. **New comedy**, as Hellenistic comedy is now called, told domestic tales of middle-class life structured as a series of episodes interrupted by incidental choral songs. New comedies took as their subjects such things as love, money, and family, often including intrigues involving long-lost children and happy reunitings. They resemble some of the situation comedies of today's television. Although there are many fragments, only one complete new comedy remains, *The Grouch* by Menander.

Actors remained exclusively male. They became professionalized, organizing themselves into a performing guild called the Artists of Dionysus. From changes in the plays (and also in theatre buildings, costuming conventions, and masks), we can infer that the acting style changed, becoming grander, showier, and more formal in tragedy and probably less boisterous, more restrained, and more representational in comedy.

HOW WE KNOW

Menander and *The Grouch*

New texts and fragments of texts from Hellenistic Greece continue to emerge from their eccentric hiding places. The Greek playwright Menander, from the late fourth century BCE, is said to have written more than one hundred comedies. None of his plays were extant prior to the twentieth century CE. All that was available of his writings were some fragments quoted by other writers. Through discoveries made in the last one hundred years, virtually all of one Menander play is known; there are substantial chunks—enough to surmise the plots—of five others.

THE BODMER PAPYRI

Here, a page from the twenty-two papyri that Martin Bodmer bought in 1952. Originally discovered in Egypt, the collection contains three plays by Menander.

The chronology of discovery tells a compelling story of how time and technology has played a part in a detective story.

In 1907, a papyrus called the Cairo Codex of Menander dating from the fourth century CE was discovered. This document gave the text of parts of four Menander plays.

In 1952, essentially all of another play, *The Grouch*, and substantial parts of two more were found in a hoard of documents known now as the Bodmer papyri. This cache of documents dates to the seventh century CE and earlier, having been placed in a clay jar to protect the writings from invaders.

In the late 1960s, parts of another play turned up in papyrus that had been used as filling in a mummy case. One person's packing material became an historian's treasure.

As recently as 2003, extensive parts of two Menander plays were found on palimpsest manuscripts within the collection of the Vatican museums. Palimpsest refers to a document where a piece of parchment was erased so it could be used again. Parchment was manufactured from goat or sheep skin and was costly. In this instance, in 886 CE the texts of Christian sermons were written over the Greek comedies, originally copied on the parchment in the fourth century CE. Special cameras and computer pattern-recognition are enabling experts to read the erased text. This discovery is allowing scholars to refine the text of *The Grouch* and other Menander fragments.

The discovery of the palimpsest manuscripts holds out hope that more ancient Greek texts may already be in our libraries and museums and will emerge as technology advances.

Theatre buildings also changed. Great stone theatres sprang up both on the Greek peninsula and on conquered lands and they tended to share common features:

- A two-storied skene.
- A long, narrow, high stage attached to the skene, usually with steps or ramps at the ends but sometimes with entrances and exits only through the skene.
- An orchestra, as before, but now of uncertain use.

Unfortunately, we do not know how plays were staged in Hellenistic theatres. Were actors on stage? In the orchestra? Some combination of the two? Where was the chorus?

Costumes and masks also changed. Those in tragedy tended toward greater size and grandeur. Unlike the masks of the golden age, based on our limited information about the golden-age masks, the masks of tragedy during the Hellenistic period are the familiar masks of cliché, having a high headdress termed an **onkos** as well as exaggerated, often distorted, eyes and mouths. Footwear for tragedy may have featured a high platform boot, called a **cothurnus**, rather than the soft slipper of former days. Such changes enlarged the physical appearance of the actor and brought him greater focus, suggesting an altered acting style. Comic masks ranged from somewhat lifelike to quite outrageous, matching the types of characters that began to repeat in comedies of the period.

Truth be told, drama and theatre from the Hellenistic period would not be of much importance to theatre historians except for three things:

- The promulgation of Aristotelian theory (when it was rediscovered beginning in the fifteenth century).
- The mistaken assumption that the buildings and practices of the Hellenistic theatre represented the buildings and practices of fifth-century BCE Athens.
- The strong influences of these plays, buildings, and practices on Roman theatre.

Aristotle's *Poetics*

Of far greater consequence than the drama itself during these years was Aristotle's theory of drama, the **Poetics**, written very early in the Hellenistic period (335 BCE). Providing a theoretical definition of the form tragedy, Aristotle set the boundaries for the next two thousand years of dramatic theory, with the following major points:

- Tragedy imitates "action that is serious, complete, and of a certain magnitude."
- Tragedy is told in language that is "embellished with...artistic ornament."
- Tragedy takes "the form of action, not narrative."
- Tragedy produces "pity and fear and the catharsis"; the last being a word meaning "cleaning" or "purging."

The meaning of Aristotle's definition has been endlessly debated, especially the phrase about catharsis, which some scholars believe refers to the response of audiences (though elsewhere Aristotle said he did not intend to talk about audiences), and other scholars think refers to emotions embedded within the episodes of the play itself.

Aristotle then defined and discussed the six parts of a play, the **elements of drama**. The following are just a few of his many comments on drama, especially tragedy:

- Plot: Plot was the most important to Aristotle. He therefore discussed it in the most detail, considering its *wholeness* (having a beginning, a middle, and an end, connected by causality); its *unity* (so that if any part is removed, the whole is disturbed); its *materials* (suffering, discovery, and reversal, meaning a change in heart for the protagonist); and its *form* (complication, climax, and the events that follow the climax which later came to be called, from the French for "unraveling," the **denouement**).

- Character: The main character of the tragedy, the protagonist, is best if he is a great man who causes his own downfall through some great tragic error (*hamartia*), according to Aristotle.

- Thought: The ideas that are encompassed in the play, the thought or reasoning that is spoken by the chorus or characters.

- Language: The play's language should be both clear and interesting.

- Music: The choral odes that were sung and danced to musical accompaniment. The chorus should be treated as part of the tragedy and add to its effect.

- Spectacle: Spectacle is the business of the stage machinist rather than the poet, Aristotle said. Again, spectacle must match the play in quality for the play to be successful with audiences.

The order of the six parts is important because it suggests the precise nature of the relationship among them, plot being primary.

The six parts should not be thought of as boxes into which sections of the play are placed; rather, they are parts of a system, a network of interrelationships so connected that a change in any one effects all others. For example, plot controls the kinds of characters that must appear in it, the kinds of characters control the kinds of ideas possible in the play, and so on. Note that Aristotles's theory treated neither comedy nor mixed forms.

Because the *Poetics* is so packed with ideas and its translation is so difficult because the ideas are so complex and concentrated, its meaning has been debated for centuries. Certainly, it remains the base from which most discussions of dramatic theory proceed, through either acceptance or rejection of all or some of its primary tenets.

Mime

There existed alongside the state-supported festival theatres another kind of theatrical activity, the **mime**, which refers to the presentations performed as well as those who performed them. Very little is known about mimes except that they seem to have been popular, professional, and perhaps slightly disreputable. Its troupes included women, its actors apparently often played barefoot, and mime troupes were not allowed to perform as part of the state-supported festivals. This fact may explain why so little evidence about them has come down to us. What little evidence there is indicates troupes performed short plays (skits?) and paratheatrical entertainments such as mimetic dance, singing, acrobatics, imitations of animals and birds, and juggling at banquets and other special occasions.

The literature of the Hellenistic era is little known, and thus, Western theatre makers are dazzled by the drama of the earlier classical era. Yet, the Hellenistic period is the one that spread Greek arts and culture to distant lands and established them as models to be emulated by civilized Western countries. When Rome accepted Greek models, they were often those of the Hellenistic era.

GREEK MIME
This detail from a painted vase may show a dramatic scene from mime as played in Greek outposts on the Italian peninsula. The appearance of comic nudity, including the oversized phalluses of many male comic figures, was likely achieved through costume tights and padding.

The Shift to Rome

After Alexander died, his Hellenistic empire soon collapsed. By a hundred years before the Common Era, Greece had fallen within the sphere of a spreading Roman influence. Roman theatres were built on Greek lands and Hellenistic theatres began to be remodeled to make them more like Roman theatres, producing hybrids that we now call Graeco-Roman theatres. The era of transition between the dominance of Alexander and the centrality of Rome is sometimes referred to as the **Graeco-Roman period**.

Although records show that theatre performances persisted in Hellenistic Greece, the center of cultural influence—and with it the theatre—had clearly shifted west to Rome itself.

KEY TERMS

Key terms are in boldface type in the text. Check your understanding against this list. Persons are page-referenced in the Index.

chorus, p. 17

cothurnus, p. 32

denouement, p. 33

eccyclema (eh-KIH-kleh-ma), p. 26

elements of drama, p. 33

facade stage, p. 25

Graeco-Roman period, p. 35

Great Dionysia (dye-un-NEE-see-uh), p. 18

Hellenistic period, p. 29

mechane (MEH-kah-neh), p. 27

middle comedy, p. 29

mime, p. 33

new comedy, p. 30

old comedy, p. 23

onkos (AHN-kohs), p. 32

orchestra, p. 24

pinake, p. 26

Poetics, p. 32

protagonist, p. 26

satyr play, p. 18

skene (SKEE-nee), p. 24

Chapter 1 at a Glance

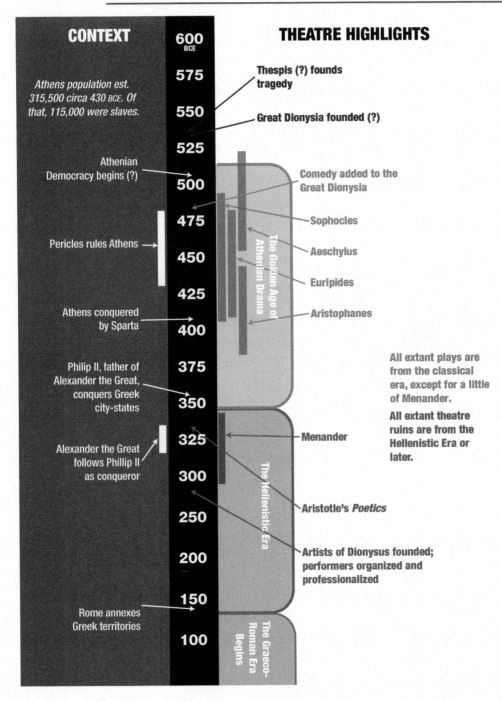

CONTEXT

THEATRE HIGHLIGHTS

600 BCE

575

Athens population est. 315,500 circa 430 BCE. Of that, 115,000 were slaves.

550

525

Athenian Democracy begins (?)

500

Pericles rules Athens

475

450

425

Athens conquered by Sparta

400

Philip II, father of Alexander the Great, conquers Greek city-states

375

350

Alexander the Great follows Phillip II as conqueror

325

300

250

200

150

Rome annexes Greek territories

100

Thespis (?) founds tragedy

Great Dionysia founded (?)

Comedy added to the Great Dionysia

Sophocles

Aeschylus

Euripides

Aristophanes

The Golden Age of Athenian Drama

Menander

The Hellenistic Era

Aristotle's *Poetics*

Artists of Dionysus founded; performers organized and professionalized

The Graeco-Roman Era Begins

All extant plays are from the classical era, except for a little of Menander.

All extant theatre ruins are from the Hellenistic Era or later.

Roman Theatre, 240 BCE–550 CE

Context

Roman theatre divides into two periods, roughly coinciding with Rome's two different forms of government, the republic and the empire. Throughout both periods, the Romans admired and emulated the older Greek and Hellenistic cultures.

The people of the Italian peninsula were mostly self-sufficient herders and farmers, who early established a republican form of government, a system in which the citizens elect people to represent the citizens and form the government. Having relatively little interest in arts, literature, and philosophy before the peoples of the Italian peninsula were organized into the Roman nation, they excelled instead in practical activities, becoming superb agriculturalists, soldiers, engineers, builders, and rhetoricians. They also had

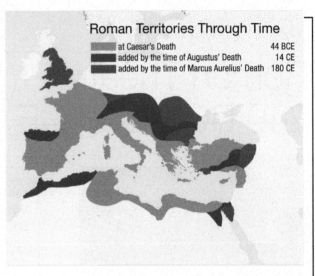

ROME

During Athens's golden age (400s BCE), Rome was simply one small city among many on Italy's peninsula, less important than the Etruscans to the north and the Greek colonies to the south. During Greece's Hellenistic period, however, a distinctly Roman culture emerged in Italy; it overtook the Greek culture by the start of the Common Era. In the empire, Rome grew and grew.

a gift for adapting useful ideas from other cultures, whose practices they modified to suit Roman tastes and needs. Their religion was polytheistic, with many Roman gods having clear Greek equivalents: Bacchus corresponded to Dionysus and Jupiter to Zeus, for example. Like the ancient Greeks, the Romans' religion was not based on a central book, so religious observances were highly varied, from region to region and family to family.

Even before the golden age of Athenian drama when the city of Rome was only one small town among many in its area, Greek culture had penetrated parts of the Italian peninsula. Later while Alexander the Great was building his Greek empire in the east, a distinctly Roman culture began to coalesce. First, Rome unified much of the Italian peninsula and then, having built a navy, began to expand to other lands around the Mediterranean Sea, which was soon thought of as the "Roman Lake." By the third century BCE (200s), Rome was a leading Mediterranean power. When Alexander's Hellenistic empire began to break apart, Rome moved to fill the void.

About a hundred years before the beginning of the Common Era, Rome's republican government gave way to an imperial one, ruled by an emperor. The process took place in several phases and was probably a response to civil war within the Roman republic. It was in this period that Rome began conquering greater and greater areas of land. Within three hundred years, the Roman Empire spread as far north as England, through parts of Africa and the Middle

East, and as far east as Syria. This expanding empire traded widely, importing luxury items from the East and exporting mass-produced, useful articles. They spread their language, religion, organization, engineering, and culture wherever they went. The sprawling empire encouraged more roads, better water management, a strong civil service, and a permanent military class. Travel, encouraged by both war and trade, promoted a kind of cosmopolitanism.

It was in republican Rome around 240 BCE that theatre and drama is first recorded as a feature in Roman festivals. It was also about this time that Rome had its first continuing contact with Hellenistic civilization as a result of the Punic Wars between Rome and Carthage in North Africa. Regrettably, the same major problem haunts the study of Roman theatre as of Greek theatre: For the periods when we know most about plays (i.e., for Rome in the years before the Common Era), we know least about theatres because they were most likely built of wood and have not lasted; conversely, when we know most about theatre buildings (the Common Era), we know almost nothing about plays.

Roman Festivals and Theatre of the Republic

Although paratheatrical entertainments developed independently in the north and south of the Italian peninsula—dancing, juggling, and forms of mime and pantomime—Roman dramatic and theatrical practices mostly reproduced those of Hellenistic Greece. Roman festivals, called **ludi**, differed from Greek festivals by having activities, such as acrobatics and rope dancing, compete directly with plays for public attention. At first, there was a single play presented at a ludi, but the number of plays grew steadily over time. Theatres of the ludi were free festivals and open to all, and probably somewhere between ten and fifteen thousand people attended. There was no formal competition among the playwrights or actors in Roman theatre. Acting companies were professional, engaged by the local organizer of the festival. In both respects, Roman theatre echoed Hellenistic theatre, not the theatre of classical Athens.

Tragedy and Comedy, Mostly Comedy

No Roman tragedy that was meant to be performed survives. However, fragments suggest that Roman tragedy resembled Hellenistic tragedy. Some plays presented upper-class Greeks in which actors wore Greek costume; others told of upper-class Romans dressed in Roman attire. Tragedy was never very popular in Rome, perhaps because as a people the Romans lacked deep interest in philosophy and ethics, the usual emphasis in Athenian tragedy. A number of literary tragedies from the Common Era, the later period of Rome, do survive but it is believed they were not intended for performance; rather they were read in homes and social gatherings. These "closet dramas," meaning a work of literature that has the form of a play but was never intended to be staged, are discussed in the section on Seneca.

Comedy was far more popular and, like tragedy, divided into two types: that written about Greeks and that about Romans. In both instances the characters were from the middle or lower class and so costumed. In addition to many titles, fragments, and names of comic playwrights, twenty-seven complete comedies survive, all by two authors: Plautus and Terence, both of whom wrote during the second century BCE (100s). Both drew heavily from Greek new comedy for their stories and approach. In fact the characters are usually drawn from the Athenian middle class. Neither playwright used a chorus. Like Greek new comedy, the extant Roman comedies by Plautus and Terence used stock characters in comic situations. Despite these strong similarities, the two authors differ from each other in significant ways and so suggest quite a range within Roman comedy.

The Theatre of Marcellus (left) was one of the first stone theatres built in Rome, c 17 BCE. This engraving from the late 1700s shows much of what then remained of the theatre. The site is today a popular tourist stop. This cross section of a Roman theatre drawn in the 1750s shows a raised stage backed by a neutral facade. The seating area is connected to the stage forming a unified structure. Roman theatres were not built on hillsides as were Greek theatres.

THE PLAY'S THE THING

Plautus's *The Menaechmi*

Written by Plautus, *The Menaechmi* is probably the most often revived Roman comedy. It has also served as a source for other works, most notably Shakespeare's *Comedy of Errors* and two US musicals, *The Boys from Syracuse* and *A Funny Thing Happened on the Way to the Forum* (which drew material from other Plautine comedies as well). The play's appeal probably comes from its farcical story, strong visual gags, and such familiar comic characters as the wily servant who outsmarts his master; the parasite, a person who tries to live off the main character's politeness; the courtesan, a cross between a high-class call girl and a mistress; and the nagging wife.

The Story of the Play A businessman from Syracuse takes Menaechmus, one of his identical twin sons, on a business trip, where the youngster disappears in a crowd. After a fruitless search, the father returns home alone, where, grief stricken, he dies, and the grandfather renames the remaining twin Menaechmus in honor of the lost brother. When this second Meneachmus grows up, he leaves with a servant to search for his long-lost twin. This information is revealed in a prologue before the action begins.

After years of searching, Menaechmus 2 arrives in the city of Epidamnus, where Menaechmus 1 has been living with a wealthy but quarrelsome wife. Following yet another argument with his wife, Menaechmus 1 storms out of the house, stealing a dress to give to his mistress, Erotium. Menaechmus 1 gives his present, orders a feast, and then leaves with his parasite to attend to business. Thus is the stage set for dual confusions.

Erotium, seeing Menaechmus 2, insists that he sit down and eat a feast that she has prepared (for Menaechmus 1); when Menaechmus 2 has eaten, she asks him to take a bracelet (a previous gift from Menaechmus 1) to a jeweler. He's happy to oblige. Meanwhile, the parasite, having become separated from Menaechmus 1, returns and sees Menaechmus 2 leaving the feast with the bracelet. Angry at Menaechmus for eating without him,

MILES GLORIOSUS

At least seven of Plautus's plays were incorporated into the 1962 musical A Funny Thing Happened on the Way to the Forum, *including the play* Miles Gloriosus *or* The Braggart Soldier. *Here, this character in Virginia Commonwealth University's production of* A Funny Thing....

he tells the wife about the gifts to Erotium, so that when Menaechmus 1 returns, he finds that his wife is in a tizzy and his mistress has locked him out of her house. He leaves just as Menaechmus 2 returns, carrying the dress and bracelet. He encounters the angry wife, who first attacks him and then decides he's crazy, ties him up, and carts him off to a doctor. Menaechmus 2, of course, has no idea what's going on: He's had a splendid free meal and tried to do a favor in return, only to be assaulted and called crazy.

The mistaken identities are finally sorted out by the servant of Menaechmus 2, who thus earns his freedom. Menaechmus 1 announces that he will sell everything he owns (including his wife) and return with his brother to Syracuse.

Plautus

Plautus (c. 254–184 BCE), the older of the two authors, was an actor as well as a playwright. Of the more than one hundred titles credited to Plautus, twenty-one play scripts have survived. Some commentators argue that the large number of surviving play scripts is a tribute to his popularity. Probably his experience as an actor accounted for the theatrical as opposed to literary qualities of his comedies. Plautine comedies are noted for:

- Loosely linked episodes.
- Many visual gags and much verbal wordplay.
- Characters who are ludicrous in appearance as well as behavior.
- Direct address to the audience, breaking dramatic illusion.

Among his many plays, *The Braggart Warrior, The Menaechmi* or *The Twins, Pot of Gold*, and *Amphitryon* were used and adapted by Shakespeare, Molière, and others.

Terence

Terence's (185?–159 BCE) comedies were more refined than those of Plautus. His plays were more elegant but also less robust and free. They were more thoughtful but less fun. Terence's comedies are characterized by:

- Plots that often combined two or more of the "new" Greek comedies into a single, highly complicated dramatic action.
- Prologues that were not part of the action of the play. Terence prologues sometimes argued matters of dramatic theory, encouraged audiences to behave politely, or defended the playwright from the attacks of critics.
- Carefully contrived actions that seemed to proceed by cause and effect, thus avoiding the episodic quality of Plautus's comedies.
- Characters that appeared more conventional and human than Plautus's and thus more sympathetic.

It may help to distinguish Terence from Plautus to know that, although Plautus is occasionally performed today, Terence almost never is. But Terence, not Plautus, was used in schools during the Middle Ages as a way to teach the Latin language and proper Latin usage. Plautus pleased audiences; Terence interested scholars.

Although comedy had always been more popular than tragedy in Rome, its popularity waned within fifty years of Terence's death. Therefore, by the time the first stone theatre was built (55 BCE), the great period of Roman tragedy and comedy was over, to be replaced by paratheatrical entertainments.

Three Important Texts

Works by three writers are extant from the later, Imperial Roman period, which, although having little impact on ancient Roman theatre, had a major influence on theatre long after Rome fell. Two how-to manuals, both written near the turn into the Common Era, are of special importance to theatre and drama because, when they were rediscovered during the Italian Renaissance (c. 1400s), their advice on how to build theatres and write

TERENCE CHARACTERS
These four comic actors are performing in Terence's play, *Andria*. The drawing survives in a medieval manuscript from a late Roman picture-cycle. Father (Simo) and son (Pamphilus), *center*, confront each other over an arranged marriage. The son's scheming servant (Davos), *far right*, gives advice.

plays was put into practice. As the Western theatre remains influenced by Renaissance practice, the Roman past comes into the present in part through the impact of these three texts.

Vitruvius

The Roman architect Vitruvius (70? BCE–15? BCE) wrote a ten-volume work, *De Architectura*, on how to lay out a city. As a part of this larger work, written around 25 BCE, he set down guidelines for building both theatres and the scenery to go in them. Without illustrations and with descriptions that were often ambiguous, the books were easily—and badly—misinterpreted by Renaissance designers. Rightly or wrongly, Vitruvius greatly influenced later architects.

Horace

The Roman poet Horace (65–8 BCE) described how to write good plays in his *Ars Poetica*, a work that was to exert even more influence during the Renaissance than Aristotle's *Poetics* did, which it superficially resembles. Horace and Aristotle were separated by country and background but even more by time. The two books were written a little more than three centuries apart. *Ars Poetica* was written in 18 BCE and Aristotle's *Poetics* around 335 BCE. Unlike Aristotle's work, a philosophical inquiry into the nature of the form of tragedy, Horace's is a practical guidebook aimed at people who want to write plays. As such, it is considerably more prescriptive than *Poetics*, suggesting such things as:

- The importance of keeping comedy and tragedy separate.
- The need to have a unity of time and of place as a way of achieving unity of action.
- The need for drama to teach as well as please and to appeal to the feelings of the audience.
- The need to show incidents, not narrate them, unless they are horrifying or incredible.

Ars Poetica had no immediate influence on Roman practice. Its importance, like Vitruvius's, comes from its powerful influence much later on Renaissance theory and drama.

Seneca

The third important text is really a set of texts. Although Roman tragedy and comedy were not played in public theatres by the 100s CE, dramatic readings were apparently given at banquets in private homes. Ten such literary tragedies—**closet dramas**—have come down to us, nine by Seneca (c. 4 BCE–65 CE), who wrote them just after the turn of the Common Era. Seneca's subjects were identifiably Greek, as shown by some of his titles including *Agamemnon*, *Oedipus*, *Medea*, and *Phaedra*.

Seneca's plays display five characteristics:

- A chorus that is not well integrated into the action, and so the choral odes—songs—divide the plays into parts, generally four odes yielding five parts.
- Protagonists that are often driven by a single dominant passion that causes their downfall.
- Minor characters that include messengers, confidants, and ghosts.
- Language that emphasizes rhetorical and stylistic figures, including extended descriptive and declamatory passages, pithy statements about the human condition (called in Latin *sententiae*), and elaborately balanced exchanges of dialogue.
- Spectacular scenes of violence and gore.

The importance of Seneca's tragedies rests neither on their literary excellence nor on their position among contemporary Roman audiences, but on their monumental effect on later writers, who discovered, translated, and copied them, probably because they were both linguistically and physically more accessible than the previous Greek tragedies. Although Seneca's plays are now rarely performed, they are important. Like the writings of Vitruvius and

Horace, they profoundly influenced Renaissance writers. Seneca's tragedies were the first dramas to be known to them, and they tried to follow Seneca's model in writing their own tragedies.

Theatre Buildings, Scenery, Costumes, and Masks

Roman theatres, like Greek theatres, were facade stages. As far as is known, their basic arrangement remained the same: scene house, aisles, and orchestra. Assuming that Rome's early theatres that do not survive resembled its later stone ones that do exist, Roman theatres differed from Hellenistic theatres in several ways:

- They stood on level ground rather than hillsides, with built-up, stadium-style seating.
- Their orchestras were half-circles, rather than full circles or rectangles.
- Their long, deep stages were closed at both ends by the building itself, which jutted out and connected to the seating. The theatre was one unified building.
- They used a front curtain; they were first to do so. The curtain descended below the stage rather than being raised above the stage as is the custom today.

As in Greece, the facade of Roman theatres served as background. In tragedy, the doors of the facade represented separate entrances to a palace or other public building, with the stage floor representing the ground in front of the building. In comedy, the doors were entrances to separate houses, with the stage representing a street running in front of them. There were **periaktoi**, three-sided devices that could be rotated to reveal painted scenes. Records tell of two periaktoi, one near each end of the stage. Because they could not possibly have hidden the whole facade, they must have served simply to inform the audience of location, not to portray any place in a realistic way. The early wooden theatres were quite spectacular, according to ancient accounts.

As in Greece, all actors of comedy and tragedy wore masks, and the masks resembled those of Hellenistic Greece, with high headdresses (onkos) and distorted eyes and mouth for tragedy and a range from somewhat realistic to comically distorted for comedy. The conventions of costuming were also rooted in Hellenistic conventions, with actors wearing a version of either Greek or Roman dress, depending on the kind of tragedy or comedy.

THE ROMAN THEATRE IN AFRICA
This partially restored Roman theatre in Tunisia, North Africa illustrates the nature of the three-story, highly decorated facade of columns and niches.

Starting in the Common Era, Rome built great stone theatres, first on the Italian peninsula and then throughout its empire. Remains are still visible in Libya, Turkey, and elsewhere. There are more than 120 known theatres. Five are on the African continent. The farthest north in is today's Germany. The sites differ in size and ornateness. Some are just ruins, decipherable only by experts, and others are complete and are still used today for theatre and music. The Romans also remodeled many stone theatres of the Hellenistic era, further complicating the investigations of future theatre historians. Stone theatres were *probably* more ornate than previous wooden ones. Now used by audiences rather than choruses, the aisles separating the scene house from the seating area were covered, causing the buildings to form a single architectural unit, rather than two as in Greek theatres. The facades were decorated with statuary, niches, and columns. A roof extended over part of the stage, both protecting the elaborate facades and improving acoustics. Audience comfort was a high priority, with awnings sometimes protecting audiences from sun and rain and, in at least one theatre, a primitive air conditioning system consisting of large fans blowing over ice brought down from mountaintops.

Paratheatrical Entertainments

Into these theatres of the Common Era came new theatrical entertainments that replaced comedy and tragedy. An indigenous rural Italian farce, called **Atellan farce** after the region in which it originated, was popular for a while. It featured four grotesquely masked characters. **Pantomime**, a solo dance performed by a nonspeaking performer (wearing a mask with a closed mouth), could be comic but was more often serious. We imagine that serious pantomime filled the void left by tragedy.

Most popular of all, however, was mime, which may have come from Greece because Greek mime (the word refers both to the form and the performers) had a long history, although it was never performed at Greek festivals. In Greece, mime seemed unimportant, but Roman mime became so popular during the empire that it drove all other forms of theatre from the stage.

Several traits of mime make it important:

- Mime included women as performers, and was the only theatrical entertainment in Greece or Rome to do so.

- Performers in the mime did not usually wear masks, so their faces were both noticeable and important. Indeed, mime performers were often successful because of their looks: either the very good looking or the extraordinarily grotesque and ugly.

- Mimes could be either comic or serious, simple or spectacular, but whatever their form, they usually dealt with contemporary life.

Mime became both Rome's most popular and its most notorious theatrical entertainment during the empire. Some female mime actors set fashions in clothes and behavior; one, Theodora, married an emperor; some became the equivalent of movie stars. Despite this popularity, few if any complete mime scripts have been passed down to us. The assumption is that they, perhaps like sitcom scripts, were thought to have no lasting value by those who kept libraries. (Modern mime—the silent, white-faced street clowns—should not be confused with the spoken Roman mime. Same word, different meaning in the past and the present.)

Christian Opposition to Theatre

In its early years, the Roman Empire confronted the growing challenge of a new religion, Christianity, which had arisen in one of its own territories. Rome had routinely adopted the gods of any culture with which it came into contact. For example, the ruins of Pompeii, buried by a volcano in 79 CE, contain the standard temples to Jupiter, Juno, and Minerva and also a small, well-maintained temple to the Egyptian goddess, Isis. But Christians refused to allow their god to be assimilated into the Roman pantheon. Indeed, they insisted that their god alone should be worshipped, rigidity unwelcome in a culture whose religion depended more on traditions than passions. (For the same reasons, Judaism refused to be assimilated and suffered

LASTING STRUCTURES
Here a Roman coliseum in Verona, Italy, being set up for a concert in the summer of 2012.

persecution by the Romans.) This Roman resistance to Christianity eventually reversed with the conversion of Emperor Constantine to the new Christian religion. He issued the Edict of Milan in 313 CE, which proclaimed religious tolerance of Christians throughout the empire.

Christianity's opposition to theatre was not to Roman comedies or tragedies, which Christians had not seen and did not know because comedy and tragedy were not performed publicly during the Common Era. The opposition was to mime. Because some mimes included sex and violence as part of the performance and because many of them mocked Christianity, Christian writers and believers demanded—unsuccessfully—the outlawing of the theatre of their time, which is to say, mime and pantomime. The past antipathy between theatre and the church, which dates from the early Roman Empire, finds fainter echoes in the present.

Mime was not the only paratheatrical entertainment sometimes characterized by excesses; equally popular were chariot racing, gladiatorial contests, animal fights, and mock sea battles in which violence and death—in many cases, real violence and death instead of pretend violence and death—were also expected and applauded. Although these entertainments took place in special buildings such as the **amphitheatre** (e.g., Rome's Colosseum) and

HOW WE KNOW

Theatre in an Ordinary Roman Town

Mount Vesuvius erupted on August 25, 79 CE, burying two small Roman cities in twelve to sixteen feet of ash and pumice: Herculaneum and its larger, better known neighbor, Pompeii. Fitfully since the seventeenth century, the city of Pompeii has been excavated. The ash and pumice were hot, but not as hot as lava, so much of the city remained underneath the fallout. Tomb robbers stole and World War II bombings exploded but many artifacts survived. Artworks, household articles, erotica, advertisements painted on walls, graffiti, and charred loaves of bread remained. Even the castings of some of the dead have been found, the bodies long gone but still outlined in the pumice and ash. These three-dimensional molds included people, horses, and pet dogs. There is a wealth of information for one city on a specific day in the first century CE. But Pompeii, for all its excavated remains, reveals very little about Roman theatre.

Pompeii was a small city, in many ways an ordinary place, with a population estimated from

Here, an exaggerated mask of a tragic character found as a mosaic in Pompeii.

(continues)

HOW WE KNOW   Theatre in an Ordinary Roman Town *(continued)*

Although this theatre has undergone various modifications over the years, it dates from the Hellenistic era.

6,400 to 30,000. It seems that theatre had a significant place in the citizens's lives. Pompeii housed two theatre structures, an open-air Roman theatre seating about 5,000 and a covered theatre, an odeon, seating up to 2,000. Mosaics and wall paintings that decorated Pompeian houses sometimes show images of theatrical performance. One house has a portrait that is inscribed as Menander, the playwright. Mosaics from another home show two scenes from Menander comedies. All the actors pictured wear masks. A painting in yet another house represents a scene from one of Euripides's plays. Another mosaic shows actors getting ready to go on stage in a satyr play. The actors have parts of costumes on and masks rest on a table to be donned later. Note that all of these images are of Greek and Hellenistic theatre, at least three centuries in the past by the time of the eruption.

Despite this pictorial and physical record, there is no hard evidence for what live theatre the Pompeians would have attended in their two theatres. Some scholars conjecture that either indigenous comedies known as *Atellan* farces or Roman comedy by Plautus and Terence were staged or possibly all three. There is a bit of evidence for the popularity of mime and pantomime and other paratheatrical expressions. Other scholars believe the covered theatre was not for performances at all but was an assembly hall for the citizens.

Pompeii walls exhibit graffiti and painted advertisements for political campaigns and entertainments. Advertisements promoting a five-day festival of gladiatorial battles and wild-beast hunts held in the Pompeian coliseum are found on several walls. No advertisements survive regarding theatre. Very little writing survives except for the advertisements and graffiti on walls. The other writing that remains, written on wax tablets, concerns finance, tax records, and loan agreements.

If there were scripts of plays in Pompeii before the eruption, none have been found. Parchment or papyrus was valuable and literature may well have been taken with those who fled the volcano in time. Or the only performances may have come from traveling troupes who knew their parts by heart or took their scripts with them when they moved to the next town.

Pompeii's theatre evidence is an illustration in miniature of the ephemeral nature of the sources for theatre history. Historians can testify that this first-century Roman town knew about theatre but can not say with certainty what kind of theatre they attended in performance.

Found in Pompeii, this mosaic, probably from the second century BCE, shows three actor-musicians in masks playing the double flute (left), cymbals (center), and tambourine (right). An unmasked youngster looks on. This mosaic, believed to be a scene from Menander's play The Possessed, *along with many other theatrical artifacts from the Naples Archeological Museum, suggests that Pompeii was a city that embraced theatre.*

circus (the Circus Maximus), theatres may have been appropriated for such events, reinforcing the arguments of those who wanted to ban theatre. That mime had to compete directly with these other kinds of performance probably explains its occasional rawness. That mime replaced comedy and tragedy in Rome's public theatres surely offers hints about Romans and their culture.

The Breakup of the Empire

By the early 300s CE, the Roman Empire had become too large and unwieldy to rule effectively. It was therefore broken into two administrative units, with the Western unit claiming Rome as its capital and the Eastern unit being ruled from Constantinople (modern Istanbul, Turkey), a new city built by the Emperor Constantine. Constantine moved to this new capital in 476, taking much of the population of Rome with him, thus tilting the empire's center of gravity far to the East. The result was a shift in power and cultural influence. Constantinople grew more powerful and turned eastward. Rome, now a much smaller city, once again found itself on the western fringe of the civilized world.

By the middle of the sixth century (500s), the Western empire was disintegrating, its system of roads and waterways crumbling, its trade sporadic, and its security destroyed. Whatever unity remained in Western Europe came mostly from the Christian church through a network of churches and religious houses bound through the pope in Rome, but the center of the Western empire had fallen.

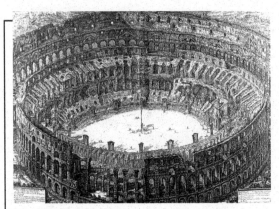 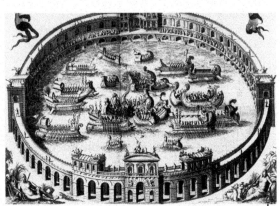

ROMAN ENTERTAINMENTS
During the Roman Empire, elaborate entertainments with animal fights, chariot races, and even naval battles became popular and drove traditional theatre from the center of cultural life. The left hand image is of the Colosseum in Rome as it appeared in the 1750s when this etching was made. The right hand image is an imaginative rendering from the seventeenth century of a mock naval battle in a Roman structure.

The Eastern (Byzantine) Empire and Theatre

Constantinople and the Eastern empire, on the other hand, flourished. Considering themselves Romans, the citizens for a time continued to speak Latin, to enjoy chariot races and theatre, and to trade with such Italian satellites as Ravenna (in today's Italy), but increasingly trade was with countries to the East. The Eastern Romans soon adopted Greek for official documents; established a Christian church, now called the Orthodox Church, which was tied more closely to the government than to the pope; and gradually adopted elements of more Eastern culture. Later called *Byzantine* (after the early town of Byzantium, which Constantinople had replaced), this empire had a thriving trade, a successful military, and a highly developed culture that included theatre.

Constantinople never entirely lost contact with the West; it continued to send gifts, receive envoys, and marry its leading families with those of the West. Still, its major interests lay increasingly to the East. This rich Byzantine culture persisted for almost another thousand years. Weakened by one of the Western crusades in the thirteenth century (1200s), the Byzantine Empire was finally overwhelmed by Muslim Turks in the fifteenth century (1453), just as the former Western empire—Europe—was beginning to grow out of the middle ages and enter its great Renaissance.

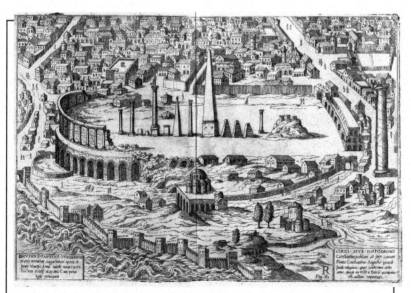

BYZANTINE EMPIRE CONTINUED ROMAN STYLES
This is a seventeenth century engraving of the ruins of the Roman hippodrome in Constantinople, which would have housed horse races and other mass entertainments.

The Eastern Church fathers preached against entertainments, including theatre, but did not quite succeed in closing them down. Professional entertainers were excommunicated from the church, yet entertainments are known to have been given at royal festivals and the emperor sometimes blessed the races at the hippodrome. Most importantly for the history of Western theatre, the Byzantine Empire preserved ancient Greek texts, including those of tragedies and comedies, which with other Greek documents eventually helped fuel the European renaissance. With the conquering of Constantinople by Muslims in the 1450s, theatre was suppressed as a sin of idolatry under Islam. Still, buildings associated with entertainments survived in the Eastern and Western empires from before the fall of Rome, and in many places, stone remains still exist of theatres, colosseums, and hippodromes (horse-racing tracks).

Byzantine theatre is not well known in today's Western world, for a couple of reasons. The languages in which its records appear are not those in which most Western scholars are competent, and many of the records were, until the late 1980s, inaccessible because they were held behind the so-called Iron Curtain. With the fall of the Soviet Union and the political realignment of Russia and the United States, however, more information is now becoming available. The recent scholarship suggests that Byzantine theatre included:

- The continuation of mime.
- An interest in Greek tragedy, which may have been literary only, without public performances.
- The exportation of performances and an idea of performance to Asia Minor and what is now Ukraine.

Roman theatre of the West left a legacy for the Renaissance in Western Europe, and so may have the Byzantine theatre, although the record is unclear. There are tantalizing hints that Byzantine theatre may have influenced both Italian popular theatre and the medieval theatre of Europe.

KEY TERMS

Key terms are in boldface type in the text. Check your understanding against this list. Persons are page-referenced in the Index.

amphitheatre, p. 48
Atellan farce, p. 46
circus, p. 50
closet drama, p. 44

ludi (LOO-dee), p. 39
pantomime, p. 46
periaktoi (peh-ree-AKH-toy), p. 45

Chapter 2 at a Glance

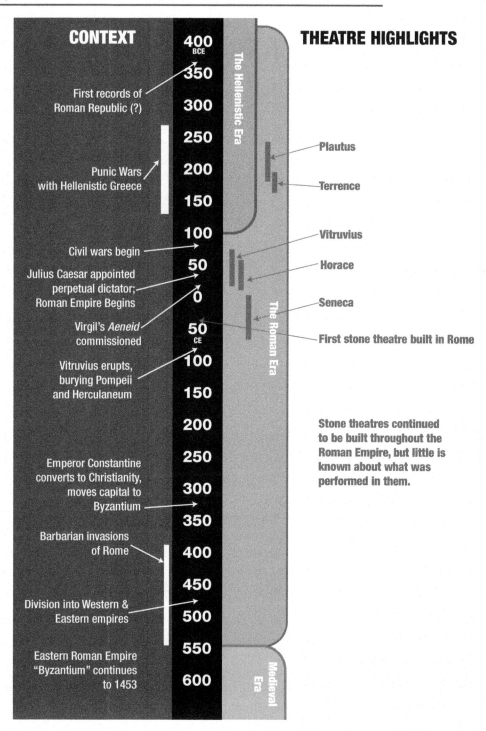

CONTEXT

THEATRE HIGHLIGHTS

The Hellenistic Era

The Roman Era

Medieval Era

400 BCE	
350	
300	First records of Roman Republic (?)
250	
200	Punic Wars with Hellenistic Greece
150	
100	
50	Civil wars begin
0	Julius Caesar appointed perpetual dictator; Roman Empire Begins
50 CE	Virgil's *Aeneid* commissioned
100	Vitruvius erupts, burying Pompeii and Herculaneum
150	
200	
250	Emperor Constantine converts to Christianity, moves capital to Byzantium
300	
350	
400	Barbarian invasions of Rome
450	
500	Division into Western & Eastern empires
550	Eastern Roman Empire "Byzantium" continues to 1453
600	

Plautus

Terrence

Vitruvius

Horace

Seneca

First stone theatre built in Rome

Stone theatres continued to be built throughout the Roman Empire, but little is known about what was performed in them.

3

Early Theatre of Asia, 200 BCE–1800 CE

OBJECTIVES

When you have completed this chapter, you should be able to:

- Trace the development of early theatre in India, China, and Japan.
- Discuss the ways in which early Asian drama is linked to religion.
- Describe Sanskrit drama.
- Discuss the importance of the *Natyasastra*.
- Describe *Kunqu* opera.
- Explain the characteristics of *Noh* drama.
- Describe a *Noh* stage.
- Describe the essential characteristics of *Kabuki*.
- Explain the characteristics of *kyogen* performances.

Context

The first civilizations with recorded language, cities, and a sustainable culture arguably began in Asia. China left written records of a feudal society dating from the seventeenth century BCE (1600s). Mesopotamia, the west Asian area around the Mediterranean and reaching into part of the Indian subcontinent, hosted what is now called the cradle of civilization, dating from about 3000 BCE to the fall of Babylon in 536 BCE. *Asia* is a word from ancient Greek, signifying all peoples east of the Mediterranean, which, except for the Persian Empire, were unknown to the Greeks. All parts of Asia have been broken into feudal regimes of varying sizes, combining at times, and being conquered by neighboring peoples at other times.

One of the seven continents, Asia covers just less than 30 percent of the earth's landmass. At present, 60 percent of the population resides there. Asia includes India, China, Japan, and the southeast Asian countries. It also covers what is now called the Middle East—Israel, Lebanon, Jordan, Iran, Iraq, and the countries of the Saudi Arabian peninsula—plus Afghanistan, Turkmenistan, neighboring states, and the eastern parts of Turkey and Russia, the large area of Siberia.

Theatre in Asia often grew out of religious organizations because religious orders were the seats of learning, religious texts offered stories ripe for performance, and the priests or monks may have seen performance as a way to propagate the religion's ideas to illiterate people.

Areas under the governance of Islam typically did not develop theatre. Theatre was usually forbidden because of the Qur'ān's proscription of idolatry, interpreted in much of Islam as any representation of people in art. Shadow puppet performances, two-dimensional jointed puppets manipulated with sticks from behind a cloth, were not universally suppressed in Islamic countries. In a shadow puppet show, only the shadow is seen by

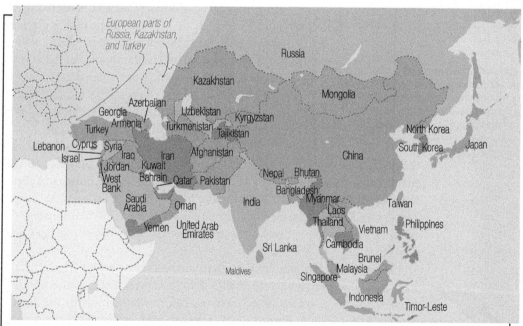

MAP OF ASIA

Most continents are separated by bodies of water, but parts of the border of Asia is on land. Asia includes a large part of Turkey and Russia and also the countries usually called the Middle East today.

SHADOW PUPPET

Shadow plays now can be found in dozens of countries around the world, especially in Muslim societies where human actors are not allowed. Shadow puppets have articulated limbs. The bodies are manipulated by the puppeteer.

the audience so, it might be said, no human is impersonated. Shadow puppet plays are still found in much of Asia, including Islamic countries.

In this short history of the theatre of early Asian areas, many different regimes and varying local, indigenous traditions are conflated and truncated. As an example of the breadth of the performing arts in Asia, it is estimated that there have been, over time, seven to eight hundred different types of theatre and paratheatrical genres in Asia. This chapter samples the theatres of India, China, and Japan from about the 200s BCE to the 1800s.

India

The Indian subcontinent (today including India, Pakistan, and Bangladesh) has been, since the sixth century BCE (500s), divided into many kingdoms of varying sizes, with borders changing through local strife. To the extent that India had any shared identity among these local populations, it was based on the dominance of the Hindu religion and the language of the religion, Sanskrit. In several eras, Indian rulers conquered significant parts of the subcontinent but the land was not continually under a unified administration.

The Indian subcontinent has a long history of theatre production. The earliest fragments of play scripts are dated to the first century CE and show enough sophistication to lead scholars to believe that Indian theatre started before that time, perhaps as early as the second century BCE. This theatre is called **Sanskrit drama** for the language in which it was written. It was a theatre connected to religious practices and court life.

All of the hypotheses for the origin of theatre applied to Greek theatre have generally been applied to India's theatre as well. There is also another possible source. Alexander the Great reached northern India in the fourth century BCE (300s BCE) and some scholars have put forward the notion that Sanskrit drama owes its origin to Greek theatre. Alexander was known to spread Greek traditions wherever he roamed and *may* have had a theatre troupe travel with him to entertain his troops. The evidence offered is minimal.

The *Natyasastra*

There are no surviving Sanskrit theatre buildings or ruins and no depictions of the theatre in drawings or paintings. There is, however, the **Natyasastra**, a book whose title is sometimes translated in English as "Theatre Science." Written between 200 BCE and 200 CE, the *Natyasastra* describes in great detail play construction, theatre building architecture, musical scales, and types of dance. Music and dance were integral parts of the drama. Individual chapters specify makeup, costume, acting, and directing. To give a sense of the level of detail, the *Natyasastra* specifies thirteen head positions and thirty-six glances for an actor to employ. Emotions are said to be communicated through specific movements of the eyes, eyelids, and eyebrows, as well as the nose, cheeks, lower lip, chin, mouth, and neck. The book prescribes posture, hand movements, and the motion of the major limbs as well.

According to the *Natyasastra*, Sanskrit drama was invented by the Hindu god of creation, Brahma, who declared, "The drama will...be instructive to all,...It will give relief to unlucky persons who are afflicted with sorrow and grief or [over] work." Sanskrit drama continued to be performed into the tenth century CE (900s) and still influences much of the regional folk drama in India today, including play structure, makeup and costumes, and styles of movement.

The *Natyasastra* offers three designs for theater space: a square, a rectangle, or a triangle. It focuses, however, on the rectangular space, which should be divided into two squares, one for the audience and one for the actors. The actors' space is further divided into two areas, one the playing space and one the backstage space.

The *Natyasastra*'s basic assumptions align with those of Hinduism: a universe of unity expressed through multiplicity, therefore aesthetically an art of multiple forms—dance, song, and poetry—unified through performance into a form that would induce empathy, or understanding, in a receptive audience. The viewer would appreciate the **rasa**, a word meaning *juice* or *essence*, which is the dominant emotional theme of the work. There are nine rasas: love or attractiveness, anger, laughter, disgust or aversion, heroic mood, compassion, fear, wonder or amazement, and

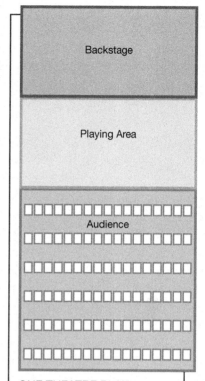

ONE THEATRE PLAN DESCRIBED IN THE *NATYASASTRA*

The rectangular version of a theatre for Sanskrit drama resembles in many ways a Western proscenium theatre. The dimensions given in the *Natyasastra* suggest audiences would have numbered two to five hundred persons.

A *KATHAKALI* PERFORMER

Indian dance drama features intricately costumed actors with fully painted faces presenting stories of Hindu gods Rama and Krishna. Here a modern actor in traditional costume of the Kathakali dance drama of southern India. Some scholars believe *Kathakali* is a direct descendant of Sanskrit drama.

peace or tranquility. *Natyasastra* provides valuable theatrical evidence of

- Professional acting companies that toured and included both men and women performers.
- Performances that included song and dance, accompanied by onstage musicians.
- Permanent indoor theatres built of wood and stone, seating two hundred to five hundred spectators, with elevated stages.
- Rigid caste limits, restricting viewing of Sanskrit drama to the elite caste of Brahmins.
- Although termed Sanskrit drama, low caste or comic characters often spoke a local dialect and not Sanskrit.

At least a thousand Sanskrit dramas were written but only about fifty or sixty scripts survive. The most highly regarded play is *Shakuntala*, a fantastic assortment of mythology, the supernatural, poetry, and serious drama with comic scenes interspersed. Subtitled *The Recovered Ring*, the play is in seven acts and a prologue with at least twenty-three named characters.

No one knows for certain why Sanskrit drama declined and disappeared in the ninth and tenth centuries CE. It may be related to successive invasions of India from central Asia that ultimately resulted in the land being ruled by the Mughal Empire, an Islamic regime unsympathetic to theatre and Hindu culture.

Indian Folk Theatre Traditions

India has extensive folk theatre traditions that date back to at least the tenth century (900s), probably much earlier. Folk theatre traditions are local, highly varied, and specific to the respective geographic area. One scholar of Indian theatre writes, "In India performances...are known by genre-specific names in their local language—*yakṣagāna, rās līlā, terukkuttu, cavittu nāṭakam*—an endless stream of names, each with its own history and reasons for having been given that name." Except for contemporary Western-style theatre, even today Indians do not go to an event called *theatre*, but to their specific indigenous folk theatre genre. Folk productions vary from dance-dramas that are strict extensions of Hindu worship conducted only in temples, to public works performed in any number of

THE PLAY'S THE THING

Shakuntala

Shakuntala, the best known of the Sankrit dramas, was written by the playwright Kalidasa, whose birth and death dates are questioned, with surmises ranging from the fourth to sixth centuries. As with many Sanskrit dramas, the story comes from the Hindu sacred poem, the *Mahabharata*, a text of nearly two million words.

Shakuntala begins with a benediction and prologue, a dialogue between the stage manager and an actress:

> Stage Manager: Lady, if you have arranged your costume, please come forward.
>
> Actress: Here I am, sir. Command me. What shall be done?
>
> Stage Manager: This is for the most part a refined audience, my lady. We must now represent the new play by Kalidasa called "The Recognition of Shakuntala." May each actor endeavor to do his best.

This exchange shows that Sanskrit drama was often presentational, not illusionistic. Every scene is interrupted by songs and poems, expressing the character's profound response to the sensations of sight, sound, and smell.

The Story of the Play King Dusyanta is chasing a deer by chariot.

Two hermits tell him the deer belongs to the holy hermitage nearby and so it should not be hunted. The hermits invite him into the saint's hermitage, where the leader is away but his daughter, Shakuntala, will offer the king hospitality. Upon entering, the king spies Shakuntala watering the sacred bushes and is struck by her beauty. Thus begins a romantic fable of the love of the king and shy Shakuntala that includes the intercession of gods, a curse, and a ring that is lost and then found in the belly of a fish.

The king is distraught. When his advisors discover that the king's problem is lovesickness, they get him back to the hermitage. Similarly, Shakuntala's handmaidens recognize her lovesickness, as well, and transpire to leave the king and Shakuntala alone. The two kiss after they speak of their erotic longings.

The king must return to the court. Meanwhile, an unseen guest is disturbed at not being better welcomed to the hermitage and casts a spell: the king will forget Shakuntala, until he sees the ring she wears with the king's name on it. Not knowing this, Shakuntala and her maids prepare for the wedding and she travels to court, sung on by a chorus of wood nymphs. At the court, the king, as foretold, does not recognize her but he can see that she is pregnant.

She insists that they are betrothed; he remembers nothing. She goes to produce the magic ring and discovers it is lost, slipped off when she scooped up water to pour on her head during the journey. Not knowing of the spell cast by the unseen visitor, Shakuntala says, "I have been deceived by this perfidious man." Her friends lead her away and report that once out of site of the king she vanished in a shaft of light.

A fisherman, a comic character, is arrested for trying to sell a ring with the king's name on it. He swears he found the ring in the belly of a fish. On seeing the ring, the king's memory is wholly restored. The king travels above the clouds in the chariot of the god of thunder, a gift to the king for some virtuous action of his. It stops at a somewhat mystical place known as the retreat of the truly pious.

The king sees a rambunctious, heroic child whose face looks like his own. The king realizes that this is his son and the son's mother is Shakuntala. The god of thunder appears, divulges that Shakuntala is the daughter of a goddess, and their son will rule the world. The god directs the king, Shakuntala, and their son to remount the god's chariot and return to the king's court. The god of thunder has been directing the story all along.

HOW WE KNOW

Shakuntala's First Translation

In 1789 *Shakuntala* became the first complete work in Sanskrit to be translated and published in English. Over the next seventy years, there were translations into German, French, Italian, Dutch, Danish, Swedish, and Polish and a partial translation into Russian.

The play had an impact beyond its literary importance. It altered the opinion of the European intelligentsia of the value of Indian culture. A land that had been prized only for material wealth was found to have a great literary masterpiece. *Shakuntala* became one small piece of India's ancient and enduring literature now open to exploration.

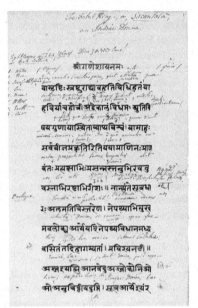

The first translator was not a literary man, however, but an English jurist sent to serve on the Supreme Court in Calcutta, Sir William Jones. He knew many languages—eventually twenty-eight in all—and had already published a translation from the Persian. He started to study Sanskrit to translate Hindu texts on law and justice to better administer justice in India. He collected many Sanskrit dictionaries. When told that there were Sanskrit works performed, similar to what the English called "plays," Jones asked which was regarded the best of them; he was pointed to *Shakuntala*.

First, he translated from Sanskrit into Latin, a language he thought similar in structure to Sanskrit. From the Latin, Jones made his English translation. A page from his working translation is seen here, with his notes in the margins.

Jones' late-nineteenth-century translation has been supplanted by later ones that are judged to be more accurate. Still, he started a revolution in European attitudes toward India and Hinduism arising out of his curiosity to read the best ancient play written in a language he hardly could comprehend when he started.

spaces. Some traditions are strictly professional, with performers undergoing extensive training and apprenticeship. Others are wholly amateur. Almost all include exaggerated makeup or masks and flamboyantly colored and shaped costuming. During the rule of Great Britain (mid-nineteenth through mid-twentieth centuries) some of these folk traditions declined. Since India's independence in 1947, folk theatre traditions have experienced some renewed popularity.

China

China was made up of kingdoms of varying sizes, not unlike Greek and Roman city-states but was successfully unified by the Han dynasty from 206 BCE to 220 CE. Han rulers established a shared language and began trade with the West via the Silk Road, a modern name given to a number of trade routes from the farthest eastern trading centers through India to the countries of the Mediterranean. After centuries of divided rule, China was again unified in the seventh century (600s). From about 1271 to 1368, the Mongol leader Kublai Khan replaced Chinese rulers. Khan was in turn replaced by the Ming, Shun, and Qing dynasties, in series, ruling some, most, or all of today's China, leading up to the twentieth century.

Paratheatrical Beginnings

Paratheatrical performances associated with religion have a long tradition in China, going as far back as the eighteenth century BCE (1700s). Court entertainments included elements of storytelling dance, jesters, and musical performances. Beginning around the second century BCE (100s), the "horn butting game" entertainments developed, reenacting battles between animals or a man and an animal. From origins at court, many of these paratheatrical entertainments spread to marketplaces.

During the Tang period in the eighth century CE (700s), the emperor founded a school for the training of singers, dancers, and other paratheatrical performers called the Pear Garden. Even today, Chinese actors are sometimes called "students of the Pear Garden."

Slapstick plays of domestic strife that included music and dance or stylized motion are documented from the Song dynasty, dating from the tenth to thirteenth centuries CE (900–1299). Men and women performed, with women being more common as actors, sometimes performing male roles. Roughly in this period, Buddhism moved from India into China, following the Silk Road. India was a lynchpin in the trade in both directions, and there is general belief that Chinese theatre owes much to the theatre of India.

Eventually, two forms of music drama emerged in China, a southern drama and a northern drama, both combined song, dance, and the spoken word. All classes of people attended. The oldest extant Chinese play script is from this era, and the first buildings dedicated to theatre were built in this period (i.e., tenth to the thirteenth centuries). No theatres from this period survive but they are described in contemporary writings as fenced areas surrounding a raised stage on three sides.

The Chinese theatres were within entertainment districts of a town, which offered theatre with other forms of entertainment. For example, the largest entertainment region in early twelfth century CE (1100–1150) Kaifeng, the capital of the Henan province, had at least fifty theatres.

Kunqu Opera

The two regional styles, northern and southern, were combined in the mid-1500s, in **Kunqu opera**, which was a nationally important genre for more than one hundred years. Kunqu stories were generally romantic

THE PLAY'S THE THING

Li Xingdao's *Chalk Circle*

As a *Zaju* play of the Yuan dynasty (1259–1368), *Chalk Circle* has several distinctive characteristics. Zaju plays have four acts and a short bridging section, sometimes used as a prologue and sometimes as a transition between acts. There are songs but usually only a single character in any act will sing. Characters speak directly to the audience, telling them about themselves, their pasts and plans, especially when they first enter.

The Story of the Play Mrs. Ch'ing's son tells her how upset he is that his sister is supporting the household by an "infamous trade" of courtesan. Mrs. Ch'ing replies that she would be happy if her son would go to work and support the family. The son sings as he leaves the family.

The daughter Hai-t'ang argues with her mother that it would be better to let Hai-t'ang marry the rich Ma Chun-shing, who is so enamored of her than to let her remain a courtesan. Later, Ma Chun-shing tells Mrs. Ch'ing that should she allow her daughter to marry him; he will give the mother many gifts and always support her. And if Hai-t'ang gives Ma a son, then even though she is his second wife, he will treat her as if she were the first wife. All are agreed. Left alone Mrs. Ch-ing speaks of her happiness and rushes to tell her aunt and sisters the good news.

Five years have passed and Hai-t'ang has given birth to a son. The first wife, Mrs. Ma, is not happy about this or her loss of status in the household. She asks her lover, a clerk of court named Ch-ao, to procure poison for her.

Hai-T'ang's brother returns, poor and hungry, to beg help from his sister. She refuses, saying everything she has really belongs to her husband. When Mrs. Ma hears of this, she encourages Hai-T'ang to give her brother some jewelry and rich clothing, for when Mr. Ma hears of her generosity, he will gladly buy Hai-T'ang new things. Hai-T'ang does so. The brother leaves vowing to be a better person than before. Mr. Ma returns and

Mrs. Ma lies, telling him that Hai-T'ang gave the missing valuables to Hai-T'ang's secret lover. Mr. Ma believes the lie and beats Hai-T'ang. Exhausted, he calls for broth. When the broth is returned, Mrs. Ma stirs the poison into the broth. Mr. Ma drinks and dies.

Mrs. Ma tells Hai-T'ang that if she will leave without the son, then Hai-T'ang may go. If she insists on keeping the child, Mrs. Ma will have her prosecuted for Ma's murder and prove to the court that the boy is really Mrs. Ma's child. Hai-T'ang will not give up her child.

Mrs. Ma, conniving with her lover who is clerk to the local judge, bribes the witnesses, and Hai-T'ang is convicted but only after beatings from the judge's guards.

She is taken to the Supreme Court for sentencing. On the trip, Mrs. Ma has bribed the guards to kill Hai-T'ang, but Hai-T'ang's brother appears. He is now a respected clerk of the Supreme Court. With her brother's protection, Hai-T'ang is safely delivered to the Supreme Court's justice.

The governor of the court in preparation for hearing Hai-T'ang's case, has summoned all the accusers and witnesses from the lower trial. Hai-T'ang defends herself with her brother's help. The governor decides to test the truth. He has a chalk circle drawn on the floor and places the five-year-old boy in the circle. Only the real mother will be able to draw the child out of the circle. In the first try, Mrs. Ma grabs the boy and pulls him out; Hai-T'ang does nothing. Second time, the same result. The governor is about to have Hai-T'ang beaten, but she tells him of her tender feelings for the boy who she nursed and raised. "If I cannot, Honored Sir, obtain my son without dislocating his arm or bruising his baby flesh, I would rather perish than make the least effort to take him out of the circle." The governor sees the truth in what Hai-T'ang says and releases her and arrests Mrs. Ma and all those who helped her to falsely convict the real mother.

and the music sentimental. Whereas most characters speak in Mandarin Chinese, comic characters speak in regional dialects. In this mix of languages between high and low characters, Kunqu resembles Sanskrit drama. Kunqu came to be called the "elegant drama," especially because of the qualities of its music: melodious, delicate, and even melancholy.

KUNQU MASK
A mask of Zhang Fei, a historical general and a fictional character in the Chinese opera, Kunqu. This mask dates from the Qing dynasty, from 1644–1912.

Kunqu was primarily the entertainment of the educated classes. Religious and governmental officials would sponsor companies and take the companies of actors with them as they moved about the country.

The most popular drama from this period is *The Peony Pavilion* written in 1598. (For context, the first performances of Shakespeare's *Henry IV* parts 1 and 2 and *Much Ado about Nothing* were given in 1598 and 1599.) In its full version, the opera runs for about eighteen hours. The audience might come and go throughout the presentation, its numbers growing for particularly beloved scenes or songs. The complete work was presented at the Lincoln Center Festival in New York City in 1999 in a lavish production, which was enacted over multiple evenings. This production later traveled the world. In 2010, an hour-long condensed version opened in Shanghai.

Japan

Japan is an archipelago of more than six thousand islands in the Pacific Ocean off the coast of China and Korea. Politically and culturally, Japan's history has alternated between periods of being heavily influenced by other cultures and periods of strict isolation. Although historically Chinese, Korean, and Indian culture inspired much in Japanese art, Japan has developed those seeds into a distinct expression.

Paratheatrical Beginnings

Little is recorded about the arts in Japan prior to the eighth century CE (700s). Masked dances, called *bugaku*, were more-or-less imported from the Asian continent sometime around the sixth to eighth centuries CE, and are still performed on state occasions today. Around the beginning of the twelfth century, an indigenous form of circus-like entertainment called **sarugaku**, meaning "monkey music," was modified by Buddhist priests for use as a teaching tool. (This emphasis on theatre for teaching restates a position of the Roman Horace and the Indian *Natyasastra*, although there is no known influence between the cultures. Theatre as a

THE PLAY'S THE THING

The Peony Pavilion

*T*he Peony Pavilion, developed near Shanghai in 1598, is a fifty-five scene Kunqu opera lasting about eighteen hours and sometimes performed over several days. The central story is a romance that starts in dreams and ends by conquering death. Some of the poetry was seen as shockingly erotic in its time. There is also an extensive subplot regarding Chinese military history. The opera is sometimes called *The Return of the Soul* because the female lead character is resurrected in the final scenes. *The Peony Pavilion* shares traits with *Shakuntala*: both are romantic stories where love survives supernatural impediments.

The Story of the Play A sixteen-year-old girl, Du Liniang, walks in the garden where she falls asleep. In a dream she meets a young scholar, Liu Mengmei, who carries a willow branch as he walks by the peony pavilion, a garden feature.

They fall in love and consummate the relationship in the peony pavilion as flower fairies dance and hide them from audience view. Once awake, the girl is so rapt by thoughts of the dream love affair that her health declines. Comic passages of the attempts to cure her alternate with sober scenes of her parent's concern. Eventually, she dies.

The president of the underworld questions her, asking, "When did anyone die from a dream?" When he confirms her story, he is moved to return her to life so she can pursue Liu Mengmei. Meanwhile, the real-life scholar Liu Mengmei discovers a portrait of Du Liniang and falls in love with her. He falls asleep and is passionately reunited with Liniang in his dreams. In his dreams, the girl sets a test of his love: he must dig up her body if she is to live again. Liu Mengmei is repulsed by the thought at first and a comic interlude follows as a character named Scabby Turtle helps with the digging. When the grave is opened, Du Liniang lives again.

Du Liniang's father doesn't believe the story of her resurrection and has Liu Mengmei imprisoned as a grave robber. Even when his daughter returns, the father refuses to believe it is she. But the emperor pardons all and decrees the two should be married. The play ends with a paean to the power of love to overcome all troubles. The flower fairies return to celebrate the happy ending.

The Peony Pavilion *as performed in London in an abbreviated three-night, nine-hour version in 2008.*

teaching tool is also one reason for the development of liturgical drama in Europe in the middle ages, covered in Chapter 4.) As the performances started to attract large audiences, priests hired others to perform the plays. Guilds of these professional performers developed in the twelfth and thirteenth centuries.

Noh Drama

Sarugaku paved the way for the development of **Noh** drama in the fourteenth century. *Noh* is probably the oldest major theatre art still regularly performed. Poetic and austere, it is a theatrical expression of Zen Buddhism. Its originators were a father and son, Kanami (1333–1384) and Zeami (1363–1444), both professional actors attached to a temple. They wrote many of the more than two hundred extant *Noh* plays, creating a body of work with certain rigid characteristics. Zeami also penned a treatise on the theory of *Noh* drama.

Each *Noh* play has a three-part structure (*jo, ha,* and *kyu*) that depends on the interaction of two characters: the protagonist (*shite*) and an accidental confidant (*waki*). Each play deals with one of five topics: god, man, woman, insanity, or demon. A *Noh* performance includes five plays, one of each of these subjects, in that order.

The shape of each plot is roughly the same: In the first part (jo), the confidant introduces himself and travels to a destination symbolized by a pillar on the stage; the protagonist enters and the two characters exchange questions and answers until the protagonist's concern and his reason for being at the place are clear. In the second part (ha), the protagonist performs a dance that is related to the concern, either by expression or narrative or symbol. In the third part (kyu), the protagonist appears as a new self, one called forth by the first two sections, thus resolving the play. Between acts of *Noh* plays, **Kyogen** are performed: short, comic performances derived from sarugaku.

Noh plots are simple; their abundant exposition seems natural to a form that is concerned not with actions but with the effects of past events. The protagonists are usually tormented figures—dishonored warriors, crazed women, guilty priests—whose appearance in the final section (kyu) in a different form is, to a Westerner, a kind of exorcism or transformation. Profoundly influenced by Zen Buddhism, however, *Noh's* ideology is intuitive, not rational. A major tenet of Buddhism is that human suffering comes from accepting the physical world as reality when the physical world, according Buddhist doctrine, is illusion. In *Noh*, the protagonist makes a mental leap from worldly appearance to eternal reality and is transformed. The protagonist's understanding that the physical world is illusion and his confrontation with the hidden reality of the eternal world resolves the play.

Noh **Staging Practices** The staging of *Noh* is emblematic and highly conventionalized. Performances unfold on a small, raised stage, with all entrances made along a raised passage (***hashigakari***) at one side; at the rear is a wall with a pine tree painted on it. The meaning of the pine tree is lost and is the subject of much scholarly surmise. Two common suppositions are that it represents a pine tree of the Kasuga Shrine in Nara or that it is an emblem of a natural backdrop once used for *Noh* presentation. Onstage musicians (three percussionists and a flutist) and a chorus soberly dressed and not masked, help establish the very deliberate tempo of the performance. Costumes are

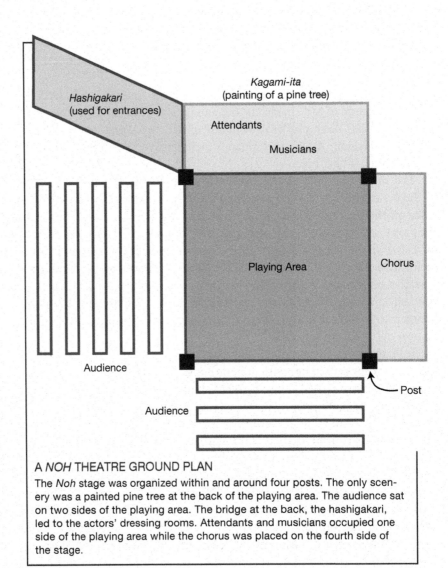

A *NOH* THEATRE GROUND PLAN
The *Noh* stage was organized within and around four posts. The only scenery was a painted pine tree at the back of the playing area. The audience sat on two sides of the playing area. The bridge at the back, the hashigakari, led to the actors' dressing rooms. Attendants and musicians occupied one side of the playing area while the chorus was placed on the fourth side of the stage.

elaborate and include masks for some characters, but there is no scenery and very few symbolic properties.

All performers are male, with the male voice undisguised for female roles. Originally, *Noh* costuming reflected street wear appropriate to the character but in the late sixteenth century, the costumes became elaborate and highly conventionalized and exaggerated. Some characters wear masks made of clay, cloth, paper, or wood. Stage attendants work as stagehands do in the Western theatre except they are always visible. When an actor needs a prop, an attendant offers it to him in full view of the audience.

Dance was fundamental to *Noh* and other Japanese drama, a trait shared with Indian but not Chinese plays. Indeed, Japan's dramatic theatre apparently developed from or alongside dance, incorporating intricate forms of movement that demanded special training.

Kabuki

Noh was reserved to the aristocracy, but **Kabuki** developed as a popular entertainment. Generally dated to public performances in 1603, the theatre grew rapidly. By 1616 there were seven Kabuki theatres. Women were the first Kabuki performers but were quickly considered too risqué. They were replaced by boy actors who then came under the same charge. From about 1650, Kabuki was performed only by men. Perhaps because of this concern with appropriateness kabuki developed an intricately conventionalized and arresting style of acting.

Kabuki as it eventually developed was a variety entertainment, typically consisting a of play written for the Kabuki stage, a comic play adapted from *Bunraku* puppet theatre scripts, and a dance drama. In its mature form, Kabuki featured long, fully developed actions that unfolded in many acts, with many characters and scenes. Kabuki performances lasted as long as twelve hours The stories came from diverse sources, and they were often heroic and romantic. The controlling convention, however, was illusionism, with Kabuki directly imitating contemporary Japanese life—that is seventeenth-century Japanese life—albeit in a stylized way.

The Kabuki stage includes two raised walkways connected by a third walkway at the rear running

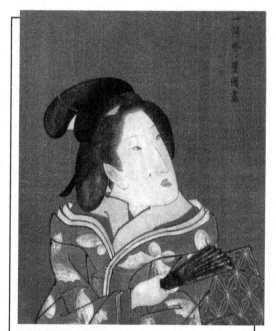

A KABUKI ACTOR, 1852
Bold, polychrome woodblock prints of Kabuki actors were very popular in the nineteenth century. Copies are still made today because the originals are highly prized and widely collected. Note the actor's extremely white makeup.

A KABUKI THEATRE, 1740
This woodblock print is titled "A Scene from a Play" and depicts a Kabuki theatre in Edo, Japan. Here one can clearly see the *hanamichi*, the long walkway into the audience used for dramatic entrances and exits.

through the audience to a large raised stage. Actors became famous for the quality of their long, silent but emotion-laden exits on the walkway through the audience. The stage featured spectacular scenery, including a trap door, and a front curtain. (After about 1750, there was even a revolving stage, the first in the world.) The costumes were complex, beautiful, and spectacular, featuring some costumes, **hikinuki**, constructed so that at a gesture they could change completely, turning themselves inside out to reveal, for example, a man in armor where a woman once stood. Makeup, though elaborate, was essentially illusionistic. Some actors specialized in female impersonation, raising it to a high art with meticulous attention to detail. Kabuki acting is considered a profession requiring prolonged study and apprenticeship and roles tended to be hereditary. Indeed, despite its spectacular scenery and costumes, Kabuki was an actor's art most of all, with the greatest actors declared national treasures, as if they were great paintings or great buildings.

Today Kabuki is still performed but not whole plays in one performance. Tickets are expensive and much of the audience is made up of visiting foreigners.

OPENING NIGHT THEATRE DISTRICT
A late-1700s woodcut print of crowds at the entrance to the theatre district on opening
night in Edo, Japan. Theatre was a popular diversion in Japan at this time and this area
hosted two competing theatres.

KEY TERMS

Key terms are in boldface type in the text. Check your understanding against
this list. Persons are page-referenced in the Index.

hashigakari, p. 66

hikinuki, p. 68

Kabuki, p. 67

Kunqu (KUN-koo) opera, p. 61

Kyogen (kee-OH-gehn), p. 65

Natyasastra (naht-ya-SAS-trah), p. 57

Noh (NO), p. 65

rasa (RAH-sah), p. 57

Sanskrit drama, p. 56

sarugaku (sah-ru-GAH-ku), p. 63

Chapter 3 at a Glance

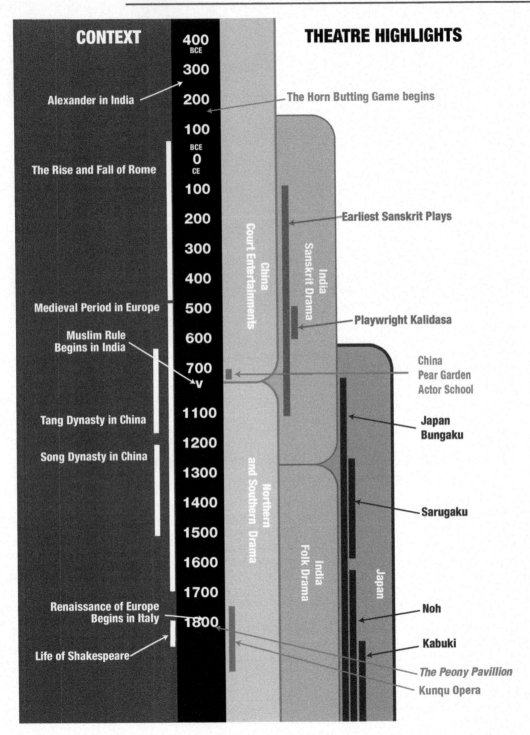

CONTEXT

THEATRE HIGHLIGHTS

400 BCE

300

Alexander in India — 200 — The Horn Butting Game begins

100
BCE
0
CE

The Rise and Fall of Rome — 100

200 — Earliest Sanskrit Plays

300

400

Medieval Period in Europe — 500

Muslim Rule Begins in India — 600 — Playwright Kalidasa

700
V — China Pear Garden Actor School

Tang Dynasty in China — 1100 — Japan Bungaku

Song Dynasty in China — 1200

1300

1400 — Sarugaku

1500

1600

1700

Renaissance of Europe Begins in Italy — 1800 — Noh

Life of Shakespeare — Kabuki

The Peony Pavillion

Kunqu Opera

China Court Entertainments

India Sanskrit Drama

Northern and Southern Drama

India Folk Drama

Japan

The European Middle Ages

When you have completed this chapter, you should be able to:

- Explain how and when a new kind of theatre came into being several hundred years after the fall of Rome in the West.
- Discuss how the medieval theatre was part of its culture.
- Trace the changes in medieval theatre from its beginnings to its end.
- Describe the physical types of medieval theatres.
- Discuss how the various theatres were funded and organized.
- Define simultaneous staging.
- Explain the use of emblematic costumes and properties.
- Describe at least one preexisting or "found space" used to house performance.

Context

Even after the 500s, Constantinople continued as a center of trade and civilization. Increasingly less Roman and more bureaucratized, the Byzantine Empire had a highly developed culture, one focused on luxury and one that looked east rather than west for its markets and goods.

Western Europe, on the other hand, was in increasing disarray after the fourth century, and after its collapse in the sixth century, Rome had no political successor. Some city-states of the Italian peninsula avoided the general decline by maintaining strong trading connections with Constantinople or other cultures. Western Europe however, continued to crumble as various forces that had before served to unify Europe weakened or disintegrated. The Roman system of roads and waterways fell into disrepair, and transportation and communication became at first troubled and at last almost impossible.

Laws were ignored and order broke down, replaced by the rule of force: bands of pirates and brigands grew wealthy and influential enough to challenge rulers and lords of manors. Without the support of a government, the monetary system failed, and barter, with all its cumbersome trappings, became the basis of trade. Out of this disarray emerged a different kind of Europe, one with different languages, traditions, and cultures—one that was fragmented and local, lacking the connective social and cultural fabric Rome had provided.

The prevailing social organization was feudal, in which the social base was not the town but the manor, a self-contained agricultural unit that could offer security to those within it. On the manor, each serf owed absolute allegiance to the lord, the owner or grantee of the land. Serfs worked the land and maintained the manor in return for protection by the lord, who would fight to maintain safety for those within. Just as serfs owed allegiance to their lord, lesser lords owed allegiance to more powerful ones, who could call on them to raise armies. Travel among manors was irregular, a fact that worked against unity within Europe.

The Christian church, on the other hand, was a weak unifying force because its services were conducted in Latin rather than the numerous local languages; its pope led the whole church; and its priests, especially its monks,

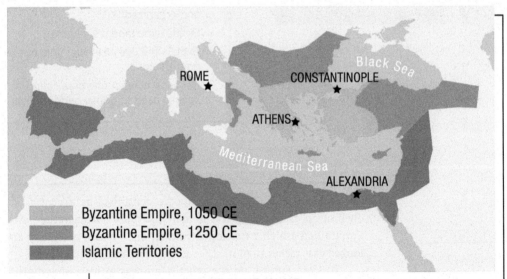

Byzantine Empire, 1050 CE
Byzantine Empire, 1250 CE
Islamic Territories

THE BYZANTINE EMPIRE AND ISLAM

While western Europe was in disarray, the eastern Roman Empire, centered in Constantinople, flourished and traded with both Europe and Asia. After the seventh century CE, Islam dominated the Middle East, the northernmost parts of Africa, and southern Spain.

occasionally traveled among church centers. Like social organization, church organization was hierarchical, with priests reporting to bishops, bishops to archbishops, archbishops to cardinals, and cardinals to the pope. This hierarchy ensured relatively orderly governance of the church in an otherwise chaotic world, and its teachings gave it a substantial base of power.

The power hierarchies of both feudalism and Christianity were essentially pyramidal: with one man at the top, relatively few men immediately under him, and so on, until at the base of each pyramid were the peasants, that great mass of people who tilled the land and provided all those above them with the necessities and amenities of life. The life of the medieval peasant was one of work, ignorance, and want; the life of people above the peasant varied. Previous historians saw this extended period in Europe as a lesser one between two greater ones, Rome, ending in about the middle of the fifth century, and the Renaissance or "rebirth," beginning in about the middle of the fifteenth century. Thus, they called this the **Middle Ages** or the **medieval**, meaning middle, period.

Early Medieval Drama and Theatre: 476–1200

For many years, historians believed that no theatre or drama outlived the collapse of Rome in 476 CE, but it is now certain that theatre continued in the Byzantine Empire and that remnants of professional performers traveled about in Italy, France, and Germany. Scattered references to performances called *mimi*, *histriones*, and *ioculatores* surface periodically in Western medieval accounts, but the degree to which such performers performed actual plays, as distinct from such paratheatrical entertainments as juggling, tumbling, dancing, and rope tricks, is not known. If theatre, as distinct from performance, existed at all, it was feeble.

CHURCH DRAMA
During the European Middle Ages, dramas were staged inside churches, in front of churches, and in the center of towns. Here, a scene from a cycle of plays staged in the early 1980s in the ruins of St. Mary's Abbey in York, England.

Hroswitha in Germany and Bishop Ethelwold in England

Two almost simultaneous events toward the end of the tenth century (900s) marked the reentry of theatre into western Europe. The first, the plays of Hroswitha, offers incontrovertible evidence of continuity with Roman drama; the second, the liturgical manual of Ethelwold, shows the Roman Catholic church staging a small play as part of a worship service.

Hroswitha This religious leader and noblewoman was attached to a Benedictine monastery near Gandersheim in modern Germany. She wrote six plays in Latin (c. 950), the earliest still-extant dramas since the first years of the Roman Empire. Based on the comedies of Terence, Hroswitha's plays sought to celebrate "the laudable chastity of holy maidens" and *may* have been performed at court and at the monastery. Hroswitha is important on three counts:

- As the first known female playwright.
- As the first known post-Roman playwright.
- As proof of an intellectual continuity from Rome to the Middle Ages.

For reasons not entirely clear, Hroswitha's contributions made little impact at the time. Yet, with little to no theatre infrastructure, it is hard to imagine how Hroswitha's plays would have had influence outside her monastery. Her classically styled plays were largely overshadowed by a different strand of theatre, an ecclesial theatre that also emerged in the tenth century.

Ethelwold, Bishop of Winchester, England This Bishop issued in 975 the *Regularis Concordia*, a monastic guidebook, which, among other things, described in detail how one part of an Easter service was to be performed. For about a hundred years before Ethelwold, the church had been decorating and elaborating several of its practices. Music, vestments, art, architecture, and **liturgy** (rites, public worship) had all changed in the direction of greater embellishment. Liturgy has elements that resemble the drama, including a script; costumes and props in the form of ecclesiastical clothing, incense, and the like; and a set of "performers" of the rite often on a raised podium before an audience-like congregation. But liturgy is ritual, not drama. One sort of liturgical embellishment that emerged in the early Middle Ages was the **trope**, an interpolation into an existing text. One Easter trope was sung by the choir antiphonally, a call and response, and began, "*Quem quaeritis in sepulchro, o christocole.*" Translated from Latin, the trope read in its entirety:

Angel: Whom seek ye in the tomb, O Christians?

The Three Marys: Jesus of Nazareth, the crucified, O heavenly beings.

Angel: He is not here, he is risen as he foretold;

Go and announce that he is risen from the tomb.

The *Quem Quaeritis* is still used in some churches. It was this trope to which staging directions were added in Ethelwold's *Regularis Concordia*, which became a standard text describing the liturgy for the Christian church in England. This document added not only stage directions but also costuming and properties to the dialogue, reestablishing many of the essentials of drama.

HOW WE KNOW

Bishop Ethelwold's Stage Directions for the *Quem Quaeritis* Trope

Ethelwold's stage directions turn four lines of dialogue, with an additional line or two, into a playlet that employs all the elements of theatre. There is impersonation (the monks are pretending to be people other than who they are), costuming, props, staging instructions to the actors (theatrical "business"), and movement ("blocking").

The *Regularis Concordia* directs in part: "Let four monks enter as if part of the service; one monk, holding a palm [a traditional emblem of an angel], approaches the sepulcher [tomb] without being noted and sits quietly. Later the remaining three monks, all of them wearing copes [long cloaks] and carrying incense, follow slowly as if seeking something." These monks are imitating the angel before the tomb and the three women coming to anoint the body of Jesus, as told in the Gospel of Peter, part of the Vulgate Bible of the time.

The four monks speak or sing a slightly elaborated version of the *Quem Quaeritis*, ending with the angel's instruction to proclaim that Christ is risen. "Let the three monks turn to the choir and in obedience to the Angel say, 'Hallelujah! The Lord has Risen!'" The angel, Ethelwold directs, is to open the sepulcher. In it is only bare cloth that had robed the body of Jesus.

The Lord is risen from the sepulcher,

Who for us hung on the cross.

(Let them put the cloth on the altar. The song finished, the Prior [a high ranking member of the clergy], sharing the joy at the Lord's victory in having conquered Death, stands and starts the hymn:)

We Praise Thee, O God.

(This started; the bells are all rung together.)

Here, then, is one of the earliest known albeit exceptionally brief, extant scripts for drama since the fall of the Roman Empire. In the description of these

This illustration from an illuminated manuscript from Bamberg, now in Germany, from the eleventh century CE depicts an angel showing the three Marys the empty tomb after the resurrection of Christ. Although this is not a specific illustration of Bishop Ethelwold's stage directions, it does suggest the popularity of this now apocryphal gospel story.

ceremonies, the *Concordia* notes that some priests "had introduced this custom, in order to fortify the unlearned people and newcomers in their faith." Here is evidence for what is believed to be the purpose of early medieval drama: it was a moving picture so that the general people of the congregation who did not speak Latin could see what they might otherwise little understand.

Ethelwold's text (less so Hroswitha's) expresses three staging conventions that characterized much of theatre in this period and operated in European medieval theatre. Medieval staging was:

- **Simultaneous:** That is, several different locations were present in the performing space at the same time, hence **simultaneous staging**. Locations were not illusionistic. Such an arrangement meant conceptualizing two different kinds of space: small scenic structures that served to locate the specific places (eventually called **mansions**) and a neutral, generalized playing space (called **platea**).

- **Emblematic:** That is, meanings from the performance reached the audience through costumes and properties that were signs or symbols whose meanings communicated easily. They were not illusionistic. Among mansions, for example, an animal mouth signified hell and a revolving globe stood for heaven.

- **Environmental:** That is, performed in available spaces rather than in structures specially built and set aside for the purpose.

Although Hroswitha's plays had no immediate successors, from the tenth through much of the sixteenth century, many dramas such as **Quem Quaeritis** were performed inside monastic and later cathedral churches as a part of the liturgy. Thus, they are called **liturgical drama**. Such plays were chanted or sung rather than spoken and were given in the language of the church—Latin—and so are also called **Latin music drama**. They were acted by clergy, choirboys, monks, and occasionally traveling scholars, schoolboys, and sometimes, nuns; the actors, then, were almost always male except in convents.

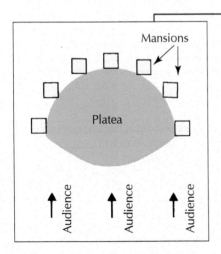

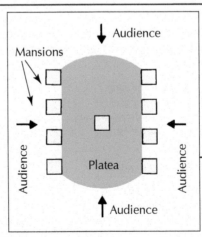

SIMULTANEOUS STAGING

Medieval staging used two kind of spaces: a generalized playing space (called a *platea*) and several specific locations (called *mansions*), which appeared simultaneously in or around the platea.

From the very short *Quem Quaeritis*, Latin music drama blossomed into many plays of varying lengths and degrees of complexity. The subjects of most such plays were biblical, usually drawn from events surrounding Christmas and Easter: the visit of the three Marys to the tomb, the travel of the Magi, Herod's wrath. Other Latin music dramas depicted such diverse stories as the life of the Virgin Mary, the raising of Lazarus, and Daniel in the lion's den. Almost all were serious, but at festivals like the Feast of Fools and the Feast of the Boy Bishops, the usual dignity was abandoned and in its place was substituted considerable monkey business. Latin music dramas continued to be performed in churches well into the sixteenth century (1500s), overlapping other types of drama by hundreds of years.

Production inside the Church

Plays performed in the church were produced by the church. Actors were churchmen except in convents, where churchwomen performed. Costumes were based on church vestments. A key identified Saint Peter; a hood signified a woman; wings or a held palm branch meant angels; wallets and staffs identified travelers, for example.

Staging depended on existing church architecture. For example, the choir loft might represent heaven, the crypt hell, and the altar the tomb of Christ. For elaborate plays, special mansions might be constructed, some small but others large enough for several persons to hide inside. Special effects required machinery capable of flying objects and actors in and out of the playing area. For example, angels and doves flew about, Christ rose to heaven, and the three kings followed a moving star that led them to the stable of the Christ child.

Although early audiences consisted only of those residing in the monasteries or convents, when the plays began to be performed in cathedral churches as well as monastic ones, general audiences attended.

Later Medieval Culture and Theatre, c. 1200–1550

Several shifts within medieval culture began to coalesce by 1200. Population increased rapidly. Towns grew up around monasteries and manors to provide goods and services, serving as centers of trade. Towns allowed for a third lifestyle, neither serf nor lord, but tradesman and professional, that is to say, a middle class. Increased trade encouraged the development of still more towns, many now located where goods that had been shipped by water were transferred to land. Water was preferable because roads were mostly terrible. The names *Oxford* and *Cambridge* reflect this origin. ("Ford" means a river or stream shallow enough to cross.) Trade expanded again when a series of crusades against Muslims and others, including inhabitants of Constantinople, prompted new shipbuilding, opened new sea routes, and established new trading ports and new markets, all aided by improved sea manuals and the invention of the compass.

Commercial theory changed. Early medieval theory was grounded in theology. Usury, now meaning an exorbitant rate of interest but then referring to all lending for interest, was condemned; merchants were supposed to work for the benefit of society; and profit was considered a kind of parasitism. No more. Merchants began to form monopolies; maximum profit rather than a just price became the goal. Modern commercial structures emerged, such as banking and partnerships. Because merchants and tradespeople lived outside the feudal system, they gradually undermined it by providing refuge for serfs seeking to escape their lords. Towns sponsored fairs to bring people from great distances and so facilitate trade. Thus, towns and commerce competed directly with manors and agriculture for social leadership. The growth of a middle class in the growing towns of Europe undermined the pyramidal structure of the Middle Ages.

At about the same time, the domination of the church and its monopoly on matters of faith began to erode, with Martin Luther later posing the most direct threat (1521). The separation of religion from everyday life was under way.

As religion became somewhat less central to the culture, the allegiance to kings and country grew. With the decline of feudalism and the authority

MEDIEVAL PLAYS IN MODERN PRODUCTION

Since 1951, the York mystery plays have been produced in York, England. Now the plays are staged periodically by the National Centre for Early Music at St. Margaret's Church in York. Performances are given both at single locations and on pageant wagons, like the *Noah and the Flood* shown here.

of the church, and with the emergence of towns and nascent nationalism, the era was metamorphosing into a new kind of culture: That is, after about 1200, western Europe was in a transition between medieval culture and a new one that would coalesce by 1550 as the Renaissance. (The Renaissance began one hundred or so years earlier in Italy.)

Religious Drama outside the Church

After about 1200, medieval drama reflected these cultural shifts in several ways. New kinds of religious drama appeared. These dramas differed from Latin music drama in several ways:

- They were performed outdoors rather than inside churches.
- They were spoken rather than chanted or sung.
- They were in the vernacular (e.g., French, English, or German) rather than in Latin.
- Laymen, rather than priests and clerics, served as actors.
- The stories and themes, no longer limited to liturgical sources, became more far-ranging.
- The performances tended to cluster in the spring and summer months, especially around the new Feast of Corpus Christi, established in the fourteenth century, rather than spreading throughout the church year, as before. They became known as **Corpus Christi plays**.

Of these changes, the most significant was the shift from a universal language—Latin—to the various national tongues because with this shift came two things important to the future of both theatre and drama: the beginning of several national dramas and an expansion of the potential audience and subject matters for plays.

The plays remained decidedly religious, if not always scriptural. In general, they were:

- **Mystery plays** or mysteries: events in the life of Christ (e.g., *The Second Shepherd's Play*) and stories from the Old Testament (e.g., *Noah*).
- **Passion plays**: the trial, suffering, death, and resurrection of Jesus Christ.
- **Miracle plays** or *miracles*: the lives of saints, both historical and legendary.
- **Morality plays** or *moralities*: didactic allegories, often about the struggle for salvation (e.g., *Everyman*).

Although the plays differed in subject matter and form, they shared several characteristics. First, they aimed to teach or to reinforce belief in church

A SAINT'S PLAY IN PERFORMANCE
Scholars believe the central figure holding a book and a baton is the master of secrets who appears to be cueing the musicians on an upper level. This engraving, from a miniature painting in a medieval manuscript by Jean Fouquet of *The Martyrdom of St. Appolonia,* dates from about the mid-1460s. Note in the background the audience under the scaffolds that perhaps hold musicians and other performers. The color image is an enlargement of a section of the original miniature. It shows more clearly the master of secrets in a blue robe and the hell mouth, to the right.

doctrine. Second, they were formulated as melodramas or divine comedies—that is, the ethical system of the play was clear: good was rewarded, evil punished. Third, the driving force for the action was God and his plan. This is different from the driving force of, say, the drama of Sophocles, focused as it was on the choices of human beings. To a modern reader, the plays often appear episodic, with their actions unmotivated, their sequences of time and place inexplicable, and their mixture of the comic and the serious unnerving.

In fact, their traits expressed the medieval view. The plays presented the lure and strength of sin, the power and compassion of God, and the punishment awaiting the unrepentant sinner. They called for all people to repent, to confess, and to atone for their sins.

THE PLAY'S THE THING

The Second Shepherd's Play, Anonymous

The town of Wakefield, England, presented a cycle of thirty-two short mystery plays based on bible stories yearly during the late Middle Ages through 1576 CE. In its complete form, the Wakefield Cycle survives in a single manuscript, now the property of the Huntington Library in California. This manuscript was written in the fifteenth century (1400s) but the individual plays are believed to have been written over a long time, perhaps over a century or two.

Of the thirty-two plays, the best regarded is *The Second Shepherd's Play* because of its fresh invention on a familiar story, its humor, and its social comment. Author unknown, it is the *second* shepherd's play because there are two other shepherds' plays in the Wakefield Cycle. At heart, *The Second Shepherd's Play* it is a variation on the story of shepherds in the fields with their flocks to whom an angel appears, heralding the birth of Christ and urging the common shepherds to follow the star to the manger in Bethlehem.

The Story of the Play Three shepherds, as night falls, complain of the weather and their fate to be poor commoners. The shepherds are met by a local character of questionable virtue, Mak. When they fall asleep, Mak makes off with one of their sheep. At Mak's rude hut, Gil, his shrewish wife, connives with him to prevent the shepherds from discovering the animal should they come look. She wraps the lamb as an infant in a cradle. The shepherds come and search for their lamb but do not find it.

Starting to depart, the shepherds realize they have offered no gift to the newborn. They return with a coin for the baby only to discover the missing lamb. Says a shepherd, "Let me kiss him...What the devil is this? He has a long snout." Mak and Gil claim the child just has a birthmark. The shepherds are unconvinced. Mak and Gil then claim the child was bewitched by an elf. Upon closer examination of the "babe," the shepherds recognize their owner's mark, clipped in the lamb's ear. Although the shepherds could do far worse to Mak, their only punishment is to toss him in a blanket, until Mak is sore all over and the shepherds' muscles ache.

As the shepherds depart from Mak and Gil's hovel, an angel appears, singing beautifully, "Rise, gentle shepherds, for now he is born..." Singing and rejoicing, the shepherds follow the star, come to Mary and the Christ child, and offer three gifts: a bunch of cherries, a bird, and a ball.

The creativity and mixed but integrated comedy and drama are the wonder of this unknown author's work, distinguishing this version of the shepherds' story from other similar ones in graceful ways. The lamb disguised as a child in a cradle is a comic mirroring of baby Jesus, the Lamb of God, asleep in a manger. The shepherds' gifts echo those of the wise men and symbolize the blood of the crucifixion in the red cherries, the holy spirit often represented as a dove shown by the bird, and the child's kingship in the ball, an orb in miniature.

Because history was God's great lesson to humankind, the drama that expressed his plan was nothing less than the entirety of human history, from creation to doomsday. Any combination of events, any juxtaposition of characters, and any elasticity of time or place that would illuminate God's plan and make it more accessible and compelling was suitable drama. The great dramas of the 1400s and 1500s that showed this history are called **cycle plays**, or **cosmic dramas**, and some took days, even weeks, to play from beginning to end. Cycles would be made up of a number of plays of varied lengths and different Biblical subject matters. Existing manuscripts show the number of texts in one cycle ranging from twenty-two to forty.

THE PLAY'S THE THING

Everyman, Anonymous, c. 1490

*E*veryman, a popular morality play rediscovered in 1900 after a lapse of more than four hundred years, is simply structured: Everyman is called by Death to the next world. Everyman then searches for a friend to accompany him on this journey. All but one forsake him. Each character is a personification of an abstract quality—Knowledge, Beauty, Strength, and so on. *Everyman* is an allegory, then, a story where abstract ideas are represented as characters. The play's structure is a string of episodes rather than a causally organized progression of incidents. Today *Everyman* is the most often produced of medieval plays.

The Story of the Play God sends Death to summon Everyman, who must bring a "sure reckoning." When Death gives the message to Everyman, saying he must "go on a long journey," Everyman cries that he is not ready; he begs for time; he tries to bribe Death, who tells him he must make the journey and should find what friends will go with him.

Everyman asks various friends—Fellowship, Kindred and Cousin, Goods—to go with him, and they agree until they learn what the destination is; then they depart.

Good Deeds speaks "from the ground." He cannot go because he is too weak to walk, but he calls his sister, Knowledge, who says, "Everyman, I will go with thee and be thy guide."

Knowledge takes him to Confession; after confessing, Everyman whips himself as a penance, and Good Deeds is able to rise and walk.

Knowledge gives Everyman a "garment of sorrow" to wear instead of his worldly clothes. She tells him to call his Five Wits, his Beauty, his Strength, and his Discretion. Everyman receives the sacrament and then journeys to his grave, where Beauty refuses to enter with him; then Strength, then Discretion, then Five Wits desert him, but Good Deeds remains at the graveside. They pray, and then Everyman goes into his grave alone.

An angel appears, saying his reckoning is "crystal-clear," and a doctor (learned man) gives a short speech to explain the play.

This woodcut from a printed edition of Everyman *from the mid-1500s shows Everyman* (left) *and Death.*

Why such dramas came to be done outside the church building has been endlessly debated. Some thought the plays had been forced out of the church because of abuses such as those at the Feast of Fools, in which young people impudently impersonated important clerical positions, such as the archbishop, bishop, or abbot. Others argued that the plays' appearance outdoors merely reflected the changing needs of the plays and their audiences for more space and freedom. More likely is the increasing power of towns,

which fastened on plays and other public shows as expressions of their new status. Play production also drew new business to the towns in the form of audiences from neighboring areas. Before substantial towns existed, the only locus for performance was the church or the manor of a lord. Whatever the reason for the development, records of religious plays given outside of churches appear by 1200 and are common by 1350.

Staging Religious Plays outside the Church

Although churches continued to produce Latin music dramas throughout the period, other religious plays had different producing arrangements. Sometimes town officials took charge; sometimes special committees did the job. Sometimes labor and religious organizations, **guilds** or **confraternities**, assumed responsibility, often under the town's protection. A guild is a group of craftsmen in a single trade, operating as a mix of a trade union, a standard-setting body, and a secret society that preserved the methods of the trade.

Guilds were frequently called on to produce a single play in a group, sometimes on the basis of particular skills or association with the play's subject: Noah plays, which required a real ship although perhaps half-size, went well with shipbuilding, for example. Because of both financial investment and tradition, plays tended to stay with the same guild for many years. As the plays and processions showed the wealth of the town, so the individual play and its properties showed the wealth of the guild.

Roles in the plays were open to all male members of the community (in France, women might perform occasionally) and were generally performed without compensation. As in any primarily amateur operation, the quality of the performances varied considerably, and it was probably in an attempt to upgrade the general level of acting that many cities after about

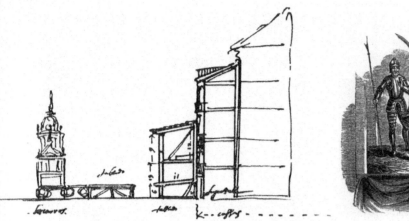

MOVEABLE STAGING

In parts of England and Spain, mansions were set on wagons that traveled from place to place thus moving the plays to audiences gathered in prearranged places. On left, a seventeenth-century sketch of a Spanish pageant wagon in front of an audience area. The engraving, on right, of a pageant wagon dates from about 1560.

1450 hired professional "property players" to take the leading roles and to instruct the others. Although these few actors were paid, they were not looked down on as socially undesirable, as professional actors in secular plays would be in later times.

There are no textbooks of medieval acting. Scholars believe that it was, like the costumes, emblematic. It probably depended on reducing the character to large, symbolic strokes, without the actors' "inner" work or the character's "psychology" found in illusionistic productions in the modern era. How amateurs handled the problem of being heard and understood outdoors is unknown. Some pictures of the period show prompters or directors, book in hand, standing among the actors; this professional may have been literally cueing gestures and turns of voice.

Some plays and some roles suggest a tradition of satirical or comic playing, with caricature an established technique. The traveling actors of the countryside probably emphasized low comedy and passed on techniques and traditions that would flourish later with clowns in the theatre of Shakespeare's time.

Fixed and Movable Staging

The staging of religious plays outside the church took two major forms, still within the conventions of emblem, environment, and simultaneity: either fixed staging or movable staging, the latter used most often in parts of Spain and England.

Scaffolds   In fixed staging, mansions or **scaffolds** were set up, usually outdoors, in whatever spaces were available—courtyards of noble houses, town squares, or the remains of Roman amphitheatres. Scaffolds differed in size, structure, and use. Some were elevated and resemble small stages but were not necessarily used as stages. Some were tiny houses, thrones, or just a tree. They were emblematic of a place but not full scenery. Depending on the space, the mansions were arranged in circles, straight lines, or rectangles, and the platea—the unlocalized playing area in front of the mansions— and the audience area were established accordingly. Although the individual arrangements varied, heaven and hell, ordinarily the most ornate mansions, were customarily set at opposite poles.

HOW WE KNOW

Oberammergau Passion Play through the Years

The passion play performed at Oberammergau in southern Germany is a tenuous link to the medieval tradition of ecclesiastical drama. The city made an oath in 1633 to perform a passion play every ten years if their town could survive the virulent plague then ravishing the area. The first performance was in 1634. Oberammergau joined a large number of German cities presenting religious drama at this time, encouraged by the Catholic Church.

The story presented as the passion play has changed in small and large ways throughout these four centuries. The history of the Oberammergau passion play is one characterized by stops, starts, and many textual revisions.

The earliest script still extant is from 1662. Scholars now know that this first script was assembled from pieces of preexisting scripts from other communities. In 1680, the community moved the performance year to the first year of each decade. A new script was crafted in 1730, which introduced the allegorical figures of Envy, Avarice, Death, and Sin as Jesus's adversaries. By 1750, church fathers became concerned that the holiest stories of Christendom should not be performed on stage. The script was rewritten again. The church and the government banned passion plays in 1770, and the play was not performed in that decade.

In 1780, a completely revised script was allowed to be staged. The villagers performed the play three times that decade and five times the next and they charged admission grossing much more than the production's cost. The ban on passion plays was revived again in 1791—with a special exception for Oberammergau.

Again in 1811, a new script was devised. All the allegorical characters were excised. Only the bible story would be put on stage. Now the play was more firmly based on the Gospel of Matthew, in which the Jews ask for the crucifixion of Jesus and, when Pilate washes his hands of the affair, the Jews exclaim, "His blood is on us and on our children!" The Jews thus became the villains. (There were no Jews as *performers* and few Jews lived in the Oberammergau vicinity. You had to be a Catholic and a lifetime resident to appear in the play.) In 1830, the first permanent theatre was built for the play; it seated five thousand. It was in this period that Oberammergau became an international destination in play years for Catholics and Protestants.

Adolf Hitler, Germany's fürher, saw the 1934 performance, saying afterward, "It is vital that the Passion play be continued at Oberammergau; for never has the menace of Jewry been so convincingly portrayed..." In the aftermath of World War II and the disclosure of the systematic murder of some six million Jews by the German government under Hitler, the town fathers sought and obtained a *missio canonica*, an official declaration of the Catholic Church that the play conformed with church doctrine, and the passion play continued with only slight script revisions.

Beginning in 1970, Jewish organizations such as the American Jewish Council and some Christian organizations as well began to protest the play's depiction of the

(continues)

HOW WE KNOW   Oberammergau Passion Play through the Years *(continued)*

Jewish people. The church connection to the play was dissolved: the play became solely a municipal activity. In 2000, the script was again rewritten in an attempt to minimize the anti-Semitism perceived by many, but few critics were satisfied. Despite revisions, discussions, and debates, the effect of Oberammergau's passion play on religious intolerance is still in question.

The conflict has not stopped the performances. About one-half of the citizens of the town are involved in the production. Performances run from 2:30 to 10:30 P.M., with a three-hour dinner break. In 2010, the town presented the show 102 times. Over a half-million visitors saw it, bringing significant money to the city. The Oberammergau passion play continues, part piety, part commerce, connected in a broken and jagged way to medieval times but also in many ways very modern.

In the United States, passion plays, sometimes called Easter plays, are performed each year in about twenty states.

This engraving shows the temporary uncovered seating and stage area in 1789. A permanent theatre was built for the play in 1830 to seat about five thousand spectators.

Pageants   In movable staging, **pageants (pageant wagons)** may have allowed the audience to scatter along a processional route while the plays were brought to them and performed in sequence, much like a parade with floats. Each play, then, was performed several times. A likely pattern was for the first play (e.g., creation) to be presented at dawn at the first station; when it moved to the second station to perform, the second play (e.g., the fall of man) was then presented at the first station. For most of the day, several plays were performing at once. The word *pageant* is important in a discussion of movable staging because it was used to describe the play itself, the spectacle of the plays in performance, and also the vehicle on which the presentation was staged.

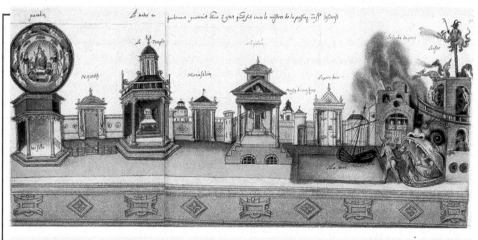

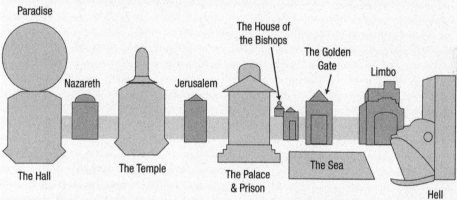

FIXED STAGING

Most fixed performances on the European continent took place in open spaces like city squares or the remains of Roman arenas. Mansions remained fixed throughout such performances. Here, a drawing of the stage for the passion play in Valenciennes, France, in 1547. The drama took twenty-five days to perform, and the mansions were changed as the play progressed. Note the elaborate Hell's mouth on the right.
The key below identifies various mansions shown in the original drawing. The area in front of the mansions is the platea.

The enormous complexity of some late medieval dramas also required specialists to oversee the production and to serve as the medieval counterpart of the modern producer. Although responsibilities differed with circumstances, the tasks of one medieval producer in France included:

- Overseeing the building of a stage and the use of the scenery and machines.

- Overseeing the building and painting of scenery and the construction of seating for the audience.

HOW WE KNOW

Pageant Wagons

The appearance of pageant wagons has been much discussed by scholars, but, as available evidence is scant, few firm conclusions are possible. Only one English description of a pageant wagon has survived but its reliability may be suspect:

> Every company has its own pageant, or parte. The wagons were of two levels, a higher and a lower, upon four wheels. The lower level is where the actors dressed; they acted on the higher level which was uncovered so that all might hear and see them. The places where they played them were in every street.

The language of this description has been modernized.

Here, a conjectural reconstruction of a pageant wagon.

HELLMOUTH
The entrance to hell in medieval church plays was represented by a mouth big enough for the actors to pass through. Smoke and fumes would often issue from the hellmouth during the play. Here, a German woodcut depicts a particularly ferocious hellmouth.

- Checking all deliveries to ensure accuracy.
- Disciplining the actors.
- Acting in the plays whenever necessary.
- Addressing audiences at the beginning of the play and at each intermission, giving a summary of what had happened and promising greater marvels to come.

Because special effects in the dramas were so extraordinary, some men, called **masters of secrets**, became specialists in their construction and workings, which included:

- *Flying*: Angels flew about; Lucifer raised Christ; souls rose from limbo into heaven on doomsday; devils and fire-spitting monsters sallied forth from hell and back again; platforms made to resemble clouds (**glories**) bore choruses of heavenly beings aloft.

- *Traps*: Appearances, disappearances, and substitutions were popular, as when Lot's wife was turned into a pillar of salt and tigers were transformed into sheep.

- *Fire*: Hell belched smoke and flames and buildings ignited on cue. In 1496 at Seurre, France, an actor playing Satan was severely burned when his costume caught fire.

Costumes

Costumes were primary carriers of meaning within the convention called emblematic: They indicated, symbolically and clearly, the nature of the wearers. In one parade of the seven deadly sins, Pride was dressed entirely in peacock feathers, the feather's "eye" symbolizing the love of display and self-admiration. A costume for Greed recorded for a late morality play had symbols of coinage embroidered all over it. In the guild-produced plays, large sums were spent on such costumes, which were then used year after year. Masks were rare, probably being restricted to devils.

Audiences

Audiences for these great outdoor performances of the towns comprised a broad spectrum, from local religious figures to town officials to ordinary citizens. The audience was not universal, however, because a fee was usually charged, and so some of the population was most likely excluded. The well-to-do paid extra to sit in stands or special scaffolds or, when pageant wagons were used, in the windows of selected houses. Those who paid the least stood to watch the plays. Those who paid nothing may have been able to see the processions, if not hear the plays.

Audiences were subject to the weather, and they saw the plays against a backdrop of their fellow citizens and their own town. Food and drink were probably available. Toilet facilities were provided in at least some sets of stands erected for the upper classes.

Secular Drama

At about the same time that religious dramas appeared outside the church, the first records of secular dramas appear. Secular drama, plays clearly not religious, may have been an outgrowth of outdoor religious drama, or it may have developed quite independently, growing out of traditions from early pagan paratheatrical performances. When the great religious plays were at their zenith, this secular tradition was moving tentatively toward maturity. Several principal venues of secular drama existed.

At court and in the homes of the wealthy, performances were given at tournaments and on holidays, especially Christmas and Mardi Gras. There, theatre pieces might be presented within another activity—for example, between the courses of a formal banquet. Such short dramatic entertainment was called an **interlude**. Other occasions for theatre included:

- *Street Pageants and Entries*: Towns staged street pageants and entries in connection with various special occasions, often during the visit of an important dignitary. As a part of these events, plays were combined with elaborate processions. Entries were accompanied by elaborate scenic structures, often a triumphal arch, to welcome an important visitor.

- *Roman Plays*: In schools and colleges, Roman comedies and tragedies were studied, copied, translated, and performed beginning in the fifteenth century.

MODERN STREET PERFORMERS
These soldiers dressed in medieval uniforms are part of a modern street pageant in Padua, Italy. Along with this contingent of marchers were street performers and short plays staged outside.

- *Farces*: For ordinary people in the towns and countryside, farces poked fun at all manner of domestic tribulations, particularly infidelity and cuckoldry.
- *Morality Plays*: In many instances, secular morality plays featured classical gods and heroes rather than Christian virtues and vices. Occasionally morality plays were drawn into the religious battles of Martin Luther's Reformation: For example, anti-Catholic morality plays costumed devils as Catholic prelates and Christian figures as Protestant ministers; anti-Protestant moralities did just the reverse.

Toward the end of the period (after c. 1450), a class of professionals appeared to put on such shows, including writing and staging them.

Production of Secular Plays

Producing arrangements for secular dramas varied enormously. Towns produced some (e.g., street pageants), courts produced others, and schools produced their own. Audiences varied with venue: audiences at royal banquets were very limited (courtiers) as were those of rural villages (peasants). But like audiences of the great religious dramas, most comprised men and women of different social classes. The degree of spectacle also varied widely with the venue, with those produced by towns and courts being most spectacular because they were considered an index of the power and prosperity of the producer. In fact, theatre became a vehicle for displaying power, its opulence a sign of the importance of the town or court producing it. On the other hand, popular farces acted by tiny troupes, often families, were performed with slim production values wherever the actors could get permission—no easy thing in the restrictive medieval world. They have left few records.

Medieval secular theatre, although never as grand as the religious, was nonetheless important because from it came the major thrust toward developing a theatre that was both professional and commercial. Theatre became a kind of commodity that some people (audiences) paid to see other people (performers) do.

The End of Medieval Religious Theatre: The Transformation of Medieval Secular Theatre

By the sixteenth century (1500s), a series of factions splintered away from the Roman Catholic Church; this religious Reformation quickly became political as rulers and nations found reasons to break from Rome or stay with it. The religious theatre was a visible annoyance to both Protestant and Catholic authorities, offending the one with doctrines already rejected, offending the other with doctrines better kept in church, at least until things quieted down. In place after place, religious plays were outlawed by both Protestants and Catholics: Paris, 1548; England, 1558; and the Council of Trent (Italy), 1545–1563.

The end of medieval religious drama was quick. It had reached its height only shortly before it was banned by the middle of the sixteenth century. Much of the best and most elaborate medieval religious theatre came between 1500 and 1550.

KEY TERMS

Key terms are in boldface type in the text. Check your understanding against this list. Persons are page-referenced in the Index.

confraternities
  (kohn-FRAH-tuhr-nih-tees), p. 83
Corpus Christi plays, p. 79
cosmic dramas, p. 81
cycle plays, p. 81
emblematic, p. 76
environmental, p. 76
glories, p. 89
guilds, p. 83
interlude, p. 90
Latin music drama, p. 76
liturgy, p. 74
liturgical drama, p. 76
mansion, p. 76
masters of secrets, p. 89

medieval, p. 73
Middle Ages, p. 73
miracle plays, p. 79
morality plays, p. 79
mystery plays, p. 79
pageants, p. 86
pageant wagons, p. 86
passion plays, p. 79
platea, p. 76
Quem Quaeritis
  (KWEHM-KWAY-rah-tis), p. 76
scaffolds, p. 85
simultaneous staging, p. 76
trope, p. 74

Chapter 4 at a Glance

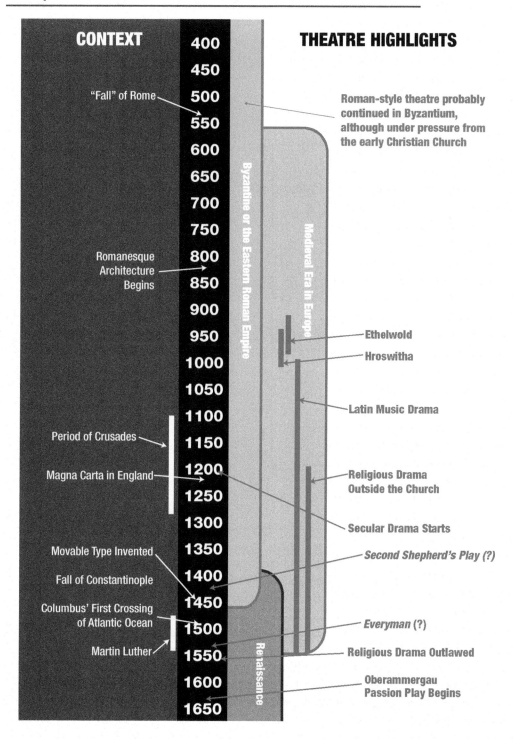

CONTEXT

THEATRE HIGHLIGHTS

400
450
500 — "Fall" of Rome
550
600
650
700
750
800 — Romanesque Architecture Begins
850
900
950
1000
1050
1100
1150 — Period of Crusades
1200 — Magna Carta in England
1250
1300
1350 — Movable Type Invented
1400 — Fall of Constantinople
1450
1500 — Columbus' First Crossing of Atlantic Ocean
1550 — Martin Luther
1600
1650

Byzantine or the Eastern Roman Empire

Medieval Era in Europe

Renaissance

Roman-style theatre probably continued in Byzantium, although under pressure from the early Christian Church

Ethelwold

Hroswitha

Latin Music Drama

Religious Drama Outside the Church

Secular Drama Starts

Second Shepherd's Play (?)

Everyman (?)

Religious Drama Outlawed

Oberammergau Passion Play Begins

5

The Italian Renaissance

OBJECTIVES

When you have completed this chapter, you should be able to:

- Discuss the major traits associated with the Renaissance.
- Define and discuss the tenets of neoclassicism.
- Explain how neoclassicism departed so radically from medieval theatre.
- Describe Italianate staging.
- Trace Italianate staging from Vitruvius through Serlio and Torelli.
- Explain and discuss the importance of Roman ideas and their interpretation to Renaissance theatres.
- Describe commedia dell'arte, the concept of a scenario, and its major masks.

Context

New ideas, social organizations, attitudes, and discoveries began to peek through the medieval order at different paces in different places and taking different forms in the theatre. For the next two hundred years, these new ideas took hold and spread throughout Western Europe, heralding the arrival of the **Renaissance** ("rebirth"). Italy experienced it first, a hundred years before England and Spain. By c.1550 (when medieval religious drama ended), the Renaissance had already revolutionized many former attitudes and practices throughout Western Europe, including politics, religion, art, and social organization. Regardless of date or location, however, several traits distinguish this new Renaissance culture from the medieval culture preceding it.

Humanism

People of the early Middle Ages—at least Christian peoples who dominated Europe—had believed that the temporal world would be destroyed, that the unrighteous would be purged, and that the righteous would be transported to a world of bliss. In the Renaissance, however, new secular and temporal interests joined previous divine and eternal ones. A love of God and his ways, long the basis of human behavior, was joined by a newfound admiration for humankind, whose worth, intelligence, and beauty began to be celebrated. This new concern for people and their earthly lives was called **humanism**.

Secularism

At about the same time, the older theology, a complete moral and ethical system based on divine revelation, gave way to competing philosophical systems that stressed **secularism**. A secular system advocated ethical conduct as an end in itself rather than as a prerequisite to heaven, and secularists argued for logical systems of thought independent of divine revelation. In science, an earth-centered astronomy was challenged by a sun-centered universe in which human beings were relegated to life on a relatively minor planet, no longer at the center of creation. This Copernican revolution, named for the Polish astronomer Nicolaus Copernicus who first promoted the idea, is one example of an essential Renaissance revolutionary insight: that careful observation and experiment could overthrow received rules from the past. Put another way, an opening was made to consider that truth existed not only in the Bible and not only in the books of ancient Greek and Roman authors, but could also be perceived by the senses.

Reformation

Within the church, demands for reform led to breaks with Rome: Some Christians, such as Martin Luther in Germany, protested against the church at Rome and launched what came to be called the *Reformation*. The Reformation put new attention on scripture that could be interpreted without the intercession of Rome. For example, Luther translated the Bible into vernacular German, and the new printing press allowed for wide distribution.

   In sum, although God, his church, and his theology remained a central fact of human life in the Renaissance, they were no longer absolute and unquestioned for issues outside religion itself. Humanism and secularism were competing with the church for acceptance.

A Widening World

By the Renaissance, exploration and discovery had increased commercial areas far beyond the Mediterranean and close-in Atlantic. Marco Polo had opened Asia, Columbus had opened the Americas, and a series of West African ports

Italian City-States During the Renaissance

Bishopric of Trent

Savoy - Not an Italian City-State

Asti, mostly under French control

Marquisate of Saluzzo

Marquisate of Montferrat

Republic of Genoa

Duchy of Milan

Republic of Venice

Mantua
Duchy of Ferrara
Duchy of Modena

Parts of Venice on the Dalmation Coast - not now part of Italy

Duchy of Lucca

Republic of Florence

Papal States

Siena

The island of Corsica is now part of France

Kingdom of Naples

Territory of Spain during the Renaissance

—— Current Border of Italy

A DIVIDED ITALY

Italy was not a united country as it emerged from the Middle Ages and developed into the Renaissance. Here, a map showing Italy's various partitions. By 1500 there were fifteen states, each with its own government.

hop scotching to the Cape of Good Hope opened a feasible sea route to India. Improved navigation aids and some road improvements joined with new postal systems to improve both transportation and communication. For example, a trip of seventy-five miles that took eight days in 1500 took only six by 1600. For trade, new organizations arose for raising capital and insuring against catastrophic loss. Joint stock companies were examples of the former, and associations among merchants were examples of the latter. Wholesalers and middlemen transformed the nature of trade and took their share of the growing profits.

The Fall of Constantinople

Along with goods, trade led to the exchange of ideas. At the center of most of the various trade routes of the fourteenth century were the city-states of Italy, which soon became centers of an international commerce in ideas, skills, and products. When Constantinople fell to the Muslim Turks in 1453, many scholars and artists came to Italy, and with them came plays and treatises from ancient Greece and Rome, which were rescued from endangered libraries, including manuscripts by Aeschylus, Sophocles, Euripides, Aristophanes, and Aristotle. Their study and interpretation began almost at once.

The Printing Press

The introduction of the Gutenberg printing press to Italy in about 1440 allowed the rapid reproduction of documents arriving from the East as well as of the interpretations and imitations of these documents. Certainly, the printing press allowed a veritable explosion of accessible information, so much so, that by 1500, numerous academies in the city-states of Italy were devoted to the study and production of Roman plays. Shortly thereafter, Italians began writing their own plays in imitation of Roman models.

The Arts and Theatre

Patronage of the arts during the Renaissance was a major and acknowledged source of prestige, and because the nobles' courts engaged in rivalries over which was to become the cultural center, painters, musicians, sculptors, architects, and writers flourished. Such changes in viewpoint, technology, and funding predictably brought changes in theatre and drama.

The first one hundred years or so of the Renaissance in Italy, unlike the same years in England and Spain, revolutionized theatre and drama. In their efforts to recapture the practice of Greece and Rome, Italian artists set theatres in Europe on a new path—a path toward **illusionism**. Theatre was thereafter to seek an illusion of real life, at least, real life within the confines for that time of Italian theatre conventions.

Four contributions of the Italians were to have far-reaching effects:

- The neoclassical ideal in playwriting and criticism.
- The Italianate system of staging and architecture.
- A popular theatre known as commedia dell'arte.
- The still popular, theatre-related genre opera.

Theory: Neoclassicism

Neoclassicism literally means "new classicism," but in fact it was based far more heavily on Rome than on Greece. Neoclassicism in the theatre, as first developed by the Italians and later adopted throughout most of Western Europe, rested on five major points:

- Verisimilitude and decorum.
- Purity of genres.

- The three unities.
- The five-act form.
- A twofold purpose—to teach and to please.

Verisimilitude

Central to neoclassical doctrine was a complex concept called **verisimilitude**—literally, "truth seeming." But the meaning of *verisimilitude* is more involved than its facile definition might suggest because artists have always aimed to tell the "truth." Thus, the critical problem for a student of neoclassicism is to understand what truth meant to the neoclassicist.

Truth for the neoclassicist resided in the essential, the general, the typical, and the class rather than in the particular, the individual, or the unique. To get at truth, a neoclassical artist had to cut away all that was temporary or accidental in favor of those qualities that were fundamental and unchanging. To be "true" meant to be usually true. The humanness of one person, for example, rested in those essential qualities that he or she shared with all other people, regardless of place, century, or ethnicity. Individual differences were not important because they were not essential to humanness. Such a view of truth placed a premium on classification and categorization, and in verisimilitude, truth had a meaning different from that ascribed to it by our own age's view of the importance of individuality and uniqueness.

Neoclassical truth implied other matters as well. Verisimilitude in drama required the elimination of events that could not reasonably be expected to happen in real life. Although an exception was made when ancient stories or myths incorporating supernatural events were dramatized, even then the dramatist was expected to minimize the importance of such events, perhaps by putting them offstage. Because in real life people generally talk to one another rather than to themselves, monologues and soliloquies were customarily abandoned in favor of dialogue between major characters and their **confidant**, persons in whom the central characters confide feelings, information, or relationships.

Characters in neoclassical drama were expected to embody the traits normally held by members of their group in manners and conduct; that is, they were to behave as was appropriate for their sex, age, social class, and so on. Such characters were said to display **decorum**. Although indecorous characters often drove the plots of neoclassical plays, they suffered either tragic consequences or comic ridicule.

Finally, because it was believed that God ruled the world in accord with a divine plan and that he was a good God, verisimilitude required that dramatic actions be organized according to moral principles—good was rewarded and evil punished. Although in daily life good occasionally went unrewarded and evil unpunished, such observable events were believed to be aberrational and therefore unsuitable subjects for drama.

Purity of Genres

Verisimilitude also inspired **purity of genres**, meaning that the two major forms, tragedy and comedy, must not be mixed. The injunction against mixing did not mean merely that funny scenes were improper for tragedy or that unhappy endings were inappropriate for comedy. Both tragedy and comedy were far more rigidly defined than today, and the rule against mixing the forms meant that no element belonging to the one should appear in the other. For example, **tragedy** was supposed to depict people of high station involved in affairs of state; its language was to be elevated and poetic; and its endings were to be unhappy. **Comedy**, on the other hand, was supposed to display persons of the lower and middle classes embroiled in domestic difficulties and intrigues. Its language was always to be less elevated, often prosaic, and its endings were to be happy. Purity of genres meant, then, that a prose tragedy or a domestic tragedy could not exist—both were a contradiction in terms. It also meant that kings and queens could not appear in comedies, nor were affairs of state suitable subjects for comedy.

The Three Unities

Verisimilitude and interpretations of classical examples created the neoclassical notion of the **three unities**—time, place, and action. Although Aristotle had argued cogently for plays with a unified action, neoclassical theorists were more concerned that their plays unfold within a reasonable time and a limited place so that verisimilitude would not be strained. No audience would believe, the neoclassical argument went, that months had passed or oceans had been crossed while the audience sat in the same place for a few hours. Theorists varied in the strictness of their requirements for unity: some argued for a single room and others for a single town; some required that the playing time of the drama equal the actual time elapsed, and others that no more than twenty-four hours elapse. Most Italian theorists accepted some version of the three unities after about 1570.

The Five-Act Form

By then, as well, neoclassicists had adopted the five-act play as standard for drama, a norm probably derived from the theories of Horace and the practices of Seneca (five sections separated by four choruses), although neither had used the "act" as a dramatic unit.

A Twofold Purpose: To Teach and to Please

The neoclassicists found a justification for drama and theatre in the ability of these to teach morality while entertaining an audience. The idea of a drama existing only for its own sake or as an expression of an individual artist was not accepted.

Razullo.   Cucurucu.

THE POPULAR COMMEDIA
DELL'ARTE
Commedia troupes developed a form of
theatre in Italy that did not reflect neoclassic
ideals nor did it reflect the "erudite drama" of
the Renaissance academies. Here, an etching from about 1620, in which two commedia
characters frame an outdoor performance on
a temporary booth stage. On the stage, five
commedia characters are performing.

By 1600, neoclassical ideals were being accepted in other parts of Europe and they remained dominant for the next two hundred years among educated and courtly audiences. Neoclassicism's limits to dramatic expression may account for its lack of appeal to many people, who sought more spectacle than the three unities permitted. Thus, despite the acceptance of neoclassicism as an ideal, its tenets were undercut in a variety of ways—by spectacle, for example.

Practice: Italian Renaissance Drama

Renaissance dramatists studied plays of Aeschylus, Sophocles, Euripides, Aristophanes, Seneca, Terence, and Plautus and used them as models, particularly after these texts were first printed in Latin, and later, Italian. From that study came a series of pale imitations of Greek and Roman models that were literary rather than theatrical, written for the academies, not the theatre.

Erudite Drama

During the 1500s, dramas were written in Italian rather than Latin even though the sources were Greek and Roman plays, especially the comedies of Terence. This output, known as *Commedia Erudita*, followed the precepts of Horace and Seneca. These plays, comedies as well as tragedies, were performed at courts and schools. A third dramatic form concerned with the lives of shepherds and shepherdesses, called *pastorals*, became popular. Pastorals usually had elements of drama but ended happily and so were often called tragicomedies. Pastorals are also called *satyric* plays, a reference to ancient Greek and Roman satyr plays, which were not truly understood in the Renaissance. Satyric in this era refers to rural and should not be confused with *satiric*, meaning reflecting satire, a literary form that uses wit and sarcasm to expose human vices and stupidities.

At least two Italian playwrights distinguished themselves. Niccolò Machiavelli completed in 1518 a scabrous comedy, *La Mandragola* (*The Mandrake*), about the seduction of a young wife by a lustful man who arranges to make her believe that taking a potion made from mandrake root will enable her to conceive a child. The potion, she is told, has the deadly consequence that it will kill the next man she sleeps with. Under the guise of protecting her ancient husband from death, she is convinced to sleep with an anonymous young man who, of course, is the lustful young lover in disguise. The old man has an heir—whose?—and once learning the truth, the young wife takes the young man as her lover. The play pokes fun at the corruption of Italian society. *The Mandrake* is still sometimes revived.

Torquato Tasso's pastoral *Aminta* (1573), set in the time of Alexander the Great with a cast of shepherds and nymphs, is admired but rarely revived. The central character Aminta, a shepherd, is in love with Sylvia, a nymph. When Aminta thinks Sylvia is dead he attempts to kills himself but fails. Sylvia finds Aminta and they are married (happy ending). The play is written in a complicated verse form much admired at the time.

Illusionism

Theatres during the four hundred years from about 1550 to about 1950 shared several important theatrical conventions that make up *illusionism*. Their major collective traits are:

- Theatre buildings with a proscenium arch, which frames the action on stage.
- Scenery and costumes that seek to create the illusion of fidelity to life outside the theatre.

These new conventions took hold first in Italy and then spread through Western Europe and its colonies, where they dominated theatre practice through much of the twentieth century.

The Italianate theatre and its illusionistic system of staging, like neoclassicism itself, developed as a mixture of ideas and techniques from ancient Greece, Rome, and contemporary Italy. Most important from the ancients was the work of Vitruvius.

Vitruvius in the Renaissance

Early in Italy's Renaissance, Vitruvius's Roman work on architecture, which had existed only in manuscripts, was printed. By 1500 it was the acknowledged authority in the field, and interpretations and commentaries in Italian followed. Although he had written about architecture and scenery, Vitruvius had provided no illustrations. As a result, the Italians translated him and provided illustrations in terms of their practices, most notably a fascination with *linear perspective*—a means of representing spatial depth (three dimensions) on a two-dimensional surface. On the stage, perspective became a means of representing greater depth than in fact existed.

Perspective

Although known to the Romans, **perspective**, when rediscovered by Italian painters, caused an artistic revolution. Artists worked to master the "new" technique, and spectators hailed its ability to trick the senses. The "vanishing point," to which objects receded away from the viewer, became, in stage design,

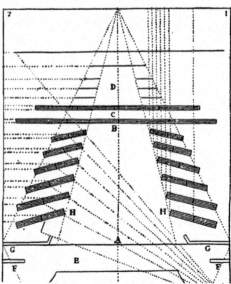

ONE-POINT PERSPECTIVE STAGE LAYOUT
Behind the Renaissance forestage, a single vanishing point was the apparent meeting place of lines that created an illusion of depth greater than the actual theatre could offer. The staged is raked to increase the perception of depth.

the key to false, or forced, perspective, through which a stage depth of thirty feet could be made to seem three hundred. On the stage, achieving this sense of depth often meant constructing three-dimensional objects (usually build-ings) in **false perspective**. In false perspective, a building or line of buildings or trees is distorted, shortened as the line moves upstage. Thus, from the audi-ence point of view, the depth of the stage seems greater that it really is as long as no actor moved to the depth of the stage. An actor would dwarf the upstage buildings if he appeared up there. So acting took place in front of the scenery.

In 1545 an Italian, Sebastiano Serlio, published *Dell'Architectura*, an inter-pretation of Vitruvius that dominated theatre architecture and design for the next century. Vitruvius, of course, had described the circular, outdoor Roman theatre. But wealthy Italians wanted plays done indoors in wealthy homes. Therefore, when the first indoor theatres were designed, the task was to adapt Vitruvius to rectangular spaces and to accommodate them to linear perspective.

Vitruvius's scanty descriptions of tragic, comic, and satyric scenes be-came, in Serlio's books, detailed illustrations in false perspective. A brief comparison of Vitruvius and Serlio will show their differences.

Of the satyric scene, Vitruvius said, "Satyric scenes are decorated with trees, cavern, mountains, and other rustic objects delineated in land-scaper style." Of the same scenes, Serlio said, "The satyrical scenes are to represent Satyrs wherein you must place all those things that be rude and rustic." He then went on to quote Vitruvius as calling for "trees, roots, herbs, hills, and flowers, and with some country houses." If the scenes were to be constructed in winter, when there were few green trees, herbs, and flowers to be found, "then you must make these things of silk, which will become more commendable than the natural things themselves." In the remainder of *Dell'Architectura*, Serlio provided tips on the use of colored lights, fire effects, fanciful costumes, and pasteboard figures in a perspective setting.

Renaissance Theatre Structures

The production of plays by courts and academies was sporadic before about 1550. Thus, temporary theatres were erected to meet the occasional need for a theatre space. Sometime after 1550, productions were offered with enough regularity that permanent theatres were called for. The designers of these spaces tried to incorporate Serlio's precepts for theatre buildings.

Teatro Olimpico

An early solution paid homage to Serlio's understanding of Roman theatres described by Vitruvius. The result was the Teatro Olimpico, the first permanent theatre built in the Renaissance. Located in Vicenza, the Olimpico was designed by the great architect Andrea Palladio to be fitted in an already existing rectangular building that housed the Olympic Academy. The project was begun in 1580 but Palladio died shortly after construction began and the theatre was completed by Vincenzo Scamozzi. The first performance in the Teatro Olimpico was *Oedipus Rex* in 1585.

The facade stage, echoing an ornate *scaenae frons* from Roman models, had five onstage doorways (corresponding to Vitruvius's five stage openings). Behind each doorway was a vista in perspective, each with its own vanishing point. These scenic alleys were added to Palladio's original design by Scamozzi. This early solution satisfied the Italian demand for perspective. Its multiple vanishing points satisfied its patrons, a wealthy gentlemen's academy. With five vanishing points then there were five "perfect" places to sit in the audience and have the illusion of depth.

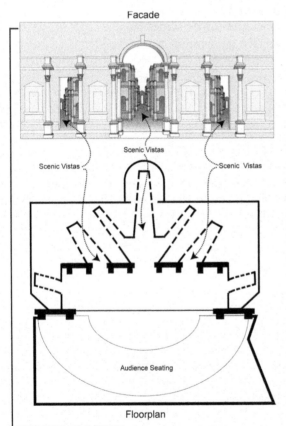

Facade

Scenic Vistas

Scenic Vistas

Scenic Vistas

Audience Seating

Floorplan

TEATRO OLIMPICO

The Teatro Olimpico was an early compromise between a Roman facade stage and the Renaissance passion for perspective. Each of five doors framed a three-dimensional vista in false perspective, giving each member of the audience a view down at least one. Actors worked on the stage; they probably used the doorways but did not walk into the false-perspective structures. Compare the diagram with the picture of the actual space (*right*). Note the slightly widened semicircle of the orchestra.

Although the uniqueness of the Teatro Olimpico fascinates scholars, the facade stage with perspective alleys became an anomaly. Architects explored other options.

Sabbioneta Theatre

After the completion of the Teatro Olimpico, Vicenzo Scamozzi was invited to build a small court theatre for a nobleman in Sabbioneta, a town near Parma. This theatre, called *Teatro all'Antica* became the first purpose-built theatre of the Renaissance. Scamozzi abandoned the idea of a Roman-style facade stage like the one Palladio designed for the Academy in Vicenza. Although the Sabbioneta theatre did not have a formal proscenium arch, it did have a series of angled flats in diminishing size, each increasing the illusion of depth. A raked stage floor helped the illusion of depth. The auditorium was horseshoe shaped. This 250-seat intimate theatre, completed in 1590, may well be an intermediate step in the development of a fully articulated proscenium arch.

The plan of a third wooden theatre, the Teatro Farnese, built in 1618–1619, in Parma, became the model for architects for hundreds of years.

Teatro Farnese

The Farnese theatre shares some of the architectural attributes of the Teatro Olimpico. Both are wooden structures (set inside of a preexisting stone building) in which theatres inspired by Roman models were fitted into a large, rectangular room. Much of the architectural detail in both

THE FIRST PURPOSE-BUILT THEATRE
The theatre in Sabbioneta, Italy, may be an intermediate step in the development of the proscenium arch. The model of the theatre was built based on Scamozzi's floor plan and elevation, a document in the Naples Museum. This view of the stage gives an approximation of the angled wing setting without a formal proscenium. The setting is a modern interpretation of Scamozzi's plan.

THE PROSCENIUM ARCH ARRIVES

The Teatro Farnese at Parma is the first theatre with a
permanent proscenium arch. The engraving from the
1730s shows the stage with a full set. The people in
front of the stage suggest a height about five feet. The
model of the seating area was devised from contemporary drawings and etchings. The etching (right) shows
a schematic of a horse parade during a court entertainment as well as the size of the area in front of the stage.

theatres reflects the ornate facades—the scaenae frons—of many Roman
theatres.

The Farnese, built about thirty-five years later than the Olympico, made
a bold leap in theatre architecture by installing a permanent **proscenium**
stage, complete with a mechanism under the stage to change scenery.

The Farnese is the first permanent indoor proscenium-arch theatre.
Designed by Giovanni Battista Aleotti and built between 1618 and 1619, the
theatre was never much used. It was largely destroyed during a bombing raid
during the Second World War. Reconstruction, based on drawings and engravings, began in 1952 and was completed about a decade later.

A model of the horseshoe-shaped seating was used in the reconstruction of the theatre. The flat floor in front of the seats could be used for balls or equestrian displays or was sometimes flooded for mock naval battles. The proscenium view shows the intricate facade that echoes its Roman antecedent.

Stage Settings for Illusionistic Theatre

Serlio's scenography—his misinterpretation of the Roman Vitruvius—was the basis for what we now call **Italianate staging**. With certain modifications related to place and date, Italianate settings throughout Europe shared the

SERLIO

Combining Vitruvius's writings on the Roman theatre with the Renaissance interest in perspective, Serlio created his own ideal scenery for tragedy (top left), comedy (bottom left), and pastoral (satyric) (above) plays. These drawings greatly influenced the design of scenery.

following features during the sixteenth, seventeenth, and early eighteenth centuries:

- Scenery placed behind both a proscenium arch and the actors, forming a background rather than an environment to surround them.

- Scenery painted in **single-point perspective** (all objects recede to the same vanishing point), as calculated from one seat toward the back of the orchestra (usually the seat of the most important noble or patron).

- Scenery consisting of **wings**, which were paired flats (wooden frames covered with fabric and painted), each pair closer together as they were farther from the audience, so that the lines of the inner edges of the flats receded toward the vanishing point. The setting culminated upstage in a **backdrop** (painted two-dimensional hanging) or a **shutter**, a pair of wings pushed together. Shutters could be opened to reveal even deeper perspective space or pierced to make a *relieve* through which greater depth was glimpsed.

- A **raked stage**, slanted upward from front to back to increase the sense of depth. Sometimes only the stage behind the proscenium arch was raked, sometimes the entire stage, causing the actors to climb or descend (hence our terms *upstage* and *downstage*).

- Machinery and rigging hidden overhead by **borders**, framed or unframed fabric painted like sky, clouds, leaves, and so on.

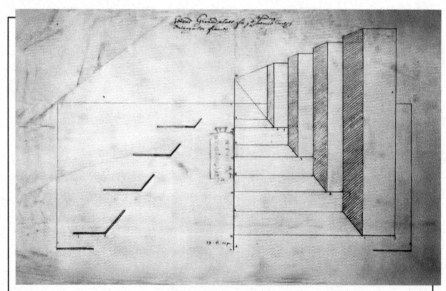

A static scenic arrangement of angled flats on the right with the corresponding ground plan on the left is from a drawing of about the 1630s.

Movable Scenery

Having developed this static scenery system, Italian artists set about almost at once to give it movement, to shift scenery, and to allow rapid changes of place. Two techniques predominated.

The Groove System The first method developed is called the **groove system**. At each side of the stage were three or four nests of scenic flats. Each nest contained a series of flats placed into tracks on the floor—grooves—and a corresponding set of grooves above the flats to facilitate the moving of the scenic pieces on or off stage, much like a sliding closet door found in some houses. With a stagehand at each nest, the flats could be manipulated—pulled or pushed—to change the scene. Sometimes winches and ropes would have aided stagehands in moving the flats. The flats were painted in single point perspective. At the back of the stage was another set of larger flats, called shutters, that would meet in stage center to complete the scenic illusion. When a signal was given—a whistle blown or a gong struck, for example—the stagehands would change the scene. The groove system was efficient but somewhat intrusive.

Chariot-and-Pole System The most effective system was shown in 1645 when Giacomo Torelli astonished audiences with fluid, fast, and apparently magical changes. The secret was his **chariot-and-pole system**. Small wheeled wagons ran on tracks under the stage, each with a pole that extended through a slit in the stage high enough to support a flat. The idea was elegant and simple: As the chariots moved below the stage floor, so the flats moved in view of the audience. Pulling a chariot toward the center brought a flat into view; pulling the chariot away from the center caused a flat to disappear. With the chariots harnessed by ropes and pulleys to the same winch, stage mechanics

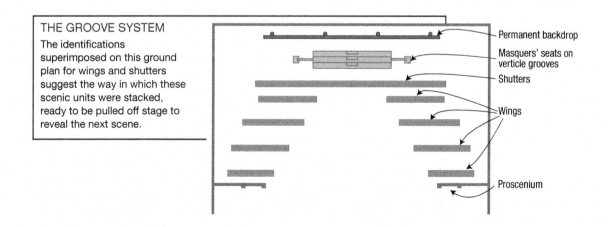

THE GROOVE SYSTEM

The identifications superimposed on this ground plan for wings and shutters suggest the way in which these scenic units were stacked, ready to be pulled off stage to reveal the next scene.

Permanent backdrop

Masquers' seats on verticle grooves

Shutters

Wings

Proscenium

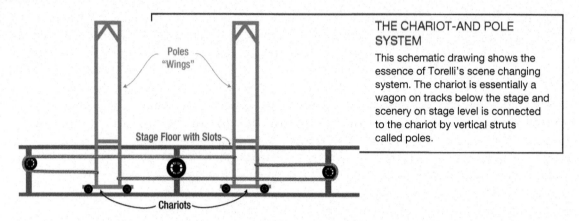

THE CHARIOT-AND POLE SYSTEM
This schematic drawing shows the essence of Torelli's scene changing system. The chariot is essentially a wagon on tracks below the stage and scenery on stage level is connected to the chariot by vertical struts called poles.

Poles
"Wings"

Stage Floor with Slots

Chariots

could turn one wheel to change an entire setting. Torelli, no stranger to self-promotion, earned the title "The Great Wizard" by coordinating these changes with special effects, such as flying, lightning, and explosions.

Contradiction in Mainstream Theatre

A contradiction clearly existed between the ideals of theory—the unities of time, place, and action and an avoidance of the supernatural—and the ideals of scenic design, whose artists increasingly emphasized rapid change of place and spectacle. This tension was resolved by keeping an austere style for neoclassical plays while expending creativity and money on operas, ballets, and lavish *intermezzi* (entertainments given between the acts of a neoclassical play)—a way of having cake and eating it at the same time.

By the mid-seventeenth century, Italian opera had become the most popular and spectacular form of entertainment in Italy. One early Italian opera called for fifteen separate locales, a challenge easily met by the chariot-and-pole system. As opera was exported to the rest of Europe, so were its scenic techniques. In English in this period, the word *opera* probably signified as much about scenery as it did about music.

An Alternative Theatre: Commedia dell'Arte

Neoclassical dramas and elaborately staged operas were primarily the entertainment of the noble, the wealthy, and the educated. Among other classes, another, very different kind of dramatic entertainment flourished in Italy: the **commedia dell'arte** ("professional playing"). Although neither the origins nor the sources of commedia are well understood, its major characteristics were well established by 1550, and Italian troupes were touring Western Europe by 1600.

HOW WE KNOW

Commedia Scenarios

Flaminio Scala (1547–1624) was a commedia actor who committed to print fifty scenarios as *Il Teatro Delle Favole Rappresentative* in 1611 (*Theatre Tales for Performance*). His publication is important because it documents a large cache of scenarios printed by the artist himself and because together the scenarios represent a part the repertory for the important company, I Gelosi.

Scala's published scenarios outline the action by acts and scenes. A scenario laid out the bare story lines, what information must be given by each performer in each scene so that the play could find its way to an ending. Actors would elaborate on the scenario, with whatever gags, poetry, songs, or bits of comic business they could fit in. Some exchanges were elastic and could be extended by the actors if the audience encouraged the performers with laughter.

Act one of *Flavio's Good Fortune* has sixteen scenes. 1: Flaminia and her servant agree that Orazio is a good man. 2: Capitano Spavento sees Flaminia and believes she is a prostitute. She enters her house....

Matt Orton

SCRIPTED COMMEDIA

Lazzi lives in this picture from a 2009 production at the University of Montevallo of Scapin, *Moliére's play based on commedia models.*

4: Pantalone leaves his house and the Capitano thinks he is one of Flaminia's lovers—he is actually her father. Capitano tells Pantalone that he is too old to be frequenting whores. Pantalone takes justifiable offense, and both go for their weapons. 5: Pantalone's servant draws his halberd and the innkeeper enters with a kitchen spit. 6: Before they can fight, the Capitano's servant pulls his master away. Pantalone considers that his daughter's virtue is at stake and so he will abandon his plan to forestall her marriage...

7: Orazio enters, with his servant. His servant tells Orazio that Pantalone is rich but unhappy because of the loss of his son, Flavio. Hearing this, Orazio weeps....

9: Graziano, a scoundrel, a person who makes money from gullible people, asks the innkeeper for his dinner so he can set up his platform and make some sales. The innkeeper asks Graziano to set up his stage right here, in front of the inn. They exit. Orazio has his servant knock on Pantalone's door. 10: Flaminia leans out the window. Orazio asks to speak with Pantalone. She does not know where Pantalone is. Orazio tells her that he loves her and intends to ask her father for her hand. Flaminia tells Orazio that her father is the master of her body and soul, and exits sighing.

11: Arlecchino and other scoundrels set up their platform and call for the rest of the group. 12: Graziano and his retinue mount the platform and sing....
15: Pantalone and his servant enter to watch. Graziano makes his sales pitch, followed by more singing.
16: The Capitano enters with his servant...Orazio draws a sword to fight the Capitano who draws his sword as well. Graziano's group runs off, followed by the Capitano who is followed by Orazio, Pantalone, and his servant, as the scoundrels' platform collapses and everyone else runs into his or her respective house and the first act ends.

By itself, this first act of the scenario seems dull. Improvisation and lazzi would make it highly effective. For example, the conflict between the Capitano and Pantalone about whether Flaminia is a whore could be expanded with mugging, clowning business, comic sword fight, and such. This act has a great visual concluding moment that would lead the audience to want to stay to see what would happen next: the improvised stage collapses and everyone runs offstage in different directions.

Commedia players—both male and female—worked from a basic story outline, a **scenario**, within which they improvised much of their dialogue and action. This approach to playmaking required inspired ensemble performers of great skill and virtuosity. The scenario would be filled out with singing, dancing, and with bits of comic business called *lazzi*, broad physical comedy. One *lazzo*—the singular Italian form of the word—might be that a character is insulted but because his hands are full, he slaps the insulting character with his foot. Or lazzi might be near-acrobatic: a character holding a glass of wine who turns a somersault without spilling it. Sometimes the lazzi could be crude, as exemplified by the "water lazzo": An inamorata has fainted and her servant calls for water. A *zanni* brings all kinds of water to revive her—orange water, jasmine water, mint water, etc.—but to no avail. Finally he urinates in a cup and splashes it on the prostrate woman. This revives her so she sings the praises of "the water distilled by the rod."

Each actor in the troupe played the same stock character in almost every scenario and therefore wore the same costume and mask, reused the same lazzi, and even repeated some of the same dialogue from scenario to scenario. Most troupes had at least ten members that included one (or two) sets of unmasked young lovers and a number of masked comic characters. The masks usually covered the face from the hairline to just under the nose, leaving the mouth free for speaking. Male actors outnumbered female. Both mask and costume became traditional for each character except the lovers.

Commedia Characters

The roles required in a scenario included four main character types. Other minor characters as required by the scenario were added.

- The Young Lovers (*Innamorati*), one or two pairs. These characters were unmasked. The Innamorati and their love affairs were often the driving force of a commedia scenario. The old men (*Pantalone* or *Dottore*) refused to see them wed or wanted the young single woman for themselves. Beauty in the female lover (*Innamorata*) and handsome virility in the male lover (*Innamorato*) were a plus. Both Inamorata and Innamorato were able to recite beautiful poetry beautifully and spoke in a standard Italian dialect. Many could sing and dance with great skill. Their costumes were the fashionable dress of the time made from rich fabrics.

- The Elders. Pantalone (usually a wealthy but miserly Venetian merchant) and Dottore Gaziano (the doctor, an educated pedant who often spouted Latin inaccurately) were the central old codgers in most scenarios. They tried to thwart the young lovers. Pantalone's costume included a black flowing cape over red tights and shirt, heelless slippers often with a curly toe, and a black skull cap. He spoke in a Venetian dialect. The Dottore wore a black academic costume of a gown and a floppy hat. He spoke with a Bolognese dialect with garbled Latin combined with gibberish.

- The Crafty Servants, called zanni. These were a collection of low-life characters—Arlecchino (Harlequin), Brighella, Pedrolino, Scapino, Coviello, Scaramuccio, and Pulcinello—for example. A company would have as many zanni as they could afford because these characters provided big laughs. A small company would have at least two clownish servants, no matter what they were named. These characters, all uncultivated peasants, were dishonest, cunning, and lustful, and most of all, hungry. Their talk was laced with vulgarity and scatological exclamations. Their dialect was either Venetian or Bergamoese. The serving maid to the inamorata, sometimes played by a man but usually a woman, wore a large apron and was quite buxom; she was often quite impertinent. The convention of the smart-talking, cheeky sidekick continues in film and television today.

- The Braggart Soldier—Capitano (the captain who boasts of his military exploits but is at heart a coward), sometimes called Capitan Spavento. Some Capitanos would wear extraordinarily expensive finery whereas others dressed shabbily to belie their exaggerated military conquests. He often carried an oversized sword. This character would have at his command a litany of excuses as to why he would not fight an opponent. He usually spoke with a Spanish accent.

- Other Minor Characters as needed. They included porters, policemen, old women, and even ghosts. They spoke in a variety of dialects. Clearly much fun ensued from the mixture of dialects, educational backgrounds, and motivations.

COMMEDIA CHARACTERS

These five commedia characters exemplify the traditional costumes for masked characters (from *left* to *right*): Tartaglia (a zanni), Pantalone, Dottore, Brigella, and Coviello (both zannis).

Organized as commercial sharing companies where each member had a prearranged share of the income, such troupes toured constantly as they tried to scratch out a living without the protection or the financial support of noble houses. Although the influence of commedia extended throughout Europe, France was especially welcoming to companies. The ephemeral nature of commedia dell'arte militated against its leaving a lasting record—there were essentially no written-out scripts although scenarios survive. Still this popular Italian comedy has been revived and imitated in many more recent cultures.

The most popular and famous commedia company was I Gelosi ("The Jealous Ones"), the first commedia company to be patronized by nobility thus earning them financial stability. They performed before Louis XIV in Paris and toured throughout Europe. Perhaps the company was founded by Flaminio Scala, but eventually I Gelosi was headed by the husband-and-wife team of Isabella and Francesco Andreini. Other companies were named *Confidenti*, *Accessi*, *Uniti*, and *Fideli*, among others.

Commedia's Influence

Although ephemeral and transitory, commedia had a lasting effect on other dramatists. (These playwrights are discussed in more detail in other chapters.)

- Molière, who shared the Hotel de Bourgogne in Paris with a commedia company, appropriated characters and lazzi to incorporate into his plays. In *The Miser*, for example, the title character, Harpagon (a Pantalone figure), is given a tirade when he discovers he has been robbed. Similar tirades were set pieces in commedia. Harpagon has a son, who serves the role of an Innamorato, who wants to marry the Innamorata that Harpagon wants for himself. In *Scapin's Deceits*, the title character is based on the commedia character of Scapino. There are many other examples.

- Shakespeare borrowed the Capitano character for use in *Love's Labors' Lost* in the person of Don Adriano de Armado. Shakespeare described him as a "fantastic Spaniard." Falstaff from *Henry IV* and *The Merry Wives of Windsor* is another typical braggart soldier.

- Carlo Goldoni (1707-1793) and Carlo Gozzi (1720-1806) are playwrights who gave literary form to commedia scenarios, turning them into scripted plays. Goldoni wrote more than a hundred plays and librettos for operas. His commedia-like comedy, *The Servant of Two Masters* (finished in 1753), is often performed today. The cast includes the characters of Truffaldino, Pantaloon (Pantalone), Capitano, Doctor Lombardi (Il Dottore), and a set of lovers (Florindo and Beatrice).

Commedia's Roots

Just as commedia dell'arte left its imprint on other dramatists, so the commedia itself borrowed heavily from contemporary Italian drama and plays from the distant past. The plays of Aristophanes, Menander, Plautus, and Terrence were especially useful to commedia companies. These Greek and Roman scripts, newly published and thus available, could become the basis of scenarios, suggest new lazzi, or offer new characters.

Italy: Eclipse

Despite Italy's unquestioned leadership in dramatic theory and scenic display and in spite of its unique popular comedy, by 1750, except for opera, Italy was no longer a world leader in theatre. Both England and France had outstripped their teacher and attained an international reputation by the end of the seventeenth century, and both achieved a lasting acclaim never given to the Italians from whom they drew. Perhaps in part this was because of the Italian-speaking peoples living in various small rival political units. Italy was not a unified country until the mid-1800s. Britain and France were each united under monarchs and the monarch's bureaucracy, focused on a capital city where theatre could be sustained and develop.

KEY TERMS

Key terms are in boldface type in the text. Check your understanding against this list. Persons are page-referenced in the Index.

backdrop, p. 108
borders, p. 108
chariot-and-pole system, p. 109
comedy, p. 99
commedia dell'arte (koh-MAY-dee-ah dehl-AHR-tay), p. 110
confidants, p. 98
decorum, p. 98
false perspective, p. 103
groove system, p. 109
humanism, p. 95
illusionism, p. 97
intermezzi, p. 110
Italianate staging, p. 107
lazzi (LAHT-zee), p. 112
neoclassicism, p. 97

perspective, p. 102
proscenium, p. 106
purity of genres, p. 99
Renaissance, p. 94
raked stage, p. 108
scenario, p. 112
secularism, p. 95
shutter, p. 108
single-point perspective, p. 108
three unities, p. 99
tragedy, p. 99
verisimilitude (veh-rih-sih-MIHL-ih-tood), p. 98
wings, p. 108
zanni, p. 112

Chapter 5 at a Glance

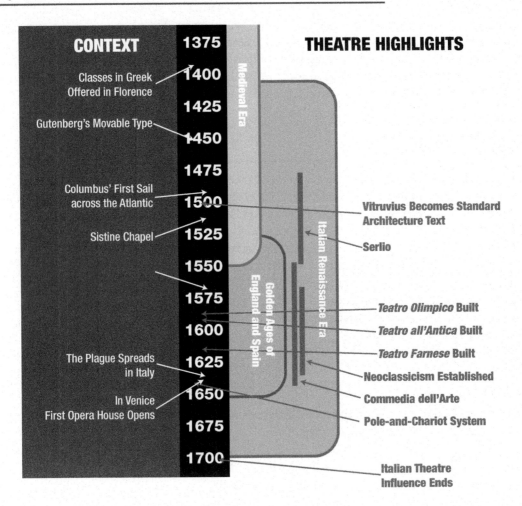

CONTEXT

THEATRE HIGHLIGHTS

1375

1400 — Classes in Greek Offered in Florence

Medieval Era

1425

Gutenberg's Movable Type — 1450

1475

Columbus' First Sail across the Atlantic — 1500 — Vitruvius Becomes Standard Architecture Text

Sistine Chapel — 1525 — Serlio

Italian Renaissance Era

1550

1575 — Teatro Olimpico Built

Golden Ages of England and Spain

1600 — Teatro all'Antica Built

— Teatro Farnese Built

The Plague Spreads in Italy — 1625 — Neoclassicism Established

In Venice First Opera House Opens — 1650 — Commedia dell'Arte

— Pole-and-Chariot System

1675

1700 — Italian Theatre Influence Ends

The Golden Ages of England and Spain

When you have completed this chapter, you should be able to:

- List the principal kinds of drama, some important playwrights, and plays from the age of Shakespeare and the Spanish Golden Age.
- Distinguish between public and private theatres in England and Spain.
- Describe the major staging conventions of Shakespeare's theatre, and compare them (i.e., note similarities and differences) with medieval conventions.
- Compare the physical theatres of Shakespeare and the Spanish Golden Age.
- Compare the role of women in the theatres of Shakespeare and Spain.
- Explain the importance of masques in English theatre history.

Context

Spain and England, both strong naval powers and vigorous traders at the Renaissance start, were early rivals. Spain, importing gold from its Central and South American colonies, pulled money to its profligate central government and clung to Roman Catholicism and absolute monarchy. England, on the other hand, developed a strong merchant class, broke with Rome, and moved toward constitutional monarchy. In both places, economic growth led to the growth of cities and the growth of theatre.

In England and Spain, a new, commercial theatre developed that exploited Medieval secular conventions in staging (i.e., emblem, environment, and simultaneity as discussed in Chapter 4). The stories told on their stages reflected

117

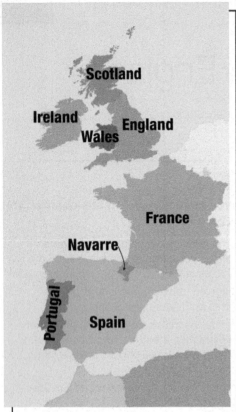

ENGLAND AND SPAIN

The sea and France separated England and Spain, as religion separated the two countries during this era. Still, the two countries both had great ages of early Renaissance theatre at roughly the same time.

characters and themes quite different than those of the Middle Ages. Theatres in both England and Spain, although influenced by Renaissance ideas, also built on conventions of the late Middle Ages.

Both England and Spain produced glorious dramas and robust public theatres soon after the end of medieval religious drama by about 1550. By 1600, with politically stable and economically sound circumstances, both countries were enjoying their **Golden Ages** of theatre and drama, with new freestanding theatres, professional players, paying audiences, and expansive plays of great complexity.

England and the Golden Age

The reign of Elizabeth I (1558–1603) brought greatness to England. With her ascent to the throne, the nation achieved the political and religious stability that permitted its arts and literature to thrive. When, in an attempt to mute religious controversies, the government outlawed religious drama, it opened the way for the rapid development of a secular tradition of plays and playgoing. When the queen finally agreed to the execution of Mary Stuart (1587), her chief rival for the throne and the central figure of Catholic assaults on the church and throne, Elizabeth's political situation was secured, and the domination of Anglican Protestants worshipping within the Church of England was affirmed. The English navy defeated the Spanish Armada in 1588 and established England as ruler of the seas and leader among the trading nations. England, for the first time in generations, was at peace at home and abroad and was filled with a national confidence and a lust for life seldom paralleled in history.

About twenty years after Elizabeth outlawed religious drama in 1558, commercial theatres began to open in London. They maintained some medieval conventions, but with one great difference: For the first time since Romans built theatres in England, the English were building special structures and setting them aside for use as theatres. In short, the age of staging in found environments was ending.

Theatre Architecture

In 1576, two commercial theatres opened in London, one outdoor—or "public"—called The Theatre and the other indoor—or "private"—known as the first Blackfriars Theatre. Therefore, when Shakespeare arrived in London about

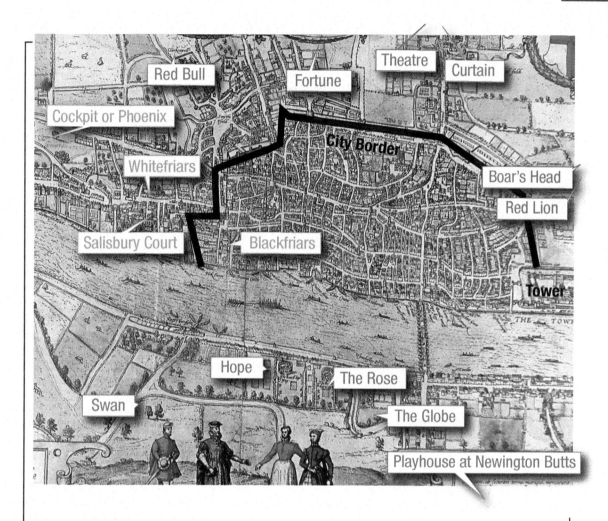

THEATRES IN LONDON

Superimposed on this map from about 1572 are the approximate locations of the theatres in Elizabethan London. Note that all but the Blackfriars theatre are outside the city borders. Public theatres are in blue; private theatres in orange.

fifteen years later, these two sorts of theatres were well established, and he wrote for and acted in both. Although their precise appearance cannot be known, their general features are known.

Public Theatres

Between 1576 and 1642, a number of outdoor **public theatres** were built. They consisted of a round or polygonal, partially roofed, multileveled auditorium that surrounded an open **yard**, into which jutted a platform raised to a height of four to six feet. The entire yard (or **pit**) and part of the stage platform were unroofed. Lighting was provided by the sun. The audience, probably numbering as many as

HOW WE KNOW

The Swan Drawing

This drawing is the only visual contemporary evidence we have of the interior of an identifiable English public theatre. It was made in 1596 by

A rare piece of visual evidence for an Elizabethan public theatre.

Johnnes DeWitt, a Dutch visitor to London, and included in a letter to his friend Arend van Buchel. De Witt's original drawing does not exist. The Swan image that survives is a copy made by van Buchel discovered in a German library in the late 1890s. Clearly the perspective and scale are askew. Yet the drawing tells much about a theatre in Shakespeare's time.

The Swan sketch shows a round theatre, a raised stage with three people on stage, a musician in the central structure (seen in the upper right-hand area), and three galleries. The parts of the theatre were identified in Latin; this version of the drawing translates those labels for clarity. DeWitt noted in his letter, in Latin, that the Swan was the largest and most magnificent of London theatres; He estimated it could seat three thousand spectators. DeWitt described the two columns, made of wood, as so artistically painted that they looked like real marble.

Even if this copy is an accurate reproduction of the original, several questions remain unanswered: Is a performance or a rehearsal pictured here? Where is the discovery space, said to be an important part of English public theatre of this time? Who are the people watching from the area above the stage? Was the perspective and scale in the original drawing by DeWitt as inaccurate as it appears in the copy by van Buchel?

2,500, surrounded the playing area on three sides, some standing in the pit and others seated in the **galleries** or the still more exclusive **lords' rooms**.

The actors worked on a raised stage and apparently awaited cues and changed costumes in a **tiring house**, located at the rear of the platform. Covering part of the stage in many theatres was a roof (the **heavens**) supported by columns resting on the stage and perhaps decorated on its underside with pictures of stars, planets, and signs of the zodiac. Gods and properties flew in from the heavens.

The stage floor was pierced with **traps**, through which characters could appear and disappear. Connecting the tiring house with the stage were at least two doors, which often represented widely divergent locations (as, for example, when one led to the fields of France and the other to the shores of

England). Atop the tiring house, a flag flew on days of performance, and at a level just below, in an area called the **hut**, were probably housed the various pieces of equipment and machinery needed for special effects. A **musicians' gallery**, visible in the Swan drawing (see page 120), was apparently located just below the hut, at the third level above the stage.

Other points are less certain. The plays clearly required two playing levels, an upper and a lower, and some sort of **discovery space**, a place where objects and characters could be hidden from view and revealed at the appropriate time. Most scholars agree that the discovery space was located between the two doors, but some conceive of it as being a permanent architectural part of the theatre, whereas others conceive of it as a portable unit to be added or deleted as required. Yet other scholars see it as a pavilion that jutted out into the stage. Obviously, any decision about the conformation of the space at stage level had implications for the upper acting level as well. Obviously, too, the degree of permanence of the discovery space would radically affect the general appearance of the theatre. The whole problem has been made thornier by the absence of such a space in the Swan drawing, the one extant sketch of a public theatre, and by the appalling problems with sight lines that any sort of discovery seemed likely to introduce. Because the available evidence will not permit the issues to be resolved, ideas about the appearance of Shakespeare's playhouse must remain tentative.

PUBLIC THEATRES
A view of the Globe Theatre from a contemporary map. Note the building shows three levels and is multisided with a structure over the stage area. The people in the foreground may suggest the scale.

HOW WE KNOW

Four Public Theatres

Documents and archeological excavations shed light on the physical features of the Fortune, Globe, Rose, and Curtain—four important public theatres erected between 1576 and 1642.

Philip Henslowe and Edward Alleyn entered into a contract in 1599 with a carpenter-builder, Peter Street, to erect a new square-shaped theatre, the Fortune. Street had been the carpenter/builder of the Globe two years previously. The contract for the Fortune gives specific dimensions for the theatre, some of which are shown here. Yet in many instances the contract instructs Street to build the Fortune *in the manner of the Globe*. Thus, a close reading of the Fortune contract reveals some construction details of the Globe.

The contract adds evidence to the notion that the Globe was *not* square nor were the dimensions of the theatre, the yard, and the stage the same as the Fortune. Henslowe specified that the area below the stage should be "paled in" with strong boards or

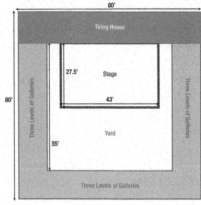

THE FORTUNE THEATRE

This modern plan is based on the dimensions found in the contract Philip Henslowe made with the carpenter-builder Peter Street.

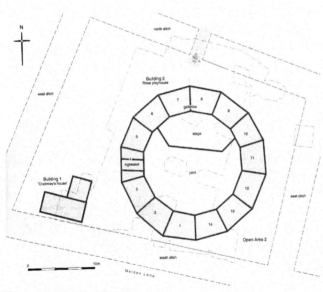

THE ROSE THEATRE

Archeologists were able to determine the shape and size of the Rose Theatre based on careful excavation of the site.

permanently covered by wood. This specification suggests that the space below the Globe stage was not boarded over but was covered by a cloth during performances. These details are not profound, yet the information is helpful in understanding the Globe.

An archeological dig in the area of the Globe and Rose theatres in 1989 provides significant factual information about dimensions and configurations of these theatres. The remodeling of a century-old warehouse on the Southbank in London resulted in a series of trenches being dug in the basement, where the remains of the Rose were found. In each case, the remains are fragmentary with some of each site destroyed by later construction. Both the Globe and Rose were polygonal. Excavations revealed that the Rose had at least fourteen sides whereas the Globe may have had sixteen or eighteen sides. Thus, in long-view maps of the late 1500s and early 1600s, they appear

(continues)

HOW WE KNOW   Four Public Theatres *(continued)*

circular. There is evidence that the Rose had a relatively small stage with no covering, or heavens, over it. Evidence from this dig suggests than that the Globe did have a covering over the stage.

The same group of archeologists that excavated the Globe and Rose, the Museum of London Archeology, discovered the foundations of the Curtain theatre in 2012. Scholars believe that two of Shakespeare's plays, *Henry V* and *Romeo and Juliet,* were first performed at the Curtain in about 1597. The Lord Chamberlain's Men left the Curtain for the newly built Globe Theatre in 1599.

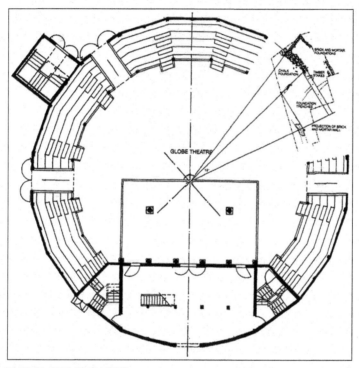

THE GLOBE THEATRE

The layout of the Globe differs greatly from that of the Rose. Note the way in which the stage is placed. Clearly the Globe had better sightlines.

The Globe (1599), the Rose (1587) and the Fortune (1600) were important London public theatres because they were home to important actors, managers, and playwrights. The Globe housed Shakespeare's company, called the Lord Chamberlain's Men, later the King's Men. The Globe burned in 1613 but was immediately rebuilt. The Rose and later the Fortune housed the Lord Admiral's men led by the actor Edward Alleyn. The manager, Richard Henslowe, has earned a place in theatre history for the survival of his "Diaries," extensive and revealing business records from the Fortune.

PRIVATE ELIZABETHAN AND JACOBEAN THEATRE
Here, the Blackfriars Playhouse at the American Shakespeare Center in Staunton, Virginia. This modern, speculative reconstruction of the Second Blackfriars Theatre is based on documents from the period, none of them visual. Note the two audience galleries that go around three sides of the theatre; the original may have had three galleries. The audience here, as in the London Blackfriars, sits on benches in an auditorium that is not darkened. Like the original Blackfriars, some audience members are also seated on the stage.

Private Theatres

Even less is known about the indoor **private theatres**. They were roofed, smaller, and therefore more expensive to attend than the public playhouses. Despite their name, they were open to anyone caring to pay. Initially, the private theatres attracted the most fashionable audiences of London, who came to see erudite plays performed by troupes of boy actors. As the popularity of children's troupes waned, the adult troupes that performed in the public theatres in the summer took over the private houses for their winter performances. The fact is significant because it indicates that the arrangement of the stage spaces in the theatres was probably similar.

Audiences

Audiences for the public theatres were like medieval audiences but more urbanized and probably more sophisticated. They did not include the very poor or the very rich. (Sometimes the very rich would hire companies to play in their manor houses for invited audiences.) Audiences were sometimes rowdy, easily distracted, and they were probably heavily male. A good portion of the audience was educated enough to get jokes and learned allusions; most of them were fascinated by language, and so sat (or stood) rapt through long soliloquies and much lyric poetry.

Private theatres supposedly attracted a more discerning and probably a more affluent audience. They sat indoors, were warmer in winter, and less bothered by rain and slush. Probably mostly male, they were self-aware of themselves as embodiments of the "new" in Elizabethan culture.

Production Practices

Both the physical arrangement of Elizabethan theatres and the medieval features of the plays—particularly the numerous short scenes and settings—argue against the use of elaborate scenery. In the theatre, there were few places to store scenery and no way of moving it on and off stage quickly; the action moved from place to place rapidly, with little or no break in the flow from scene to scene. Small properties were therefore important, and we find stage directions for the use of ladders, chairs and tables, tapestries, a freestanding arbor, and other small items. The underlying staging conventions were clearly medieval, with a chair emblematic of a throne room, for example, and an arbor for a garden. The onstage columns and the two doors also sometimes represented specific locations, thus resembling medieval mansions. On the other hand, such things as "a view of Rome" appeared on lists of properties, and so perhaps some locations were illustrated in paintings. Most of the stage platform worked like a medieval platea, serving alternately as a bedroom, a throne room, and a rampart in quick succession.

Costuming was probably more important to spectacle than scenery. Contemporary accounts mention rich fabrics in many colors. Again, the basic convention was medieval, undoubtedly emblematic, with real Elizabethan dress the basic look. Nonetheless, other periods, countries, and races were signified by emblematic costume pieces—a turban, a Roman breastplate—but historical accuracy was unknown.

Most actors wore contemporary dress, some of it the castoffs of patrons or wealthy friends. Actors mostly supplied their own costumes, and building up a stock would have been important to an actor; however, unusual characters—devils, angels, allegorical figures, Turks, savages—would have called for costumes from the theatre company. Masks were used rarely, and then only for specific reasons; they were no longer a major convention of theatre.

Actors and Acting

A royal official, the Master of the Revels, licensed acting companies. The license protected actors from harsh medieval laws against players, often called "rogues and vagabonds." Actors in the London troupes were further protected by nominal servant status in noble households: Servants "belonged" to a household and found a medieval—feudal—shelter there. Despite this status, a few actors became wealthy. Shakespeare was able to retire as a gentleman, that is, a wealthy man of property.

The troupes themselves were organized as self-governing units—**sharing companies**—whose members shared expenses, profits, and responsibilities for production. A very few members owned a part of the theatre building itself; these were called **householders**. The most valuable members of the company held a whole share in the costumes, properties, and other company possessions; lesser

HOW WE KNOW

Philip Henslowe's Inventory

Philip Henslowe, the principal business manager of the Lord Admiral's Men, inventoried the properties, set pieces, and costumes of this company in 1598. He recorded the totals paid for admissions to the theatre and noted payments to twenty-seven Elizabethan playwrights. He variously commissioned, bought, and produced plays by, or made loans to, Ben Jonson, Christopher Marlowe, Thomas Middleton, and others.

His record also tells much about the theatrical conventions of the English Golden Age. The inventory notes one rock, one tomb, one hell mouth, one tomb

of Guido, one tomb of Dido, one bedstead, one pair of stairs, eight lances, one golden fleece, two rackets, a bay tree, a tree of golden apples, a small altar, two moss banks, and a "chain of dragons" among other items.

Henslowe's inventory also lists specialty costumes: a Neptune costume, Tamberlaine's breeches in crimson velvet, a Phaeton costume, gowns for Dido and Juno, and "a robe for to go invisible"—a ghost costume. This inventory of set pieces and costumes lets us know that some three-dimensional properties were employed in the production of plays in Shakespeare's era.

members owned only half or quarter shares, with their influence and income reduced accordingly. In addition, each company hired some actors and stagehands (**hirelings**), who worked for a salary rather than for a share of the profits.

The precise style of acting is unclear, but vocal power and flexibility were prized. Plays of the period offered ample opportunity to display breath control and verbal dexterity in the monologues, soliloquies, complicated figures of speech, and symmetrical and extended phrases. On the other hand, oratorical and rhetorical techniques did not seem to overpower the actors' search for naturalness. Contemporary accounts, including lines from Shakespeare's *Hamlet*, speak of an acting style capable of moving actors and audiences alike. The goal was apparently a convincing representation of a character in action performed by an actor with a well-tuned vocal instrument.

Because all actors (and playwrights as well) were male, the roles of women were taken by men or young boys, many of whom were apprenticed to leading actors in the troupe. Boys then created the roles of Juliet, Cleopatra, and Lady Macbeth. Among the adult actors, most specialized in certain kinds of roles (e.g., clowns, comic older women, or heroes), and many were widely admired in Shakespeare's day: Richard Tarleton and Will Kempe as clowns, and Richard Burbage and Edward Alleyn as tragedians.

Acting Companies

Two London-based adult theatre companies tower in prestige and achievement, the Lord Admiral's Men and Lord Chamberlain's Men, each headed by widely admired actors.

The Lord Chamberlain's Men This acting troupe, founded in 1594, became, in 1603, the King's Men under the patronage of King James I. This is the company that Shakespeare joined as actor and playwright when he came to London in about 1590. The troupe played first at the Rose, then at the Theatre, and at both Globe theatres. In the winter months it often performed at Blackfriars, at court, and on the road, traveling England and playing in the courtyards of inns or at grand houses of the titled. In addition to the plays of Shakespeare, the company performed plays by Ben Jonson, Thomas Dekker, Francis Beaumont, and John Fletcher. The Lord Chamberlain's Men's greatest actor was Richard Burbage (c. 1567–1619) who originated the leading roles in Shakespeare's plays: *Richard III*, *Hamlet*, *King Lear*, and *Othello*. An important actor of clown roles was also with this company, Will Kempe the original Dogberry in *Much Ado about Nothing*. He left the company in 1599 to seek work in Europe.

The Lord Admiral's Men Under the leadership of Philip Henslowe, the manager, and Edward Alleyn, the company's leading actor, the Lord Admiral's Men was the only important rival to the Lord Chamberlain's Men (Kings Men). Alleyn, considered an important rival to Burbage, originated important roles in plays by Christopher Marlowe. He played the original Tamburlaine, Dr. Faustus, the title role in *The Jew of Malta*, and, probably, *Edward II*. Alleyn, married to Henslowe's stepdaughter, preserved many of Henslowe's business records thus providing a wealth of information about London theatre and its practices.

EDWARD II'S DEATH SCENE
In this modern-dress production, Edward II is confined to a mental institution. Here, he is about to be assassinated by the insertion of a red-hot poker in his rectum. Death by red-hot poker is a well-known myth of Edward II's death, which is not found in contemporary accounts.

Tudor Plays and Playwrights

Adding to the general well-being of the nation was the vigor of the court, the schools, and the universities, where scholars were remaking Italian **humanism** and classical documents with an eye to English needs and preferences. In particular, some university students, called the University Wits, were applying classical scholarship to the English public stage and laying the foundations for the vigorous theatre to come. These University Wits, including Christopher Marlowe and Thomas Kyd, brought the erudition of humanistic scholarship to the English stage.

Shakespeare Shakespeare was not a University Wit. Born in 1564 in provincial Stratford-upon-Avon, a day's journey from London, Shakespeare was a middle-class boy who grew up as the nation moved from a medieval to a Renaissance culture. Not university educated, Shakespeare nonetheless received the solid basics of village schools: Latin, the classics, and the foundation of writing style.

His early life appears to have included acquaintance with powerful local families; his father, although a tradesman (a glover), was a man of position in the town.

Shakespeare (1564–1616) married a local woman but did not stay long in his hometown. By his mid-twenties, he had gone alone to London to take up the perilous profession of acting, putting his father's trade behind him. He took with him, however, the rural England and the English characters of his youth, which would inform his plays and poetry for his entire life.

Rich and famous, he retired from the stage in about 1612. He returned to Stratford, there to purchase a handsome house and display the gentleman's coat-of-arms his financial success justified.

Shakespeare is the greatest playwright of the English-speaking world and one of the greatest dramatists of Western civilization. Between 1590 and 1613, Shakespeare wrote thirty-eight plays, which for convenience are customarily divided into three types:

- History plays (those treating English history): *Richard II, Henry IV* (Parts 1 and 2), *Henry V, Henry VI* (Parts 1, 2, and 3), *Richard III,* and *Henry VIII.*

- Tragedies: *Romeo and Juliet, Julius Caesar, Hamlet, King Lear, Othello, Macbeth,* and *Antony and Cleopatra.*

- Comedies: Ranging from popular romantic works, like *Love's Labor's Lost, As You Like It, Twelfth Night, Much Ado about Nothing,* and *A Midsummer Night's Dream,* to the darker tragicomedies, such as *All's Well That Ends Well* and *Measure for Measure.*

Shakespeare's plays, and those of his contemporaries in England and Spain, shared more ideas and techniques of playwriting with the Middle Ages

TWELFTH NIGHT IN MODERN PRODUCTION

This unusual production scheme at Kutztown University uses a series of mirrors to underscore the cross-dressing comic episodes in this popular Shakespeare comedy. It seems to ask the question, "Is what we see what we get?" Note the two vertical columns that might reflect the columns in the original production on the Elizabethan stage.

than with Greece and Rome. Six important traits of the golden age of English plays (including those of Shakespeare) are:

- An Early Point of Attack: Plays begin near the beginning of the story, with the result that the audience sees the story develop onstage rather than learning about it secondhand through messengers or reporters.
- Several Lines of Action ("Subplots"): Early in the plays, the various lines appear to be separate and independent, but as the play moves toward its resolution, the several lines gradually merge so that, by the play's end, the unity of the various lines is evident.
- A Large Number and Variety of Incidents: The mixing of tears and laughter is not uncommon, nor is the close juxtaposition of tender scenes of love with brawling scenes of confrontation.
- Free Use of Time and Place: Action unfolds across several months or years and in several locales.
- A Large Number and Variety of Characters: Casts of thirty characters are common, and among the characters can be found kings and grave-diggers, pedants and clowns, old people and youths, city dwellers and rustics, rich people and poor.
- A Varied Language: Within the same play are found lyric passages, elegant figures of speech, ribald slang, witty aphorisms, and pedestrian prose, all carefully chosen to enhance the play's dramatic action.

The art of Shakespeare and his contemporaries was an expansive one that filled a large dramatic canvas with portraits of a wide cross section of humanity engaged in acts ranging from the heroic to the mundane. In this aspect, Elizabethan plays contrasted greatly with the medieval. The texture of Elizabethan plays is rich, detailed, linear, and allusive, whereas medieval plays were often simplistic. Classical plays such as *Oedipus Rex* had late points of attack, unity of action, and relatively few characters, locations, and incidents, Shakespeare and his contemporaries told their stories from the beginning and included many details in several developing lines of action, each with its own characters. Whereas classical plays adopted rather restricted patterns of time, place, and dramatic action, Elizabethan plays ranged freely. Whereas the power of classical tragedy rested on intensity achieved through concentration and sparseness, in the plays of Shakespeare and his contemporaries, power emerged

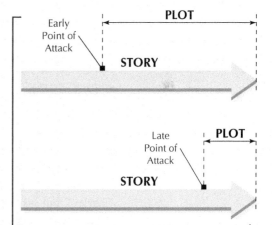

PLOT, STORY, AND POINT OF ATTACK
Plot is the arrangement of the incidents, the way the story is told. When plot and story begin at about the same point, the play has an early point of attack. When the plot begins late in the story, the play has a late point of attack.

through the wealth of detail, the range and contrast of emotion, and the sweep of the playwrights' vision.

Two other playwrights of Shakespeare's era, Christopher Marlowe and Thomas Kyd, were greatly admired in their time.

Christopher Marlowe Marlowe is ranked among the most talented of English playwrights even though his output was limited by an early death from a stabbing in a tavern brawl. Unlike Shakespeare, Marlowe (1564–1593) had a university education. He is noted by critics for his vigorous command of blank verse and the brilliance of his language. When he died in 1593, he had written about as many plays as Shakespeare. They include *Tamburlaine*, Parts 1 and 2, *Dr. Faustus*, *The Jew of Malta*, and *Edward II*. Although *Dr. Faustus* was influential, *Edward II* is his most often revived play in the modern era.

Thomas Kyd Like Marlowe, Kyd (1558–1594) was university educated. He wrote the most popular play of the Elizabethan era, *The Spanish Tragedy*. This play of murder and revenge used a model established by Seneca that included a chorus of one, ghosts, soliloquies, and an episodic structure that straddles many locales. Revenge tragedy is a genre that includes a murder, a visit by the victim's ghost to his avenger who is usually his son, a phase of intrigue by the murderer and the avenger, real or faked madness by the avenger, a climax of great violence that leaves the murderer, the avenger, and many bystanders dead. For example, Shakespeare's *Hamlet* follows the conventions of a revenge tragedy.

Stuart Plays and Playwrights

When Elizabeth I, a Tudor, died in 1603 without children, James I, a Stuart, ascended the throne to guide England's fortunes. His son, Charles I, came to the throne on the death of James I in 1625. In this Stuart period, England enjoyed the works of several important playwrights. Yet drama had changed. Shakespeare's heroic themes had given way to ones of depravity and pessimism. Melodrama replaced tragedy.

Ben Jonson After Shakespeare, Jonson (1572–1637) is considered the finest Elizabethan playwright. He wrote nearly twenty plays, almost forty court masques, and eleven other books. His career spanned the reign of Elizabeth I, James I, and Charles I, but his most productive period was during the Jacobean era, the era that saw the productions of *Volpone, or The Fox* (1605) and *The Alchemist* (1610), immediately successful in first performances. ("Jacobean" refers to the reign of James I as King of England.) These plays are only sometimes revived today.

John Webster Although he was a prolific writer for the stage, collaborating with other playwrights, John Webster (c. 1580–c. 1634) is best known for two plays that reflect the dark, violent, horror-filled turn of drama after Queen

Elizabeth's death. *The Duchess of Malfi*, first produced by the King's Men in 1614, became a quick success. Although the play begins as a love story, it ends as a violent tragedy.

The Duchess has two brothers, a cardinal and a duke, who forbid her to remarry after her husband dies so that they might usurp her lands. She secretly marries her steward. As a result the Duchess, her children, and her second husband are murdered. The wicked brothers die as well. Another of Webster's plays, *The White Devil*, is remembered today. A revenge tragedy, *The White Devil* failed in its initial presentation but later achieved success.

Beaumont and Fletcher Francis Beaumont and John Fletcher coauthored plays for almost a decade during the reign of James I, usually tragicomedies (serious events followed by a happy ending) and comedies of manners, none particularly memorable today. Their collaboration was so admired that a folio of more than fifty "Beaumont and Fletcher" plays was published in 1679, including ones Fletcher wrote himself and others on which he collaborated. Recent scholarship suggests Beaumont and Fletcher, however, wrote no more than fifteen plays together. Beaumont retired from the theatre in 1613. Fletcher then wrote plays independently and with as many as eleven additional collaborators, including Shakespeare, usually for the King's Men. He is suspected of teaming with Shakespeare on *Henry VIII* and *The Two Noble Kinsmen*.

Shakespeare's Legacy

Once printed and distributed, Shakespeare's language, along with that of the King James Bible of about the same time, did much to establish modern

TWO NOBLE KINSMEN
This play is generally accepted as a collaboration between Shakespeare and John Fletcher in 1613. It was first presented at the private (indoor) Blackfriars theatre. These images from Butler University Theatre show the two dominant moods of the play.

English. Successive generations only rarely revived plays by other Elizabethan playwrights, but Shakespeare took hold. Productions of Shakespeare are notable throughout the history of Western theatre. That said, for many years there was little reverence for Shakespeare's writing as each generation rewrote Shakespeare freely to fit its notion of what theatre should be. In the mid-nineteenth century (1800s), the British actor William Charles Macready began once again to perform the plays as written.

In frontier America in the nineteenth century, literate households, if they owned any books, had a Bible and a collected Shakespeare. Itinerant troupes played Shakespeare on barges along the Mississippi and in gold rush towns in California territory. Many of the catchphrases of Shakespeare—*Neither a borrower nor a lender be*—entered common usage, even among English-speaking people who had never seen a Shakespeare play. German translations of Shakespeare in the 1700s fit with the country's romantic style and made Shakespeare, in English and translation, among Germany's three most popular playwrights.

In the twentieth century, troupes in totalitarian countries sometimes staged Shakespeare as a way to criticize their own society but safely, behind the undeniable value of the classic author. In the twenty-first century, productions of Shakespeare, some with film actors in leading roles, have been commercial successes. With Shakespeare, the past is very much in the present.

Court Masques and New Conventions: Inigo Jones

Not all theatre was performed in public and private playhouses. A courtly audience gathered by invitation only for plays and spectacles staged in royal and noble houses. Although both Henry VIII (Elizabeth's father) and Elizabeth had supported theatrical entertainments, it was the Stuart kings who followed them, James I and Charles I, who perfected splendid court **masques** (short for masquerades). These ephemeral entertainments were performed once or twice, usually at Christmas and Twelfth Night celebration or when visiting royalty was present. Then they disappeared, never to be revived. Masques were performed only at court often in the Banqueting Hall at Whitehall; masques were never presented in the public or private playhouses.

Stuart masques were allegorical stories with song, poetry, music, and, most importantly, dances designed to compliment a particular individual or occasion. Their texts were little more than pretexts for elaborate scenic displays and lavish costumes. Although the major roles and all of the comic or villainous characters were played by professionals, the courtiers themselves performed the heart of the masques, the three spectacular dances. Great sums of money ensured the splendor of the entertainments; one such

INIGO JONES CHARACTERS IN COURT MASQUES

These two sketches for masque characters are among the very few colored ones that Jones produced. He usually drew a quick monochrome sketch, made a few notes about color and fabric, and then passed it on to the costume construction crew. The first is a torchbearer used to lead the dancers to the main floor for their featured appearance; the second is a winged dancer. The third drawing is an Inigo Jones scene for an unknown masque.

masque cost a staggering £21,000 at a time when the average *annual* wage for a skilled worker was about £25.

Many leading dramatists wrote masques, including Ben Jonson. Annoyed that the text assumed such a clearly secondary position to the scenery, Jonson stopped writing masques in 1631.

The star of the masques was not the playwright but the scenic and costume designer, Inigo Jones (1573–1652). An Englishman by birth, Jones studied in Italy twice during the early years of the seventeenth century, where he learned the newest techniques of illusionistic stage painting, machinery, rigging, and design. He introduced many of these into the English court when in 1605, he staged his first masque for James I, *The Masque of Blackness*. By the end of his career, Jones had introduced into the English courts—but not into the commercial theatres—all the major elements of Italianate staging then developed (see Chapter 5): illusionism, false perspective, and quick-change scenery using shutters and grooves.

Masque Production Practices

Inigo Jones's responsibility for the design and production of masques was enormous. He designed the temporary picture-frame "theatre"—the stage itself—that was installed in preexisting spaces such as banqueting halls. The masques, including scenery and machines, were engineered to be set up quickly and then be quickly dismantled. The productions, performed at night, were lit by candles with reflectors to increase power but also with shields to diminish the illumination as needed. The stage was four- to six-feet high and relatively shallow.

Machinery Jones also designed all of the scenic machines used in the presentation of a masque. Cloud machines and flying devices were significant elements in almost all of his designs. The scenes, in one-point perspective, were changed using the Italian groove system. Single-point perspective, of course, seemed most illusionistic from those seats in the center of the audience space, the most central seat always occupied by the monarch. Only the King, seated in the center and far enough from the stage to see the spectacle and enjoy the dances staged on the floor, had the most perfect view of the entertainment.

Costumes A hallmark of a masque was the elaborate, often fantastic, costumes Jones designed for the professional actors, court performers, and dancers. Many of these costume sketches exist today in the archives of the Duke of Devonshire. They reveal the quick hand of an accomplished artist able to give enough detail so the costume could be fabricated. Only four of Jones's extant costume drawings are in color.

Significance

Stuart masques have significance in theatre history that is greater than one might suppose given the number of persons who saw them:

- First, they used Italianate systems of staging during the first half of the seventeenth century (1600s), when the English public and private theatres still relied on scenic practices that were essentially medieval.

- Second, the close association of extravagantly expensive masques with the monarchy was a goad for the suceeding Puritan regime to close theatres following the civil war.

The Closing of English Theatres

In 1642, a civil war broke out. To oversimplify the many contentious issues to the point of caricature, the civil war pitted those in favor of monarchy, courtiers, and an Anglican Church that echoed Roman Catholicism against those who favored Parliament, merchants, and a much simplified Anglicanism. The parliamentarians under Oliver Cromwell won, deposed the king, seized power, and closed the theatres, in part because they had been so closely associated with the monarchy.

Music, however, was not banned, and so a writer of masques named William Davenant (c. 1606–1668) produced operas, staging them using the Italianate system. Thus were Italianate conventions of illusionistic staging introduced to the English public, having by then been used at court masques for almost forty years.

With the closing of the theatres in 1642, an English secular theatre based loosely on medieval conventions closed as well. When English theatres reopened in 1660, England adopted the Italianate conventions, especially illusionism, already in use on the continent.

Spain in the Golden Age

During the middle ages, Spain's theatre had paralleled England's in important ways. Its medieval dramas included Latin music drama, religious plays, comedies and farces, school and university plays, and court interludes. Spanish religious plays, called *autos sacramentales*, combined many of the characteristics of the morality and cycle plays. They were one-act allegories, for example, illustrating the mystery of the Eucharist for performance during the feast of Corpus Christi. Pedro Calderon de la Barca was the most prolific and popular writer of autos.

Staging conventions of Spanish medieval dramas were similar to those in Medieval England; both used movable more often than fixed staging. During the transitional period from the Middle Ages to the Golden Age, small troupes of professional players toured until permanent theatres were built in Madrid in the early 1580s.

Women as Audience and as Actors

The Spanish theatre's acceptance of women was significantly different from the English, at the same time more permissive and more restrictive. It allowed women to act after the mid-1580s but put women audience members in a separate gallery with its own entrance—guarded—from the street. Many women went there masked, perhaps to avoid being recognized.

Legal permission for women to act was also shaky. Attempts were made to rescind the permission to act as early as 1587; in 1589, churchmen made a determined push to remove them and replace them with boys—so long as the boys wore no makeup. The governing council thought that the risk of boys in makeup was greater than the risk of women and so said the women could stay. Spanish actresses, however, like actresses in many countries, were long considered immoral and a threat to male morality.

Spanish Public Theatres

The public theatres of Spain, like the English theatres, remained essentially medieval in staging conventions. The earliest permanent public theatres were outdoor theatres with thrust stages. Audiences stood in a central yard or sat in galleries and boxes on three sides of the stage. The stages, whose backgrounds were pierced with entrances, were partially roofed (held up by two columns), were served by traps and flying machines, and featured both a discovery space and a secondary acting area above the stage. Conventions of scenery, costume, and playwriting also resembled those of England. As in England, the Spanish **court theatres** used the newer, Italian conventions.

The location of Spanish public theatres, called *corrales*, was a telling difference between English and Spanish theatres. Spanish theatres were inserted into the interior yard at the center of a block of private houses instead of being the freestanding purpose-built structures developed in London.

The *Corral del Principe*

In the early 1580s, two new theatres were built in Madrid, the *Corral del Cruz* and the *Corral del Principe*, to replace those that had existed since the 1560s. Both were owned by a religious confraternity to raise money for its hospitals; this connection also gave the theatres some needed legitimacy. The Corral del Principe became the city's dominant theatre for more than a century.

Corral—the word for the open space among several houses—became the synonym for a permanent theatre. It was the Spanish solution to the problem of creating an enclosed space where audiences could be controlled and thus made to pay a fee to enter. Inside the rectangle enclosed by the houses, builders put up at one end a stage twenty-eight-feet wide and twenty-five-feet deep. It was raised above the *patio* (pit), the cheapest area (standing room behind, benches in front), which was only the width of the stage and about fifty-feet long. Along its sides ran a raised level of boxes or loges, preferred and more expensive seating. Opposite the stage at the end of the patio were more boxes and, above them, a separate seating area for women with its own entrance from the street. From the back of the women's gallery to the back wall of the stage and from side to side, this was an intimate theatre—the size of the in-bounds area of a modern basketball court. The stage was roofed. Part of the patio could be covered with an awning, although this seems to have been for sun, not rain.

Like other corrales, the Principe also used windows in the houses on each side, behind which were high-end boxes—rooms, really—owned and controlled by the house owner. Their privacy apparently attracted upper-class women. At the back of the stage was a two-level area that could be curtained; there seem also to have been doors there and on the sides. The stage floor was trapped, and overhead was fairly sophisticated flying machinery. Music was common, but it is unlikely that either musicians or audience members sat on the small stage.

Scenery in the Corral del Principe was selective but sometimes complex: fountains, trees, a ship's mast and rigging (presumably for the actors to climb), the superstructures of a Moorish and a Christian ship. Costumes by the first third of the seventeenth century were often expensive and showy, although with only emblematic historical accuracy, such as turbans for Moors or togas for Romans. Mostly, however, actors wore contemporary clothes.

The Corral del Principe may be taken as typical of Spanish theatres of the Golden Age. It was small, rather medieval in its arrangements, and often rowdy, but some of the greatest of Spanish plays were first performed there.

Plays and Playwrights

Spain's Golden Age, like England's, was noted not for its theatrical practices but for its plays. During this one-hundred-year period, Spanish playwrights wrote thousands of plays, called **commedias**—any full-length play, no matter if it was serious or comic. Like medieval and contemporaneous English plays, they featured a welter of characters and events, spanned many times and places, and mixed laughter and tears. Secular tragicomedies, plays on religious subjects, cloak-and-sword plays, and farces were all popular.

Lope de Rueda   The earliest important playwright and Spain's first actor-manager, Lope de Rueda (c. 1505–1565) specialized in writing farces and religious plays. He was known for his farcical short plays, called *pasos*, or prose interludes, which used simple situations (often racy), trickery, and practical jokes. His company performed them and other plays in found spaces and important houses throughout Spain. Twenty-six of his pasos survive.

Lope de Vega   By far the most popular Spanish playwright, Lope de Vega (1562–1635) may have originated the cape-and-sword plays, swashbucklers that subsequently influenced both English and French dramatists. Cape-and-sword plays—*comedia de capa y espada*—were romantic plays featuring courtly manners and duels in which the characters wore capes and carried swords. The author of more than five hundred works, Vega is now best known for his play *Fuente Ovejuna* (*The Sheep Well*). Vega is the first Spaniard to make his living solely as a playwright.

Calderón de la Barca   The most respected Spanish playwright of the Golden Age, however, was probably Pedro Calderón de la Barca (1600–1681), whose *Life Is a Dream* epitomized the poetry and intellect of his best works. Calderón wrote more than a hundred commedias, eighty autos sacramentales, and twenty short comedic works called *entremeses*. Calderón stopped writing for the stage about 1640; the theatres were closed shortly thereafter for royal mourning (1644–1649). When they reopened, the Golden Age had passed, although the public theatres remained in use into the eighteenth century.

THE PLAY'S THE THING

Calderón de la Barca's *Life Is a Dream*, 1635

Pedro Calderón de la Barca was the last playwright of Spain's Golden Age of Theatre, and for many critics, he is the summation of this era. *Life Is a Dream*, first published in 1635, shares with Elizabethan plays a mixed tone, a large variety of characters, two major subplots, and is written in verse. Unlike many English Renaissance plays, it has a late point of attack with much exposition needed to cover antecedent action. The action of the play takes place in a few days and in only a few locations.

In other characteristics, *Dream* resembles the theatre of its time: a traveling woman is disguised as a man (Shakespeare's *As You Like It* and others); a king performs a fateful experiment with his heir(s) (*King Lear*); and the central character undergoes changes that bewilder him and put him under extreme personal and moral stress (*Hamlet*). Moreover, the action is placed in a mythical country with a real name—Poland—but in the play "Poland" is a country of Calderón's mind, as are Shakespeare's cities of Vienna or Verona (*Measure for Measure* and *Romeo and Juliet*, respectively).

The Story of the Play Rosaura, dressed as a man for protection, and her sidekick, Fife, struggle on their journey to the capital of Poland from their native Moscovy. They discover a tower where Segismundo has been imprisoned since birth. He knows not why. Moved by his plight, Rosaura tosses Segismundo a sword he might use in his escape.

King Basilio calls everyone together to announce an extraordinary hidden history: when the Queen died in childbirth the child she was carrying did not die as had been announced. Instead, the King believed that the child, Segismundo, was fated by the stars to be a wicked ruler and, eventually, Basilio's killer. To thwart this fate, the king had his son imprisoned since infancy. He has a plan to see if he was right to lock Segismundo away. If he is confirmed in his suspicions, then he will give the throne to two cousins. If not, his son will inherit the throne.

His scheme is to drug Segismundo, bring him to the capital, dress him as a prince, and upon his waking, instruct everyone to treat him as a prince. Segismundo is to be told that his memories of captivity are a dream.

When Segismundo awakens from the drug he is bewildered. Told what the king has directed, Segismundo is enraged. When later Segismundo sees Estrella, the first female he has ever seen as a woman, he falls in love with her. Her fiancé, Astolfo, defends her virtue and the two men fight. The king enters and decides that his prediction was correct. Segismundo must again be drugged and returned to the tower.

When he wakes in chains, Segismundo is told that his day as prince had just been a dream. Meanwhile, many citizens, learning that they have a hidden prince, rally to Segismundo's aid, urging him to overthrow Basilio and take his rightful place as king.

In the ensuing civil war, Segismundo comes upon King Basilio. In his second encounter with freedom, Segismundo sees his father as a well-meaning man

(continues)

This modern interpretation of de la Barca's Life Is a Dream *was staged at Old Dominion University, designed and photographed by Anita Easterling. The pavilion suggests the tower in which Segismundo is imprisoned.*

THE PLAY'S THE THING   Calderón de la Barca's *Life Is a Dream* (continued)

who put too much faith in the evidence of the stars. Segismundo not only spares the king, but places him back on his throne. The restored King Basilio weds Estrella and Segismundo.

Life Is a Dream is of particular interest to modern and postmodern critics and theatre practitioners for its insinuation that reality may not be wholly known while we live because a dream can convince the dreamer that the dream is an actual occurrence. Later this theme excited the imagination of the Romantics, the psychological moderns, and the postmodern absurdists, among others.

KEY TERMS

Key terms are in boldface type in the text. Check your understanding against this list. Persons are page-referenced in the Index.

autos sacramentales
   (AW-tohs sa-crah-mehn-TAH-lehs),
   p. 135
commedia, p. 138
court theatres, p. 136
corral (ker-RAL), p. 136
Corral del Principe (ker-RAL del
   PRIN-cee-pee), p. 136
discovery space, p. 121
galleries, p. 120
Golden Age, p. 118
heavens, p. 120
hirelings, p. 126

householders, p. 125
humanism, p. 127
hut, p. 121
lords' rooms, p. 120
masques, p. 132
musicians' gallery, p. 121
pit, p. 119
private theatres, p. 124
public theatres, p. 119
sharing companies, p. 125
tiring house, p. 120
traps, p. 120
yard, p. 119

Chapter 6 at a Glance

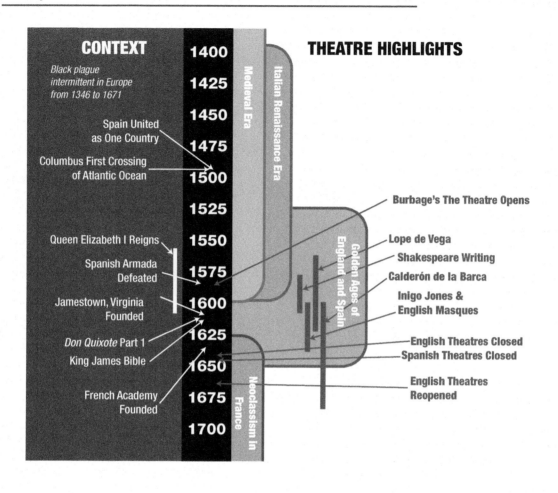

CONTEXT

1400

*Black plague
intermittent in Europe
from 1346 to 1671*

1425

1450

Spain United
as One Country

1475

Columbus First Crossing
of Atlantic Ocean

1500

1525

Queen Elizabeth I Reigns

1550

Spanish Armada
Defeated

1575

Jamestown, Virginia
Founded

1600

Don Quixote Part 1

1625

King James Bible

1650

French Academy
Founded

1675

1700

Medieval Era

Italian Renaissance Era

Golden Ages of
England and Spain

Neoclassism in
France

THEATRE HIGHLIGHTS

Burbage's The Theatre Opens

Lope de Vega

Shakespeare Writing

Calderón de la Barca

**Inigo Jones &
English Masques**

English Theatres Closed

Spanish Theatres Closed

**English Theatres
Reopened**

7

Neoclassicism: Triumph and Decline in France and England

OBJECTIVES

When you have completed this chapter, you should be able to:

- Explain the significance of the production of *Le Cid*.
- Discuss the different performances likely to have been seen in the public and the court theatres of France.
- Sketch events leading to the formation of the Comédie Française.
- Explain how sentimentalism affected French drama and theatre.
- Discuss the relationship between French theatre and English Restoration theatre.
- Describe the major conventions of English Restoration theatre.
- Name the major kinds of drama existing during the English Restoration.

Context

The ideas and practices of the Italian Renaissance reached France early, but politically unstable France had little energy for developing a strong secular theatre. The French Wars of Religion—a series of conflicts between Catholics and French Protestants called Huguenots and among royal houses—had raged off and on from 1562 to 1598. In 1593, King Henri IV of France converted to Catholicism. In 1598, he published the Edict of Nantes, which offered tolerance to Protestant believers, a tolerance not always honored in actuality. These essentially civil wars left France financially and socially weakened. Henry IV restored order and strengthened agriculture and education in his country. He financed the expeditions that gave France claims on what is now

Canada. Henry was followed by Louis XIII and the Thirty Years' War, between France and Austria, which was one of the most destructive of European wars and further strapped France's well-being. The next monarch, Louis XIV, known as the Sun King, reigned from the age of four in 1638 until he was seventy-six. The land was nearly bankrupt when Louis XIV was crowned, but it prospered under his long rule. Louis XIV's was a reign characterized by ostentatious royal wealth and royal patronage of the arts.

Two cardinals of the Catholic Church served as ministers to the monarchs during this era and had great influence on finances, politics, and the arts. Cardinal Richelieu was chief minister from 1624 to his death in 1642. As such, Richelieu did much to consolidate royal power. He was also a lover and supporter of the arts. He founded the *Académie Française*, which is still the official arbiter of the French language today. Richelieu was followed by Cardinal Mazarin, who, because of Louis XIV's young age at attaining the throne, and Mazarin's close relationship with Louis's mother, Queen Anne, acted very much as regent. Mazarin was less an art lover than Richelieu had been, although he did amass a collection of jewels, much of which he left to the king on his death in 1661.

French Theatre through Its Golden Age

Because of the religious civil wars, the early steps of French theatre were tentative. Medieval religious theatre in France, however, was bolstered by the *Confrérier de la Passion* (Confraternity of the Passion), an amateur group organized and endorsed by Charles VI in 1402 to present mystery plays in Paris. Although highly regarded by some, the *Confraternity* was increasingly attacked by clergy who objected to the addition of apocryphal matter to the mystery plays and by the production of what were considered indecent pantomimes and farces. The group at first played in various theatres but built their own space in 1548, the Hôtel de Bourgogne. (*Hôtel* literally means "town house.") That same year they were forbidden to perform religious plays and were dissolved in 1676.

Through the early 1600s, French theatre practices remained essentially medieval. Farces performed by traveling actors were the mainstay of a scattered French theatre. Its audiences were famous for their unruliness. At about the time of Shakespeare, the first notable (and extremely prolific) French playwright, Aléxandre Hardy (1570?–1632), appeared; his plays resembled those of England's and Spain's Golden Ages (e.g., many characters and sprawling actions). Like those of his contemporaries, Hardy's plays used simultaneous settings and emblematic costumes. Although his audiences were more genteel than those for the previous farces and included women as well as some people from the court, his theatre was still a pretty rough place.

FRENCH THEATRE IN THE EARLY 1600s

French theatre remained mostly emblematic and simultaneous, with scenery still scattered rather than gathered in one place. Note the various mansionlike set pieces. This space, converted from a tennis court, was long and narrow. Seats were installed on each side with a covered stagelike structure at one end.

With increasing political stability, Paris became France's theatrical center. The first professional acting troupe established itself there permanently in 1625. Its theatre was the *Hôtel de Bourgogne*, the space built seventy-five years previously for the production of mystery plays, just as they were being banned. When rival professionals began to settle in Paris, however, they chose indoor tennis courts for their theatres. A theatre converted from a tennis court had a long, narrow auditorium with a small stage at one end, probably with an upper level and some sort of "inner stage" below. The resulting theatres were small and intimate, holding six or seven hundred people. Staging conventions remained basically medieval.

Thus, at a time when the English and Spanish theatres were well into their Golden Ages and Italian theatre was revolutionizing theory and scenery, the French theatre was only just establishing itself.

By the 1630s, however, French theatre and its audience were sufficiently important to make them a focus of government interest. Because the French court of the time was closely linked by marriage and policy to Italy, Italian practices became the model for France, in theatre as elsewhere. In theatre, Italian practice meant promoting neoclassicism and Italianate staging.

Neoclassicism: Corneille and *Le Cid*

A number of well-educated men began to write for the theatre. Chief among them was Pierre Corneille (1606–1684), whose play *Le Cid* (1636) marked a turning point. Based on a Spanish play of the Golden Age, *Le Cid* was reshaped by Corneille to bring it closer to neoclassical ideas but not into strict conformity with them: The original six acts were reduced to five; its several years were compressed into a single day; the many locales were squeezed into a single town. Still, the play had a happy ending, and its numerous incidents strained neoclassical verisimilitude. The recently formed French Academy—itself an example of aggressive neoclassicism, a literary society supported by those in power—praised the elements of *Le Cid*

HOTEL DE BOURGOGNE

By 1630, a commedia company and Moliere's company were sharing this theatre. The visualization of the setting may not be accurate.

that conformed to the rules but condemned those that strayed. French playwrights, including Corneille, got the message: Critical acclaim and approval from those in political, financial, and social power would come from lining up with neoclassicism.

After 1636, neoclassicism dominated French drama for more than a hundred years. In 1641 the first Italianate theatre was built in Paris. Giacomo Torelli was brought to Paris from Italy by Cardinal Mazarin in 1645 to install a chariot-and-pole system. His productions marked the acceptance

SPECTACULAR STAGECRAFT

Giocomo Torelli's design for Corneille's 1650 play *Andromède* illustrates the use of aerial appearances, popular in both Italy and France.

of all Italianate scenic practices in Paris: Almost immediately, the tennis court theatres had to adapt or die; they installed some form of Italianate scenery. Thereafter, simple neoclassical settings competed with lavish operas, ballets, and **machine plays**, plays written specifically to exploit the new stage machinery.

Italianate Staging: Public versus Court Theatres

Italian theory and staging played out differently in France, however. The triumph of neoclassicism was manifest primarily in the French *public* theatres, where a distinct French style of drama developed. The public theatre was emotionally compressed, austere both in action and in language. The triumph of Italianate staging, on the other hand, found its fullest expression in the *court* theatres, where plays from the public theatres were restaged with ballet interludes, movable scenery, and gorgeous costumes. King and courtiers played heroes of romance and mythology in purpose-written entertainments that moved out into parks and gardens, sometimes with mock tournaments and battles. Italianate scenery in the public theatres was more modest. Commercial theatre did not have the King's deep pockets.

The Sun King and the Golden Age

Both the court and the public theatres reached their peak during the reign of Louis XIV, a king who "drew power to himself as the sun attracts the planets" as one contemporary noted. Calling himself "The Sun King," Louis XIV declared, "I am the state," and he believed it. Absolute power, ego, and show were summed up in the word *gloire* (glory), which carried over from war into theatre; it also extended to the building of great follies, such as Louis's palace at Versailles, where he surrounded himself with France's nobility. Louis pursued an aggressive campaign of

THE PALAIS ROYALE

King Louis XIII and Cardinal Richelieu, the powerful advisor to the king with Anne of Austria looking on. This image from about 1641 represents a view of the first French fixed proscenium theatre with a stage using flat wings rather than angled ones. Richelieu had the theatre constructed in his palace. The space was later renamed the Palais Royale.

national self-display, not only through military adventures but also through the arts, including theatre.

Theatres benefited. They got both royal subsidy and royal patronage but not enough to survive without public support, and so they were sometimes in the position of serving two masters at once. Their position became even more complex when, with the opening of Versailles, the court moved there, leaving the public still in Paris. Yet this robust theatre played for court and public, men and women. (Favored male audience members even sat on the stage.) At its best, this theatre offered great variety and superb quality, satisfying an audience that became the most demanding and sophisticated in Europe. French theatre replaced Italy's as the model for Europe.

In addition to the continuing dominance of neoclassicism and enthusiasm for Italianate staging, the pinnacle of French theatre meant:

- The emergence of two great playwrights to join Corneille.

- The expansion to five permanent—later reduced to three—professional theatres in Paris, with strict government control through monopolies.

THE SUN KING
Lavish court entertainments including theatre flourished under Louis XIV's patronage. Pictured here is a ballet costume worn by Louis XIV as Apollo, The Sun King.

Playwrights

Racine Although Pierre Corneille continued writing, his fame was eclipsed by that of Jean Racine (1639–1667). Born three years after the first production of *Le Cid*, Racine was educated by Jansenists, a Catholic sect with an overriding preoccupation with sin and guilt, concerns that permeated Racine's major plays. Trained in the classics, Racine based his only comedy, *The Litigants*, on Aristophanes's comedy *The Wasps*. His most esteemed tragedy, *Phèdre* (*Phaedra*), was based on Euripides's *Hippolytus*. (See Introduction.) Racine's other important plays include *Andromache* (1667) and *Bernice* (1670).

Phèdre is a model of neoclassicism. Because the play's major conflicts occur within the character Phèdre, the neoclassical requirements for unity are easily accommodated, and because Phèdre's passion leads to her downfall, neoclassical commitment to the punishment of evil is satisfied. *Phèdre*, unlike *Le Cid*, is neoclassical through and through, and its achievement in plot, character, and diction placed it among the masterpieces of dramatic literature. France had accomplished what England would not: lasting and popular drama based on neoclassical theory.

Molière French comedy found its genius in the actor-dramatist Molière (born Jean-Baptiste Poquelin in 1622, died 1673). At about the time that

THE PLAY'S THE THING

Jean Racine's *Phèdre*, 1677

Racine (1639–1699), Corneille, and Molière were the greatest French playwrights of the latter half of the seventeenth century. In Racine's *Phèdre*, based on Euripides's *Hippolytus*, the title character lusts after Hippolytus, her stepson. *Phèdre* is the quintessential neoclassical tragedy, embracing all of the elements of neoclassicism including a five-act structure written in verse. The play also observes the three unities of time, place, and action. In keeping with neoclassic doctrine, Phèdre is punished for her evil desires by death.

The Story of the Play In Troezen, Hippolytus, son of Theseus, the king of Athens, sets out to look for his long-absent father; he confesses he is doing so partly to avoid Aricia, whom he loves despite "glorying in his chastity."

Phèdre, Theseus's wife and Hippolytus's stepmother, is said to be "dying in her nurse's arms." She appears—weak, distraught—but the mention of Hippolytus rouses her, clearly causing pain. She confesses to her nurse, Oenone, that she loves him and is dying of that love.

Word comes that Theseus is dead. Phèdre tells Hippolytus she loves him and begs him to kill her. However, Theseus suddenly returns; the rumor of his death was wrong. Phèdre is guilt stricken, horrified, and frightened, but her nurse advises her to protect herself by accusing Hippolytus of having tried to seduce her. Given permission by the frantic Phèdre, the nurse then does so; Theseus confronts his son, who refuses, as a matter of honor, to tell his father the truth about Phèdre. Theseus asks Neptune to avenge him on Hippolytus.

Hippolytus rides off alone in his chariot. A messenger brings the news that Neptune has sent a monster from the ocean that so terrified Hippolytus's horses that they have dragged him to his death. The nurse drowns herself. Phaedra commits suicide.

The great French actress Mademoiselle Rachel played the title role in Phaedra *throughout Europe and the US to great acclaim in the nineteenth century.*

theatres were closing in England, Molière was leaving home to join a traveling theatrical troupe in France. By 1660 he was head of the troupe, was writing most of its plays, and was firmly established as a favorite of Louis XIV. Perhaps the greatest comic writer of all times, Molière used his own experiences as an actor as well as his knowledge of Roman comedy, Italian commedia, and French farce to create comedies that ridiculed social and moral pretentiousness.

Molière's comedy typically depicts characters made ludicrous by their deviations from decorum. Although his dialogue is often clever, verbal elegance and wit for their own sake do not form the core of his plays. Some comedies depend heavily on farcical business (resembling commedia's

THE PLAY'S THE THING

Molière's *Tartuffe*, 1669

Born Jean-Baptist Poquelin (1622–1673), the actor, dramatist, and company manager took Molière as his stage name. Molière's first great success in Paris was his performance before the young king Louis XIV of *The Doctor in Love*, which he wrote and in which he played the title role. His strength as a comic actor was quickly recognized. He wrote more than thirty-six plays, many of which, including *Tartuffe*, are regularly staged today.

The Story of the Play Orgon has made Tartuffe, a supposed religious zealot, a pampered guest in his house. Orgon is obsessed by Tartuffe despite Tartuffe's being despised as a hypocrite by Orgon's

Molière was an active member of his troupe and acted many key comedic roles. Here, he is the title character in Sganerelle.

brother-in-law, Cléante; his wife, Elmire; his son, Damis; and the witty servant, Dorine. Cléante pleads that Orgon use moderation and restraint, but Orgon is unmovable. Orgon tells his daughter, Mariane, that he wants her to marry Tartuffe, but Mariane loves Valère and is disgusted by Tartuffe.

Tartuffe tries to make love to Elmire; he is overheard by Damis, who tries to expose him to Orgon. Tartuffe turns the accusation upside down by saying he is too humble and too pious to defend himself. Orgon turns against his son and throws him out of the house, swearing he will strike him out of his will and make Tartuffe his sole heir. He urges Tartuffe to be with Elmire constantly to show Orgon's faith in him.

Elmire, disgusted, tells Orgon that until then she had passed off men's advances as something a wife dealt with herself, but his actions toward Damis are too much: She will show him the truth about Tartuffe. She hides Orgon under a table and then calls Tartuffe into the room and pretends to welcome his advances. Tartuffe is eager, lustful; he wants "tangible proof" of her feelings. Elmire coughs to get Orgon's attention, but he does not come out from under the table. She asks about Tartuffe's piety; he tells her that he can "remove Heaven's scruples" about adultery. She keeps coughing. Finally, unable to get Orgon to come out, she sends Tartuffe to make sure nobody is nearby and then all but pulls Orgon out. He is stunned. Elmire is sarcastic: "What, coming out so soon? Why don't you wait until the climax?"

Orgon, his obsession ended, confronts Tartuffe and tells him to leave the house, but Tartuffe instead orders Orgon and the family out: Tartuffe owns the house through Orgon's deed of gift. Worse, Tartuffe has private papers that Orgon entrusted to him that can ruin Orgon with the government.

A process server arrives, threatening Orgon's arrest. The police follow, but they arrest Tartuffe instead; the king knows the truth of Tartuffe's hypocrisy and is just.

lazzi) and visual gags. Of his more than twenty plays, the best known are probably *The School for Wives* (1662), *Tartuffe* (1664), *The Misanthrope* (1666), *The Miser* (1668), *The Would-be Gentleman* (1670), and *The Imaginary Invalid* (1673), whose leading role Molière was playing when he was stricken with a final illness. Denied last rites by the church because he was an actor, he was granted Christian burial only through the direct intervention of Louis XIV.

Theatre Companies

By 1660 there were five permanent, professional troupes in Paris, including Molière's, a commedia troupe from Italy, and the opera, music, and dance troupe headed by Jean-Baptiste Lully. All were sharing companies and all included women. France had no householders—actors who, in England, owned parts of the theatre building. The most talented actors settled in Paris as members of these troupes; the rest toured.

Within fifteen years, however, government control and a tendency toward centralization affected the acting companies. With Molière's death, his troupe was joined with two others to form the Comédie Française, which became France's national theatre. Membership in this sharing company was fixed; therefore, new members could not be elected until others had retired or died. Because of its financial rewards, including a substantial pension for retired members, the list of applicants was long.

The Comédie Française was granted a monopoly on the (legal) performance of tragedies and comedies in Paris. Lully's company held a monopoly on musical entertainments and spectacles. The Italian troupe—after a short banishment for a political indiscretion—got exclusive rights to what came to be called **comic operas**. Thus, less than a century after the freewheeling days of the first professionals, French theatre was rigidly structured, with three legal troupes that were expected to continue their traditions, not to initiate the new. The result was a highly polished but conservative theatre—and the suppression of competition.

The life of French actors, even those settled in Paris, was not easy. Some troupes were granted royal subsidies, and the king tried to improve their reputation and social acceptability by royal edict. Nonetheless, French actors were denied civic and religious rights throughout most of the seventeenth and eighteenth centuries, a situation that led many to adopt pseudonyms to spare their families. "Molière" is a pseudonym, for example.

Acting style was formal, more concerned with fidelity to theatrical tradition than to everyday life. Great emphasis was placed on vocal skill, necessary in part because of the highly poetic, even rhetorical quality of the plays. Actors were conservative in the approach to their craft. They apprenticed or hired into a company and learned to act from other actors whom they sought to emulate. Once trained, they tended to specialize in a limited range of roles throughout their career, a trend that became more pronounced with time.

Toward 1750, some new kinds of plays began to appear, their traits seemingly driven by two forces: a changing set of moral values and a reaction against neoclassical dramaturgy.

Sentimentalism

As Louis XIV became both more conservative and more religious with advancing age, French culture in general shifted toward conservativism, adopting a set of values now called **sentimentalism**. According to this view of the world, each individual is basically good. This doctrine contrasted with the previous, neoclassical, view that human existence was a continuing struggle between good and evil. According to the sentimentalist, evil came about through corruption; it was not part of human nature at birth. Sentimentalism thus implied that, although people might not be perfect, they were perfectible. Literature should therefore show virtuous people acting virtuously in their daily lives. Heroic behavior and ethical perfection need not be restricted to some idealized world of pastoral poetry or exotic tragedy.

Sentimentalism affected both serious dramas and comedies. The philosopher and writer concerned with many subjects, Voltaire (1694–1778) tried to introduce Shakespearean features to French plays, including more spectacle and wider-ranging subjects, but his efforts were mostly frustrated. The plays of Shakespeare remained almost unknown on the French stage until the 1800s. Molière's ideal of social sanity as the basis of comedy was replaced by virtue, and audiences wept at comedies as much as they laughed.

Changes in Production Practices

Design, likewise, began to change. Although the basic conventions of costuming remained unchanged (contemporary rather than historical), the costumes themselves were prettified and

A DANCING LESSON

Le Bourgeois Gentilhomme, or *The Would-be Gentleman*, was one of Molière's most successful productions, a play intermingled with music, dance, and singing. Molière played the title role of Monsieur Jourdain, clothed in bright colors trimmed with silver lace. Here, the aspiring aristocrat is given a dancing lesson in this production from about 1850.

sentimentalized, even in commedia. In scenery, the introduction of **multipoint perspective** (moving the vanishing point away from a single center point by adding several vanishing points toward the side) not only allowed actors to work closer to the scenery but also increased the number of "perfect" seats in the audience, suggesting the acceptance of more than one perception of "truth."

Changes in Performance Practices

Acting, too, grew ever more conservative. The previous tendency of actors to specialize in certain kinds of roles became gradually more rigid until, by 1750, clearly defined **lines of business** emerged. New actors, both male and female, were hired as **utility players** and gained their experience by playing a great number of small and varied roles. They then declared a specialty in a specific kind of role: a "walking" lady or gentleman (third line); a specialist in low comedy, or "stage eccentric" (second line); a hero or heroine (first line). Once committed to a particular line of business, actors did not stray far from it, regardless of age.

Along with lines of business came a practice known as **possession of parts**, an agreement that an actor who played a role in the company owned that role for as long as he or she remained in the company. Both practices placed a premium on tradition—and, often, on age—and inhibited innovation.

Acting style depended heavily on vocal power and versatility and on formality and elegance rather than "truth to life." For example, some actors apparently intoned or chanted the poetic and lyrical passages of tragedies, much as the recitative of opera is delivered today, and many actors played for *points*, expecting to receive applause for passages particularly well delivered (in which case, the actor might repeat the passage).

With no outlet for the talents of the many actors and writers who did not get into the Comédie Française, and with dwindling enthusiasm for neoclassicism, French men and women began to work in illegal theatres—that is, theatres other than the monopolies. Joining jugglers, dancers, and others who had worked at fairs for centuries, theatrical troupes began to play outside the law, practicing all kinds of tricks to avoid open conflict with the monopolies. From

MULTIPOINT PERSPECTIVE

Adding second and third vanishing points and shifting the main vanishing point off center extends the vista behind the proscenium arch. Compare this stage set by Giovanni Battista Piranesi with the single point perspective found in Chapter 5.

HOW WE KNOW

A Forgotten Theatre Recovered

In the 1920s, a Swedish theatre historian, Agne Biejer, rediscovered a unique opera theatre dating from 1766 at the Palace at Drottningholm, an island in the western part of Stockholm that is home to the Royal Family. This theatre was virtually intact and untouched since its abandonment in about 1792. He began a two-year campaign to restore the theatre for use.

This forgotten theatre held scenery for fifteen stage settings with parts of scenic elements for other effects along with the original machinery under the stage to make the scenery move using the chariot-and-pole system. Biejer also found a wave machine, a thunder machine, and a flying chair. Drottningholm then became a place of pilgrimage for theatre historians because although Europe held other theatres of the era, they had been in continuous use, altered repeatedly as the times demanded. The Drottningham theatre was one time forgot.

The theatre is a long rectangle, 176 feet by 80 feet, divided in half as stage and auditorium. The scenery, all from the same era, can sometimes seem an extension of the hall's architecture. A musician's pit fronts the stage, then a level floor with benches and chairs for royal audience members, and two raked sections with benches behind. There are two open boxes and two boxes with latticework, in case the royals wanted to attend unnoticed.

Operas are still performed at Drottningholm, albeit fewer now in the worldwide recession. A fast-paced video showing the chariot-and-pole system in action above and below the stage is available on YouTube, titled, "Drottningholms slottsteater," http://www.youtube.com/watch?v=EdRUdoKfPvo. It's worth a watch.

The Drottningholm Theatre as it appeared after Biejer's restoration.

the experiments of these "illegitimate" theatres came a robust alternative to the government theatres—a theatre that was strictly commercial, one supported by a paying audience. Housed in the fairs (it would move to the boulevards in city center in the next century), this theatre aimed to be entertaining and to attract the largest number of spectators possible, their money paying the actors and providing the spectacle.

English Restoration Theatre (1660–c. 1750)

While France had enjoyed the leadership of Louis XIV, England had been without a monarch for twenty years, as the English Commonwealth had been ruled by Cromwell. During this time, the theatres were closed. Although the English theatre had been closed, William Davenant had produced his few "operas," introducing Italianate staging, long a staple in court masques, to the English public for the first time. Another Stuart king, Charles II, (son of Charles I) was restored to the throne in 1660, hence the name of the period—the Restoration.

English Public Theatre

With the return of Charles II from exile in France, English theatres reopened in 1660. Their model, however, was not the theatre of Shakespeare's London; it was now the theatre of Paris. The English theatre now included at least four French traits:

- Women actors, who quickly assumed all female roles except witches and comic old women, which continued to be played by men (as they were in Molière's company). The presence of women onstage encouraged, fairly or not, the risqué reputation of Restoration theatre.
- Conventions of Italianate staging.
- Newly designed theatre buildings that met the needs of Italianate staging.
- New, French-inspired producing arrangements. The English king granted two monopoly patents, one to Davenant and another to Thomas Killigrew, thus limiting London to only two "legitimate" theatres. Although often challenged, these patents were reaffirmed through most of the 1700s.

Theatre Architecture

When theatres first reopened in 1660, they used either old, rather dilapidated theatre buildings, such as the Red Bull, or they adapted tennis courts (Lincoln's Inn Fields, Gibbon's Tennis Court), as in France. As new theatres were built, however, they blended Shakespearean and French features.

DRURY LANE, AS REBUILT IN 1794
The interior of the Drury Lane theatre reflected the general organization of most theatres in England: A pit area with seats slightly below stage level, several seating galleries (usually three to five), and a very high open seating area at the top of the theatre.

The auditorium was divided into box, pit (now with benches), and gallery. Favored audience members now sat on the stage itself, as in France. The stage comprised both a proscenium arch with a raked stage behind it and a forestage that thrust into the pit. Most scenery was located behind the proscenium arch, where grooves were installed to facilitate scene changes, but most acting took place on the forestage, which was roughly the size of the area behind the proscenium. Early Restoration playhouses were intimate, with as little as thirty feet from forestage to rear boxes.

Staging conventions were Italian by way of France. Wings, borders, and shutters formed stock sets appropriate for comedies, tragedies, and pastorals. For costumes, most actors wore a sumptuous version of contemporary fashion. Acting depended heavily on vocal power and versatility and on formality and elegance rather than truth to life. Lines of business and possession of parts determined which actors played which roles, contributing in England, as in France, to an increasingly conservative style of acting. Lighting was still by candle, and so audience and actors were equally visible.

The Theatre Royal, Drury Lane, first built in 1674 exemplified the new characteristics of London theatre architecture.

Restoration Drama

The period between the reestablishment in London of commercial theatre in 1660 and the ascension to the English throne of William and Mary in 1689 was dramatically rich. The plays were markedly different from those seen in the theatres in 1640. Many new forms of drama appeared, including heroic tragedy, refined tragedy, burlesques, pantomimes, opera, and several varieties of comedy.

Restoration dramas, likewise, showed French influence. Plays written during the age of Shakespeare continued to be produced, but they were often adapted to bring them into closer accord with neoclassical theory. In Restoration productions, Lear and Cordelia, for example, were happily alive at the ending of "Shakespeare's" *King Lear*. Newly written plays differed in both content and form from the Elizabethan. The worlds they embodied were those of a highly artificial, aristocratic society, probably influenced by life at Louis XIV's court, and their dramaturgy more closely reflected continental neoclassicism than Shakespeare. But from 1660 to 1700, comedy prevailed.

Comedy of Manners

Most famous today are the Restoration **comedies of manners**, plays whose witty dialogue and sophisticated sexual behavior reflect the highly artificial, mannered, and aristocratic society of the day. The heroes and heroines are "virtuous" if they succeed in capturing a lover or tricking a husband. "Honor" depends not on integrity but on reputation, and "wit," the ability to express ideas in a clever and apt way, is prized above all. The admirable characters in the plays are those who can operate successfully within an intricate social sphere; the foolish and laughable are those whose lack of wit or upbringing denies them access to social elegance. In short, the comedies depict the mores and conventions of a courtly society in which elegance of phrase and the appearance of propriety were more highly prized than morals and sincere feelings. Among the most important authors of Restoration comedies were William Congreve and William Wycherley.

William Wycherley William Wycherley's (1640–1716) reputation as a leading Restoration playwright is secured by only four plays written in a five-year period: *Love in a Wood* (1671), *The Gentleman Dancing-Master* (1671), *The Country Wife* (1675), and *The Plain Dealer* (1676). *The Country Wife*, considered lewd and immoral even in Restoration England, is often revived. The central character, Margery Pinchwife, is newly married to a much older man who brings her to London and tries to protect her from the city's licentious ways. The seducer, Horner, has his doctor, Quack, spread the word that Horner is a eunuch—impotent due to a sexual disease contracted while in France—and thus not a sexual threat to the women of his set. With that blatant lie, Horner goes about merrily seducing the ladies of London. He is successful and unremorseful.

William Congreve The dramatic reputation of Congreve rests upon four comedies: *The Old Bachelor* (1739), *The Double Dealer* (1694), *Love for Love* (1695), and *The Way of the World* (1700). William Congreve

(1670–1729) also wrote a tragedy, *The Mourning Bride* (1697). Although *Love for Love* was his most successful play when first produced, critics now cite *The Way of the World* as sophisticated and brilliant, the highlight of Restoration comedy of manners. Two young lovers, Mirabell and Millamant, wish to marry. To receive her dowry, Millamant must gain the approval of her brittle, foolish aunt, Lady Wishfort. But Lady Wishfort wants her nephew to wed Millamant. Complications arise but the young lovers are to wed providing Mirabell accepts Millamont's quite modern prenuptial "provisos:"

Mirabell	Have you any more conditions to offer? Hitherto your demands are pretty reasonable.
Millamant	Trifles; as liberty to pay and receive visits to and from whom I please; to write and receive letters, without interrogatories or wry faces on your part; to wear what I please, and choose conversation with regard only to my own taste; to have no obligation upon me to converse with wits that I don't like, because they are your acquaintance, or to be intimate with fools, because they may be your relations. Come to dinner when I please, dine in my dressing-room when I'm out of humour, without giving a reason. To have my closet inviolate; to be sole empress of my tea-table, which you must never presume to approach without first asking leave. And lastly, wherever I am, you shall always knock at the door before you come in. These articles subscribed, if I continue to endure you a little longer, I may by degrees dwindle into a wife.

Not as dissolute a comedy as *The Country Wife, The Way of the World* is peopled with brilliantly conceived characters and peppered with wit that still resonates in the modern world.

Comedy of Intrigue

The first woman to make her living as a writer, Aphra Behn (1640–1689) wrote almost twenty plays, several novels and short stories, and poetry. *The Rover*, her most successful play, is sometimes revived today. Its plot, often racy, features as protagonist Angellica Bianca, a famous courtesan who falls in love with an unfaithful noble and swears revenge on him for his betrayal.

Tragedy

"Heroic" tragedies presented a conflict between love and duty. In a world far removed from that of the Restoration comedies, tragic heroes were flawless and heroines chaste. The dialogue was based on heroic couplets, two-line units of rhymed iambic pentameter. The idealization and formality of this kind of tragedy made it unusually susceptible to parody, and so burlesques of it soon appeared. Succumbing to both the onslaught of burlesque and the changing tastes of audiences, heroic tragedies declined in public favor, their place being filled by neoclassical-inspired tragedies.

John Dryden (1631–1700) excelled in both forms of tragedy. He was a poet, translator, critic, and playwright who dominated English literary culture so much so that his era is sometimes referred to as "The Age of Dryden." Dryden wrote at least thirty plays, some well-received comedies, and translated the works of the Roman poet Virgil, among others.

Dryden's *All for Love*, a rewriting of Shakespeare's *Antony and Cleopatra*, brought it closer to the principles of neoclassicism. While using only the plot of this tragedy, Dryden observed the unities of time, place, and action, if liberally interpreted.

Audiences

Restoration theatres were small, seating about 650 at the beginning of the Restoration, and the audience was fairly cohesive—young, courtly, and self-confident. Regularly in attendance were royalty and the upper aristocracy, many of them veterans of exile in France with the king. Some women in the audience wore masks, as much to increase their attractions as to hide them. This theatre was a place to be seen as well as to enjoy the plays. Within fifteen years, however, noncourtiers began to take up theatre as a leisure-time activity in ever-larger numbers, causing a shift in audience taste. By 1700 theatres seated two thousand or more.

Acting Companies and Actors

Acting troupes were larger, included women, and were organized quite differently than they were before the Restoration. The sharing system of Shakespeare's day gave way to the contract system. That is, actors no longer shared in the profits of the company; they were, instead, hired for a specific period of time at a specific salary. This economic restructuring meant that actors lost artistic control of London's theatres. Outside of London and in colonial America, the sharing system continued.

Actors were hired by someone much like a modern producer. This entrepreneur set the salaries, managed the theatre building, and selected the repertory. Although two patent holders were reaffirmed in 1663 after Charles II returned to the throne, by 1694 John Rich became the holder of both theatre patents because of the financial ruin of Thomas Killigrew, the other license holder.

Important actors (and some other theatre personnel) were sometimes granted yearly "benefit performances," meaning they could keep the profits from that presentation. The benefit system still operates today in some cities, including New York; instead of individuals receiving the profits, organizations benefit. New York producers often schedule benefit performances for

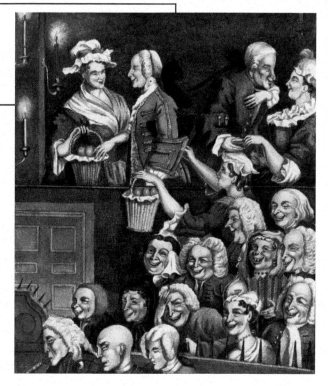

A HAPPY AUDIENCE COMPLETE WITH ORANGES

This Hogarth black-and-white engraving, colored in 1733, shows orange sellers plying their wares, much as Nell Gwynn did at Drury Lane before she became an actress there.

the Actors Fund, a human services group that helps performing arts professionals in need.

The Restoration was a period of important actors, male and female. Four "greats" exemplify the era.

Nell Gwynn The story of Eleanor "Nell" Gwynn's acting career is a short one. She was an actress for about five years, making her debut in a play by Dryden in 1664 and retiring from the stage in 1669 as the mistress of Charles II. Records indicate Nell Gwynn (1650–1687) was considered a vivacious, charming, good-looking woman at a time when women were first accepted on the English stage. She was an excellent singer and dancer.

Her life story, however, is intriguing. Her mother kept a whorehouse, and she grew up in poverty. From an early age she worked as an orange seller at the Drury Lane Theatre and shortly thereafter became the mistress of an actor in the company there. She then went on the stage specializing in "breeches parts," parts where a woman dressed in form-revealing men's clothing somehow required by the plot. She excelled in the speaking of prologues and epilogues and caught the fancy of Charles II. Gwynn then retired from the stage, bore Charles II children, and was a popular hostess.

Thomas Betterton Considered the greatest actor of the Restoration, Thomas Betterton (?1635–1710) was also a company manager and adaptor of plays. He excelled in roles by Shakespeare, especially Hamlet. He adapted many of Shakespeare's plays to meet the neoclassical preferences of the era. Much in demand, he also originated dozens of roles in plays by Dryden and other prominent playwrights of the time. He married the actress Mary Saunderson, who became the first actress to play many of Shakespeare's female roles.

Betterton was an active director and manager during most of his acting career, beginning with the Duke's Company in 1668. With the financial ruin of Killigrew's company, the two licensed theatres merged into the United Company in 1682 under Betterton's guidance but headed by the stingy management of John Rich. The actors rebelled in 1695 and set up a sharing company in Lincoln's Inn Fields in a converted tennis court under Betterton's management.

Anne Bracegirdle Quite unlike Gwynn, Anne Bracegirdle (c. 1671–1748) was a model of propriety on stage and off, called by some the "celebrated virgin." The daughter of Justinian Bracegirdle, a coachman or coach-maker, and his wife, she was raised from childhood by Thomas Betterton and his wife. The Bettertons, who were acknowledged for their training of young actors, probably coached Bracegirdle. She became one of the best actresses of the time, especially in comedic roles, making her debut in 1688 and retiring from the stage in 1707. She created the role of Millamant in *The Way of the World* and other witty, sophisticated characters. She excelled, as did Gwynn, in breeches parts showing to advantage her fine figure. Bracegirdle was also a gifted singer.

Anne Oldfield Anne Oldfield (1683–1730) was a much-admired actress at the height of her career in small parts in the Theatre Royal, Drury Lane, where her beauty—rather than her acting skills—earned her favor. A decade later, Oldfield was a star, inheriting the accolades first given to Bracegirdle.

The Rise of Sentimentalism: 1700–1750

In England as in France, the eighteenth century brought with it a change of values. Between about 1700 and 1750, society steadily grew more conservative, middle class, moralistic, and sentimental.

The amoral tone of the **Restoration comedy** of manners became offensive to many, and in its place developed the view that drama should teach morality. At first, the change was merely in the plays' endings: Young lovers philandered and cuckolded throughout four acts of the play but in the fifth, repented and declared their intentions to lead a moral and upright life henceforth.

Sentimental Comedy

By the 1730s, however, heroes and heroines were becoming embodiments of middle-class values, struggling cheerfully against adversity until, at the

THE LONDON MERCHANT

The London Merchant or *The History of George Barnwell*, first performed in 1731, follows a young apprentice who falls under the spell of a prostitute. After stealing money from his employer to fund his relationship, Barnwell robs and murders his uncle—a scene pictured here. *The London Merchant* is considered the first domestic tragedy.

end, their courage and persistence were rewarded. Prized especially were characters able to express their insights into human goodness in pithy statements, called sentiments. Thus, the label "sentimental hero" implied not only one who embodied virtue but also one whose speech was rich in sentiments. The audiences of the day experienced "a pleasure too exquisite for laughter," and **sentimental comedy** dominated English and French comic drama by the middle of the eighteenth century—a clear break with neoclassicism.

Serious Plays: Domestic Tragedy

Heroic and neoclassical tragedy were increasingly replaced by a kind of serious drama, alternately called **domestic tragedy** and middle-class tragedy. George Lillo's *The London Merchant* (1731), for example, was a major break with the neoclassical ideal: A middle-class hero is led astray by a prostitute and is ultimately punished. Although the play aimed to teach morality by showing the punishment of evil, it was nonetheless a far cry from strict neoclassicism because it was written in prose, featured a middle-class hero, and dealt with affairs of the heart and the marketplace rather than affairs of state. None of these more serious plays, however, satisfied the English taste for scenic splendor and spectacular effects.

Minor Forms

Opera and a number of so-called minor forms provided outlets for visual display. Native English opera was gradually replaced by spectacular Italian opera, whose popularity soared in the eighteenth century. As well, English **pantomimes** combined elements of commedia dell'arte, farce, mythology, and contemporary satire with elaborate scenes of spectacle in short **afterpieces** (short entertainments performed after the evening's play). Often, the dialogue was merely an excuse for major scenes of **transformation**, in which Harlequin, for instance, by a wave of his magic wand, changed

places and people into new and dazzling locales and characters. Because new scenery was often commissioned for pantomimes, many innovations in the design and execution of settings in England can be credited to pantomime.

Changes in Production and Performance Practices

Changes in drama were accompanied by changes in production and performance practices. As more middle-class people came into the audience, existing theatres were enlarged, and new theatres were built larger; within a hundred years, the intimate theatre of the Restoration, seating fewer than seven hundred playgoers, had been superseded by those seating two thousand or more. Theatres began to commission painters to provide new settings for some plays (especially those featuring familiar named locations), and these painters, adopting new techniques for suggesting depth, made it possible for actors to work closer to scenery than before. Increased emphasis on scenery led to a gradual decrease in the size of the forestage and a need for more space behind the proscenium arch. As a result of these shifts, there was little difference in appearance between English and continental theatres by 1750. Both countries had adopted the conventions of Italianate staging. Women were now on stage and in the audience. Both cultures had developed theatrical centers in their capital cities, where their kings maintained monopolies over a strictly limited number of theatres. Actors talented and experienced enough to perform in the monopoly theatres lived good lives; others, however, lived precariously, working in small cities and towns and touring outlying areas.

IMPERIAL THEATRE, VIENNA
By the 1700s, theatre architecture seemed international. Here, a theatre in Vienna in about 1670. Note the royalty in the front row with seating on the ground floor behind. This theatre features four galleries fitted into a rectangular space.

By the mid-1700s, European audiences (including those of a just-developing German theatre) had already begun to tire of the austerity of neoclassical dramas. As audiences became increasingly middle class, sentimentalism and spectacle began to be prized; both found expression in opera, ballet, and new dramatic forms. When monopoly theatres disdained the innovations, commercial theatres sprang up to house them, first at the fairs of London and Paris (hence, **fair theatres**) and later in London's West End and Paris's boulevards.

KEY TERMS

Key terms are in boldface type in the text. Check your understanding against this list. Persons are page-referenced in the Index.

afterpieces, p. 161
comedy of manners, p. 156
comic opera, p. 150
domestic tragedy, p. 161
fair theatres, p. 163
lines of business, p. 152
machine plays, p. 146
multipoint perspective, p. 152

pantomimes, p. 161
possession of parts, p. 152
Restoration comedy, p. 160
sentimental comedy, p. 161
sentimentalism, p. 151
transformation, p. 161
utility players, p. 152

Chapter 7 at a Glance

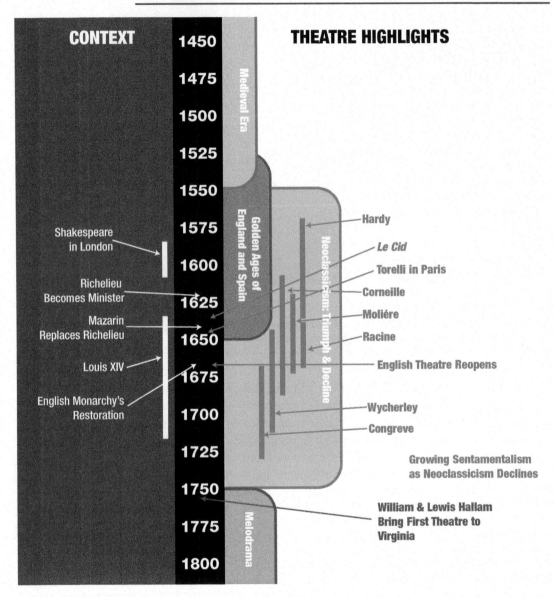

CONTEXT

THEATRE HIGHLIGHTS

1450
1475
1500
1525
1550
1575
1600
1625
1650
1675
1700
1725
1750
1775
1800

Medieval Era

Golden Ages of England and Spain

Neoclassicism: Triumph & Decline

Melodrama

Shakespeare in London

Richelieu Becomes Minister

Mazarin Replaces Richelieu

Louis XIV

English Monarchy's Restoration

Hardy

Le Cid

Torelli in Paris

Corneille

Moliére

Racine

English Theatre Reopens

Wycherley

Congreve

Growing Sentamentalism as Neoclassicism Declines

William & Lewis Hallam Bring First Theatre to Virginia

Melodrama and the Rise of Commercialism, 1750–1900

When you have completed this chapter, you should be able to:

- List and explain the major traits of melodrama.
- Compare romantic and realistic melodrama
- Name some major writers of serious and comic drama from the mid-eighteenth century to the start of the twentieth century.
- Name and discuss several important actors of this period.
- Describe the nature of commercialism.
- Suggest how changes in English law facilitated the beginnings of English-speaking theatre in the American colonies.

Context

From the mid-eighteenth century until the early-twentieth century, theatre in Europe and America achieved popularity and commercial success never before equaled. This period saw many tumultuous economic, social, and political changes. The middle-class grew in size and influence. (Middle-class refers to those people who are manufacturers or trades people as contrasted to landed nobles and serfs or laborers—the upper class and the lower classes, respectively.) Farming became more efficient so farms supported fewer laborers. These displaced people moved to cities and factories in search of a livelihood and cities grew at an extraordinary rate. Cities were good and terrible, good because they offered people a new freedom; terrible because decent housing, waste disposal, disease control, and the like were slow to develop. For most, cities were dirty, crowded, and unsafe.

THEATRE ROYAL COVENT GARDEN
An etching from 1810 shows a pit orchestra surrounded by four balconies; in the center back, above the fourth balcony was yet another seating area. Note the proscenium door and the two boxes above the door.

Steam power was perfected around 1775, making manufacturing and transporting goods no longer dependent on only human, animal, or water power. Steam power, the engine of the Industrial Revolution, was replaced by internal combustion engines beginning in the mid-1800s. Literacy expanded and so did the availability of the printed book. When paper became truly inexpensive because of steam power, printed materials such as books and newspapers also became cheaper and more widely available.

Perhaps related to the growth of cities and literacy, the period between about 1750 and 1850 came later to be called the "age of revolutions." Gradually and not without bloodshed and counterrevolutions, a number of governments changed from absolute monarchies to constitutional governments and republics. This period includes the American Revolution, the French Revolution, the revolt of slaves in Haiti and elsewhere in Latin America, and independence movements in Latin America. Of course, these political changes led to change in theatre as well.

The years from 1750 to the twentieth century were the period of commercialization—the triumph of capitalism and the glorification of wealth. "Captains of industry" made fortunes in railroads, steel, oil, textiles, canals, road building, manufacturing, and mass communications. New technologies made long-distance transport, mass production, and mass consumption possible. New ideas of business organization and new laws made big business and big fortunes possible.

Theatre Becomes Commercial

The theatre could not ignore the new working-class audience that poured into cities, the expanding middle class that occupied new urban developments, or the more distant audiences now reachable by railroad and steamship. Nor could it ignore profits, now possible on a scale never imagined by Shakespeare or Molière.

For the theatre, it is important to remember that this was a time before any technology competed with the drama. There were no movies. The only place to experience dramatic or comedic storytelling with scenic spectacle was the live theatre. The phonograph started to bring recorded sound into the home in the 1870s. The first stage to be lighted by electricity was London's Savoy Theatre, home of the Gilbert and Sullivan comic operettas, in 1881.

Theatre's biggest competition did not develop until after World War I, a period in theatre history that will be explored in future chapters. Commercial radio did not start until the 1920s. The first successful theatre for silent movies opened in 1905. Movies with synchronized, recorded sound were first shown in the late 1920s. Commercial television as we know it began only after World War II in 1946. Before these competing technologies developed, theatre had a clear stage for commercial development.

Theatre in Four Countries, c. 1750–c. 1850

Germany

Germany's theatre experience was different from England's and France's in this period. "Germany" was still a hodgepodge of small states, duchies, and principalities linked by little except language. Something like the current German nation was not unified until the 1870s. Despite a glorious tradition of music, the various countries speaking German had no permanent theatres at the beginning of the 1700s. Such traveling players as there were played low comedy or blood-and-thunder bombast for illiterate audiences. In 1725, however, Johann Gottsched, a neoclassicist and playwright, and Carolina Neuber, head of an acting troupe, introduced the first "serious" German drama and theatre. Other permanent theatres quickly sprang up in Germany

INSIDE THE STATE THEATRE, HAMBURG, GERMANY

This rendering of the interior is crude (the people are erratically out of scale), but the theatre in the early 1800s had a pit orchestra with box-pit-gallery seating. The large candelabrum in the audience area illuminated the audience as well as the stage.

(sixty-five of them by 1800). But they were spread all over the German-speaking area. In the eighteenth and nineteenth centuries, German theorists and artists tried to assert a cultural centrality that German theatre had never known, and they used the language of art and seriousness. They tilted toward English models. German audiences knew Shakespeare from touring seventeenth-century English companies. As a neoclassicist, Gottsched promoted neoclassical French ideas but failed.

England and France

By the early 1700s, the theatre had begun to lose its ties to the old monarchies in England and France. At the same time, the audience base started growing, first into the middle class and then into the working class. Before this time, monopolies granted by government tied the theatres to power. This tie weakened as royal power ebbed. Now came large audiences who had not power but *money*, which they used to buy entrance to new "illegitimate"—not licensed by the government—commercial theatres.

For all these reasons, by the mid-1700s, theatrical energy was shifting to the commercial theatres, which offered new kinds of plays in spectacular settings.

America

English actors squeezed out of the London theatre brought theatre to the colonies. Rather than tour rural England, brothers William and Lewis Hallam chose to assemble a company made up mostly of family members and sail to a distant English province, an outpost of the New World. In 1752 the troupe arrived in the Royal Colony of Virginia, and after building a theatre, opened with Shakespeare's *The Merchant of Venice*. This group (although reorganized and enlarged after the death of Lewis Hallam and renamed the American Company in recognition of America's break with England) toured the towns of the East Coast with almost no competition until the 1790s. In some towns it could not appear because not all colonial communities welcomed theatre, seeing it as decadent and sinful. The American Company's repertory, acting styles, and production conventions were English, with appropriate adjustments made for the needs of almost constant touring. The American Company had the distinction of staging the first native U.S. comedy (Royal Taylor's *The Contrast*, 1787) written to be performed by professional actors. By 1800, there were playhouses in New York, Philadelphia, Baltimore, Williamsburg, and Charleston.

The Walnut Street Theatre, Philadelphia, was founded in 1809 and remains the oldest theatre building in the United States. Its first theatre production in 1812 was Richard Brinsley Sheridan's comedy *The Rivals*, which had been first staged in London in 1775. It is said that

EARLY THEATRE, PHILADELPHIA
The Walnut Street Theatre, Philadelphia, opened in 1809 and claims
to be the oldest continuously operating theatre in the United States.
Here, an exterior view of about 1820. Many of the United States'
most important actors appeared on its stage over the years.

President Thomas Jefferson and the Marquis de Lafayette attended this first
performance.

Commercial Theatre Develops

The fully developed **commercial theatre** was one in which profit was the
primary goal, with income from ticket sales the principal source of revenue.
Capitalization came either from individual wealth or from limited companies
created for the purpose. The creators of theatre—actors, directors, and designers—
became employees of financiers—mostly men—eventually called "producers."

At first glance, it might seem that the theatre had been commercial since
the Renaissance, an enterprise to make money by selling tickets. Molière's
players in France and Shakespeare's in England were fully profit-making
endeavors. However, commercial pressure on theatre was long muted by support, censorship, or licensing from a crown, from aristocrats, from local governments, or from the church. In the decades leading up to 1750, however,
those subsidies declined, the licenses weakened or dissolved, and the need to
pursue profit increased. (Censorship continued under many governments,
but its power was only to say "No!") The financial setup and managerial
forms for commercial theatre varied over time.

Actors and Actor-Managers

Throughout the long early history of commercialism, key performers came to prominence. They captured the spirit of the changes of the era and accelerated the pace of change through their artistic and entrepreneurial boldness. Four are considered here in brief.

David Garrick

David Garrick (1717–1779) was the son of a French Huguenot, a Protestant who emigrated to England when religious protection was abolished in France. Thus, Garrick always spoke with something of a foreign accent. He began as a wine merchant, but from childhood the theatre attracted him. He first appeared out of London, using a pseudonym, which was not unusual at the time because acting was seen as a louche profession. His breakthrough performance was as Richard III in an unlicensed theatre, one without a royal patent.

Garrick's style is impossible to fully capture today. Clearly, he contrasted with what came before—an acting style that was smooth, rhythmic, attaining to the quality of music—which at its worst was sometimes termed *bombastic*. Garrick was seen as more natural and more relaxed with his approach changing suddenly as his character's objectives changed. As with any change in style, not every critic liked his work. And acting in general did not immediately change after Garrick. For example, Garrick regularly hired an actor of the old school, James Quin, who never really changed in style at all. Quin is quoted to have said, "If this young fellow be right, then we have been all wrong."

DAVID GARRICK

One of the most influential actor-managers of his era, he steered the acting style away from bombast to a more "natural" approach. Here, in a 1774 painting by Philip James de Loutherbourg, David Garrick in *The Chancers* by John Fletcher.

Garrick was hired to play in one of the patent theatres, the Drury Lane, and went on to become co-owner of the patent. Beginning in 1747 until his retirement in 1776, he solely held the patent and as such, was the manager-director of productions there.

Garrick was noted for having a particular respect for the plays of Shakespeare, although he continued to play them in bastardized versions and sometimes inserted his own lines and scenes. As an actor-manager-director, he was a reformer in physical production, bringing some consistency to set design and costuming. It was under his aegis that chandeliers with their general stage lighting were replaced with oil lighting on poles from the wings, with metal reflectors that could be turned to direct or vary the lighting, and with colored silk coverings to change the color. He engaged Philip James de Loutherberg as scene painter and gave him the freedom to experiment with new realistic techniques.

Edmund Kean

Edmund Kean (1789–1833) first appeared on stage at age four. A poor student from a family we would call dysfunctional, Kean had little education but was taken up by his uncle, Moses Kean, a variety performer, and the actress Miss Charlotte Tidswell. In his teens, he moved among jobs. Once, as a rider of a circus horse, he broke both his legs and he suffered from that injury all his life. In 1814, the financially desperate management of the Drury Lane hired him to play Shylock. He was a meteoric success.

As an actor, Kean had a limited range, with little taste for comedy. The poet Samuel Taylor Coleridge said of Kean, "Seeing him act was like reading Shakespeare by flashes of lightening." The French actor François Joseph Talma called Kean, "an uncut gem." He restored the tragic ending to *King Lear* but audiences would not accept it.

Kean was mercurial in real life, in intermittent battle with friends, coworkers, playwrights, and critics. For a while, he kept a tame lion in his dressing room. He was the first English actor to play in the United States as Richard III in 1820, taking advantage of new, faster ship passage. He returned to the United States in 1825 to a mixed reception from audience and critics. He was tried as a correspondent in an adultery case in 1825, found guilty, fined, and afterward, booed off the stage and pelted with fruit. This scandal ended his career.

EDMUND KEAN
Edmund Kean as Sir Giles Overreach in Phillip Massinger's *A New Way to Pay Old Debts* in a painting from 1820. One contemporary critic noted of Kean that, "Seeing him act was like reading Shakespeare by lightening."

Charles Macready

Unlike either Garrick or Kean, William Charles Macready (1793–1893) grew up in relative privilege. He was educated at Rugby, a centuries' old independent school, and was to attend Oxford, but instead helped his father's teetering provincial theatre business. As an actor, the growth of

STAR POWER

William Charles Macready became one of London's great stars, playing not only Shakespeare but also in plays by contemporary authors. Here, in an 1821 painting, he is seen as Macbeth.

his fame was slow with the first big success *William Tell*. He traveled to the United States in 1826, 1843–1844, and 1849 and Paris in 1828 where he is said to have returned Shakespeare to the French stage.

In fact, over the course of his stage career, Macready gradually returned to staging Shakespeare as written. (The exception was *Macbeth*; the audience would only accept the "old" adulterations, including added scenes, music, and witches dancing.) His performances were notable for their intellect and culture. Although he could be as bold as Kean, his boldness was backed by his understanding of the text. As an actor-manager, Macready paid attention to all the performers; when he traveled abroad, he took most of his company with him.

On his last trip to the United States, Macready played Macbeth at the Astor Place Theatre while the US actor Edwin Forrest was playing the same role just blocks away. Perhaps as publicity, perhaps as genuine dispute, there had been a public argument about which was the better Shakespearean actor. More importantly, there was an anti-British feeling in the lower classes, fed in part by memories of the War of 1812 and in part by class antipathies, with the upper class being Anglophile and thus pro-Macready. By the time the play was to start, there were perhaps ten thousand people in the streets by the theatres. The government called out troops and the resulting riot, called the Astor Place Riot, killed between twenty-one and thirty-one rioters and injured forty-eight. Of police and troops, none were killed but fifty to seventy police and 141 troops were injured. Macready returned to England. Forrest's career was damaged by the memory of the event. The Astor Place Theatre did not get over the scandal either, becoming a library in the next year.

Ellen Terry

Ellen Terry's parents were touring comic actors. Four of her siblings were actors and two others were in theatre management. (There were eleven siblings in all.) Her daughter Edith was a director, producer, and costume designer. Terry's illegitimate son, Edward Gordon Craig, was a path-breaking stage designer. By the mid-nineteenth century, commercial theatre could be a business and it was for the Terry family.

Ellen Terry (1847–1928) first appeared on stage at the age of eight, with Charles Kean, the son of Edmund Kean, connecting her to a tradition of acting in the age of commercialism. Her first adult successes were in Shakespearean roles, a revival of *The School for Scandal*, and in various contemporary plays. At the age of thirty in 1878, she joined famed actor-manager Henry Irving's company and thus became the leading actress of Shakespearean roles. After Irving's death, Terry admitted that they had been lovers for awhile; Irving was married. She had a long epistolary and chaste love affair with George Bernard Shaw, and when she ran her own company beginning in 1903, she staged Shaw's plays and those of Ibsen. Terry toured the United States seven times in the plays of Shakespeare and Shaw and in popular contemporary plays, many of which were based on history. Critics acclaimed her beauty, charm, grace, simplicity, and her easy movement and laughter on stage. Terry's last full stage performance was the nurse in *Romeo and Juliet* in 1919 aged seventy-two.

ASTOR PLACE RIOTS

Macready played Macbeth on May 10, 1849, while his US rival, Edwin Forrest, played the same role on the same night at another theatre. Thousands of New Yorkers protested Macready's performance in a riot that killed many. Theatre seemed very important to US culture on this day.

From Actor-Manager to Producer

As commercial pressures increased, theatres organized themselves differently. Previous sharing companies that had toured or located in small cities had led perilous lives. In sharing companies the performers held various-sized shares in the theatre company and so shared in the company's receipts according to the shares they held. When income went down, all the shares went down so all in the company received less money. Collecting capital was difficult. Sharing companies were lucky if they owned decent costumes, much less scenery or a theatre. To reduce these risks, actors came to prefer salaries to shares, even though this change made them employees rather than part owners. This shift, however, required a changed business organization. In some companies, a leading actor, called the **actor-manager**, now operated the company, made decisions once made by the group of sharers, and paid the others. In other, somewhat later companies, the company was managed by the director who was called a **director-manager**. Ultimately it was the person who managed investors' money who led the theatre company, called a **producer**. The producer was not necessarily creative on the stage but probably creative in attracting and enticing investors for a theatre production. The successful producer could recognize talent in other people and foster it to appear at its best on stage.

The Star System

Through the 1700s, theatre companies tended to stay together in one place or in a few places reachable by horse. Changes in technology broke this pattern. By the early 1800s in the United States, for example, actors were playing a circuit of theatres up the Mississippi River from New Orleans as far north as Lexington, Kentucky, on the Ohio River, stopping wherever there was promise of an audience and repeating the circuit the following season, something possible only with steam power. With an expanding rail system after the 1840s and faster steam ocean travel, national and even international stars could move fairly quickly between cities, where they usually played with resident companies. This **star system** brought William Macready, for example, from London to US cities first in 1826 and to Paris in 1828. At first, stars traveled essentially alone, picking up the rest of an acting company in the cities where they appeared. Stars later began to travel with their own supporting actors and then their own production units; somewhat later still, actors formed **combination companies** to travel the nation and the world. Combination companies were complete producing units with actors, scenery, costumes, and props, generally touring a single play. Combination companies began in the 1860s and were common by 1900. They could produce a single play because when the audience dwindled in one place, they would move to another instead of mounting a new show. **Repertory** companies remained—companies that mounted multiple plays in one town—but they were the exception. Combination companies were and still are the norm in commercial theatre touring today, colloquially called "the road."

SHOWBOATS
Steam-powered paddle wheel boats plied the Mississippi River from the early 1800s bringing entertainment to riverside towns. Here, "William Chapman's Floating Theatre" in about 1847.

Theatrical Syndicate in the United States

The theatre was also affected by the way the rest of society did business. The late nineteenth century saw money and power increasingly concentrated in fewer hands. Monopolies were created as large businesses swallowed small ones, until few rivals remained, which marked the age of the robber barons and the great "trusts" in the United States. Trusts are today more often called *monopolies*. Trusts created counterreactions in the early twentieth century: Working people organized to secure safer conditions, more money, and more power, and the labor union movement began.

Theatre was part of this change, at least in the United States. Since Shakespeare's day, entrepreneurs had owned theatre buildings. By the 1800s, a businessman might own several theatres in different cities and send combination companies from one to another, creating an efficient touring circuit. Toward the end of the nineteenth century, one group in the United States, the **Theatrical Syndicate**, realized that if they could own all the theatres, they could control all theatre, including ticket pricing and actors' salaries. The syndicate bought buildings, organized the buildings into circuits based on transportation routes, centralized the booking of combination companies in New York which caused actors to have to live there, and created a near-monopoly by the early twentieth century. It effectively ended the tradition of stock or sharing companies. The power of the Theatrical Syndicate was absolute: artists who defied it found that virtually no theatre in the United States would house their performances. Several stars who stood up to the Syndicate—including Sarah Bernhardt and Minnie Maddern Fiske—were reduced to touring in tents.

Theatre's increasing commercialization had other consequences. As theatre depended more on ticket sales and was managed more and more by businesspeople, profit trumped art, committing commercial theatre to popular culture and a mass audience.

Drama in the Commercial Theatre

Since around the 1750s, as many as twenty thousand plays have been staged in commercial theatres around the world. Of this number, few have ever been revived. Many of the scripts are lost. Timeliness and subject matter were often more commercially important than quality. This is not to say that plays from the commercial theatre were bad. Commercial plays had to be *accessible*—without ideas that would offend or challenge a mass audience or cause it to ponder. The commercial audience went to the theatre for escape, for thrills, laughs, and tears, but not necessarily to have to think.

THE PLAY'S THE THING

Augustin Daly's *Under the Gaslight*, 1867

Augustin Daly (1836–1899), playwright, director, critic, and theatrical manager, was one of the most influential figures in US theatre during the last half of the nineteenth century. He wrote or adapted more than ninety plays. *Under the Gaslight* is the quintessential realistic melodrama, a play in five acts in which social status is prominent. The famous railroad scene, in which the comic man is tied to the railroad tracks but rescued by the heroine just before the oncoming locomotive is about to kill him, became a staple in many other realistic melodramas and in many early films.

The Story of the Play In an upper-class New York drawing room, Laura Courtland, engaged to Ray Stafford, is confronted by the villainous Byke. Laura tells her flighty cousin Pearl to tell Ray the truth that Byke threatens to reveal: Laura is not a real Courtland but an adopted former street child. Ray decides to break off the engagement, writes Laura a letter (saying he loves her), then crumples the letter and shoves it into a pocket. Later, however, at a gathering at swank Delmonico's Restaurant, the letter falls out, and sneering society women read it and banish Laura. This time, Ray fails to stand by her and she is an outcast.

Three months later, Laura is living incognito in a basement with Peachblossom, a street child. Byke

and his female accomplice, Old Judas, try to kidnap them but are foiled by Snorkey, a one-armed Civil War veteran who leads Ray to Laura. Ray pleads for a second chance, but Byke and Old Judas return and kidnap the women and then try to get Laura to a New Jersey hideout from a Hudson River pier. Snorkey and a gang of street boys thwart them; Laura is thrown into the river, and Ray dives in after her.

Some time later, at an elegant country house, Ray is now engaged to Pearl. Laura is a reclusive guest, but she flees, still loving Ray. In a nearby woods, Snorkey overhears Byke and Old Judas plotting to murder Laura and rob Pearl. At a railroad, the fleeing Laura is exhausted and arranges to spend the night locked in a signal shed; Snorkey appears, but Byke captures him and puts him, tied, on the railroad track. Laura hacks her way out of the locked shed with an axe and rescues Snorkey just as the train roars by.

Back at the country house, Byke is stealing Pearl's jewels when Laura, Ray, and Snorkey catch him. Byke states that Pearl, not Laura, is the adopted child thief; Laura is a real Courtland. Peachblossom announces that Old Judas has been killed in an accident. Ray switches his engagement from Pearl back to Laura, and Snorkey is to marry Peachblossom.

Shifts in Western Drama after c. 1750

Three major cultural changes can be seen as underlying the shifts in drama after 1750.

The Rise of Sentimentality **Sentimentality** is the arousing of feelings out of proportion to their cause—"easy tears." Most often the cause is the situation or type rather than an individualized character, calling up a stereotype to which the sentimental feelings are already attached—the helpless child, the threatened virgin, or the faithful dog. Sentimentality reflects strong ideas of good and evil; believes in love, happiness, and virtue; uses many words and overblown language. Sentimentality emphasizes values that suited the age of commercialism: family, fidelity, loyalty, work, and obedience to superiors. There is nothing wrong with sentiment. Sympathy, feeling with others, is a human trait. Sentimentality is excessive feelings, evoked too easily.

To audiences new to the theatre, sentimentality was a satisfying response that let them feel at home in the medium. To the rising middle class, sentimentality allowed for easy tears that cost nothing: A businessman could weep over a hungry child, applaud the happy ending, and then go home and ignore his servants who had emigrated from the Irish famine only months before. Sentimentality became popular with audiences not interested in subtlety. Usually, it was socially conservative.

The Shift from the Active to the Acted-on Sentimentalism, unlike previous drama, was concerned with victims as much as with heroes. The result was a 180-degree turn from heroic drama to what one critic has called "losers' stories." The focus became victimization and the reaction to it instead of heroic effort in the face of opposition. Such victims were usually presented as single cases and were not generalized to cause the audience to think about a real social problem: The rural virgin threatened by the evil young aristocrat was not connected to larger issues, such as poverty and the exploitation of women.

The Collapse of Genre With the end of the "rules" of neoclassicism, the idea of genre started to crumble. Tragedy as the Greeks defined it pretty much ceased to exist except as "closet drama" (plays meant to be read but not performed) because the ideas that had

SENTIMENTAL VICTIMS
Melodrama thrived on victimization. Here, two stereotypical victims, the mother and the weeping child—caught in a snowstorm, no less.

defined tragedy had died. Melodrama took its place. Comedy became little more than a play with a happy ending or a funny play with gags.

Melodrama in the Commercial Theatre

Melodrama was the most popular dramatic style of the nineteenth century, although melodrama began even earlier. What audiences loved was its exploitation of unquestioned good and evil, with the good always under threat from evil but triumphing at the end. Almost as important was melodrama's sentimentality. Both the good-evil dichotomy and the sentimentality in which it was enveloped typified its audience's search for stability in a time of great change. In 1895, Oscar Wilde would lampoon this clear distinction of good and evil, having a character say of the plot of a novel, "The good ended happily, and the bad unhappily. That is what Fiction means."

Nineteenth-century stage melodrama has gone out of fashion and is even found funny now, so it is seldom revived. That said, what has to be remembered is how enjoyable melodramas were. They were full of energy, whipping from adventure to adventure; they had thrills, emotions, and a good deal of laughter—many of the melodramas were full of comic sequences. Their playwriting was often clumsy, the plot coincidences transparent, the language overblown, but melodramas gave enormous pleasure. Melodrama lives on in movies and television today, especially in action adventures.

Music

Melodrama means "music drama," a term taken from the widespread use of music within the plays. Melodramas used emotional music underscoring a scene, a technique that is still used in movies and television and some plays to push mood and to announce surprise or to build suspense. Music also appeared as **signature music**, the same theme played whenever a certain character entered or left or performed some

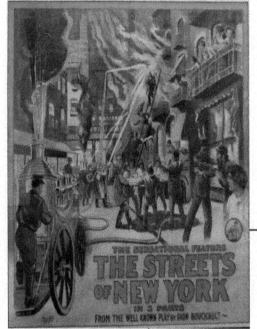

MELODRAMA

This genre dominated the popular theatre of the 1800s and early 1900s. Fires were great theatre; so were volcanoes, shipwrecks, threatening trains, floods, and disasters of all kinds. Here, a poster for *The Streets of New York* by Dion Boucicault. Melodramas, like this one, moved seamlessly into movies and then into television.

audience-arousing feat. A pit orchestra was essential to early melodrama; some melodramas also used vocal songs.

A Simplified Moral Universe

Melodrama presented a simplified moral universe in which good and evil were clear and were embodied by easily recognizable characters. Physical attractiveness typified the hero and heroine, usually in love with each other. Costume also announced their character types. These characters are often called **stock types** because they are not individualized, as if they were picked off a rack, from existing stock. Helping the hero was the comic man or sometimes comic woman, who often saved the hero and frustrated his enemies. It was evil, however, that propelled the action in the person of a villain, also recognizable by costume and physique and sometimes by social rank—a nobleman or landowner. He initiated the action by threatening the hero or heroine; he or she escaped, often saved by the comic man; the villain threatened again, and again there was an escape, and so on. The structure was thus episodic, progressing by threat and escape, each more extreme than the one before until the final incident, when hero and heroine might move from certain death to happy marriage within minutes.

Spectacle

Many romantic melodramas also depended on spectacle—fires, explosions, drownings, or earthquakes—as threats to the good characters or as obstacles to the villain. Many also featured animals, horses and dogs, and so were termed "equestrian dramas" and "canine melodramas." Movies such as *Lassie Come Home* and *National Velvet* thus had a long theatrical pedigree.

STOCK TYPES

The villain drove the action of melodramas. The comic man sometimes frustrated him and saved the hero or heroine for another attempt on them by the villain. Note the clothing; it clearly defines the character without a word of dialogue spoken.

The Stage Villain.

The Stage Comic Man.

Romantic interest in the sea and the navy during the Napoleonic Wars gave rise to "nautical melodramas." These, and "rustic" melodramas that took place in rural settings, "gothic" melodramas that we would call horror stories (e. g. *Dracula*), and others, filled the theatres. After 1850, middle-class theatres increasingly played **realistic melodramas**, and romantic melodramas increasingly became the fare of the lower-class theatres; but romantic melodrama persisted right through the period and moved seamlessly into silent movies.

Realistic Melodrama after c. 1850

Realistic melodrama began to appear about 1850. (The theatrical style known as Realism would not appear in the avant-garde theatres until the 1870s, although it had a few precursors that went back to the 1700s.) The **box set** of the 1830s was a step toward realistic interiors. A box set is a setting of a room with three visible walls; the proscenium is the fourth wall of the room, which is invisible so the audience can see the action in the room. The rise of a practical-minded business class shifted attention from the exotic and the never-never to the familiar and the utilitarian. The middle-class drawing room was a place to dramatize issues of money and status, including moral status and "belonging" in society. Thus, this realistic melodrama, also called **gentlemanly melodrama**, became a feature of middle-class theatres. It was less lurid in language and incident than romantic melodrama, its incidents themselves more carefully linked by cause and effect. Less reliant on violent spectacle, it put melodrama into middle-class costume but kept the action of threat and escape—for example, a well-to-do woman

THE BOX SET
The full placement of walls, doors, cornice, and ceiling define the box set. The furniture and properties are dimensional and "real."

threatened with revelation of her shady past—but sometimes extended a single threat and its resolution across the entire play. So common were the coincidental resolution of melodrama plots—scenes of the finding of a long-lost child or the reunion of long-separated mothers, children, brothers, or sisters, recognized by a locket or some other external sign—that they became a cliché satirized in comic plays such as Oscar Wilde's *The Importance of Being Earnest* (1895).

Most realistic melodramas remained wedded to victims, sentimentality, and social conservatism. No matter how realistic such plays might get, however, they remained a form of wish fulfillment, driven by an idea of how the audience *wished* people behaved rather than by how they *knew* they generally behaved. In essence, the wish fulfillment was the wish for social and cultural stability as defined by a patriarchal, commercial society—the ideas that long-lost children should be united with their parents, erring wives should be saved from themselves, or a bankrupt father should be rescued by secret benefactors. It was this social conservatism that kept melodrama from truly attacking social problems as realistic drama eventually did. Despite many plays about laboring people in laboring settings—mines, factories, ships, or farms—and despite a recurring tendency to make the villain an owner or a boss or an aristocrat, melodramas did not suggest that poverty, bad working conditions, or prostitution had systemic causes. Such a larger issue would require more of the audience than just a sentimental tear. Rather, the cause was always the villain—an individual, evil boss, or corrupt factory owner or seducer.

The Most Important Melodrama in English: *Uncle Tom's Cabin*

Probably the most important melodrama in the English language was *Uncle Tom's Cabin* (1852) based on the novel by Harriet Beecher Stowe. Published before the age of copyright in the United States, it was pirated, adapted, and translated without permission wherever there were theatres. The play remained strong through World War I (1914–1918), when more than a dozen companies were still touring it in the United States. Some actors spent their lives touring the play, and *Tomming* was a recognized actors' term that meant to appear in a staging of *Uncle Tom's Cabin*. The play included an escape across an ice-clogged river by a runaway slave pursued by dogs; a dead child being carried to heaven by angels; and virtuous Uncle Tom being beaten by the villain, Simon Legree. However, unlike most melodramatic plays, *Uncle Tom's Cabin* was tied to a social and moral issue: the horrors of slavery. When President Abraham Lincoln met Stowe during the US Civil War, he is reported to have said, "So you are the little woman who wrote the book that started this great war!"

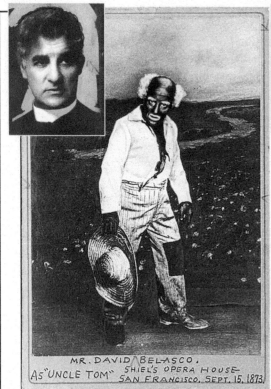

MR. DAVID BELASCO,
AS "UNCLE TOM"   SHIEL'S OPERA HOUSE
SAN FRANCISCO. SEPT. 15. 1873.

Miss "LOTTA" CRABTREE
AS "TOPSY"
PIKE'S OPERA HOUSE N.Y.
8TH AVE. & 23rd St.
1868 .

WHITE ACTORS, BLACK FACES

David Belasco and Lotta Crabtree were two of the most famous US white actors who appeared in blackface makeup in *Uncle Tom's Cabin* in the latter half of the nineteenth century. The images on these souvenir photos may be laughable (or insulting) today, but audiences of the time took white performers in black makeup seriously, at least in this play. Audiences could cry at the plight of African American slaves before the Civil War without noticing the continuing segregation that led to white actors making a living acting out black heartbreak. The inset pictures show the actors as they generally appeared.

Playwrights of Melodrama

Most melodramas, both romantic and realistic, were written by hacks hired by the theatres. Only specialists recall their names. Buffalo Bill Cody, for example, toured for years in hack melodramas about the West before he started the Wild West Show. Gentlemanly melodramas, on the other hand, were sometimes written by eminent but now forgotten literary people. An author important to subsequent playwrights was the Irish-American Dion Boucicault. His first success was *London Assurance* (1841), a farcical comedy, with crossed lovers, people in disguise, plots, and ploys, all by city people in a country house. Boucicault's plays are rarely revived although they can be fun. He wrote a great variety of melodramatic plays, including a gothic play, *The Vampire*

THE MOST FAMOUS MELODRAMA IN THE WORLD
Uncle Tom's Cabin toured the world for generations in various adaptations. Here, it is being played in Paris about 1900. The poster advertises a US production about 1890.

(1852), and topical melodramas placed in the United States, including *The Poor of New York* (1857) and *The Octoroon or Life in Louisiana* (1859). He continued to write plays until the early 1880s.

The Octoroon—the word means a person who is one-eighth African American—takes place on a plantation. A nephew of the plantation owner returns from France and falls in love with one of his uncle's daughters, a girl born of the uncle and a slave woman. The plantation is under threat from an unpaid mortgage. McClosky, the evil man causing the plantation to go under, kills a slave boy who arrives with legal papers to halt the sale. At a crucial moment, someone appears with a photograph proving that McClosky killed the boy. McClosky escapes jail and sets on fire a steamboat that carries slaves from the plantation. In the US version, the octoroon despairs and drinks poison. In the British production, the nephew and the octoroon are united in a happy ending. With either ending, that is a lot of plot—and typical of melodrama of this era.

Boucicault is important in the history of playwriting because he demanded a percentage of box office receipts instead of a flat fee, thus starting the practice of **royalties**. By 1866, the first international copyright agreement was made, partly because of Boucicault, allowing playwrights to share the spoils of commercialism.

Melodrama after 1900

Melodrama remained a dominant genre into the last third of the twentieth century, although toned down in its excesses of both action and language by the development of realism. For example, the plays of Lillian Hellman (active in the theatre from 1934–1960) are largely melodrama. Melodrama is still, for

example, the genre of soap opera on television and the suspense thriller on film, as well as of many plays in which an unquestioned assumption of goodness is threatened by unquestioned badness, with goodness and badness more recently defined not in moral terms but in terms of power—the sensitive loner oppressed by heartless prudery or the AIDS victim oppressed by small-minded fear.

Comedy in the Commercial Theatre

With the collapse of genre, the comedy of this period was not the comedy of Greece, Hellenism, or neoclassicism. "Plays with happy endings" might better define many comic plays of the period from 1750 through 1900 and perhaps as late as 1950. But most melodramas had satisfying endings as well. So comedy must be understood to include a wide range of other than melodramatic plays, from satire to situation comedy and farce, with happy endings and a predominantly light tone.

Shakespeare was a dominant figure in comedies in this period. His romantic comedies, with their stellar female roles, offered the nineteenth-century culture female examples who were attractive, often witty, virtuous, and ultimately subservient to males—Viola (*Twelfth Night*), Rosalind (*As You Like It*), Isabella (*Measure for Measure*), Beatrice (*Much Ado about Nothing*), and Portia (*The Merchant of Venice*). They became nineteenth-century icons throughout Europe and the United States.

Sheridan and Goldsmith: English Comic Playwrights

Early comic plays, created in either monopoly theatres or theatres in transition to commercialism, partook of the older sentimental comedy but often made gentle fun of sentimentalism itself. They kept some of the character types and stock scenes of Restoration comedy, but their characters were mostly less aristocratic and their concerns more middle class. In England the leading comic authors before 1800 were Richard Brinsley Sheridan (1751–1816), whose plays included *The School for Scandal* and *The Rivals*, and Oliver Goldsmith (1730–1774), author of *She Stoops to Conquer* and others. Both authors are regularly revived today.

The Rivals, for example, was a favorite play of the British royal family and of George Washington. A comedy of manners set in fashionable Bath, its primary story is of two lovers, Lydia and Jack. Because Lydia longs for a pure romantic love, Jack pretends to be an ordinary army officer instead of what he is, the son of a wealthy and titled man. There are promises; interfering parents; arranged betrothals, which are unwanted by at least one party; a duel; and a happy ending. *The Rivals* includes a secondary character whose comic errors have been imitated in plays, television, and film comedies throughout time, and her name is used for a type of syntactical error now called the *malaprop*. Mrs. Malaprop can be relied on to choose a word that sounds like what she means but is very much the wrong word. She says of Jack, "He is the very pineapple of politeness!" meaning, of course, "pinnacle." Another of many instances: "I hope you will represent her [Malaprop's daughter] to the captain as an object not altogether illegible." She means to say "ineligible."

ENGLISH COMEDY

Richard Brinsley Sheridan's *The School for Scandal*, which was a comedy of manners like many of the comedies of the Restoration but with sentimentalism instead of cynicism, opened at the Theatre Royal in Drury Lane in 1777. Here, a production at University of Missouri-Columbia.

France and the Well-Made Play Beginning in 1815

The most popular comic playwright in Europe and the United States before 1850, however, was Eugène Scribe, who created more than three hundred plays for Parisian theatres, including for the former monopoly venue, the Comédie Française. He wrote opera librettos and some of his nonmusical plays were the basis of opera texts. The translation and international production of Scribe's plays made French comedy a model for the world. Scribe's playwriting technique—careful preparation for what is to come, meticulous networks of relationships, apparent chains of cause and effect—gave the impression of tight causality when, in fact, the plays were built around multiple lines of action that touched mostly by chance or coincidence. The expression the **well-made play** was applied to these techniques, first as a compliment and in the late twentieth century as a term of contempt. Nonetheless, it worked brilliantly for Scribe's audiences and served as an example to later, more socially engaged writers such as Ibsen. In a few plays, Scribe used these techniques to touch on contemporary problems, leading to the term *problem play*. **Problem plays**, although technically comedies, at least acknowledged contemporary social flaws; their resolutions, however, avoided suggesting how society could correct itself. Scribe could also write witty dramatic prose and sparkling farce.

Oscar Wilde

In England, Oscar Wilde (1854–1900) wrote perhaps the best and still the most often revived comedy since the Restoration, *The Importance of Being Earnest,* an apparently frivolous look at upper-class mores and duplicity. Wilde was a critic and cultural commentator before he was a playwright. His first plays were drawing room melodramas leavened with high wit. *Earnest* was another thing altogether, taking many of the conventions of melodrama and extending them into absurdity. One famous scene is when the redoubtable Lady Bracknell interviews a potential husband for her daughter.

Lady Bracknell	Do you smoke?
Jack	Well, yes, I must admit I smoke.
Lady Bracknell	I am glad to hear it. A man should always have an occupation of some kind. There are far too many idle men in London as it is....I have always been of opinion that a man who desires to get married should know either everything or nothing. Which do you know?
Jack	*[After some hesitation.]* I know nothing, Lady Bracknell.
Lady Bracknell	I am pleased to hear it. I do not approve of anything that tampers with natural ignorance. Ignorance is like a delicate exotic fruit; touch it and the bloom is gone. The whole theory of modern education is radically unsound. Fortunately in England, at

Jack	any rate, education produces no effect whatsoever....Are your parents living?
	I have lost both parents.
Lady Bracknell	To lose one parent, Mr. Worthing, may be regarded as a misfortune; to lose both looks like carelessness.

Wilde had three plays successfully running in London's commercial theatres in 1895 when he was convicted of gross indecency—essentially of being a homosexual—and sentenced to two years in prison at hard labor. This virtually ended his playwriting career. The government revoked his copyright to his writings. He died in exile in France in 1900, at age forty-six.

HOW WE KNOW

Early Theatre Photography

Photography became a popular marketing tool of the commercial theatre by the mid-1800s when photos became widely available. Photographs of theatrical personalities taken more than 150 years ago give historians access to the actual look of performers, costumes, settings, and makeup of the mid-nineteenth century. Photographs were sold as souvenirs of a performance and collected by people who might rarely see theatre but were fascinated by the lives of the famous.

Photography was invented about 1826. By about 1840 negative images on translucent materials and on glass were made that could be printed inexpensively in one copy or hundreds. From 1854, there were popular, standardized small prints called *cartes de visite* because they were the size of a calling card, about the size of a modern business card. Starting in 1870 larger prints supplanted the cartes de visite. These images were called "cabinet cards" because they were large enough to be seen when displayed on top of furniture, about 4 1/4 by 6 1/2 inches. Cabinet cards featured private individuals and families, furniture and sculpture, political and social figures, authors, circus and variety performers like Tom Thumb and Annie Oakley, and actors. The popularity of cabinet cards waned toward the end of the nineteenth century, but they continued to be produced into the early 1920s.

The cabinet card process took strong lighting and long exposure times, thus subjects were usually shot in photographers' studios, standing still. The earliest known stage photo is from 1883 when a theatre studio photographer used temporarily installed electric light to capture a scene of an otherwise forgotten play, *The Russian Honeymoon*. Photographs taken on theatre sets became common after 1900, facilitated by faster, more sensitive exposure media and the adoption of electric lighting in theatres.

Today, photography is so commonplace that it can be difficult to imagine how astounding it was in the nineteenth century, documenting history and culture with an immediacy and specificity that painting and etchings could not match.

Here, a cabinet card taken by Benjamin Joseph Falk of the 1887 melodrama The Wife, *written and produced by David Belasco and Henry C. De Mille. In this scene, someone is discovered lurking behind a curtain. The character on the right is astounded.*

Reactions to the Commercial Theatre

As a result of melodrama and the well-made-play, theatre flourished, but the more popular it became, the more predictable and vapid it seemed to some artists. A series of reformers began to try to put creativity and meaning into the theatre. They usually couched their pleas in terms of art, often asking for a return to "serious" drama and "important" theatre. All were successful in that many of their innovations gradually migrated to the commercial stage, changing its character in some ways, expanding its repertory of storytelling methods. But all failed. Theatre never recovered its cultural centrality. Political, economic, and cultural power had become decentralized and the technological innovations awaiting theatre in the twentieth century would further disperse theatre's power.

Think of 1640 and of our own time as the extremes. Cardinal Richelieu, through the French Academy, could mandate rules of art for all French-speaking culture. In twenty-first-century United States, cultural power is spread from New York to Hollywood, with other centers in sports, e-commerce, universities, and many other locations, as well as individuals as diverse as Lady Gaga, Kim Kardashian, and Mark Zuckerberg. In the United States, the one place where cultural power is *not* centered is the national capital; there is now an almost complete separation between cultural power and political power. In Richelieu's day, the two were identical.

Theatrical innovators—reformers—saw their own declining centrality, but they tried to aim their demands for seriousness and art at a world that was going or already gone. The commercial theatre, however, was happy to incorporate such innovations as pleased its audience and by doing so, create something excitingly new.

KEY TERMS

Key terms are in boldface type in the text. Check your understanding against this list. Persons are page-referenced in the Index.

actor-manager, p. 173

box set, p. 180

combination companies, p. 174

commercial theatre, p. 169

director-manager, p. 173

gentlemanly melodrama, p. 180

melodrama, p. 178

problem play, p. 186

producer, p. 173

realistic melodrama, p. 180

repertory, p. 174

royalties, p. 183

sentimentality, p. 177

signature music, p. 178

star system, p. 174

stock types, p. 179

Theatrical Syndicate, p. 175

well-made play, p. 186

Chapter 8 at a Glance

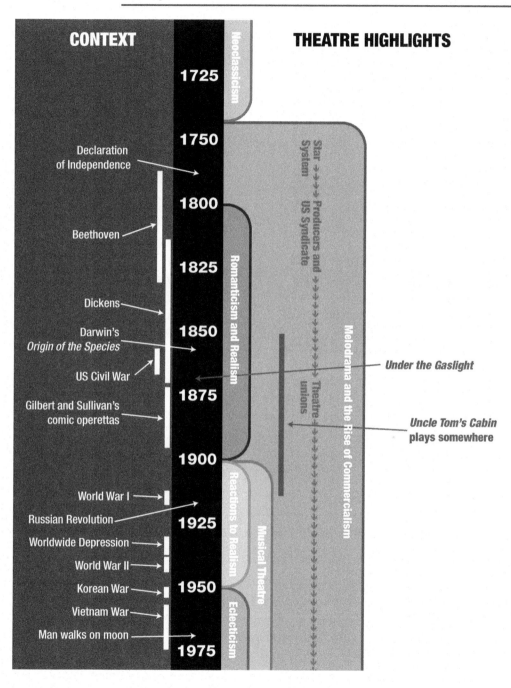

CONTEXT

THEATRE HIGHLIGHTS

Neoclassicism

1725

1750

Declaration of Independence

Star ⟶⟶⟶ Producers and US Syndicate
System

1800

Beethoven

1825

Romanticism and Realism

Dickens

Darwin's *Origin of the Species*

1850

US Civil War

Under the Gaslight

Melodrama and the Rise of Commercialism

1875

Gilbert and Sullivan's comic operettas

Theatre unions

Uncle Tom's Cabin plays somewhere

1900

World War I

Reactions to Realism

Russian Revolution

1925

Worldwide Depression

Musical Theatre

World War II

Korean War

1950

Vietnam War

Eclecticism

Man walks on moon

1975

Romanticism and Realism, 1750–1900

When you have completed this, chapter you should be able to:

- List and describe the major tenets of romanticism.
- Compare realism and naturalism.
- Discuss the major leaders of realism and naturalism.
- Sketch the arrangement of audience in the theatre before and after Wagner.
- Describe changes in acting in the shift from romanticism to realism.
- Name and discuss the major playwrights of romanticism and realism.
- Describe the box set and the "fourth wall."

Context

What do these things have in common?

- The Declaration of Independence, 1776

- *Frankenstein*, the novel by Mary Shelley published in 1818

- "'Beauty is truth, truth beauty,'–that is all / Ye know on earth, and all ye need to know." A line from John Keats' poem "Ode on a Grecian Urn," published in 1820

- *The Rights of Man*, a book by Thomas Paine, published in 1791, arguing that revolution is justified when the government does not protect the people's rights or interests

FRANKENSTEIN

Frankenstein was an 1818 novel by Mary Shelley about a scientist and his creation of a living man. The monster is a twisted emblem of two of romanticism's ideas: he is a natural man in one sense, not raised in society, so he could express the ideals of nature, and on the other hand, he is the creation of soulless science. The story has been adapted for film and many times for the stage, here in a production at the National Theatre, London, in 2011.

These disparate things are united in two ways: First, they fall into the same hundred years, and second, they are expressions of **romanticism**, a radical cultural shift that affected politics, economics, and culture.

The period from about 1750 to 1850 was when the world turned upside down. The upheavals included political revolutions, the Industrial Revolution, population migrating to cities, steam power, cheaper printed matter, railroads, and photography. For the first time, nations supported compulsory education. The international slave trade was outlawed by Britain, the ban enforced by its navy. Out of this turmoil, the cultural and intellectual cluster now called romanticism came into being.

A Cluster of Ideas and Impulses

Romanticism as a cultural phenomenon should not be confused with the words *romance* or *romantic*, referring to love or sexual attraction. *Romanticism* springs from the same historic root as "romance" and "romantic" but its meaning is unconnected to them.

We now tend to think of romanticism as a set of theoretical ideas. It is as accurate to think of it as a set of effects, which were later articulated as theoretical ideas by several people in several countries at more or less the same time. Those ideas then became causes for change in their turn, in what we might now call a feedback loop. Romanticism included political ideas as well as ideas about society, psychology, art, and the nature of the world. It was only secondarily about the theatre. Moreover, the ideas of romanticism were not necessarily consistent. Nonetheless, long after the fact we can see five certain common interests:

- Rebellion.
  Romanticism was revolutionary. In art, romanticism wanted to overturn neoclassicism. In politics, equality and the idea of a social contract binding government and governed were romantic. Socially, early feminism, personal religion, and opposition to slavery were romantic. Romanticism railed against a status quo that inhibited individualism and equality.

- Art with a capital *A*.
  Creative and intellectual romantics all but invented the idea of Art as a special activity. The Artist was a special being—a creative genius able to see truths hidden from others. The Artist was inspired. Before romanticism, artists were considered as specialized crafts people. Looking back after romanticism, the artists of periods before romanticism were also seen in hindsight as creative geniuses.

- Nature.
  Natural feelings were more reliable than reason or authority. Civilization and education corrupted nature. Children, savages, and peasants were uncorrupted, therefore nearer innocence. Nature was a window through which the child and the Artist could see Truth.

- Anti-industrialism.
  Art and beauty were "sublime"; factories were "dark Satanic mills." Cities were unnatural and corrupting. Early industrialists were seen by romantics as greedy bean counters without souls—the opposite of the Artist. Industry was ugly with its noise, smoke, and massive buildings and therefore the opposite of Beauty.

- Uniqueness.
  Truth was to be found in the particular, not the general. To establish uniqueness was to establish identity.

People at the time did not necessarily see these five ideas clearly. Political activists saw mostly their own impatience with top-down government; artists saw their own disgust with top-down "rules" of neoclassicism; middle-class people saw their own distaste for slavery or slums or dreadful working conditions. Many literate people picked up the jargon of romantic art—*sublime, picturesque, grotesque*—and, insofar as they used it, they were "romantic," but the spread of the jargon probably had more to do with increasing mass communications than with commitment. Romanticism was new, the latest thing. Depending on one's position at the time, romanticism was either tremendously exciting or decadent and dangerous.

BOOTH'S PLAYHOUSE

The interior of Edwin Booth's playhouse reveals that by 1869 some theatres had eliminated the proscenium doors. Instead there are three boxes close to the stage. Note the orchestra seating and three balconies. This watercolor reveals the bright colors and decorative detail of many nineteenth-century theatres.

Romanticism still has a contemporary feel. If you could step back right now into the world of 1740, you would find its culture and its behavior alien, but if you could step back into the world of 1820, you would find some of it familiar—ideas about individualism, freedom of choice, human rights, and the environment. To be sure, you would have to land among the right people—mostly upper middle class and educated—but if you did, you would see why romanticism is still important: It was the beginning of our world of individuals and self-expression.

Romanticism in the Theatre

The effects on the theatre were significant, if erratic. Romantic theatre artists disdained both neoclassicism *and* frivolous theatre and tried to reform both. They began slowly and unevenly, and they were rejected by conservative theatres. Contradictorily, it was in the monopoly theatres that the romantics wanted to see their ideas applied—that, after all, was where the connection with power had been and where the connection to the upper class still was.

Yet the places where romantic ideas crept on to the stage partly unnoticed were nonmonopoly theatres. The ideas were "in the air"; they had come, after all, from the same causes that led ordinary people to see and think in new ways, including to see and think in new ways as audiences in the theatre. International trade and imperialism, for example, created a knowledge of exotic places; thus, foreign locales began to show up in plays and settings. The new interest in childhood and primitivism brought children, common people, American Indians, peasants, and Africans to the stage, both as hot topics for hack playwrights and as real concerns of intellectuals. Plays were set in newly detailed scenery of forests, dungeons, jungles, caves, both because new plays required them and because visual artists were themselves now more interested in nature and detail. New technologies also made detailed scenery more convincing. The new faith in feelings brought plays that appealed to emotions rather than intellect.

Romantics Revive Shakespeare

Romantics revived Shakespeare, finding in his work the breadth and the emotional power they prized. From the 1770s until well after 1900, his plays remained among the most often produced in the world.

In England, most of all, then in Germany and the United States, Shakespeare was elevated to a cultural icon. His plays were performed from London to the California gold fields; they were read aloud in Hamburg drawing rooms and around the fires of the fur-trapping "mountain men" of the western United States. Frontier families, if they had any books, had the Bible and the works of Shakespeare. The King James Bible and Shakespeare became a binding force of English-language culture that gave it a frame of reference, a common elevated language, and a common rhythm that lasted well into the twentieth century. In France, however, where neoclassicism persisted longer, Shakespeare was not seen on the stage until an English company brought the plays to Paris in the 1830s.

Playing Shakespeare's tragic roles became the test of an actor. A great Hamlet or a great Juliet was an international star. Lines from the plays were common in everyday speech; the characters were role models. It was Shakespeare, along with the Bible, that gave a changing society connectedness. Attempts to imitate Shakespeare were generally unsuccessful, however; what audiences wanted in new plays was something emotional, prosaic, and spectacular.

Romanticism in Germany, England, and France

The most conscious efforts to introduce romantic ideas in the theatre came in dramatic theory and drama. Especially in Germany, a distinct body of "serious" romantic plays was written and is still in the German repertory. A recognizable gap appeared, however, between serious, literary, "important" plays and popular ones in France and England. Over the long haul, Art lost, in part because of the Artists' unresolved contradictory impulses. For Art to win, it would have to reach large audiences. If something reached large audiences, it was commercial theatre—the antithesis of Art.

Germany

Romantic drama found its home in Germany. Germany produced a seminal theoretical work, Gotthold Lessing's *Hamburg Dramaturgy* (1770), which rejected French neoclassicism as a model and recommended instead Shakespeare. Lessing said that the aim of drama should be to give a real representation of life. Lessing

- Recommended natural language.
- Demanded that drama should come from interesting and vigorous characters and should engender sympathy as well as surprise.
- Praised sentimental comedy and domestic tragedy.
- Argued for heroes who were human beings, not aristocratic or royal titles.
- Disparaged borrowed dramatic forms such as neoclassicism.
- Believed sincerity in character and plot to be an important requisite of drama.

Lessing also wrote several plays, including so-called philosophical dramas. The most lasting—as a literary, not a theatrical—work was *Nathan the Wise*. Set in Jerusalem during the Third Crusade, its themes are friendship, tolerance, relativism of God, and a rejection of miracles. The church forbade performance of the play during Lessing's lifetime. The Nazis banned the play as well.

Storm and Stress *Hamburg Dramaturgy*, and especially its urging of Shakespeare as a model, in turn influenced young German radicals calling themselves the ***Sturm und Drang* (storm and stress)**, an in-your-face term of the day. Two of the greatest Sturm und Drang radicals were to write German classics. Johann Wolfgang von Goethe (1749–1832) wrote the play *Faust*, an acknowledged literary masterpiece, but not a theatrical one, in part because it takes more than twenty hours to stage and the second half calls for extraordinary settings and transformations hardly possible in the technology of the time.

GERMAN ROMANTICISM
Lessing's *Nathan the Wise*, here in an English translation at Wake Forest University, is set in Jerusalem in the time of the crusades. Nathan is a wise Jewish merchant who argues for religious tolerance.

The other great German theatre romantic was Friedrich von Schiller (1759–1805), whose commitment to liberty showed in *The Robbers* and *William Tell*, both successes that led to many imitations. Much about romanticism can be suggested by the subjects of these plays—love and loss, liberty, the fight against despotism, free will and wisdom—as do the kinds of characters—robbers, rebels, lovers, questioners. Perhaps most significant is the form of the plays, whose authors demanded the right to roam freely in time and space and not be limited by "the unities" or other neoclassical notions.

England

In England, however, attempts to create a serious body of romantic drama labored too closely in the shadow of Shakespeare. Attempts to imitate Shakespeare ruined many plays. Further, serious English romantics refused to meet the needs of the theatre, including pleasing the audience. Even when England's great poets tried seriousness in the theatre, they usually failed. The internationally esteemed romantic poet Lord Byron did write a tragedy that worked, *Werner*, a lurid tale of revenge and despair, but it barely escaped the trap into which most serious romantic drama fell—that of mistaking the most extreme moments of Shakespearean tragedy as the essence of the tragedy. Shakespearean tragedy's effectiveness is found in the contrasts of crowds and soliloquies, extreme and commonplace, and the comic and the extremely dramatic. English romantics who wanted to bring a new seriousness to the theatre were not alone in thus failing to find a dramaturgy to match the emotional expression in which they believed. The resulting plays therefore often lacked internal probability and had long passages of great dullness separating moments of incredible bombast. Romantic language pushed the envelope and sometimes became wild, torrential, and overblown—a verbal eruption to match the emotional eruptions of its heroes. Few of these plays have lasted. Rather, Italian operas made from the plays have endured, in which music supplied the unity and subtlety that the spoken dramas did not.

France

In Paris, romantic dramas made it to the nonmonopoly theatres in 1790 but were shut out of the hidebound Comédie Française until 1830, when Victor Hugo's romantic drama *Hernani* was staged and caused a riot. The riot was not unprovoked. There was an antagonism between the old guard in the arts and the romantic young guard.

The theatre at this time often had *claqueurs*, paid audiences who would applaud or boo, depending on who was paying. To keep old fogies from dominating the reception of *Hernani*, Hugo got an opening night

THE AUDIENCE RIOTS

The first performance of *Hernani* caused a riot at the Comédie Française as this 1930 painting illustrates. The riot was orchestrated by Victor Hugo, *Hernani*'s author, in hopes of drawing attention to his romantic drama.

crowd of young people—poor and artistic types—to attend. These proto-bohemians came early, brought food with them, sang, and drank. When the custodians of the Comédie would not unlock the doors to the restrooms, the young people did what nature demanded in the theatre itself and made a smelly mess of it. The establishment audience members were aghast when they arrived. The scandal paid off for Hugo, and *Hernani* ran for one hundred performances. After *Hernani*, the Comédie was belatedly and briefly revived by the energy of romanticism, but romanticism itself ran out of steam a few years later, so watered down in the popular theatres by that time that storm, stress, and riot fizzled.

Romanticism Dwindles

Drama had been caught in a contradiction: Serious literary romantics wanted to create Art for a sensitive audience, therefore, a limited audience. The extreme artistic position was **closet drama,** plays written to be read, not staged. Theatres needed to bring in the largest possible audience to survive financially.

Romanticism was pretty well over as a coherent movement by the 1840s. It had succeeded in destroying neoclassicism; it had planted its flag at the Comédie Française; the English monopoly "patent" theatres had died of old age; and German theatre had had what one source calls its Golden Age. Romantic drama had not reformed the theatre on the whole, however.

What persisted was sentimentalism, which trivialized romanticism and matched Victorian taste, middle class, fussy, and "moral." Romantics established the *image* of the Artist—special, gifted, emotional, and inspired—and of Art, which entered Victorian culture as a kind of secular religion. To a great extent, many people today still share the romantic idea of the Artist and of Art.

An Aftershock: Richard Wagner, a Romantic Artist, Flourishing 1842–1882

Richard Wagner, the opera composer, had a huge ego and knew he was a genius in the romantic mold. His influence on modern theatre has been enormous for two innovations: (1) the idea of unity in production brought about by a unifying artist and (2) a separate, classless audience space in the theatre.

Unity through the Master Artwork

Wagner's concept of a unified theatrical production was called the **gesamtkunstwerk (master artwork)**, meaning a total art work incorporating pictorial art, drama, and music conceived and executed by a "master artist" who would control the whole show—ideally Richard Wagner himself. The idea would go far to pave the way for the importance of the director in the modern theatre.

The Separated Audience

In 1876, Wagner got his own theatre at Bayreuth, paid for by his former patron Ludwig II, King of Bavaria. It epitomized his ideas: several nested proscenium arches between audience and actors, not just one; a hidden orchestra pit; steam jets between audience and playing area to emphasize a "mystic chasm"—the separation of the master artwork from the audience.

Perhaps more important, Wagner put his audience in the dark and got rid of box, pit, and gallery. Now, the audience sat in a fan-shaped orchestra

WAGNER THE THEORETICIAN

The interior of Wagner's theatre in Bayreuth was an important influence on the future of theatre architecture and audience seating. Wagner eliminated box, pit, and gallery, thus creating the most common modern audience arrangement and putting the emphasis on the proscenium arches and what went on within them.

that was "classless," and every seat had an equally good view of the stage. Called **continental seating**, the arrangement became standard in the twentieth century.

The effect was in one sense a democratic one, but it had the autocratic effect of putting the entire audience in the same passive surrender to the stage—no catcalls from upper galleries, no bored aristocrats whispering in boxes. It was a theatre space in which the master artist gave and the audience received. This architectural expression reinforced the idea of the artist as genius and the audience as passive watchers-in-the-dark that has largely persisted for music and theatre to this day.

Reform after Romanticism: Realism and Naturalism, from c. 1850

The phenomenal popularity of commercial theatres with their melodramas and sentimental comedies in the nineteenth century did little to satisfy reformers. What they saw was a theatre with a huge audience, doing productions that used the best technology of the day, all of which seemed to them wasted in sheer overproduction and on the production of trivial plays. Again, a call for "seriousness" would come; this time, however, the buzzword would be not romanticism, but **realism.**

The idea that art should show real life was hardly new. It was implicit in Renaissance theory, explicit in every portrait or still life that was painted. Virtually every new art movement to this time saw itself as more real than those that came before. A literal rendering of life became available with the invention of photography about 1840. In the theatre, local color and scenic detail dated to the eighteenth century, as did the prototype of the box set, an imitation of a room with side walls rather than wings probably dating from 1841. The box set was common by the end of the romantic period. In drama, commercial playwrights were writing problem plays that seemed to examine real-life issues. Even painted scenery became more realistic. An important early artist in painted scenery was Philippe-Jacques Loutherbourg, a Swiss national working in London in the 1770s. In a forest scene on stage, for example, the green trees gradually turned red, and the moon rose lighting up the clouds, an effect accomplished by semitransparent drops that were gradually lit from behind. These effects are a commonplace in today's theatre but were stunning in the late eighteenth century.

By the 1850s, problems of inequality, industrialization, and urbanization were well known and widely discussed. Urban poverty was on the rise and with it urban crime. Fear of political instability led toward repression, which fanned dissatisfaction. The new radical realists demanded that art respond to these problems. Art should not be only about deep feelings

PAINTING WITH LIGHT

Philippe-Jacques Loutherbourg was, beginning in 1771, David Garrick's scene painter at the Theatre Royal Drury Lane. He was famed for painting specific places with dramatic lighting. His stage designs do not survive, but many of his paintings give a sense of his evocation of light through paint. Here, a painting from 1801, of the Iron Works at Coalbrookdale, England.

or sensations. Art should be a mirror of the world and ultimately be a force to change the world. Science was offering new theories that threatened old ideas. Charles Darwin proposed evolution in his 1859 book *Origin of the Species*, which left humanity without its uniqueness in creation, apparently at the mercy of environment. Psychology as a field for scientific study emerged around 1879 and at century's end, Sigmund Freud proposed the *unconscious*, which undermined the notion of good intentions. What good were one's intentions if one's actions were influenced by emotions and perceptions one was not consciously aware of? One effect of the birth of evolution and the unconscious was to displace romantic ideas, especially romanticism's optimism and faith in nature as a window on the ideal. Instead, nature was the driven by the survival of the fittest. The impact on serious Art, including theatre, was to turn art toward questioning and challenging the status quo.

Important Leaders of Realism and Naturalism

Realists—and their more extreme relatives, advocates of **naturalism**—believed that truth resided in the material objects observable in the physical, external world. The realists were also objectivists: They believed that truth could be discovered through the application of scientific observation and could be replicated by a series of objective observers, not by a single romantic inspiration.

According to the realists and the naturalists, the function of art, like that of science, was the betterment of humankind, and the method of the artist should be that of the scientist. Plays should be set in contemporary times and places, for only they could be observed firsthand by the playwright. Because the highest purpose of art was the betterment of

REALISM IN MOSCOW
Here, Anton Chekhov's *The Three Sisters* at the Moscow Art Theatre in a realistic setting from 1901.

humanity, the subject of plays should be contemporary life and its problems. This was not art for art's sake!

Although sharing with realists a belief in science as a solver of problems, the naturalists differed in their definition of what problems most needed attention and in their hope for the future. The naturalists stressed the problems of the poor and tended to be pessimistic about their solution. According to the naturalists, people were victims, not players in life. Their destiny was controlled by factors like heredity and environment, over which they had little influence. Because the naturalists attempted to give the impression that their plays were an actual record of life, the dramas often appeared formless and unstructured, traits that gave rise to the phrase "a slice of life" to describe some naturalists' plays.

Georg II, Duke of Saxe-Meiningen

One of the earliest creators of realistic staging was Georg II, Duke of Saxe-Meiningen, flourishing from the 1870s to the 1890s. (Saxe-Meiningen was a duchy in what today is Germany that covered an area of about one thousand square miles.) In some ways, the duke was merely perfecting and popularizing ideals of staging promulgated much earlier; nonetheless, he influenced later realists around the world.

Saxe-Meiningen objected to many practices of the commercial mainstream because they resulted in productions that were not internally consistent; they lacked unity and seemed artificial. For the duke and his court theatre, the art of the theatre was the art of providing the *illusion* of reality; he therefore sought methods of production that would lead to "an intensified reality and [would] give remote events the quality of actuality, of being lived for the first time." To this end, the duke stressed historically accurate scenery, costumes, and properties; lifelike acting; and unity.

Production Practices The duke believed that all elements of a production required coordination. The setting must be an integral part of the play and not just a background, and so he encouraged his actors to move *within* the setting rather than merely playing in front of it. If actors were to move within an environment, the scenic details had to be three-dimensional rather than painted, and so actual objects were used in the settings. He used authentic fabrics instead of the cheaper substitutes often seen in commercial theatres of the day. Simultaneously, the duke strove to provide several levels (e.g., rocks, steps, and platforms) so that the scenic design would not stop abruptly at the stage floor.

Although Georg II is often solely credited with the theatre's work, his wife, an actress and musician, Ellen Franz, worked with him as did the former actor Ludwig Chronegk, who under the duke's direction and financial support, created the role of theatre director.

Acting There were no stars in Saxe-Meiningen's group. Each member of the company was eligible to play any role; and each member, if not cast as a major character, was required to play in crowd scenes, something commercial stars never did. Each actor in a crowd scene was given lines and actions and put into a sub-group led by an experienced actor. Actors were to avoid

MEININGEN'S CROWDS

The new stage realism—individualized crowd members, varying levels, and varied postures and arm positions—is shown in an engraving of the funeral-oration scene in *Julius Caesar*. The Duke of Saxe-Meiningen is said to be the first director, although he had predecessors.

parallel lines on stage, to make stage crosses diagonally rather than parallel with the curtain line, to keep one foot off the ground whenever possible (by placing it on a step or by kneeling on one knee), and not to copy his or her neighbor's stance. Actors were told to look at one another rather than the audience, to react to what was said and done onstage, and to behave naturally, even if it meant delivering a line while not facing the audience. Makeup was based on historical portraits. These practices now seem obvious, but in the 1870s they were startling.

Influence Beginning eight years after the duke took over the theatre, the Meiningen company began touring western Europe and Russia. The troupe gave more than 2,800 performances in thirty-six cities. From these performances came its international reputation and its influence.

André Antoine and the *Théâtre-Libre*

André Antoine (1858–1943), an amateur actor, abhorred the commercial theatres of Paris; disapproved of the way actors were trained at France's leading school for actors, the Paris *Conservatoire*; objected to the scenic practices of the major theatres; and decried the flimsiness of contemporary popular drama. What was needed, Antoine concluded, was a theatre in which new and controversial plays could get realistic productions. Therefore, when an amateur group to which he belonged balked at producing a new play, Antoine undertook the production himself and, spurred by early success, became the full-time director of his own new theatre in 1888. He named it the *Théâtre-Libre* (Free Theatre) and described it as nothing less than "a machine of war, poised for the conquest of Paris." It was a "free" theatre because it was not beholden to government nor exposed to governmental censorship. It was, among other things, an alternative theatre. It is worth noting the differences between Antoine and Saxe-Meiningen at this point:

- Antoine was far more interested in new plays. He produced plays by Henrik Ibsen, Gerhart Hauptman, Leo Tolstoy, August Strindberg, and Ivan Turgenev, among others. Saxe-Meiningen often produced romantic plays and plays by Shakespeare in realistic styles, not the new realistic plays.

- Antoine sidestepped tough government censorship by running a subscription theatre. Because Saxe Meiningen controlled his own duchy, he was not concerned with censorship.

- Antoine had to make a theatre from scratch. Saxe-Meiningen had his own court theatre.

Plays Although Antoine produced a wide range of plays at the Théâtre-Libre, he seemed most comfortable with plays in the realistic and naturalistic styles.

THE FREE THEATRE IN EUROPE
After Antoine established the *Théâtre Libre* in 1888, the theatre closed a few years later due to financial problems. Antoine reopened the same space in 1897 as the *Théâtre Antoine*. In 1943, Simone Berriau continued the management of the theatre, adding her name to the marquee. Berriau continued the Antoine tradition of producing a wide range of European plays; her first production was by French philosopher, novelist, and playwright Jean-Paul Sartre. Here, the play being presented in 2006 is a French translation of Wilde's *The Importance of Being Earnest*.

As a members' only organization, the Théâtre-Libre was able to introduce to Parisians a wide range of French and foreign authors whose works were considered too scandalous for production in major theatres.

Production Practices: The "Fourth Wall" Antoine believed with the naturalists that environment influenced human behavior, so he made his settings as believable and lifelike as possible. He designed a room on paper and then decided which "wall" of the room was to be removed so that the audience could see in. Antoine also used actual three-dimensional objects rather than their painted substitutes. For one play, he brought real sides of beef on his stage and for another, real trees and birds' nests; and for another, a real student's room furnishings. The attention he paid to realistic detail and his reliance on actual objects led to his being called by many the father of naturalistic staging. A contemporary of Antoine's seemed to sum up Antoine's goal: "The front of the stage must be a **fourth wall,** transparent for the public, opaque for the player."

Acting Antoine believed that actors should appear to be people, not actors. He wanted his actors to say their lines naturally, just as one might engage in a conversation with friends and, at the same time, to move about the furniture and accessories as in real life. Sincerity and conviction were the qualities he sought, and so he advised his actors to ignore the audience and to speak to one another in conversational tones—in short, to try to *be*, rather than to *act*, the characters in the play. Perhaps for these reasons, Antoine often used amateurs who had not received conventional training for the commercial theatre and who were therefore more receptive to the experimental style of naturalistic acting.

Influence The major contributions of Antoine and the Théâtre-Libre were

- To popularize acting techniques leading toward greater naturalness on stage.
- To gain acceptance for scenic practices now known as fourth-wall realism, with all that implies about scenic detail and literal objects.
- To introduce a new generation of playwrights both French and foreign to the theatre-going public of Paris.
- To establish a model for a censor-free theatre.

The most significant experimental theatre of its day, the Théâtre-Libre gave rise to a number of similar noncommercial theatres throughout the world. Called the **independent theatre movement**, this blossoming of small theatres in several countries almost simultaneously propelled an international movement for theatrical reform. An unintended consequence of the movement was to instigate the ultimate acceptance of realism as the mainstream of the commercial theatre, an acceptance complete by early in the twentieth century. As we shall see, the dominance of realism in the commercial theatre led to new reactions and reform movements.

The Free Stage in Germany; The Independent Stage in Britain

In Germany, *Die Freie Bühne* (The Free Stage) was an early independent theatre founded in 1889 by Otto Braham. Dedicated to realism and naturalism, Die Freie Bühne used professional actors but performed only on Sundays when the professional theatres were closed. In London, a Dutch immigrant, Jakob T. Grein, founded The Independent Theatre in 1891 for performances of plays "which have a literary and artistic rather than a commercial value." Like Die Freie Bühne and for the same reason, the Independent Theatre performed only on Sundays. Like Théâtre-Libre, it was a subscription theatre, so it could perform forbidden works. Ibsen's *Ghosts* had been refused a license by Britain's Lord Chamberlain, so when the Independent Theatre produced the play, the controversy brought the group to prominence. The Independent Theatre also first staged the early works of George Bernard Shaw.

Konstantin Stanislavski and the Moscow Art Theatre

When the Meiningen company toured Russia in 1885 and 1890, Konstantin Stanislavski (1863–1938) and Vladimir Nemirovich-Danchenko (1858–1943) saw it perform. They decided to establish a new kind of theatre in Moscow whose goals were to remain free of the demands of commercialism, to avoid overemphasis on the scenic elements of production, and to reflect the inner truth of the play. For this, the Moscow Art Theatre established in 1898, Nemirovich-Danchenko was to select the plays and handle the administration, and Stanislavski was to serve as the production director.

Acting and Directing at the Moscow Art Theatre As a director during the early years of the Moscow Art Theatre, Stanislavski worked in a rather autocratic fashion, planning each detail of his actors' vocal inflections, gestures, and movements. But as his interest in the problems of the actor grew, and as his actors became more skillful, he abandoned his dogmatic approach and became an interpreter and helper to the actors. His ideal became for the director and the actors to grow together in their understanding of the play. Only after the group had grasped the psychology of the roles and the complex interrelationships, often a three-month process, did the actors begin to work on the stage.

By 1917, Stanislavski had developed, from personal experience and observation of others, his major ideas for training actors; ideas codified in a series of books that have since been translated into more than twenty languages: *My Life in Art* (published in the United States in 1924), *An Actor Prepares* (1936), *Building a Character* (1949), and *Creating a Role* (1961). Together, these books represent what has come to be called the Stanislavski "system" of actor training, although Stanislavski himself insisted that his was *not* the only way to train actors and that his methods should *not* be studied and mastered by everyone.

Influence of the Moscow Art Theatre What began in 1898 as an experiment in external realism was by 1906 an experiment in psychological realism, concentrating on the inner life and truth of the character. When the Moscow Art Theatre toured Britain and the United States early in the twentieth century, the word *ensemble* was used again and again to describe the company, which seemed natural and unified, without stars.

STANISLAVSKI AND THE MOSCOW ART THEATRE
Here, Maxim Gorki's *The Lower Depths*, a naturalistic play set in a flophouse. Stanislavski is center, on the table.

The Stanislavski ideal had become an established tradition in Russia by the time of the Russian Revolution (1917). A number of Russians trained in "the system" left their country because of the revolution and became acting teachers, bringing the ideas of Stanislavski to London, New York, and then Hollywood.

Plays and Playwrights of Realism

New directors, teachers, stage designers, and actors required new plays matched to their ideals of psychological realism. Realism in the drama began tentatively and cautiously. Although other writers had presaged realism, it was the Norwegian Henrik Ibsen (1828–1906) who helped launch realism as a major artistic movement.

Ibsen

With plays such as *A Doll's House* (1879), *Ghosts* (1881), and *Hedda Gabler* (1891), Ibsen assumed his controversial role as an attacker of society's values. Structurally, these plays were fairly traditional. They told a story and moved logically from event to event, just as well-made plays had done for years. But their content was shocking. When individuals came into conflict with society, the individuals were no longer assumed to be guilty and society blameless. Indeed, social customs and traditional morality were exposed by Ibsen as a tangle of inconsistencies and irrelevancies. Questions such as the proper role of women, the ethics of euthanasia, the morality of business and war, and the economics of religion formed the basis of serious probings into social behavior. Theatrical producers throughout the world who believed that drama should be involved in the social issues of the day applauded the Norwegian dramatist, and soon other artists began to translate, produce, and later, emulate his plays. Note that in addition to realistic dramas that had an international influence on the development of realism, Ibsen also wrote plays in many other genres, including symbolism, the problem play, folk drama, and epic. Ibsen's plays are often revived today.

Chekhov

The Russian Anton Chekhov (1860–1904) scored his first success in 1898 when *The Seagull* was produced at the Moscow Art Theatre. Three other Chekhov plays were later produced by the Moscow Art Theatre: *Uncle Vanya, Three Sisters,* and *The Cherry Orchard*—all about the waning days of Russian landed aristocracy. Chekhov's plays differed from those of Ibsen in their tendency toward poetic expression and symbolism. His manipulation of

THE PLAY'S THE THING

Henrik Ibsen's *A Doll's House*, 1879

Ibsen is often called the father of modern drama. He wrote more than two dozen plays in every major style of the nineteenth century—from romanticism to symbolism—but his realistic plays like *A Doll's House* are those most often produced today. When he turned exclusively to writing plays in his early forties, he was already an experienced company manager, stage manager, and director.

The Story of the Play Nora Helmer is a married woman and a mother, but some of her behavior is childlike, and her husband Torvald, a priggish bank manager, treats her as a charming toy (and, implicitly, a sexual toy). When an old friend of Nora's, Mrs. Linde, comes to ask if Torvald can give her a job at the bank, Nora confesses that she is not so childish as she appears: She has "saved Torvald's life" by borrowing money when he was ill to send him to recuperate in Italy. Torvald does not know of the debt, which she has been repaying from

her household money, so Torvald thinks she is a spendthrift, as well.

Her creditor is Krogstad, who works at Torvald's bank and is going to be fired; he demands that Nora intercede for him or he will reveal to Torvald not only her borrowing but also the fact that she forged her now-dead father's signature to the note.

Krogstad is fired; his job is to go to Mrs. Linde. He demands again that Nora help him get a better job at the bank; when she cannot, he leaves a letter for Torvald in the letterbox. Nora, recognizing that the truth must come out, believes that Torvald will stand by her, even share the blame; she tells Mrs. Linde that there will be a "miracle." Still, waiting for her husband to find the letter, she becomes more and more frantic and talks of suicide; she dances for her husband a tarantella that becomes wild, manic, a dance of seduction.

Krogstad and Mrs. Linde meet at Nora's and recognize each other—they are former lovers who now decide to reconcile. Krogstad says he will retrieve the letter, but Mrs. Linde tells him that "this unhappy secret must come out."

After a party, Nora tries to keep Torvald from the letter. Torvald is sexually aroused; he calls her his "most precious possession." He reads the letter and his mood changes: She has "ruined his happiness, threatened his future." They will have to go on living together "for public appearances," but she will not be allowed to raise his children. Nora's miracle does not happen.

The maid brings another letter. Torvald reads it and cries, "I am saved!" Krogstad has sent him the forged note to destroy and said he will keep silent.

Nora has become quieter and quieter. Now she sits her husband down at the table and, in a lengthy scene, explains how wronged she has been. "I have been your doll wife, Torvald." Finally, she leaves him and the children—coolly, calmly—telling him that her first duty is to herself. She goes out; Torvald cries out her name, then says that there is still hope, but there is the sound of the house's outer door slamming.

ANTON CHEKHOV'S *THE THREE SISTERS*

In Chekhov's lifetime, the Moscow Art Theatre produced his plays realistically. In this production by Virginia Commonwealth University, the setting is simplified and nonrealistic. The lighting manipulates brightness and shadow for emotive effect.

language, with measured pauses and artful repetitions, produced a sense of reality as well as suggesting allusions and evoking a feeling of music. In some ways, his stories foretold the Russian Revolution by depicting the isolation of the aristocracy and its inevitable extinction. Chekhov's plays are not limited in importance to Russia however but are adapted and revived all over the world today.

Naturalistic Playwrights: Hauptmann and Gorky

Naturalism was not just extra realism or superrealism. Naturalism was a fatalistic movement that saw heredity and environment as deterministic of life stories. Among the most successful playwrights in the naturalistic style were Gerhart Hauptmann and Maxim Gorky. Hauptmann's *The Weavers* (1892) uses a group protagonist to show the devastation that comes to already impoverished workers when industrialization threatens their way of life. The term *group protagonist* means that the story has not one individual main character but uses a group as the focus of the play. Gorky's *The Lower Depths* (1902), by depicting the seemingly hopeless lives of people living in a flophouse, explores whether religion or political reform offers the best chance for change.

Success and Reform

By the early years of the twentieth century, the theatre had risen to unprecedented commercial success. Counter to that success were repeated attempts to reform the essence of theatre, to make it more serious, more politically and socially engaged, and more inventive. Theatre split into commercial and avant-garde streams, but as the twentieth century continued these two streams would somewhat intertwine as theatre responded to increasing competition from new technology.

KEY TERMS

Key terms are boldface type in the text. Check your understanding against this list. Persons are page-referenced in the Index.

closet drama, p. 197
continental seating, p. 199
fourth wall, p. 204
gesamtkunstwerk (geh-ZAMT-koonst-verk [master artwork]), p. 198
independent theatre movement, p. 205

naturalism, p. 200
realism, p. 199
romanticism, p. 191
Sturm und Drang (STERM-oond-DRANG [storm and stress]), p. 195

Chapter 9 at a Glance

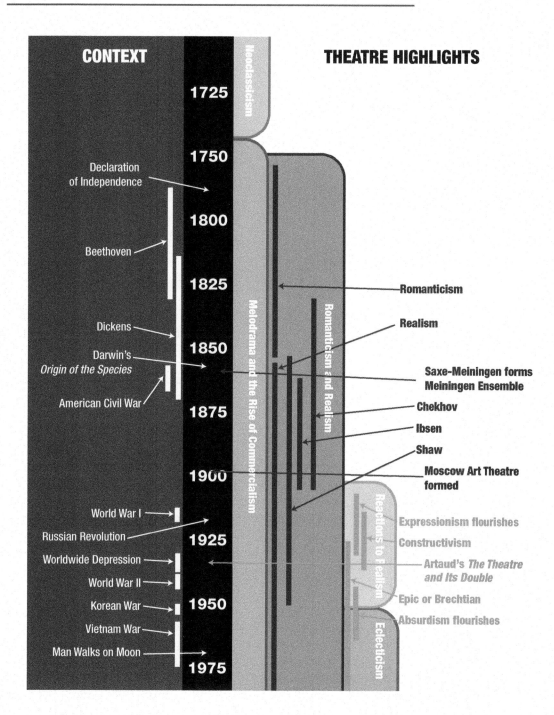

CONTEXT

THEATRE HIGHLIGHTS

Neoclassicism

1725

1750

Declaration of Independence

1800

Beethoven

1825

Romanticism

Realism

Dickens

Darwin's
Origin of the Species

1850

Saxe-Meiningen forms
Meiningen Ensemble

American Civil War

1875

Chekhov

Ibsen

Shaw

1900

Moscow Art Theatre
formed

Melodrama and the Rise of Commercialism

Romanticism and Realism

World War I

Russian Revolution

1925

Expressionism flourishes

Constructivism

Worldwide Depression

Artaud's *The Theatre
and Its Double*

World War II

Korean War

1950

Epic or Brechtian

Vietnam War

Absurdism flourishes

Man Walks on Moon

Reactions to Realism

Eclecticism

1975

10

Theatre in Africa

OBJECTIVES

When you have completed this chapter, you should be able to:

- Compare the regions of Mediterranean and sub-Saharan Africa.
- Explain the nature of the solo storytellers in Mediterranean Africa.
- Discuss the impact of missionaries on theatre in sub-Saharan Africa.
- Describe the theatre of the *Yoruba*.
- Discuss the plays of two sub-Saharan playwrights.
- Sketch the nature of theatre for development.

Context

Of the continents, Africa is second to Asia in land and population size. It stretches south of the Mediterranean and west of the Red Sea and the Arabian peninsula. Scientists are fairly certain that early humans evolved first in Africa more than two million years ago. The culture of Africa can be divided into two unequal parts: Mediterranean and Saharan Africa to the north and sub-Saharan Africa, south of the great desert.

Northern Africa

Northern Africa has been influenced from ancient times by contact with other cultures about the Mediterranean. The Mediterranean Sea eased travel, trade, and colonization among the early cultures of the area. The earliest history of a developed civilization in the area is from circa 3300 BCE in Egypt. Early Egypt traded with many nearby cultures. Trading partners included today's Libya and other African areas; the proto-Greek culture in Crete; and Canaan, known today as Israel, Lebanon, the Palestinian territories, and parts of Jordan. Egypt had a highly developed culture, which had many rituals and public entertainments and which left to us fantastic, enormous, and beautiful monuments.

Later, Hellenistic Greeks traded with and ultimately colonized Egypt. Alexander the Great founded the city of Alexandria in Egypt and set up a Greek family, the Ptolemy dynasty, as the rulers of Egypt. The famous Cleopatra—Cleopatra VII—was the last Ptolemy (Hellenistic Greek) pharaoh, her reign ending in 30 BCE. As Rome grew to power in the Mediterranean, it colonized or exploited most of Mediterranean Africa. Roman ruins, including coliseums and theatres, can be found in this area. In its time, Christianity moved from Palestine into northern Africa, and in the early seventh century, Islam, which brought the Arabic language and alphabet, dominated much of Mediterranean Africa.

At present, about 45 percent of Africans are Muslims, 37 percent are Christians, 17 percent follow indigenous religions, and about 1 percent have other religious affiliations. But the religions are not evenly divided on the continent. Northern African countries often have two hundred times as many Muslims as Christians. In sub-Saharan Africa, the proportion is generally reversed.

The peoples of Northern Africa are largely Arabs, a mixed ethnic group sharing the Arabic language. As an ethnic group, the term *Arab* is not identical to *Muslim*, which identifies a religion. There are Christian and Jewish Arabs and Arabs who follow indigenous religions. That said, Islam is the dominant religion of the Arab people.

Sub-Saharan Africa

By contrast, sub-Saharan Africa had virtually no written language until colonization and missionary contacts started in the early 1800s. The Sahara, Arabic for *great desert*, is the largest desert on Earth excluding Antarctica. It is roughly the size of the United States and so was an effective block for ancient European traders to reach the parts of Africa below the desert. Sub-Saharan Africa, comprised of more than thirty nations today, is the poorest region in the world. Many inhabitants have no access to electricity. Life expectancy is low; infant mortality is high.

It is estimated that precolonial Africa had as many as ten thousand states of differing size and political organization. The more northern of the sub-Saharan tribes largely accepted Islam between the eleventh and thirteenth centuries. Arabs took slaves from the black African people, largely those from sub-Saharan Africa, from the seventh centuries up to the early decades of the twentieth century. European and American trade in African slaves ran from the fifteenth to the early nineteenth centuries.

European colonization of all of Africa began in the late nineteenth century. At an 1885 conference called by the king of Belgium, the European

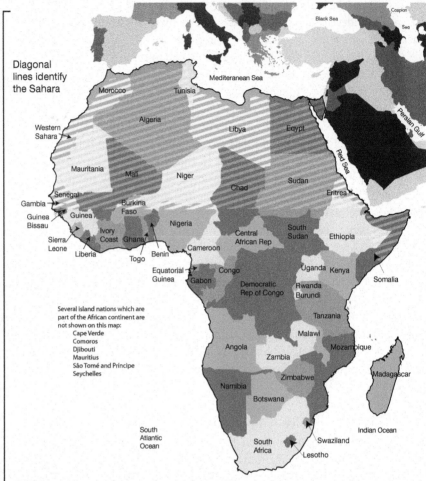

Diagonal
lines identify
the Sahara

Several island nations which are
part of the African continent are
not shown on this map:
    Cape Verde
    Comoros
    Djibouti
    Mauritius
    São Tomé and Príncipe
    Seychelles

AFRICA

The physical barrier of the Sahara effectively divides the African continent into two
parts: a northern part long intertwined with the history of other Mediterranean and
near-Asian cultures and a sub-Saharan part effectively isolated from the cultures of
other global areas until recent centuries.

powers negotiated which European country would control which parts of the
continent. Gradually after World War II, the countries of Africa became independent from European powers, often only after bloody colonial wars. The
borders of these countries were, in many cases, created for the convenience
of the European powers and did not reflect tribal or religious ties of the indigenous regions. Perhaps for this reason, much of Africa today is repeatedly
roiled by civil war and intertribal violence. In areas where survival is a daily
struggle, to speak of theatre or its lack would be bizarrely inappropriate.

Colonialism in the Country of South Africa

The breakup of colonial control was different in South Africa than elsewhere on the continent. South Africa, a large country on the southern tip of Africa, was valuable to both the Dutch and the British first as a port on the route to their Asian colonies and trading posts. Dutch and British settled in the area in significant numbers and fought over control of the area. Today, there are eleven official languages in South Africa and two of them are dialects of European languages: Afrikaans derived from Dutch and South African English. The discovery of diamonds and gold in South Africa in the 1880s made the land more valuable. Two wars between the Dutch and British, called the Boer Wars, concluded in 1902 with British ownership.

This was a society in which the races were kept separate and native Africans had no power, a social structure that came to be called by an Afrikaans word, *apartheid*. It was the European colonists who began the drive for South Africa's independence from Europe. In 1961, after a national referendum, South Africa became independent from Britain. The native peoples, largely through the political organization of the African National Congress (ANC), petitioned locally (not always peacefully) and internationally for full citizenship. In 1994, the first integrated elections were held and power was transferred to the ANC. Nelson Mendela became the country's first black president—having previously been imprisoned by the South African white government for twenty-seven years for leading the ANC antiapartheid efforts.

ROMAN LEGACY

Although little is known about what was performed in Hellenistic Greek and Roman theatres, these ancient structures dot the landscape of Mediterranean Africa. Here, a Roman facade theatre in Libya.

Theatre in Northern Africa

Hellenistic Greeks and Romans built theatres in Northern Africa. In fact, Alexandria in Egypt had its own Guild of Artists of Dionysus, the Hellenistic organization of professional actors. But we do not know what was performed in these structures. The best guess, based on what little is known about the scripts staged in more central areas of Hellenistic Greece and in the Roman Empire, is that tragedies were little performed if at all. The stage was dominated by what we might recognize today as situation comedies, mime, and pantomime.

In Egypt there are a small number of widely separate artifacts offering limited evidence of previous performances that have elements of theatre, the oldest dating from 2600 BCE. Most scholars today judge these performances to have been rituals, with many of the qualities of ritual: diffuse performance areas and times, little differentiation between performer and audience, and a functional purpose, generally related to maintaining or improving the afterlives of dead pharaohs or serving the gods. In fact, many of these performances may have been seen only by priests, high officials, and members of the royal family. It is telling that ancient Egyptian had no words comparable to *actor, theatre,* or *performance,* though a lack of vocabulary is not decisive evidence that a thing did not exist.

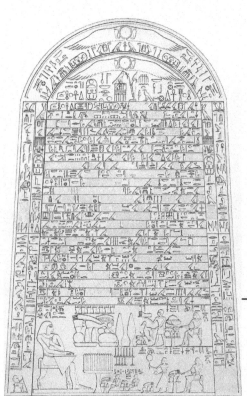

Islam generally suppresses theatre, seeing it as a form of idolatry. Thus, from the advent of Islam in the seventh century CE to the modern period, there was little or no theatre in Muslim Africa. As elsewhere in Muslim areas of the world, shadow plays were tolerated. An Egyptian in the fourteenth century CE committed some shadow play scripts to writing. From this evidence we know puppet plays were broad comedies, often filled with sexual machinations, farcical situations, and gags about bodily functions. As sometimes today, a well-timed fart could trigger a big laugh. Solo storytellers, sometimes accompanying themselves on musical instruments, were also common.

WAS THERE THEATRE IN ANCIENT EGYPT?
Here, a drawing of the Ikhernofret stele from 2000 to 1650 BCE, now in the Berlin Museum and controversially used as evidence for theatre in Egypt. New reviews of old claims within the last thirty years have led most Egyptian scholars to agree that there was no theatre in ancient Egypt, although there were dance, music, and ritual processions.

Beginning in the nineteenth century, theatre inspired by European performance started slowly to enter Northern Africa. In 1847, a prosperous businessman in Ottoman-controlled Lebanon following a visit to Italy put on a performance of his play *Al-Bakhīl* (*The Miser*) in his home. To do so he had to obtain a decree from the authorities to allow the performance. Later a Syrian dramatist, actor, and troupe manager was forced to emigrate to Egypt in 1884 after the religious authorities of Damascus objected to performances of his work. He found a welcoming regime in Egypt. The Khedive of Egypt—its ruler—was focused on modernizing Egyptian society and eager to imitate European things, including drama. He encouraged local and foreign troupes to perform at an open-air stage in gardens close to the then new Cairo Opera House (1869). Plays performed in the last decades of the nineteenth and early decades of the twentieth century included original plays, stage adaptations of stories from the *One Thousand and One Nights* and other existing tales, and adaptations of Moliére.

Tawfīg al-Hakīm, who studied in Paris and returned to Cairo in 1928 to stage serious Muslim drama, is generally regarded as the most significant Arabic literary figure of the twentieth century. He adapted stories from the *Qur'ān*, from *One Thousand and One Nights*, and from Greek myth. He continued to write into the 1960s.

Elsewhere in Muslim-dominated Africa, theatre did not much develop before the end of World War II. Only after Tunisian independence from France in 1956 did theatre become common there. An Arab Theatre Festival was established starting in 1964. The 2009 edition of the festival in Egypt featured theatre from Jordan, Tunisia, Egypt, the United Arab Emirates, Lebanon, Algeria, Syria, Palestine, Libya, Bahrain, and Yemen—countries of Mediterranean Africa and the southwestern part of Asia whose population is largely Arab.

Theatre in Sub-Saharan Africa

Many of the states of sub-Saharan Africa had rituals, storytellers, dances, festivals, and rites that shared some of the characteristics of theatre. The knowledge of performance in sub-Saharan Africa is limited because virtually none of the languages of the area had an alphabet and so there is no written record. Today most areas have at least two languages: a native language and the language of the colonizer, mostly French or English. What comes down to us of preliterate theatre-like activities in sub-Saharan Africa is almost solely from the accounts of European hunters and Christian and Islamic missionaries beginning in the nineteenth century and from practices of today; performances whose participants believe are the continuance of long historical traditions in their cultures.

SUB-SAHARAN ART
Although there was no formal written language in Africa south of the Sahara Desert, art of a high caliber was created. Here, two brass objects from the 1600s, a leopard and a female head.

The countries, tribes, and families of sub-Saharan Africa have similar performance types. The local performers and audiences probably see them as different, having different languages and local content. Did any of these performance types begin in one place and then spread through trade and warfare to other places? No record has been found.

Dances sometimes used masks and often had drumming and mimicked hunting or animal encounters. Masks are used in ancestor commemoration, in recalling the historic or mythic origin stories of a tribe, in rites related to the seasons, or as commemoration of births, deaths, or passage into adulthood. African storytellers often impersonate characters in their stories and sometimes provoke call-and-response patterns with their listeners. In some cases, storytellers are accompanied by dancers or mimes. In western Africa, a storyteller was called a *griot*. As an inheritor of an oral tradition, a griot is poet, singer, historian, and itinerant musician. Griots also shared gossip, satire, or political observation.

MODERN STORYTELLERS
African storytellers through time were poets, singers, and musicians as well as tellers of tales. Here, a modern storyteller in performance asking for a response from an audience.

With the advent of Christian missionaries in the early nineteenth century, native practices were recorded and native languages transliterated into the European alphabet. Writing came to the languages of sub-Saharan Africa. At the same time, Christian missionaries converted Africans to Christianity wherever they could, sometimes trying to suppress traditional performance and to supplant indigenous tales with Bible stories. Often, Islamic institutions continued in the same areas as Christian missionaries practiced.

Schools established by missionaries and European colonists taught drama using Shakespeare and George Bernard Shaw. Colleges taught contemporary European plays and playwrights. They had a large influence on theatre performance; in some countries, educational theatre was the only theatre available. Western-style theatre in Africa where it occurred included plays performed in English or French and plays performed in the local, native languages. One Nigerian writer noted that in his youth in the mid-twentieth century, "The same streets on which both Christian and Muslim rituals and festivals took place also constituted the playing spaces of the collective rituals and festivals of the Yoruba...." *Yoruba* refers to the religion and cultural practices of a large west-African ethnic group.

Yoruba Performance

Alongside European theatre, indigenous performance types continued to varying extents. One prominent example is the Yoruba performing troupes called *Alarinjo*. The Yoruba is an ethnic group made up of 30 to 50 million people living in western Africa, mostly in Nigeria. The performances grew out of ritual festivals and dance dramas connected to ancestor worship. Masked figures represented the dead. At some time (tradition places it about 1600 CE) the maskers' function became more like entertainment than ritual, with itinerant troupes traveling around the Yoruba territories. The troupe begins with songs, drumming, and acrobatics intended to attract an audience. The performance proper starts with an opening chorus followed by two dances, a ritual dance to honor the gods and a social dance in the latest styles. There follow dramas also of two types: a spectacle and a revue. The spectacle is based on Yoruba myths. The revue is a satire based on recent events in Yorubaland. The finale is another song and dance. Thus, the performance mixes song, dance, and drama.

A Modern Heir of Yoruba Performance Modern traveling Nigerian theatre began in the mid-twentieth century with the actor, musician, and playwright, Hubert Ogunde (1916–1990), founder of the first professional theatre troupe in Nigeria. His presentations retained many of the elements of traditional Yoruba performance. Ogunde devised the basic plot but wrote and rehearsed only the songs; the dialogue was improvised. Many of his later works featured jazzy music, dance reflecting the fashion of the times, and topical satire. Ogunde's success was a result, in part, that his plays were performed in two languages, Yoruba and English.

From the postcolonial era, largely after the mid-1960s, the extent of foreign influence has differed greatly among African countries. Some now perform Western commercial theatre, some are focused on exploring the colonial experience, some are primarily comic, and some use social and political comment and satire. In some countries, theatre is largely amateur or educational. In others, theatre is professional, sometimes centered on a national theatre. In areas with frequent war and famine, theatre is essentially nonexistent.

Nigerian Playwright Wole Soyinka

Wole Soyinka, a Nigerian playwright, critic, and poet, was the first African to win the Nobel Prize for Literature (1986). He was born in 1934 when Nigeria was still a colony of Britain. He studied at the University College, Ibadan, Nigeria, and the University of Leeds, England; then he was a play reader at the Royal Court Theatre, London, before returning to Nigeria in 1960. He was politically active and during the Nigerian civil war was jailed from 1967 to 1969 for his outspoken opinions. His plays draw

Pete Smith

MADMEN AND SPECIALISTS
Wole Soyinka's 1971 play, *Madmen and Specialists*, used a conflict between a man and his son to examine the effects of power and war on human judgment. Soyinka was educated in Nigeria and, later, in England. He is the first African to win the Nobel Prize for Literature. Here, a production of *Madmen and Specialists* at the University of Michigan.

THE PLAY'S THE THING

Wole Soyinka, *Death and the King's Horseman*, 1976

Wole Soyinka wrote plays that were adaptations of European dramas as well as plays based on Yoruba myth. *Death and the King's Horseman* is a Yoruba-centered play, based on a real incident that took place in Nigeria during British colonial rule.

Egungun costumes play an important role when donned by the colonists in the play. In yearly death commemorations among the Yoruba peoples, elaborate Egungun costumes are worn by priests, who, through drumming and dancing, are believed to be inhabited by the spirits of the tribe's ancestors. To the early colonists of Yorubaland, the costumes must have seemed like children's masquerade dress, at least until the newcomers understood the meaning of the costumes in Yoruba ritual.

Story of the Play In the market place, a women's realm, at the close of business, comes Elesin, the king's horseman. The king has died nearly a month ago. As the king's horseman, Elesin must die today, to accompany the king in the afterlife. Elesin dances and sings the "Not-I" song: Death comes and everyone says to it, "Not I"—except for Elesin. He knows that "life has an end." But in his pride for this special day he is upset to be in normal clothing. The women rush to clothe him in rich cloths. As the king's horseman, Elesin has received all good things and honor in his life.

Before he dies, he wants to engender a child with a beautiful, young girl. One woman asks whether Elesin should anchor himself to the material world by making a child.

In the district officer's bungalow, a tango melody plays from a hand-cranked phonograph while the district officer and his wife, Pilkings and Jane, dance. When the tango stops, the sounds of native drums continue. A native policeman, Amusa, is shocked to see that the English couple is wearing Egungun costumes, costumes that symbolize the dead to

Here, a production of Death and the King's Horseman *at Southern Illinois University.*

(continues)

THE PLAY'S THE THING *Death and the King's Horseman*, 1976 *(continued)*

the Yoruba. Pilkings and his wife plan to wear them to a colonists' ball that night. Amusa has come to tell them, in his broken English, that Elesin plans to commit suicide. Pilkings directs that Elesin be arrested to prevent the suicide and the couple continues to the ball.

At the market, Amusa is confronted by the women as he goes with two other constables to arrest Elesin. The women will not let the men pass. They will not let Elesin be disturbed on his wedding night. The women suddenly grab the men's batons and hats. When they threaten to grab their pants as well, the men leave. The women sing and dance in joy.

Elesin joins the women; he believes he has impregnated his new bride. He sings and dances with the women, gradually moving into a trance, later moving more smoothly and more slowly. He stops singing and the Praise-Singer describes Elesin's changes, for he is dying to join his king.

At the ball, Pilkings learns there is a riot in the marketplace and leaves to attend to it. Still at the ball, Jane meets Olunde. Olunde is Elesin's grown son from an earlier wife who has been in England to learn medicine. He has returned upon hearing of the king's death. He will inherit the position of king's horseman and wishes to see his father's body while it is still warm. Shockingly, Pilkings returns with Elesin alive in chains. Disappointed that Elesin has not followed the requirements of their culture, Olunde says he has no father.

Elesin is now in a jail cell, but thrilled that his son still clings to the beliefs of the Yoruba. Pilkings argues the irrationality of the Yoruba creed; Elesin counters with similar contradictions in Pilkings' beliefs. A group of women, singing a dirge, bring in a long bundle. Unwrapped, it is the body of Olunde. "Because he could not bear to let honour fly out of doors, he stopped it with his life," one woman says. Elesin uses the chains on his hands to garrote himself before the colonists can stop him. Pilkings asks the women if this is what they wanted to happen. They answer that it is what Pilkings caused by playing with strangers' lives.

from Western drama and from the stories and myths of his tribe, the Yoruba. For example, he adapted Euripides's *The Bacchae* for the Nigerian theatre (1973) and based *Opera Wonyosi* (1977) on John Gay's *Beggar's Opera* and Brecht's *The Threepenny Opera*.

In his Nobel Prize lecture, Soyinka made a personal, historical, and philosophical case against the apartheid still happening at that time in South Africa. Protest of apartheid was the thematic drive of another African playwright with an international reputation, Athol Fugard.

Guðmunda Jónsdóttir

NATIONAL THEATRE OF GHANA

The National Theatre of Ghana, in the capital of Accra, was a 1992 gift of the Chinese government. It houses the national symphony, dance company, and theatre players. A building is not an arts program, and theatre in the center is sparsely attended, not able to compete with film. China has invested money in a number of African nations and hopes to develop Ghana's newfound gas and oil deposits.

South African Playwright Athol Fugard

Fugard was born in South Africa in 1935 of Irish and Dutch parents. Beginning in 1958, Fugard was one of the founding figures in a number of interracial theatres and black theatres in South Africa, which performed plays of Fugard, Bertolt Brecht, and others. Publicly speaking out against apartheid in 1962, Fugard came under surveillance of the Secret Police, which led to his plays being published and performed only outside of South Africa. For four years, from 1967 to 1971, the South African government confiscated Fugard's passport so that he could not travel.

Fugard's first performance in the United States was of *The Blood Knot*, staged off-Broadway in 1964. Internationally, his most widely produced play is from the apartheid period, *Master Harold ...and the Boys*, which ran on Broadway for 344 performances beginning in 1982. Seventeen year-old Hally—Harold—spends time with two middle-aged African servants, Sam and Willie, whom he has known all his life. Their talk is warm, replete with memories of how Sam and Willie played with Hally in his childhood. But when Hally learns that his father is returning that day from the hospital, he verbally attacks and brutalizes the two servants, unleashing the racial hate of South Africa's white society in vivid language. Sam understands that Hally is causing himself more pain than he is inflicting on Sam and Willie. Sam asks Hally if they can start over the next day, offering a glimmer of hope. In the Broadway production, Sam was played by the South African actor Zakes Mokae and Willie was played by Danny Glover, later a highly successful film actor.

MASTER HAROLD...AND THE BOYS

The plays of Athol Fugard, all written in English, have been produced around the world. His mother was Irish; his father a Dutch Afrikaner. He is also a novelist, actor, and director. Here, a production of *Master Harold...and the Boys* at Triad Stage in Greensboro, North Carolina.

Fugard's plays after the fall of apartheid have focused less on political themes and more on personal ones, including such titles as *Valley Song* (1996), *The Captain's Tiger* (1997), and *Victory* (2007).

Theatre for Development

Theatre for development, also called community development theatre or theatre of social intervention, has an educational purpose aimed at small communities. Theatre practitioners, using the local languages and performance traditions, try to educate about issues such as family planning, health (including AIDS and infant inoculations), agriculture, and human rights. In areas where electronic communication is not widely available and literacy is low, theatre can be a medium to serve educational needs. Although theatre for development tries to engage locals in the creation and presentation of skits and plays, the work is not spontaneously local. Rather, it is instigated by reform-minded individuals, charitable nongovernment organizations (NGOs), or socially progressive governments. Theatre for development is a twentieth-century invention.

One technique used is called "focus theatre" where a scene shows a problem the audience faces. When the scene is repeated, individual members of the audience are encouraged to interrupt the play wherever they wish and to enter the play with their own stories, opinion, and advice. In the language of the important theorist of developmental theatre, Brazilian Augusto Boal, spectators become "spect-actors." Entering the action and improvising responses makes the topic more authentic for the person who joins in and the rest of the audience as well. Focus theatre encourages problem solving, creativity, and ownership.

For example, the Nigerian Popular Theatre Alliance (NTPA) is an NGO allied to the Department of Theatre and Performing Arts of the Ahmadu Bello University, Zaria, Nigeria. Since 1992, it has instigated and supported theatre for development about the issues of women's health, AIDS, the environment, and democracy. In each case, the theatre for development encouraged their audience or students to turn their awareness into action. For example, one issue identified was the workload of women in their local societies. With funding from Canada, a group of women who participated in an NTPA show bought a shared multipurpose grinder, which has relieved the women of the area of the labor of grinding grain manually and individually for each family.

Another example is Sponsored Arts for Education (SAFE) in Kenya. An English actor, Nick Reding, founded SAFE in 2002 to organize and fund indigenous arts groups in the development and presentation of theatre promoting AIDS education. Reding obtains funding and material support largely from European sources to support local theatres such as the Kizingo Arts Troupe of Mombasa, Kenya. The troupe's short play *Huruma* ("Mercy") has

THEATRE FOR DEVELOPMENT
Ria Coope and Liz Sweeney (left to right, both in the 2011 class at the City University of New York School of Professional Studies for master of arts in applied theatre) perform *Through the Wall*, a theatre-in-education piece, with students of the Kigali Institute of Education, Kigali, Rwanda.

been seen by more than 100,000 Kenyans. The play repeatedly teaches that AIDS can only be transmitted by unprotected sex and shared blood; it urges families and communities to accept and support members who are HIV-positive. (Parts of *Huruma* were included in the widely released 2005 film *The Constant Gardener*. A video of the complete play with English subtitles is included on the DVD of the movie as a bonus feature.)

One of SAFE's trustees, the film and stage actor Alan Rickman, described the *Huruma* performances: "The troupe arrives in a village of anywhere up to 2,000 inhabitants. With trumpets and drums some of them create a kind of Pied Piper line through the village. The town gathers around.... An hour later they go back to their homes having been wildly entertained and more importantly, informed. So you're watching the minds of a whole community being changed in front of you." After the show, the troupe hands out condoms and educational brochures.

Theatre for development is not only an African initiative. It is being used in South America and in the underdeveloped areas of Asia as well. Theatre for development is one aspect of a relatively new discipline called *applied theatre* or *applied drama*, which uses theatrical techniques to ameliorate or solve problems in a variety of nontraditional settings. Applied drama is used as an

HOW WE KNOW

Theatre in Ancient Egypt

Over the last one hundred years or so, there have been scholarly studies declaring that there was theatre in ancient Egypt long before theatre emerged in Athens. The consensus expert opinion now is that there is no credible archeological or textual evidence for the existence of theatre in ancient Egypt. The controversy arose because of

- Problems translating from the dead language used by the Egypt of the pharaohs.
- Limited extant text.
- Questions about the definition of theatre.
- No known Egyptian words for the makers of theatre.

Ancient Egyptian writing dates from about 3400 BCE. The last written example of text known in the language is dated from the fourth century CE. The current official language of Egypt is the Egyptian dialect of Arabic.

Translating Ancient Egyptian The first successful modern translation of a text in ancient Egyptian came in 1822. It was a translation of the Rosetta Stone, an unassuming granite block currently in the British Museum. The Rosetta Stone was engraved in 196

The Rosetta Stone is now in the British Museum.

BCE with a royal decree that repeated the same text in hieroglyphics, demotic, and ancient Greek. The translation of the stone was an important breakthrough, but it took years after that to develop a dictionary and grammar of the language.

Limited and Fragmented Extant Text Questions of the language aside, texts scholars used to claim there was ancient Egyptian drama are fragmented and often abbreviated. The examples also come from a broad time span, as much as three millennia or more. If there was theatre, it left few traces over such a long time.

Definition of Theatre Beginning with scholarly publications in the 1920s, those interpreting these pieces of text as drama believed that the text had dialogue and stage directions. Later others studying the same fragmentary texts disagreed. Even if the text is dialogue and actions, the critical question is whether together they constitute drama. There are dialogue and description of actions in the texts of many religions without being a play.

Some of the documents used to support the idea of ancient Egyptian drama refer to ceremonies about Osiris, a god of the underworld whose myth includes death and resurrection. Stories of death and resurrection are found in many cultures, which has made the Osiris myth attractive to non-Egyptians. Especially cited as evidence of the Osiris "drama" is the "Ikhernofret" *stele* from the nineteenth century BCE now in the Berlin museum. Ikhernofret was a member of the Pharaoh's court, sent to represent the Pharaoh at the Osiris rituals. The stele gives a veiled description of the festivities, declaring Ikhernofret's role in carrying them out: "I drove back the rebels.... I overthrew the enemies.... I followed the God in his journeyings.... " There is no dialogue.

No Word for *Actor* There is compelling evidence that there were festivals and public celebrations in ancient Egypt, and rituals performed in closed temples, some of which included impersonation. There is no known word in ancient Egyptian for *actor, theatre*, or *performance*, but there are words for professional dancers and musicians. For now, the consensus of scholars is that there was no ancient Egyptian theatre.

adjunct to psychiatric therapy, in working with the autistic, in social justice settings, even in corporations. The City University of New York offered the first master of arts degree in applied theatre, which includes the opportunity to do an internship in Rwanda aimed at supporting theatre for development that addresses reconciliation and unity there. This focus is in response to the "Rwandan Genocide" of 1994, where the primary native tribes of the country, the Hutu and the Tutsi, fought and slaughtered 800,000 people in a country of about 11 million.

KEY TERMS

Key terms are boldface type in the text. Check your understanding against this list. Persons are page-referenced in the Index.

Alarinjo (ah-lar-EEN-yo), p. 219   theatre for development, p. 224
griot (GREE-oh), p. 218   *Yoruba* (YER-uh-buh), p. 219

Reactions to Commercialism, c. 1900–1950

OBJECTIVES

When you have completed this chapter, you should be able to:

- Discuss several reactions to commercial theatre.
- Describe the ways in which the Theatre Guild and the Group Theatre were alike and the ways in which they differed.
- List and discuss several major comic and serious playwrights of this period.
- List several events that led to the decline of the US commercial theatre.
- Describe the art theatre movement in Europe and in the United States.

Context

The growth in cities, literacy, mechanization, and transportation that marks the modern epoch came to a horrifying culmination during the First World War. From the summer of 1914 to the winter of 1918, tanks, machine guns, poison gas, flamethrowers, radio communication, and airplanes changed warfare from its old reliance on just rifles, bayonets, marching, and horses. Europe was left with devastation and hunger. American soils were untouched. The experience of the war changed everyone. As a popular song put it, singing of young men from the United States who had seen the great cities of Europe, "How you gonna keep 'em down on the farm, after they've seen Paree?" US decisive involvement in the war was the first clear evidence that this new nation was a rising world power.

The 1920s saw a bogus sense of easy wealth and a constitutional amendment that outlawed the sale of alcoholic beverages in the United States from

1920 until its repeal in 1933—an era called Prohibition. Anyone who wanted a drink could find one: it just was not legal. The sense of easy money in the 1920s was an international mirage, an economic bubble; it collapsed to create the worldwide Great Depression, lasting from late 1929 until the late 1930s. Unemployment in the United States rose to 25 percent; in some countries, it was 33 percent. Many in the developed world believed the propaganda coming out of Russia about the "success" of its 1917 socialist revolution and agitated for revolution in Europe and in the United States. In this environment, Adolf Hitler became Chancellor of Germany in 1933, and the world began to move toward the Second World War. In September 1939, just twenty-one years after the First World War ended, the Second World War began.

Theatre took part in this historical moment. It could not ignore the new working-class audience that poured into cities. By the start of World War I, US commercial theatre was one of the most successful of all time. By the end of World War II, commercial theatre remained financially successful but was smaller and less central to the nation's culture. Commercial theatre was the conservative, middle-of-the-road product against which many theatre artists rebelled.

Revolts against Commercialism

The trends in the commercial theatre described in the close of the preceding chapter continued into the twentieth century. Commercial theatre was dominated by realistic melodramas and comedies, both largely forgettable, and increasingly, by a distinctly US concoction, the musical (see Chapter 12). Between 1920 and 1965, more than four thousand plays were produced commercially in New York. Of these, only a handful are remembered and sometimes revived. Nearly all of commercial theatre was ephemeral.

There were many attempts by theatre artists to create a theatre they considered to be better than the commercial theatre. Many of these artistic movements or artistic styles are also used to describe painting and sculpture of about the same time periods, but the styles as expressed in those plastic arts and in the theatre can be quite different.

Although the realists had been innovators in their time, reacting against commercial theatre, other movements revolted against realism almost immediately. The reasons for reacting against realism included:

- Realism was not *theatrical*. It was *too much* like life.
- Realism was dull: The language was mundane, the characters flat, the action—if truly lifelike—boring.
- Realism had to struggle to be significant; if no more was at stake than the fate of one ordinary individual, what was the larger meaning?

Craig Schwartz

DETAILED REALISM

Realism lived on in theatre throughout the twentieth century. Here, a moment from a 2010 revival at Los Angeles' Center Theatre Group of Frank D. Gilroy's *The Subject Was Roses* of 1964. Note the literal kitchen setting.

These objections to realism coalesced around a view that realism was opposed to art, a view that is one of the bases of "**modernism**" in all the arts. The dominant slogan of modernism came from the poet Ezra Pound, "Make it new!" Modernism was a force in the theatre, where it was believed that the theatre had to be "retheatricalized," that innovation itself was valuable, and that form or style was as important as content so long as both were *artistic*. Modernism took many styles.

In one direction, modernists redefined theatrical space by throwing out the proscenium arch and its picture-frame stage; in another, they threw out the box set and detailed settings, replacing them with varying kinds of simplified or abstract scenery, including settings of ramps, stairs, and levels. Others tried to retheatricalize acting by throwing out "ensemble" and "inner truth" and going for an impact that was bigger, more external, and more physical and symbolic. None replaced commercial realism, but several modified mainstream realism. Some of these movements, briefly defined, are discussed in this chapter. Together they describe the nature of theatre in reaction to commercialism from about 1900 to 1950.

Naturalism

Naturalism is like realism, but it sees people's fates as dictated by past causes. It identifies evil but can usually see no hope for its amelioration, so it is fatalistic.

Symbolism

Symbolists believed that the truths of life could not be expressed directly but only in metaphorical and allusive manner. It can be difficult in the theatre to differentiate symbolist plays from surrealist ones. One way to identify the two styles is that **symbolism** as a movement belongs to the last third of the nineteenth century and **surrealism** begins in the 1920s.

Surrealism

Surrealists believed that the subconscious was the main source of truth. They wanted to write or paint without thinking and were drawn to the weird "logic" and nonreal juxtapositions of dreams. Surrealist works often have a sometimes sly and sometimes overt sexual content.

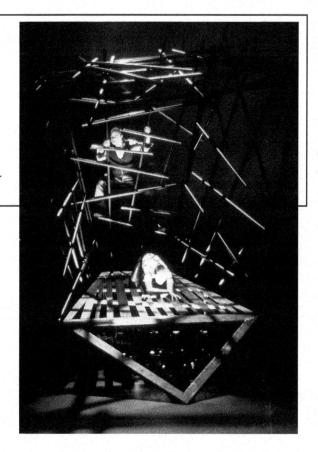

EXPRESSIONISM AND CONSTRUCTIVISM
Here, an adaptation of Franz Kafka's short story "The Metamorphosis" staged by Butler University Theatre.
In the story, the protagonist wakes up a bug. The constructivist set gives the actor the opportunity to climb the walls like a bug, an expressionistic projection of his inner feelings.

Expressionism

Expressionism in the theatre and film shows a world through the eyes of the protagonist who is either psychologically disturbed or under great stress and thus sees things in a highly distorted manner. One can differentiate **expressionism** from surrealism in that expressionism is the protagonist's distorted perception of the world whereas surrealism strives to be give universal access to the "reasoning" of the subconscious.

Cubism

Cubism began in painting with an attempt to break up representation and present fractured, abstracted versions of life. In the theatre, **cubism** was expressed primarily in design.

Constructivism

Originating in the new Soviet Union, **constructivism** reflected the machine and the factory on stage. Open platforms, wheels and gears, and primary colors in theatre design made of the stage a metaphorical machine for performance of the play. Constructivism was a theory of visual art in which scenery did not attempt to represent any particular place but provided a "machine" on which actors could perform.

Epic Theatre

Also called **alienation theatre**, or more commonly, Brechtian theatre after its foremost practitioner and theoretician Bertolt Brecht, **epic theatre** wanted to break through the audience's passive identification with realistic characters and provoke the viewers to change their beliefs, or better, to take action. The audience should always know that they are watching a play. The techniques in epic theatre involve contrast, contradiction, and interruption, often with song. Epic theatre is most often associated with the political left, especially Marxism or socialism.

Absurdism

The human impossibility of people to communicate is the root of **absurdism**. From this it follows that life is devoid of inherent value or meaning. Some people ally absurdism with existentialism—there are similarities in worldview—but existentialism is a philosophy, not a theatrical style.

A CUBIST SLANT
Painter Marc Chagall breaks up the costume in a manner reminiscent of cubism in this costume plate for a production at Moscow's State Jewish Theatre from the 1920s.

Postmodernism

Postmodernists reject that there is historical or transcultural truth or that there is cultural, economic, or political progress. They are relativists; for them there can be no one truth. Postmodernists are interested in language as it reflects social or political power and in cultural definitions such as man-woman, straight-gay, white-black, native-foreign, and high- vs. low-culture. Postmodern theatre generally eschews unity in place, time, style, or tone and undermines the idea of psychological cause. Pomo—jocular shorthand for "postmodern"—theatre often uses past stories, forms, and images in ironic ways. Once **postmodernism** was identified as a movement, some critics have maintained that absurdism is a kind of postmodernism.

Two Influential Theorists against Commercialism

Although many avant-garde styles and techniques have influenced today's theatre, the theories of Bertolt Brecht and Antonin Artaud have probably been most influential. These two theorists and playwrights operated from quite different sets of assumptions about the nature of theatre and the purpose of art, but they shared a disdain for commercial theatre. They shared as well a belief that commercial theatre lulled audiences into an artistic trance that each wanted, with different techniques, to shatter. Together, their theories inspired much of the theatrical experimentation of the 1960s and 1970s.

Bertolt Brecht and Epic Theatre

Bertolt Brecht (1898–1956) believed that theatre should educate citizens—participants in a political system—in how to bring about socially responsible change. He saw theatre as a way of making a controversial topic easier to consider. His commitment to a socially responsive theatre doubtless came, in part, from having to escape from Germany when Hitler was rising to power.

Traditional German theatres, whether those of Wagner or Saxe-Meiningen, had sought an illusion that allowed the members of the audience to believe in and identify with the onstage actions. Because Brecht was a Marxist and viewed theatre as an instrument for change, he objected to a theatre that mesmerized its audiences and made them passive observers. He, therefore, tried to redefine the relationship between the theatre, its audience, and society. He proposed that if he jarred audiences out of their identification with the feelings being evoked on stage, he would succeed in forcing them to think about the causes and cures of the situation they saw on stage. Brecht sought, therefore, alternately to engage and estrange his audiences using a technique he called *Verfremdungseffekt* (usually translated as the **alienation effect** or, simply, the **A-effect**).

The complex of staging and playwriting used by Brecht came to be called Epic Theatre. *Epic* captured many of the qualities that Brecht prized: the mixing of narrative and dramatic episodes, the telescoping of time and place, and the spanning of years and countries. Epic theatre focused on political and social content instead of just emotional response. Erwin Piscator (1893–1966), German director and producer, originated many of the techniques first associated with epic theatre: the use of elaborate scaffold-like settings, film, cartoons, still projections, signs, and treadmills. His settings, like those of the constructivist director and producer Vsevolod Meyerhold (1874–1940), were not realistic. Although Brecht was not the first to use either these techniques or the term *epic*, Brecht popularized the term and the practices through his own plays, his theoretical writings, and his productions at the Berliner Ensemble, which was, after 1954, East Germany's most prestigious theatre.

Brecht wrote more than fifty plays and adaptations. Many of Brecht's plays were adaptations of classic European and Asian works, including *Edward II* (1924), *The Good Person of Setzuan* (1940), *The Duchess of Malfi* (1943), *The Caucasian Chalk Circle* (1945), *Antigone* (1948), *Don Juan* (1952), and *Coriolanus* (1953). After his death in 1956, Brecht's plays were often staged by avant-garde theatres around the world. Today in the United States, most Brecht play productions take place in college and university theatres.

His plays were sometimes misunderstood by audiences—or at least Brecht thought so. One example is the often-produced *Mother Courage and Her Children* (1938). Mother Courage is an itinerant peddler in the

BERTOLT BRECHT'S *THE GOOD PERSON OF SETZUAN*

The play is a parable about a young woman who wants to lead a moral life, but her "friends" force her to invent an alter ego, a male, to protect herself from their avarice. The play title is sometimes translated as *The Good Woman of Szechwan*. Here, a production at Butler University.

seventeenth century trying to survive between both sides fighting the Thirty Years' War. Although she tries to protect her children, each is killed in turn. She goes on, trying to make enough money to stay alive. Audiences identified with Mother Courage, seeing her as a victim of forces beyond her control, interpreting the play as having solely an antiwar theme. Brecht intended Mother Courage to be an example of a war profiteer, a capitalist villain. Brecht's second wife, the actress Helene Weigle, played the role internationally to great acclaim. Certainly, she understood Brecht's intentions for the character, but few audiences could see Mother Courage as a villain.

Perhaps his best known and most often revived work is an early one, *The Three-Penny Opera* (Berlin, 1928), something between a musical and a ballad opera, with memorable music by the German—and later, Broadway—composer, Kurt Weill. Starting in the 1950s, the best popular US singers all took a turn at singing "Mack the Knife," from *Three-Penny*.

THE PLAY'S THE THING

Antonin Artaud's *Jet of Blood*, 1924

Artaud's *Jet of Blood* is bizarre even by today's standards. With a playing time of less than five minutes, the story (insofar as one exists) unfolds through repetitive, banal dialogue and detailed stage directions that demand startling visual effects—in keeping with Artaud's desire for sight and sound to overpower language in the theatre. *Jet of Blood* with its assault on the senses is a telling example of what would become theatre of cruelty. Young Man and Young Girl begin the play, speaking of love for nine lines. Then comes the first set of stage directions (translation by Ruby Cohn):

Silence. There is a noise as if an immense wheel were turning and moving the air.... At the same time two Stars are seen colliding and from them fall a series of legs of living flesh with feet, hands, scalps, masks, colonnades, porticos, temples, alembics, falling more and more slowly, as if falling in a vacuum....

After crying out, "The sky has gone mad," the young man exits with the girl, presumably to have sex. Knight and wet nurse (holding her swollen breasts in her hands) argue about the young couple. They exit and the young man returns, crying out that he has lost the

girl. Eight more characters enter. Then more stage directions:

At this moment night suddenly falls on stage. The earth quakes. There is furious thunder and zig-zags of lightning in every direction...all the characters can be seen running around bumping into each other and falling then getting up and running about like crazy. Then an enormous hand seizes the Bawd by her hair, which bursts into flame and grows huge before our eyes.

HUGE VOICE: Bitch, look at your body!

The Bawd's body is seen to be absolutely naked and hideous beneath her blouse and skirt which become transparent as glass.

BAWD: Leave me alone, God.

She bites God in the wrist. An immense spurt of blood lacerates the Stage, and through the biggest flash of lightning the Priest can be seen making the sign of the cross. When the lights go on again all the characters are dead, and their corpses lie all over the ground. Only the Young Man and the

(continues)

THE PLAY'S THE THING   Antonin Artaud's *Jet of Blood*, 1924 *(continued)*

Bawd remain.... The Bawd falls into the Young Man's arms.

The now flat-chested wet nurse returns holding the dead body of the girl, and the young man holds his head in his hands. The wet nurse lifts her skirt and the young man is transfixed. More stage directions:

A multitude of scorpions crawl out from beneath the Wet-Nurse's dress and swarm between her legs. Her vagina swells up, splits.... The Young Man and Bawd run off as though lobotomized.

This next line of the young girl ends the play: "The virgin! Ah that's what he was looking for."

Jet of Blood was not staged in Artaud's lifetime and only once or twice in bowdlerized adaptations since because it hardly seems possible that such a play could be constructed in the live theatre.

Antonin Artaud as Jean Paul Marat in the 1927 film Napoleon.

Antonin Artaud and the Theatre of Cruelty

Although Antonin Artaud (1896–1948) was an actor, director, playwright, poet, and screenwriter, it was as an antirealist theorist that he made his greatest impact. *The Theatre and Its Double*, a compilation of Artaud's major essays, was published in France in 1938 but was not translated into English until the late 1950s. Because Artaud believed that important ideas came not from logical reasoning or rational thinking but from intuition, experience, and feelings, he developed his ideas through images and visual metaphors:

- The Theatre of Cruelty
  Artaud called for a **theatre of cruelty**. He wanted to bombard the senses. He experimented with ways of manipulating light and sound: In both, he adopted the abrupt, the discordant, the sudden, the shrill, and the garish. Lights changed colors quickly, alternated intensity violently; sound was sudden, often amplified. Scenery was subservient

to the elements of production, with the audience placed in an environment created by actors, lights, sound, and space. Artaud preferred barns and factories to conventional theatres. The actors were encouraged to use their bodies and their voices to provide scenery, sounds, and visual effects and not be limited by notions of psychological realism and character analysis. Actors were to address the senses of the spectators, not merely their minds.

- The Theatre as Plague
  Comparing theatre to a plague, Artaud said, "It appears that by means of the plague, a gigantic abscess, as much moral as social, has been collectively drained, and that like the plague, the theatre has been created to drain abscesses collectively." He declared that theatre caused people to confront themselves honestly, letting fall their individual masks and confessing their social hypocrisies.

- The Theatre and Its Double
  Western theatre had lost its magic and its vibrancy and had become merely a pale imitation, a double of the true theatre. Artaud proposed "a theatre in which violent physical images crush and hypnotize the sensibility...as by a whirlwind of higher forces."

- The Rejection of Language
  Artaud wanted to remove the script from the center of his theatre because he believed that words and grammar were insufficient carriers of meaning. Truth came instead from spiritual signs whose meaning emerged intuitively and "with enough violence to make useless a translation into logical discursive language." Artaud wished to substitute gestures, signs, symbols, rhythms, and sounds. Theatre was intuitive, primitive, magical, and potentially powerful.

- The Centrality of Audience
  Artaud dismissed notions of art as a kind of personal therapy for the artist. Theatre was good only when it returned the audience to the subconscious energies that lay under the veneer of civilization and civilized behavior. Whereas Brecht tried to make audiences *think* about a social or political issue, Artaud wanted to make them experience a spiritual awakening, to participate in something that might be called a communion in the sense of a coming together.

Artaud's theories, in many forms and with many distortions, were appropriated and applied after 1950 by theatre artists, moviemakers, and especially rock musicians. Whatever one may think of his pronouncements, it is clear that, although long in coming, their acceptance has been widespread.

Important US Theatre Groups

Some US theatre organizations responded to the limitations of commercialism by establishing producing organizations to offer productions not limited by a need for maximum profit. Their plays tended to be realistic in style, and over time, artists in both groups were absorbed into commercial theatre and film.

The Theatre Guild

At first, the Theatre Guild from the 1920s was opposed to commercialism. It supported works by US playwrights dealing with serious artistic or political issues (e.g., Eugene O'Neill) and serious foreign playwrights whose plays were, at the time, controversial. The Guild also produced other US writers, including plays by Robert Sherwood, Maxwell Anderson, Sidney Howard, William Saroyan, and Philip Barry. In all, the Guild mounted more than two hundred plays on Broadway, including seven by O'Neill and eighteen by George Bernard Shaw. It also produced the George Gershwin-DuBose Heyward-Ira Gershwin musical-cum-folk opera *Porgy and Bess* in 1935. The Theatre Guild's early success almost persuaded Broadway that a commercial-sized audience existed for serious drama, mostly realistic in style.

In the Depression, however, the Guild lost ground. As its finances became precarious, it moved toward commercial practice. By the 1940s, the Theatre Guild was almost indistinguishable from the Broadway producers against whom it had originally rebelled. In its later years, it produced the musicals *Oklahoma!* (1943), *Carousel* (1945), and *The Unsinkable Molly Brown* (1960). The last show the Guild produced on Broadway was the 1996 musical, *State Fair*, a stage adaptation of the Rodgers and Hammerstein film musical of the same name from 1945, remade for the stage in 1962.

The Group Theatre

In the 1930s, another new organization, the Group Theatre, was at first a militant voice for noncommercial theatre in New York, driven by a strong leftist political slant. Its repertory

THE THEATRE GUILD: CLASSICS WITH IMPORTANT ACTORS

Here, Shakespeare's *Othello* with Paul Robeson and Uta Hagen in 1943. Robeson was a strong singer and actor at a time when his race often impeded his career. Hagan, a successful Broadway actor—she created the role of Martha in *Who's Afraid of Virginia Woolf?* in 1962—became one of the most important acting teachers in the United States.

focused on social issues, especially poverty and oppression. The style of the playwriting and acting was realism. The Group Theatre popularized a design style now called simplified or **selective realism**, a style that uses especially chosen elements for the setting but omits nonessential elements. Perhaps more important was its popularizing of an Americanized version of Stanislavski's acting techniques, the **American Method**, which became the US realistic acting style that still dominates US stage and film. The method emphasized that actors search within themselves for the truth of a character's life rather than using external techniques to perform. For ten years, the Group Theatre produced works by many important US writers of its time including Paul Green (*The House of Connelly*, 1931) and Sidney Kingsley (*Men in White*, 1933). In all, the Group Theatre presented more than twenty plays on Broadway. Financial and political problems ended the Group Theatre during World War II.

Clifford Odets, one of the original members of the Group Theatre, set out to be its playwright. His first play, *Awake and Sing!* (1935), is a family drama overlaid with issues of poverty and the appeal of socialism. *Waiting for Lefty* (1935) is more clearly political, focused on cab drivers considering whether to strike. Odets also wrote *Golden Boy* (1937), one of the Group's notable successes.

The Group Theatre was founded by Harold Clurman, Cheryl Crawford, and Lee Strasberg in 1931. Clurman was a director and critic, Crawford began as a casting director and later took the role of literary manager, and Strasberg was an actor, director, and teacher of acting. While the Group nurtured playwrights, theorists, and producers, it was the acting company that featured some of the best and best-known US talents: Luther Adler and his sister Stella Adler, Franchot Tone, John Garfield, Francis Farmer, Robert Lewis, Morris Carnovsky, Will Geer, Lee J. Cobb, and Sanford Meisner, among others. After the Group Theatre disbanded in 1940, these actors enriched theatre throughout the United States and film.

From the Group Theatre came the Actors Studio, one of the most important US training centers, devoted to spreading the American Method, a realistic style of acting. It was founded in 1947 by Robert Lewis, Elia Kazan, and Cheryl Crawford. Lewis and Kazan began as actors. Lewis became a renowned acting teacher, and Kazan a highly successful director on stage and film and later a novelist. Under the leadership of Lee Strasberg, who became the Actors Studio's director in 1951, the American Method of acting was developed and greatly influenced theatre and film.

The Federal Theatre Project

The Federal Theatre Project (FTP) was the closest thing to a government-supported, national theatre the United States has ever seen, but it was short-lived. Launched in 1935, the FTP was one of many federal

A VOODOO *MACBETH*

A twenty-year-old Orson Welles re-located the tragedy from Scotland to a fictional island much like Haiti. Instead of the traditional witchcraft, Welles substituted voodoo imagery. Here, a setting—probably the "cauldron/witches" scene—from the Federal Theatre Project production of 1936 in Harlem, which then moved to Broadway.

government programs initiated in the 1930s to put people back to work. Under the umbrella of the Works Progress Administration (WPA), the federal government employed millions during the Depression doing public works. The WPA is responsible for many bridges, libraries, post offices, and the hardscape of US national parks. The FTP was aimed at aiding theatre artists. Part of the program's excitement came from its national character; units were established in almost every state. Additional excitement came from its commitment to cultural diversity—there were, for example, both Jewish and black theatre companies—and part came from the quality of its innovative art.

In New York, through the auspices of the FTP, the first **living newspaper** in the United States premiered. A kind of staged documentary, living newspapers soon spread throughout the country, dramatizing society's most pressing problems: housing, farm policies, venereal disease, and war. During an anti-communist government probe, however, living newspapers were denounced as communist plots. In 1939, the government failed to appropriate money for the FTP, and so ended the nation's first far-reaching experiment in support of theatre arts. Before its demise, however, the FTP introduced a number of major new artists and theatres, among them the later film actors John Houseman, Joseph Cotton, Arlene Francis, and Burt Lancaster. Orson Welles worked in the FTP, most memorably directing an all-African American production of *Macbeth*, which was nicknamed the "Voodoo Macbeth." Welles went on to make a name for himself—and squander his fame—as an actor and director in film.

The Art Theatre Movement

Reactions to realism and to commercial theatre also came in the form of new kinds of theatres. Just as the realists had started the first "independent" theatres, reactions against those very theatres brought about a proliferation of "art" theatres, soon followed by other radical, "experimental," or "little" theatres from the late nineteenth century into the 1960s. Generally the **art theatre movement** rejected the illusionism of a traditional proscenium arch theatre.

Art Theatre Pioneers in Europe

Early creators of art theatres included:

- *William Poel*, an antiquarian—a lover of the past. Poel reacted against late Victorian commercial production by staging Shakespeare and other Elizabethan playwrights in supposedly authentic ways—a bare-stage *Hamlet* in 1881, for example. He founded the English Stage Society in 1895 to recreate the Elizabethan stage. Poel influenced both modern thinking about Shakespeare and the popularity of the thrust and arena stages. When Poel staged Shakespeare in a proscenium theatre, he used a series of bare platforms—not realistic scenery—and moved the stage area forward of the proscenium arch to diminish the arch's importance.

- *Aurélien-François Lugné-Poë* who had acted for Antoine. Later he turned to nonrealistic production at the *Theatre d'Art* (1891) working with Paul Fort and then alone at the *Theatre de l'Oeuvre* (1893), both in Paris. Lugné-Poë staged "experimentally" seeking new styles, especially for symbolist works.

- *Jacques Copeau*, an actor-director who founded in 1913 the *Vieux Colombier* theatre in Paris and "cleared out the wings and old picture frame" by building a permanent setting of levels, an inner below and an upper balcony. Although Copeau staged mostly the traditional French repertory, his productions rejected traditional, realistic scenery. Copeau founded a school in the 1920s that influenced modern French, English, and US theatre.

- *Alexander Tairov* at Moscow's *Kamerny* ("Chamber") Theatre after 1915. Determinedly antirealistic, he had no one style of his own and was called "cubist" for his modernism. He staged a wide variety of plays in several nonrepresentational ways, anticipating the eclecticism of later directors and the heretical approach to classics.

- *Vsevolod Meyerhold* at the Meyerhold Theatre in Moscow from 1922 until it was closed by the Soviet regime in 1938. Meyerhold was

THE PICTURE FRAME PROSCENIUM IS OUT

Jacques Copeau, like many of his French colleagues, favored nonrealistic productions. Here, the interior of Copeau's theatre, *Vieux Colombier*. The arches move through the auditorium but there is no proscenium arch. The stage has a permanent setting that could be adapted for various plays.

sternly opposed to a realistic theatre he saw as "academic." His approach to staging was described as "circus-like." This was the period that saw the development of constructivism (fl. 1920–1935). Although early in his career Meyerhold directed experimental works for Stanislavski, during the 1920s he devoted himself to developing a theatrical art suitable for a machine age. He relied on two major techniques: **biomechanics** and constructivism. Biomechanics was a training system and performance style for actors based on an industrial theory of work: They were to be well-trained "machines" for carrying out the assignments given them, and so they needed rigorous physical training in ballet, gymnastics, and circus techniques. He believed an actor could call up emotions by assuming certain poses, gestures, and movements, which he cataloged and taught. In practice, sets designed for Meyerhold were combinations of platforms, steps, ramps, wheels, and trapezes. Shortly after Stalin decreed that Socialist theatre could only be realistic, Meyerhold was tortured and killed by firing squad in 1940.

The art theatre movement was an after-the-fact term for these diverse approaches, which included other theatres as well, including the Abbey in Dublin, Ireland, founded in 1903 and still producing today. The "art" of the art theatres was still partly romantic but existed against the background of a changed culture, that of turn-of-the-century Europe—imperialist, stuffy, class-conscious, money-conscious. Art theatres emphasized a somewhat superficial, sometimes glib, sentimentalized belief in the power of beauty to improve life. That belief was mostly elitist, as were the art theatres.

Influential Nonrealistic Stage Designers

Adolphe Appia (1862–1928), designer, is often called a symbolist. He believed that artistic unity was the fundamental goal of theatrical production and that lighting was the element best able to fuse all others into an artistic whole. Like music, light was capable of continual change to reflect shifting moods and emotions within a play, and light could be orchestrated by variations in its direction, intensity, and color to produce a rhythm to match the dramatic action. Because he found an aesthetic contradiction between the three-dimensional actor and two-dimensional painted scenes, Appia gave the stage floor and scenery mass. He solved the problem in part by devising three-dimensional settings composed of steps, ramps, and platforms, among which the living actor could comfortably move.

Gordon Craig (1872–1966), like Appia, opposed scenic illusion and favored instead a simple visual statement that eliminated inessential realistic details and avoided photographic-like reproduction. His emphasis was on the manipulation of line and mass to achieve, first, a unity of design and, ultimately, a unity for the total production. Although Craig placed less emphasis on the importance of the actor and the text than Appia, they agreed on the importance of the visual elements of the production. Perhaps it would not be an injustice to designate Appia as the formulator of the theories that Craig later popularized. Appia and Craig influenced the new stagecraft and then commercial theatrical design. Both were enabled by technological advances, especially electric stage lighting.

CONSTRUCTIVISM
Here, a view of a 1928 for a production of *The Bath House* intended to help the lighting designer discover ways to illuminate the ramps, ladders, and treadmill.

The Art Theatre in the United States

The art theatre came a bit later to the United States. When it did, it was bound up culturally with several other fashions: the civic pageant, which was also genteel and "artistic"; the first programs in "theatre arts" at colleges and universities; and the new stagecraft.

New stagecraft was an avant-garde tendency in stage design that favored simplified, sometimes abstract settings; nonrealism; lighting as a major design component; and alternatives to the proscenium stage. European in origin and based heavily on the ideas of Appia and Craig, it surfaced in the United States when Sam Hume (a designer who had been working at the Moscow Art Theatre)

organized a new stagecraft exhibition in Boston and New York in 1914–1915. It was, in fact, the future: Designers like Norman Bel Geddes, Robert Edmond Jones, and Lee Simonson made the new stagecraft dominant in US design by 1930.

The first US art theatres arrived more or less with the new stagecraft. They soon became known as "little" theatres, which was significant because they attracted small audiences. The Abbey Theatre's US tour of 1911 seems to have inspired the first US art theatres: The Chicago Little Theatre began in 1912, the Boston Toy Theatre, and the Wisconsin Dramatic Society about the same time. By 1925, there were little theatres "in barns, barrooms, churches, studios, and other odds and ends of civilized building, all the way from Maine to California, from crowded sophisticated Greenwich Village to the open spaces of Vancouver," as an early historian of the art theatre declared. Amateur, artistic, and mostly elitist, their most famous example was the Provincetown Players, which had started in a shack in the art colony at Provincetown, Massachusetts, in the summer and moved to New York's Greenwich Village in 1915. The Provincetown Players staged the early plays of O'Neill and included people as diverse as journalist John Reed and poet Edna St. Vincent Millay. Some key people from the Provincetown Players helped found the Theatre Guild.

The little theatres became a movement and an influence because they quickly had a voice: Their organ was *Theatre Arts Magazine*, which gave national distribution to their ideas. It described individual theatres and kept readers current on what was going on in Europe and at home. By 1930, however, *Theatre Arts* was turning toward the New York–based commercial theatre for its copy. The little theatres still existed, but many had used up their enthusiasm for art and had become community theatres, often amateur theatres, which staged middle-of-the-road popular fare that had first appeared on Broadway. Art and Beauty had not proved potent at either paying the bills or solving social problems, and no wonder: They were ideas from before "the War"—World War I—and the cynicism and striving of the 1920s

NEW STAGECRAFT

Robert Edmond Jones devised this setting for *Hamlet* in the 1920s. Note the simplified, dimensional structure and the expressive use of lighting to emphasize the shapes of the setting.

was not congenial to them. The Great Depression and the rise of fascism in Europe finished Art and Beauty as ideas with impact, not least because those ideas were associated with German culture.

The fading of *Theatre Arts Magazine* marked the death of the little theatre movement but not of avant-gardism in the United States. Much of the same energy went into leftist theatre in the 1930s, only to appear again after World War II in new forms.

Playwrights: Sometimes Commercial, Sometimes Not

Eugene O'Neill

In the United States, Eugene O'Neill was the foremost early playwright who aimed to elevate the theatre to the standards of art. As a critic wrote in 2011, "Before Eugene O'Neill, America had entertainment; after him, it had drama." One approach he used was to base his plays on ancient stories. Many of his plays were first performed at the noncommercial Provincetown Playhouse and the Theatre Guild. Later his plays came to Broadway. He wrote more than thirty long plays and dozens of one-acts. *Anna Christie* (1920), *The Iceman Cometh* (1946), and *A Moon for the Misbegotten* (1947) are often revived.

O'Neill's plays were often difficult and pessimistic. Consider *Desire under the Elms* (1925), a US retelling of the Greek myth of Phaedra, or *Mourning Becomes Electra* (1931), a retelling of the Orestes myth, placed during the US Civil War. *Mourning* is a trilogy of five-act plays—a total of fifteen acts—thus rarely produced. His work was serious and ambitious: he

ROBERT EDMOND JONES
The setting by Jones for O'Neill's *Desire under the Elms*. The front of the house is raised to reveal the interior of the Ephraim Cabot house. The heart of the play is the sexual tension between Ephriam's new young wife and her stepson.

received the Nobel Prize in 1936 and four Pulitzer Prizes and was respected but, after the initial productions, not widely revived. His one comedy, *Ah, Wilderness!* (1933), is often staged. Still his example and earnest striving helped raise the US theatre to the level of literature. At his death in 1953, O'Neill left an unproduced autobiographical play, *Long Day's Journey into Night*, which, once it was staged, has been generally considered one of the greatest of US plays.

Other US playwrights of note from the first half of the twentieth century looked beyond realism for innovative styles to tell new serious stories.

THE PLAY'S THE THING

Eugene O'Neill's *Long Day's Journey into Night*, Produced 1956

Eugene O'Neill had received the Nobel Prize for Literature in 1936 and was suffering from Parkinson's disease as he wrote *Long Day's Journey into Night* in 1940. He gave the autobiographical play to his wife as an anniversary gift, writing that because of her love, he was able to "face my dead at last and write this play." O'Neill asked that it not be published until twenty-five years after his death, but his wife caused it to be published and then produced just three years after his death.

The play exactly duplicates O'Neill's family. The father in the play, James Tyrone, is an Irish American actor who had a tremendous and lasting success with one part for years, never developing as a serious actor as he had wished. O'Neill's father, also named James, played the title role in *The Count of Monte Cristo* more than six thousand times. The two sons echo the life stories to the time of the play of Eugene O'Neill and his brother, Jamie.

The mother in the play, Mary Tyrone, is addicted to morphine. Morphine was not a regulated drug until 1914, and many morphine addicts at the time of the play were middle-class women like Mary Tyrone. O'Neill's mother, Mary Ellen O'Neill, was a morphine addict.

The Story of the Play The play takes place on one day in August 1912, beginning at 8:30 in the morning and ending around midnight. The place is a seaside summer home, decidedly not luxurious. In the first of four acts, the family worries if Mary, just back from treatment for her addiction, will begin taking morphine again. Also in the first act, the family is worried whether the doctor has found that Edmund's cough and weight loss are the signs of consumption, now called tuberculosis. Early in the first scene of Act II, Mary is

(continues)

THE PLAY'S THE THING   Eugene O'Neill's *Long Day's Journey into Night*, Produced 1956 *(continued)*

using again. By Act III, the family knows that Edmund has consumption and will be going to a sanatorium.

Other than these two questions, both resolved early in the worst way, there is little story development. In various combinations, in advancing states of inebriation from morphine or alcohol, the characters talk about themselves, their pasts, and each other; they bicker and reminisce. Although the play takes place in one day, these conversations or something like them have been going on for all their lives. Character is revealed in layers. The family members say how they see themselves and how they see each other. By the end of the play, their lives of limited possibilities seem to have been nearly inevitable.

The family agrees that James Tyrone is cheap. He argues he is not cheap. Later he says he is not really well-to-do because all his money is tied up in real estate. Or, he says, maybe he is cheap but it comes naturally to him because he grew up poor and had to begin work at age ten, for fifty cents a week. Mary Tyrone was a convent girl from a well-to-do family who dreamed of becoming either a concert pianist or a nun until she met James and fell in love. Life with James as an itinerant actor-manager was one of cheap hotel rooms, no permanent home, no friends, and no social life. Mary half hopes to overdose and die, but she could never commit suicide for the Virgin Mary would not forgive her.

In the last act, the three men return home late from drinking. O'Neill equates the men's need for alcoholic escape from feeling and depression with Mary's use of morphine. Finally, Mary comes down, carrying her old wedding gown that she's fished out of the attic. She is tremendously intoxicated, lost in a reverie of her convent years. She suddenly remembers: "I fell in love with James Tyrone and was so happy for a time."

Elmer Rice: Expressionism on Broadway

Elmer Rice's *The Adding Machine* (1923) is unusual for being a noteworthy expressionistic US play mounted on Broadway. The protagonist, Mr. Zero, an accountant at a large, faceless corporation, is replaced by an adding machine, and Zero psychologically deteriorates. Rice's play was a reaction against the increased mechanization and automation in the work place that was feared to be displacing workers. In 2007 the play was the basis for a musical that premiered in Chicago and played a successful off-Broadway run. (O'Neill, too, wrote expressionistic dramas that appeared on Broadway, *The Hairy Ape* [1922] and *The Emperor Jones* [1920].)

Thornton Wilder

Another nonrealistic play, a success on Broadway, has had a long afterlife in not-for-profit and educational theatres: Thornton Wilder's *Our Town* (1938). The life of a small town is explored led by a one-man chorus named Stage Manager. The main character, Emily, dies young and is allowed to return to the Earth to relive one last day. It is no coincidence that *Our Town* is placed in the years of 1901 to 1913, the dawn of the twentieth century but before the First World War changed the United States and much of the world. Although not a dominant topic of *Our Town*, an important element is a nostalgia for a lost, quieter, more family-oriented time. It is difficult to tie the play to a specific theatrical style. Today one might see *Our Town* as

A SKEWED WORLD

The 1923 expressionist drama *The Adding Machine* chronicles the crumbling life of an ordinary accountant, Mr. Zero, who loses his job to a machine. He kills his boss and is tried for murder. Here, Lee Simonson's design for the courtroom scene. Note the angled walls and windows, a common motif in expressionistic stage design.

closest to epic theatre—although it was written before the time that Brecht's theories had wide distribution. *Our Town* is epic in having nonrepresentational scenery and costuming, emblematic staging, and a stage manager who comments on and interrupts the action, disrupting the audience's emotional involvement in scenes.

Less often revived—and even more experimental—is Wilder's 1942 Broadway play *The Skin of Our Teeth*, which tells a nonlinear story of a family, living during the ice age in the first act (a dinosaur appears as a character), a roaring-twenties-like era in the second act, and, in the third, at the end of an apocalyptic war as the family emerges from a bomb shelter. This play is of its time, spawned by the horrors of the First World War and the fears of a second war to come and acknowledging that civilization had survived by the "skin of its teeth." Again the style of Wilder's play is hard to connect to the theatrical styles of its time. Today one might see it as postmodern, before that term was devised, because of its disdain for unity.

Luigi Pirandello

An Italian, Luigi Pirandello (1867–1936) was ahead of his time. Many in his early audiences in Rome and Milan thought he must be insane. In *Six Characters in Search of an Author* (1921), for example, Pirandello acknowledged that the play was not reality but just a play. During a rehearsal for a play-within-the play, six people unexpectedly appear, telling the director that they are characters who need a playwright to make their story. *Six Characters* played in translation on Broadway in 1922. Pirandello wrote more than twenty plays. The most often revived in the English-language theatre are *Six Characters in Search of an Author, Henry IV* (1922), and *Right You Are if You Think You Are* (1917). The theatricality of Pirandello is clearly an early precursor of what would come to be called postmodernism.

Federico García Lorca

In Spain, the poet Federico García Lorca (1898–1936) wrote symbolist plays, including *Blood Wedding* (1932) and *The House of Bernarda Alba* (1936). Lorca was killed in 1936 by the fascists during the Spanish Civil War. As a leftist and critic of Spanish middle class life, Lorca's works were completely censored by Generalissimo Francisco Franco's totalitarian government from 1939 to 1953.

Comedy in the Commercial Theatre

Comedy is often topical. Even when comedy is not topical, it often reflects societal attitudes that are open to change, especially likely to change in the twentieth century, a period of rapid change. For example, humor using the stereotypes of an immigrant group for the source of its humor—Mick jokes, Polack jokes, Chink jokes, Wop jokes, and Kike jokes (Irish, Polish, Chinese, Italian, and Jewish ethnic slurs, respectively)—was popular in the early decades of the twentieth century but unacceptable today. Comedy needs constant reinvigoration although there are exceptions.

There were many successful writers of comic plays during commercialism whose works have never been remounted after their first successes. An example from the late nineteenth century is Clyde Fitch (1865–1909) who wrote more than sixty plays, most of them light comedies that were immensely popular in New York and London. He was a box-office star playwright who wrote for acting stars. His play, *Captain Jinks of the Horse Marines*, was a star vehicle for Ethel Barrymore in 1901. At one time he had five plays running simultaneously on Broadway. Today, his plays are seldom revived and then only as a curiosity.

POSTMODERN LORCA
Here, a 2002 staging of Federico García Lorca's 1932 *Blood Wedding* at Butler University. A largely symbolist work is here given a postmodernist stage set; a giant, fractured, in places transparent, guitar.

George S. Kaufman

One playwright whose comedies have lasted is George S. Kaufman (1889–1961), often called "the great collaborator." He wrote more than fifty plays, musicals, revues, films, and criticism. His work earned two Pulitzer Prizes. Kaufman was in great demand as a director of his own and other writer's works. Throughout his forty-year career, Kaufman wrote with the novelist Edna Ferber, Marc Connelly, and the Marx Brothers, among others.

Critics believe Kaufman's best work resulted from his collaboration with Moss Hart. Together, they created off-beat characters and a more democratic approach to comedy, but they remained socially conservative and somewhat sentimental. In 1936 he and Hart wrote *You Can't Take It with You*, and in 1939, *The Man Who Came to Dinner*. Both became staples of community theatres and educational theatres for decades and are still revived. They wrote large-cast plays that commercial Broadway could afford even in the Great Depression.

George Bernard Shaw

George Bernard Shaw (1856–1950), an Irishman writing in England, began in the noncommercial theatre and became successful in the commercial theatre. Shaw started playwriting in the late nineteenth century, but some of his most memorable plays came in the early decades of the twentieth century. A realist and a socialist, Shaw was paradoxically both the best comic playwright of the period and the most serious one as well; his plays are full of verbal fireworks and the collision of real ideas—poverty, industrialism, war, and nationalism—although their plots were often the old ones of love, marriage, and money. Shaw gave his villains some of his best arguments, which is one of his great strengths as a playwright. When he contrasted the upper and lower classes, both sides got a satirical drubbing. He was one of Henrik Ibsen's most vocal and influential supporters in England. Although Shaw's plays are unlike Ibsen's, Shaw shared the Norwegian playwright's concern with the unexamined life of middle-class women. His plays continue to be revived today. Among Shaw's sixty titles are *Major Barbara* (1905), *Misalliance* (1910), and *Pygmalion* (1912–1913), the play adapted into the 1950s musical *My Fair Lady*. He almost lived to see this musical produced, dying in 1950 at the age of ninety-four.

Noel Coward

Central to the style of his time was a playwright of light comedies of manners and a composer and lyricist of pithy theatre songs, the Englishman Noel Coward (1899–1973). Coward wrote comedies of wit and social mores between the two wars and even after, with plays like *Blithe Spirit*, *Private Lives*, *Present Laughter*, and *Design for Living*. Coward visited the United States in 1921 and said that the energy of Broadway theatre affected his writing and led to his first great successes in London and in the United States. Over a long

THE THEATRE GUILD'S FIRST PRODUCTION REVIVED IN CHICAGO

Here, George Bernard Shaw's *Heartbreak House*, staged in 2004 by the Goodman Theatre in Chicago. The set clearly reflects Captain Shotover's individuality, including his love of tinkering and inventing. The Theatre Guild brought the play first to the United States in 1920.

life, Coward wrote more than fifty plays, revues, and musicals. During World War II, he fed the British propaganda machine with popular songs including the ironically titled "Don't Let's Be Beastly to the Germans" and especially with a dramatic and patriotic film script about the British Navy titled *In Which We Serve*. After the war, Coward continued to write, but nothing he did was as successful as before. In the 1950s, he devised a cabaret act, singing his own songs and those of his contemporaries, sometimes with new comic lyrics of Coward's devising, which was successful in London, Paris, and Las Vegas.

One example of Coward at his most challenging was *Design for Living*, which the London censor would not allow on stage until 1939, so it opened in New York in 1933. Coward wrote the play for himself and his two friends, the internationally renowned husband-and-wife acting team Alfred Lunt and Lynn Fontanne. In the first act, Otto discovers that his wife Gilda has slept with their good friend Leo and storms away. In the second act, Gilda and Leo are living together. Otto dines with Gilda and the two reignite their love, ending the scene in an embrace. In the morning, Gilda decides to abandon them both and exits as Otto still sleeps, leaving behind a note. When Leo returns and he and Otto find the note from Gilda, they are upset. Act III takes place in New York, sometime later. Gilda has married someone else. Leo and Otto crash her party and chase the other guests away. Gilda insists they leave as well but secretly passes them her apartment key. In the last scene, Gilda's husband returns and finds Leo and Otto are lounging in his pajamas. Gilda announces that she cannot resist Otto *and* Leo, the husband storms out in disgust, and the three collapse on the sofa, laughing. *Design for Living* has some of the sexual free spirit of the 1920s, brought into the 1930s, a *ménage à trois*, just for laughs.

Theatre under Occupation and Totalitarianism

Totalitarian governments and occupying foreign powers typically restrain and censor theatre and other arts. In the early years of the Soviet regime, the experimental arts flourished. Under Stalin, the government attitude toward the arts changed. The government declared in 1932 that only **socialist realism** was appropriate for the arts in the Union of Soviet Socialist Republics and aligned countries. The basic tenet of socialist realism was that nonrepresentational art cannot be understood by working people; anything other than realism was decadent and reactionary. Only representational art could fulfill the educational and propaganda needs of the state. Many artists who ignored the demand for socialist realist creations were censored, exiled, sent to labor camps, or killed.

Before the rise of Hitler, Germany was a country wild with experimentation in the arts including theatre. In Nazi Germany, an attitude similar to that of Stalinist Russia prevailed. Moreover, because many artists were Jewish, Communist, or both those artists that could, emigrated to more congenial countries. Strangely, in Nazi-occupied Paris, the arts were allowed to continue with minimal censorship. Audiences and censors sometimes responded differently to the same work. Playwright Jean Anouilh adapted the ancient Greek tale of *Antigone* (1943) for Paris audiences. French audiences saw in the play's battle between an intransigent leader and a girl doing what she believed to be right—a parable for their situation under occupation. Nazi censors failed to see that. Jean-Paul Sartre adapted the Greek myth of Orestes and Electra trying to avenge the death of their father in a play he titled *The Flies*. The characters of the flies were the furies, the supernatural beings pestering and haunting Orestes. Audiences identified the flies with the Nazi soldiers in their city. Nazi censors failed to see that, too.

Commercial Theatre Declines

Early in the twentieth century, the theatre was faced with commercial competition of a kind it had never known: the movies. *Birth of a Nation*, the first feature-length film (1915), was a popular sensation and a box-office hit. Sound came to film in 1927. By the late 1930s, the Technicolor film of *Gone with the Wind* was on the way to grossing more than $70 million, roughly equivalent to more than $1 billion in 2011. Vaudeville stars were moving to another new medium that might compete with theatre, radio; and legitimate theatres across the United States were closing or being remodeled into movie houses. Even before television became a commercial reality in the United States in 1948, these other new rivals economically ravaged the US theatrical circuits and the "road," ending vaudeville and burlesque, and driving the last nails into the coffins of theatre stock companies.

The effect on Broadway was also severe and drawn out. At the end of World War I (1918), Broadway saw two to three hundred productions a year. Investment for a production was reasonable, as little as two thousand dollars for a small show, rarely more than ten thousand dollars. Ticket prices were low—three dollars bought the best seat in the house. Tourists and New Yorkers flocked to the theatres.

By the end of the 1930s and the Great Depression, however, the vigorous commercial theatre of the 1920s was in trouble. Despite occasional bright spots, Broadway's commercial theatre continued to decline through World War II and beyond. Increasingly, New York theatres were abandoned, torn down, or converted to movie houses or "girlie shows." Many others were dark (meaning "closed") as often as they were open.

Several other causes may be given for the decline of the commercial theatre between the wars. The Depression of the 1930s hit theatre hard, as it did every other business. Theatrical unions grew strong enough to demand higher wages and better working conditions, but now they were asking for them from a theatre less able to pay them. As the cost of producing plays escalated, so did ticket prices; therefore, some former patrons found themselves priced out of the theatre audience. Clearly, the commercial theatre was in trouble, and its death was regularly—if inaccurately—predicted. Broadway was popularly called "The Fabulous Invalid," always on its deathbed and yet sometimes so fabulously exciting. It survived, but its glory days lay back before the First World War when theatre was the primary source of popular entertainment.

THE NEW RIVAL: FILM

In 1915, D. W. Griffith released his feature-length *The Birth of a Nation*. Movies drained the mass audience out of the theatres, ending stock companies, vaudeville, and most of the road. This is the assassination of President Abraham Lincoln in Ford's Theatre as seen in Griffith's film, the photo taken from the souvenir program of 1915.

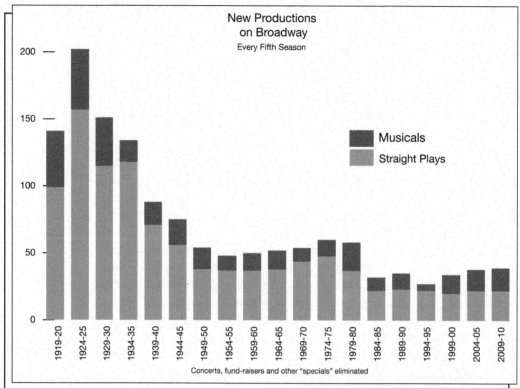

New Productions
on Broadway
Every Fifth Season

■ Musicals
■ Straight Plays

Concerts, fund-raisers and other "specials" eliminated

Numbers of productions on Broadway peaked in the 1920s. The Great Depression, sound film, and finally television reduced the demand for Broadway theatre through the rest of the twentieth century.

KEY TERMS

Key terms are boldface type in the text. Check your understanding against this list. Persons are page-referenced in the Index.

absurdism, p. 232

alienation effect or
   A-effect, p. 233

alienation theatre, p. 232

American Method, p. 239

art theatre movement, p. 241

biomechanics, p. 242

constructivism, p. 232

cubism, p. 232

epic theatre, p. 232

expressionism, p. 232

living newspaper, p. 240

modernism, p. 230

new stagecraft, p. 243

postmodernism, p. 233

selective realism, p. 239

socialist realism, p. 252

surrealism, p. 231

symbolism, p. 231

theatre of cruelty, p. 236

Chapter 11 at a Glance

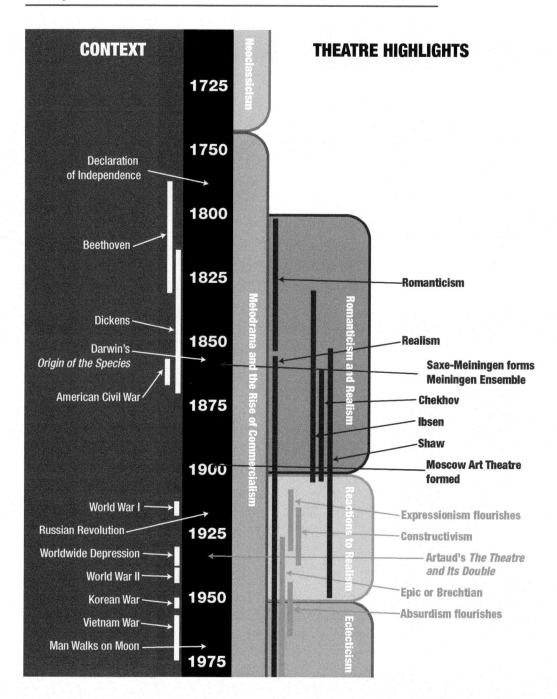

CONTEXT

THEATRE HIGHLIGHTS

Neoclassicism

1725

1750

Declaration of Independence

1800

Beethoven

1825

Romanticism

Dickens

1850

Realism

Darwin's *Origin of the Species*

Saxe-Meiningen forms Meiningen Ensemble

American Civil War

1875

Chekhov

Ibsen

Shaw

1900

Moscow Art Theatre formed

World War I

Expressionism flourishes

Russian Revolution

1925

Constructivism

Worldwide Depression

Artaud's *The Theatre and Its Double*

World War II

Korean War

1950

Epic or Brechtian

Absurdism flourishes

Vietnam War

Man Walks on Moon

1975

Melodrama and the Rise of Commercialism

Romanticism and Realism

Reactions to Realism

Eclecticism

Musical Theatre

When you have completed this chapter, you should be able to:

- Trace the emergence of the US musical from operetta to the revue.
- Compare the nature of the book musical to the integrated musical.
- Describe the qualities of a "pop opera."
- Explain the importance of Stephen Sondheim, Andrew Lloyd Webber, and Cameron Mackintosh to the development of the American musical.
- Describe the nature of the jukebox musical and give examples.

Context

Before World War I, music was essential in paratheatrical performances and in some theatre. It was a major component of melodrama. Various kinds of "ballad opera" marked the preromantic period, for example John Gay's *The Beggar's Opera* of the eighteenth century. By the early nineteenth century, operetta was popular in Paris. **Operetta** stories were romantic, with characters largely royal or at least upper class. If any common people appeared, they were the comic servants. Operettas were strewn with woozy music: marches, love anthems, and especially waltzes. They required trained voices, perhaps ones lighter than grand opera but trained nevertheless. Starting largely in France, the songs would be played throughout Europe and the United States and became the first really popular stage music. The scripts would also be produced everywhere, not so much in translation but in adaptation, for Berlin, London, and New York audiences.

The works of W. S. Gilbert and Arthur Sullivan who flourished in London from 1871 to 1896 dominated British musical theatre in shows such as *The Mikado* (1885), *HMS Pinafore* (1878), *The Pirates of Penzance* (1879), and others. Gilbert and Sullivan operettas were unlike the romantic operettas that flourished on the continent; they were wholly comic and mildly satiric, both of British society and of opera conventions. Each Gilbert and Sullivan operetta was quickly pirated in the United States, with little or no money for the authors. They are regularly revived today.

In working-class areas, music halls grew out of public houses or saloons, and **music hall** became a British term for lower-class musical variety shows, which included a master of ceremonies, songs, comedians, and dancers. Similar paratheatrical entertainment developed in the United States, which was called **vaudeville** and **burlesque**, starting during the first half of the nineteenth century. Burlesque, originally a comic form for mixed audiences, became overwhelmingly a male entertainment, especially after Lydia Thompson's "British Blondes" toured the United States in 1869. The blondes, dressed in skin-colored tights, were a sexual provocation in their time. The British Blondes' mix of comedy, song and dance, parody, animal acts, drag performers, and big stage effects mixed with naughty jokes and racy costumes changed US burlesque forever. Thereafter, burlesque featured

OPERETTA

Gilbert and Sullivan's fourteen comic operettas, written between 1871 and 1896, dominated Victorian-era musical theatre. Here, a poster for one their most often performed works, *The Mikado* (1885). *The Mikado* was nominally placed in Japan but really lampooned British culture and politics.

spectacle, song, dance, *and* female bodies. Striptease was added after World War I, pushing burlesque to the outskirts of respectability. Vaudeville, on the other hand, flourished as a family entertainment. Later, many of the stars of vaudeville moved to radio, Broadway revues, and the movies in the 1930s when vaudeville itself died, done in by movies and the Great Depression. Until then, vaudeville served as a recruiting league for the Broadway **revue**, a nonstory mix of comedy, music, and dance with opulent spectacle and lots of more-or-less-clothed female bodies. One US example of the revue was the *Ziegfeld Follies*, a yearly entertainment from 1907 through 1931, with occasional editions thereafter until 1957. Follies girls were hired because they had beautiful faces and figures and could walk across a stage with grace in

THE ZIEGFELD GIRL

The Ziegfeld Follies featured "walking girls" who were not required to sing, dance, or say dialogue. Instead they were hired for their beauty, height, and their ability to move up and down stairways wearing elaborate—and scanty—costumes topped by enormous headdresses.

elaborate, scanty costumes and out-of-this-world hats and headdresses; they were not hired for their ability to dance, sing, or tell jokes.

The US Musical Emerges

Musical theatre in the United States eventually took another direction. Incorporating songs and dance into story in new ways, it became the outstanding theatrical export of a nation that was coming to dominate the world with its popular culture.

Some theatre historians say *The Black Crook* of 1866 was the first musical. They note that it had a story, popular songs, and dances performed by actors with pleasant voices, but not the voices of trained operetta performers. The play script was by a US author, and most of the music was adapted for *The Black Crook* from existing popular songs. The production ran 474 performances—a historic run for the time—in a huge theatre, the 3,200-seat Niblo's Garden, and then toured the United States for decades.

Still, *The Black Crook* was an accidental creation. Thus, some historians think it is not accurate to call it the *start* of the US musical form. The "accident" is telling: A ballet troupe from Paris lost their New York engagement when their theatre burned. Casting about for other jobs, the dancers were put into an existing melodrama to make a five-hour-long "musical spectacle." (The "black" of the title refers to black magic, not to African Americans.) How *The Black Crook* is viewed, then, is open to critical interpretation.

A distinctly **American musical** form developed later, after about 1900, when the US musical began to separate itself from European operetta and the musical revue. The main characters in the US musical were not titled, like those of operetta; the songs were often able to be sung by average voices rather than opera-trained ones; and there was a story unlike musical revue. Sometimes, however, the story was only a minor part of the event. From its beginnings, the musical had double appeal in music and spectacle; the latter was often the female body, gorgeously costumed, often dancing—the "chorus girl."

THE BLACK CROOK
Some say this show is the forerunner of the US musical, a genre that is uniquely American. This poster shows the finale of the four-hour plus spectacle.

Composers

Most of the top Broadway composers of the first half of the twentieth century wrote for operetta or revue or both even while helping to create the new, story-based form that became US musical comedy. They worked with **lyricists** and **librettists** (writers of words to songs and writers of the play or **book**). These composers and some of their works included:

- Victor Herbert, operettas (1859–1924): *Babes in Toyland* (1903), *The Red Mill* (1905), and *Naughty Marietta* (1910).

- Jerome Kern, musicals (1885–1945): *Oh, Boy!* (1917), *Sally* (1920), and *Show Boat* (1927).

- Sigmund Romberg, operettas (1887–1951): *Blossom Time* (1921), *The Student Prince* (1924), and *The Desert Song* (1926).

- Irving Berlin, musicals and revues (1888–1989): *Music Box Revue* (1921), *Annie Get Your Gun* (1946), and *Call Me Madam* (1950).

- Cole Porter, musicals (1891–1964): *Anything Goes* (1934), *Red, Hot and Blue!* (1936), and *Kiss Me, Kate* (1948).

- George Gershwin, musicals (1898–1937): *Lady, Be Good* (1924), *Strike Up the Band* (1930), *Girl Crazy* (1930), *Of Thee I Sing* (1931, first Pulitzer Prize for a musical), and *Porgy and Bess* (1935).

- Richard Rodgers, revues and musicals (1902–1979): *Garrick Gaieties* (two editions 1925 and 1926), *On Your Toes* (1936), *Pal Joey* (1940), *Oklahoma!* (1943), *Carousel* (1945), and *The Sound of Music* (1959).

CHORUS GIRLS

These beauties were required to sing and dance in the chorus as well as look fetching.

Neither these composers' backgrounds nor their music was entirely "American," however. Herbert was born in Ireland; Romberg in Hungary; and Berlin in Russia. Their musical training was often European and classical, not US and popular—Gershwin trained with private classical music teachers; Romberg and Herbert studied in Europe; Kern at the New York College of Music and in Europe; and Porter at Yale and Harvard. The Russian-Jewish immigrant Irving Berlin, on the other hand, had no training at all and could not read music.

What distinguished their music as the century progressed, however, was the adoption of the rhythms of popular dance music. Such music often had its roots in nineteenth-century African American musical forms that, by 1900, had their own songwriters that were known throughout the United States. Mostly they were popularized in theatrical types that were patronizing to African Americans, such as the minstrel show, blackface vaudeville acts, and "coon shows."

Some have argued, too, that the preponderance of Jews among the composers affected the sound of US popular music. Cole Porter, a WASP, famously told Richard Rodgers, a Jew, that he had found the secret to writing more successful popular songs. "I'll write Jewish tunes," he said. He meant specifically he would use minor keys. Whether this anecdote is true or not, all successes, whatever their origin, were quickly copied in hopes of having a big, profitable US hit. The races and ethnicities may not have come together in the first half of the twentieth century in the United States, but popular entertainment was a melting pot.

Lyricists

Essential to the musical were the lyricists. With increasing frequency, the top composers were associated with the same lyricists in musical after musical, and the lyricists clearly shaped the tone and often the style of the music. In no composer is this clearer than Richard Rodgers. Until 1940 his lyricist was the witty, sometimes risqué, and inventive Lorenz Hart, and their musicals demonstrate Hart's nonsentimental mind. Among Rodgers and Hart song titles are "The Lady Is a Tramp," "There's a Small Hotel," and "Bewitched, Bothered, and Bewildered." Rodgers later connected with Oscar Hammerstein II, in 1943, and the musicals became more romantic,

IRVING BERLIN'S *ANNIE GET YOUR GUN*
Berlin wrote both music and lyrics for this 1946 hit and all his Broadway shows. The musical includes the song "There's No Business Like Show Business." Here, two scenes from a production by the Nevada Conservatory Theatre, Las Vegas. Annie Oakley, left, sings "You Can't Get a Man with a Gun."

sometimes even saccharine. Among Rodgers and Hammerstein song titles are "You'll Never Walk Alone," "My Favorite Things," and "It Might as Well Be Spring." With Hammerstein's lyrics, Rodger's tunes were even more popular than they were with Hart's lyrics. Not all songwriters worked with lyricists. Irving Berlin, Frank Loesser, and Cole Porter wrote their own lyrics, but they are exceptions.

Hammerstein had had much the same effect on Jerome Kern, with whom he collaborated before Rodgers, starting after 1925. The result of that collaboration best remembered today is *Show Boat*, which was a more serious and sentimental musical than Kern's previous work with others. In fact, *Show Boat* was an anomaly for its time, a musical with an unhappy ending, centering on charges of interracial marriage, which was against the law in many states at the time. Other musicals at the time might be a little satirical but never took on such serious subject matter. Most musicals focused on comic schemes in pursuit of money and romantic love.

The "Book Musical" Both the operetta and the revue faded after the 1920s; the **book musical** took their place. Still usually frivolous and with songs often more stuck in than developed from the action, such musicals were meant as entertainments whose scripts were excuses for goofy jokes and glorious melody. They produced many of the great songs of the US theatre that became popular on stage, radio, recordings, and as sheet music. Jerome Kern, for example, poured out beautiful melodies seemingly endlessly; George Gershwin, in his short life, wrote many songs that remain standards. What is perhaps most significant about these composers is that they were primarily *songwriters*. Many of them wrote songs on order for a moment in a script—love songs, novelty songs, southern songs, patter songs, and "showstoppers" (rousing musical numbers, usually comic, earning such applause that they would interrupt the action). These songs became part of the national cultural life at a time when many middle-class homes had a piano and sheet music was sold at the five-and-dime variety stores. Songs were detached from the musicals and popularized via sheet music and radio, and they were sung and played in nightclubs and supper clubs—and in homes. In later years, these songs became known as the **Great American Songbook**. Some examples include:

- "Someone To Watch over Me" by George and Ira Gershwin for the musical *Oh, Kay!* (1926).
- "You'll Never Walk Alone" by Richard Rodgers and Oscar Hammerstein II for the musical *Carousel* (1945).
- "April in Paris" by Vernon Duke and E. Y. "Yip" Harburg for *Walk a Little Faster* (1932).
- "If I Were a Bell" by Frank Loesser for *Guys and Dolls* (1950).
- "I Got Lost in His Arms" by Irving Berlin for *Annie, Get Your Gun* (1946).
- "Falling in Love with Love" by Richard Rodgers and Lorenz Hart for *The Boys from Syracuse* (1938).

The Integrated Musical

Only gradually did a more serious dramatic purpose appear, foreshadowed in *Show Boat* (1927), developed in *Pal Joey* (1940), and fully-realized with *Oklahoma!* (1943). The movement thereafter—that is, after 1940—was toward a serious comedy with a happy ending, usually centered on romantic love, mostly dealing with contemporary people, and having song arising from character and advancing the plot, hence the term **integrated musical**. Book, song, and dance were intertwined or integrated to tell the story. An example of this kind of integration is the song "If I Loved You" from Rodgers and Hammerstein's *Carousel* (1946). As sheet music, it is a typical song with two choruses, a bridge (a musical term for a contrasting middle section of a song), and a repeat of the chorus lasting about three minutes. In the show, Billy Bigelow and Julie Jordan each sing some, talk as the music continues as

THE PLAY'S THE THING

Girl Crazy, 1930

The brothers George and Ira Gershwin collaborated, beginning in 1924, on more than a dozen Broadway musicals. Together they created some of the most unforgettable songs of the twentieth century. Like *Girl Crazy*, these musicals were all early "book musicals," meaning there was a rather flimsy plot of some sort in service of the songs or a major star. Dances were included but rarely moved the plot forward; most were pleasant interruptions in what little plot there might be. *Girl Crazy* had a singing/dancing chorus of thirty women.

The bare-bones recounting of the plot of *Girl Crazy* that follows reveals the nature of the silly book. Clearly it is not meant to be believable, but only to provide a way to loosely tie together the great songs of George and Ira Gershwin, sung by great singers: Ethel Merman in her stage debut and Ginger Rogers. It also provided for the dialect clowning of the important vaudeville star of the era, Willie Howard. Six of the *Girl Crazy* songs are classics of what is now

called the Great American Songbook: "Embraceable You," "Sam and Delilah," "Bidin' My Time," "I Got Rhythm," "But Not for Me," and "Boy! What Love Has Done to Me."

Girl Crazy was filmed three times, most notably in a 1943 version starring Judy Garland and Mickey Rooney. In 1992, *Girl Crazy*, with a completely new script and additional Gershwin songs interpolated, was a Broadway and London hit under the title *Crazy for You*. It earned a Tony Award as best musical.

The Story of the Musical *Girl Crazy* is set in a tiny Arizona backwater, Custerville. Into this mostly male town rides the central character, Danny Churchill (romantic lead), a New York playboy whose father has shipped him off to Buzzards, the family ranch, hoping to save him from the fast life in the Big City. He makes the three-thousand-mile trip to Custerville in a taxi driven by Gieber Goldfarb (the lead comic character with a heavy Jewish accent).

A moment from the 1992 rewrite of Girl Crazy *titled* Crazy for You.

(continues)

THE PLAY'S THE THING Girl Crazy, 1930 *(continued)*

Danny meets Polly Gray (romantic lead), the local post mistress. Danny decides to turn Buzzards into a gambler's dude ranch replete with imported New York showgirls. The reborn Buzzards is an instant success, drawing customers from both coasts. The gambling room is managed by Slick Fothergill and his wife Kate, a sexy singer who headlines the casino's show. Two other women appear in Custerville for reasons that are nearly incomprehensible: Patsy West (the female comic), a telephone switchboard operator, and Tess Harding, Danny's former girlfriend from New York.

There are complications. Gieber Goldfarb has won the election for Sheriff and to escape the wrath of his rival disguises himself as an American Indian, Big Chief Push-in-the-Face. Later Goldfarb dresses in drag to help catch a mugger.

The locale moves to San Luz, Mexico, where Molly realizes that she has been tricked by Sam into spending the night together in a hotel where he has registered them as husband and wife. Molly then realizes her feelings for Danny. They are headed for the altar and a happy ending for all.

---

underscoring, sing some more, talk some more, and sing the song again, this time as a duet. By the end of the piece—seventeen minutes or so in length—they are in love, which the audience knows through the progression of song, dialogue, and underscoring, tightly integrated. These new musicals were sometimes as frivolous as those that preceded them, but they could address larger issues. For example, Rodgers and Hammerstein's *South Pacific* is concerned deeply with racism, at least from the standpoint of romance between men and women of European and Asian descent.

Gender and Race and the US Musical

The leading composers and lyricists listed previously were white men; so were most musical producers and directors. A few white women—Dorothy Fields and Betty Comden—were notable lyricists. Although many of the composers and lyricists were European immigrants or children of immigrants, they were all caught up in US popular culture. Thus musicals until at least the 1970s, were mostly about a white United States obsessed with romantic love and material success. The "glorification of the American girl," to borrow a marketing phrase from the Ziegfeld Follies, was a very white *male* undertaking. It reflected a society managed by white men.

Mostly invisible but essential to the music were African American musicians of both sexes. Although individual white composers often acknowledged a debt to African American music, the music industry did not as a rule. This music was already in the US grain by the time the US musical was ready to begin its evolution. African American composers rarely made it to Broadway. Exceptions included Will Marion Cook and Eubie Blake. Cook's musical comedy *Clorindy; or, The Origin of the Cakewalk* (1898) was the first all-African American show to play on Broadway. Blake was a songwriter and vaudeville performer before he cowrote the music for *Shuffle Along* (1921), said to be the first hit on

OKLAHOMA! IN THE ROUND

The Arena Stage revived this classic integrated US musical with a racially mixed cast in 2011. Here, the farmhand Curly is played by a Hispanic actor, Nicholas Rodriguez; his love interest, Laurey, is an African American actress, Eleasha Gamble. Laurey's Aunt Eller is played by Faye Butler, also African American. The chorus, seen here performing in the newly opened Mead Center for American Theater in Washington, D.C., is racially mixed as well.

Broadway with African American authors and cast. *Shuffle Along* created a mini-trend, with nine African American musicals opening in New York between 1921 and 1924. In the commercial theatre, success always spawns imitation.

Some black musicians resented such co-optings as Gershwin's *Porgy and Bess* (1935), a white version of southern African American life, using a white version of African American music. Commentators on the subject were divided when the show premiered. At least African American actors were getting work even if in a script with music neither of which were authentic reflections of African American life or song styles. As demanded by the social structures of the times, material written by African Americans for African

Americans to perform could also bow to popular, white tastes. Consider just the title of African American songwriter Eubie Blake's hit show, *Shuffle Along* of 1921. *Shuffle* in African American slang was the term for a slow movement reminiscent of complacent, obedient slaves or servants. At least one historian states that *Shuffle Along* would be offensive if staged today because it reflected the styles and assumptions of minstrel shows.

Song Forms

There soon developed a vocabulary of song forms that served the integrated musical. They included:

- The *"I" song* or *"I want" song*, sung early in the show, introduces main characters and sets out what they are striving for or against. An example, from Merrill and Styne's *Funny Girl* (1964), is Fanny's first song, "I'm the Greatest Star." A comic "I" song, as befits the woman who will become a famous comedienne, the song tells Fanny Brice's family and friends that, although they do not believe in her dream, she *will* become a stage star.

- The *rhythm song* is an upbeat number, often providing a reason for dancing that builds to a big finish. Often, this is the song that people remember and hum as they leave the theatre. An example is "Hello, Dolly," from the Jerry Herman musical of the same name (1964).

- A *comic song* is an opportunity to set laughs to music. In "Adelaide's Lament," from the Frank Loesser musical *Guys and Dolls* (1961), Adelaide, a nightclub singer trying to better herself, consults a psychology text and discovers her sniffles are a "psy-co-so-mat-ic" illness because her boyfriend of fourteen years will not marry her.

- The *ballad* is a slow song, often a love song or a lament for lost love, that expresses the characters' desires but also functions to slow down the show's pace, allowing room for the next rhythm or comic song to build again to a big finish. There are too many examples to choose just one. Consider "Some Enchanted Evening" from *South Pacific*, "I'll Know (When My Love Comes Along)" from *Guys and Dolls*, "People" from *Funny Girl*, and "It Only Takes a Moment" from *Hello, Dolly!* Ballads were the songs that really sold sheet music and that every radio singer wanted to record, making money for the composer and lyricist.

In addition to the kind of songs described, two additional songs types are traditionally placed on a musical's play list: the Opening Number and the penultimate number (still called the "eleven o'clock number" even though Broadway musicals now usually end before 11:00). The opening number, the first musical number in the production, sets the tone, time, place, and mood of the musical. The opening number of *Annie Get Your Gun* is "Colonel Buffalo Bill" sung by the full cast, touting the virtues of Buffalo Bill's Wild West Show that has come to town. It also introduces the romantic lead, Frank Butler.

The next-to-last number is usually a comic number intended to invigorate the audience and generate applause. In *Annie Get Your Gun*, the eleven o'clock number is "Anything You Can Do (I Can Do Better)," a comic challenge song between Frank Butler and Annie Oakley, the two leading players. The finale quickly follows.

Rodgers and Hammerstein's *Oklahoma!* (1943) established the dream ballet as an expressionistic storytelling dance. In a number titled "Out of My Dreams," the main female character, Laurie, dreams about her predicament, stuck between a good man she loves and another man who is threatening and probably unhinged. The fifteen-minute choreography by Agnes De Mille was so effective that the dream ballet became a cliché, often used by writers and choreographers without the talent to make it a successful storytelling device.

HOW WE KNOW

Preserving Musicals

Scholars sometimes have to dig deeply to locate original orchestrations, vocal arrangements, and scripts of US musicals. Sometimes they fail to find them. Too often, these manuscripts were not preserved so that future generations could know *exactly* what was originally performed. For example, this situation faced musicologists who were preparing an "authentic" version of the Gershwins' 1930 musical *Girl Crazy*, described elsewhere in this chapter.

It is perhaps understandable that musicals from the early twentieth century have not been preserved. Creators saw musicals as ephemeral, something to satisfy an audience for a season or to tour the United States and London maybe, not undying art. There was no market then to publish a musical orchestration. Even later, there was carelessness. The original orchestrations of big hits such as *Fiddler on the Roof* (1964), *Hello, Dolly!* (1964), and *A Chorus Line* (1975) are among the missing.

What often goes missing is the **partitur**, a single original manuscript that contains the notes for all the musical instruments on the same page. The arranger produced the partitur and then a copyist pulled out the music for each instrument from the partitur to make the individual parts. The partitur was the property of the composer at the close of a musical, but it was not always returned to the composer.

Shows were modified for productions after Broadway in most every case. Orchestrations were simplified for touring and amateur production or enlarged for film. Keys were changed for singers with different ranges. Dance breaks were inserted for stars who were better dancers than singers or omitted for those not able to dance effectively. To make these changes, an arranger often borrowed the original Broadway orchestration master and in some cases never returned it to the owner. As a result, it can be statistically more difficult to find the original orchestration of a hit musical than of a flop: no one wanted to borrow the partitur of a flop.

Original cast recordings give some historical information to theatre historians, but they are not reliable. True original cast recordings did not start until *Oklahoma!* in 1943. But the technology of the time, the 78-rpm disk, had room for about three-and-a-half minutes per side, so some songs were sped up, truncated, or just arbitrarily divided between two sides. Long-playing 33-rpm disks were an improvement, with

(continues)

HOW WE KNOW   Preserving Musicals *(continued)*

a little more than twenty minutes to a side, but they still required compromises. Because the musicians did not have to be paid for every performance, why not add more violins, more timpani, and so on? Thus, the original cast recordings cannot be relied on to reflect the musical as it was performed on stage.

Changes were also made in the script over time to reflect audience taste. One notable example comes from the groundbreaking *Show Boat* (1927). The musical, set in 1880, opens with African American stevedores hauling bales of cotton and singing of the distance between their lives and those of white people—a repeated theme of the show. The original lyrics of Oscar Hammerstein II were

Niggers all work on the Mississippi,
Niggers all work while the white folks play—

Hammerstein's in-your-face opening was intended to shock the audience. The word *nigger* was an indictment of the *times*, not of African American people. In the 1936 film, the lyric became "Darkies all work on the Mississippi," and in the 1946 revival, it was further softened to "Colored folks work on the Mississippi." To contemporary ears, *darkies* and *colored folks* are not much better than Hammerstein's original bombshell.

Now composers are more attentive to the historical value of their drafts of words and music and of each show's partitur. The largest collection of original materials on the US musical is now in the Library of Congress. But some critical information may still be in a warehouse, a film studio vault, or somebody's basement. There are gaps in what we know about how musicals originally sounded. Lucky is the theatre historian who can fill one of these holes in the historical record.

Musicals since 1950

Broadway composers and lyricists of the integrated story musical after about 1950 include:

- Frederick Loewe (1901–1988) and Alan J. Lerner (1918–1986), composer and lyricist, respectively, of *Brigadoon* (1947); *My Fair Lady* (1956); *Camelot* (1960); and others.
- Jule Styne (1905–1994), composer of *Gypsy* (1959) and *Funny Girl* (1964).
- Leonard Bernstein (1918–1990), composer of *Candide* (1956) and *West Side Story* (1957).
- Jerry Herman (1931–), composer and lyricist of *Hello, Dolly!* (1946), *Mame (1966), and La Cage aux Folles* (1983).
- Stephen Sondheim (1930–), lyricist for *Gypsy* and *West Side Story*; composer and lyricist for *A Funny Thing Happened on the Way to the Forum* (1962), *Company* (1970), *Follies* (1971), *A Little Night Music* (1973), *Sweeney Todd* (1979), and others.
- Stephen Flaherty (1960–) and Lynn Ahrens (1948–), composer and lyricist of *Once on this Island* (1990), *Ragtime* (1998), and *Seussical* (2000).

These musicals were mostly optimistic and continued the integrated musical traditions.

Concept Musicals

Some musicals late in this era were developed around a compelling idea—sometimes with a linear plot, more often without a traditional plot. Three musicals—*Hair, A Chorus Line*, and *Company*—are examples of this "concept" or idea category of the US musical.

Hair   The production of *Hair: The American Tribal Love-Rock Musical* in 1967 was an acknowledgement that time had moved on—in its use of music, its counterculture characters (antiestablishment draft dodgers), its idealism ("make love not war"), and the influence of the non-commercial, experimental theatre of the era. Galt MacDermot composed the rock score, and James Rado and Gerome Ragni wrote the book and lyrics. Developed at the Off Broadway Public Theatre, a not-for-profit theatre, *Hair* told of hippies, drugs, and the Vietnam War, and the show's popularity led to the acceptance of practices previously considered unacceptable in commercial theatre: nudity, four-letter words, and an antiestablishment tone, to cite only the most obvious.

A Chorus Line   In 1975, *A Chorus Line* was nurtured at the same not-for-profit theatre in New York as was *Hair*. The script was developed by dancers during discussions with the director and a writer, a technique courtesy of the experimental theatre. The script was then structured and expanded by James Kirkwood, Jr., a novelist and playwright, and Nicholas Dante, one of the dancers; the music was composed by Marvin Hamlisch; and the lyrics by Edward Kleban. The musical told of the difficulties faced by professional Broadway dancers. Its success re-invigorated a Broadway love affair

THE AMERICAN TRIBAL LOVE-ROCK MUSICAL

First staged in 1967, *Hair* has been a perennial favorite of college and university theatres. The Public Theatre, the original producer, revived *Hair* at its Central Park venue in the summer of 2008. It then moved to Broadway winning strong reviews and a 2009 Tony Award for best revival of a musical. The revival then toured. Here, a moment from that production.

Joan Marcus

COMPANY
Eleven short plays by George Furth became the basis of *Company*, directed by Harold Prince with music by Steven Sondheim. Here, a production by Ball State University.

with dance continuing through the 1990s and including the dynamic tap show *Bring in Da Noise, Bring in Da Funk*, also a concept musical, one which featured African American composers and performers. In both *Hair* and *A Chorus Line*, actors performed on stages mostly devoid of scenic pieces. This, too, was probably an unconscious nod to the experimental theatre.

Company Another concept musical, *Company*, opened on Broadway in 1970. With music and lyrics by Stephen Sondheim and a book by George Furth, *Company* is about a single, unmarried man, Bobby, facing his thirty-fifth birthday. Bobby cannot seem to have a serious relationship or to marry. Five married couples, his best friends, urge him to commit to a relationship/marriage. In a series of comic scenes and songs, it becomes clear that these couples are not the best representatives of married life. Bobby finally decides that marriage is "Being Alive," the climactic song. *Company* won five Tony Awards, including best musical.

Stephen Sondheim: Lyricist and Composer

The 1970s and 1980s were dominated by the composer-lyricist Stephen Sondheim. All his work integrated character and song, so much so that songs often could not be detached from the drama. To some in the audience, the gain in dramatic power was won at the cost of tunefulness and the old zesty, punchy musical show. Despite this limitation, some of his songs are regularly performed by cabaret and jazz performers, and several revues of his songs have been produced with great success.

He began his career as a lyricist for two classic musicals, *West Side Story* (1957) and *Gypsy* (1959). The first musical for which Sondheim wrote both the music and lyrics was *A Funny Thing Happened on the Way to the Forum* (1962). There followed fifteen musicals, mostly successful, including *Follies* (1971), *A Little Night Music* (1973), *Sweeney Todd* (1979), *Into the Woods* (1987), and *Assassins* (1990). His most recent musical was the unsuccessful *Road Show* in 2008.

Musicals and Popular Songs

Hit songs played on the radio often originated in Broadway musicals before the rock era, but that has changed. The last two widely played radio hits from musicals were probably "Aquarius/Let the Sun Shine In" (1967) from the musical *Hair* and popularized in a recording by The Fifth Dimension and "Send in the Clowns" (1975) from Sondheim's musical *A Little Night Music* in a recording by Judy Collins.

Although the integrated book musical remained the norm, two variations evolved beginning in the 1980s, the sung-through musical and the jukebox musical.

The Sung-Through Musical

Also known as "pop opera," the **sung-through musical** is characterized by having little or no spoken dialogue. Instead, many of these musicals used a technique from traditional opera, called **recitative**, which is dialogue set to music, half-sung and half-spoken. Or the story was suggested through staging and imagery without dialogue or recitative. For many of these shows, the score mixed the rhythms of pop music with long melodies reminiscent of arias from Verdi or Puccini operas.

These pop operas featured notable spectacle—a helicopter landing on stage (*Miss Saigon*, 1989); a chandelier falling from over the audience onto the stage (*The Phantom of the Opera*, 1986); a giant barricade erected in audience view from which a revolution was fought (*Les Misérables*, 1985); or a giant tire carrying a cat moving through the proscenium and into the rafters above the heads of the audience (*Cats*, 1981). Although these shows generally required strong voices, they did not require star personalities to sell tickets. Thus, although expensive to first produce, the weekly running cost of these shows could be quite reasonable. The 1980s were the prime of the pop opera.

Andrew Lloyd Webber British composer Andrew Lloyd Webber turned out a number of hugely successful sung-through mega-musicals with plenty of spectacle. His *The Phantom of the Opera* has become the longest-running musical in US history. In October 2010, *Phantom* celebrated its 10,000th London

NOW AND FOREVER

Based on a book of poetry, *Cats* adopted the slogan "Now and Forever." And why not? It played in New York for eighteen years. Here, a production at Southern Illinois University.

performance and, in February 2012, its 10,000th Broadway performance. By the 10,000th performance, *Phantom* had grossed $845 million in New York alone. The musical has played 145 cities in 27 countries with worldwide ticket sales of $5.6 billion.

Working with the lyricist Tim Rice (1944–), Lloyd Webber (1948–) wrote a number of pop songs before their first big success, *Jesus Christ Superstar*. *Superstar* was a two-record album that sold 2.5 million copies before being staged on Broadway in 1971. It is not a traditional musical, more like a suite of songs, recounting in rock idioms the last weeks of Jesus's life. The staging was extravagant and theatrical, and it ran for more than seven hundred performances.

Evita (1976 in London, 1979 in the United States) was also first a two-record release before it was staged as a musical. Essentially the musical is about the life of Eva Perón, the mistress-then-wife of the Argentinean President Juan Perón in the 1950s. After *Evita*, Webber and Rice ended their partnership, and Lloyd Webber's musicals became more operatic in musical style. A musical based on setting T. S. Eliot's poems written for children about cats hardly seemed promising, but Lloyd Webber's *Cats* (1982) ran on Broadway for eighteen years.

Schönberg and Boublil The French composer/lyricist team of Claude-Michel Schönberg and Alain Boublil adapted Victor Hugo's novel of 1862 *Les Misérables* as a sung-through musical. Schonberg-Boublil's musicalization, also called *Les Misérables* (1980), became a long-running international hit. By February 2012, *Les Miz*, as it is popularly called, had played in forty-two countries and had been translated into twenty-one languages. There have been 2,500 productions of a simplified version prepared for school children to perform. Later, in collaboration with the American Richard Maltby, Jr, the team wrote *Miss Saigon* (1989), inspired by Giacomo Puccini's opera

Madama Butterfly. *Miss Saigon* tells of the love affair of a US soldier and a Vietnamese girl. Unable to help her escape when the United States left the war, the soldier is despondent but goes on with life. Returning to Vietnam five years later, he discovers that he has a son and that the mother, his former love, will do anything for the former soldier to take the boy home with him. As a mixed-race child, the boy can have no future in Vietnam but could have a good life in the US.

Producer Cameron Mackintosh Cameron Mackintosh (1946–) is not a writer, director, designer, or actor; he is a producer and has been responsible for managing many enormously financially successful musicals in London, New York, and around the world. He produced Webber's *Cats*, *The Phantom of the Opera*, and others.

He heard a short song cycle in France based on Victor Hugo's novel of 1862 taking place in the years leading up to the French rebellion of 1852, *Les Misérables*, and thought it could be a musical. He convinced the French composer and lyricist, Schönberg and Boubil, to give him the rights. He hired Herbert Kretzmer to write an English libretto. The result—more pop opera than musical—was a huge international success.

The image of the waif Cosette, taken from an illustration in the original edition of the Hugo novel, has become the internationally recognized logo of the play, through Mackintosh's persistent and sometimes clever advertising. Producers may not be artists, but successful ones identify talent and manage it into profitable productions. In 2010, Mackintosh's net worth was estimated to be £635 million, equivalent to slightly more than US$1 billion.

COSETTE

Les Misérables producers used as its logo the engraving of the waif, Cosette, taken from an early edition of the 1862 novel by Victor Hugo.

Jukebox Musicals

Jukebox musicals are based on a collection of popular songs written by a well-known composer or associated with a particular singer or musical group. The creators devise a minimal story in which the songs can be used. (A jukebox was a machine found mostly in restaurants and bars, first popular in the United States around the 1940s, that played songs selected by a patron when a coin was inserted.) The songs of

Buddy Holly, Billy Joel, Frankie Valli and the Four Seasons, and ABBA have provided scores for this genre of musical. The advantage the **jukebox musical** brings, producers believe, is that the public knows and loves the songs before the musical opens.

Mamma Mia! (1999), *Movin' Out* (2002), and *Jersey Boys* (2006) are some successful examples of this genre. The disco group ABBA's catalogue of hits provided the songs for *Mamma Mia!* The story is about a daughter who sends three wedding invitations to her mother's ex-boyfriends. The daughter believes one of the men might be her father. *Mamma Mia!* features twenty-six musical numbers including the disco hit "Dancing Queen."

The jukebox musical based on the songs of Billy Joel, *Movin' Out*, is singular. It is a dance show choreographed by Twyla Tharp. The action is danced, there is no dialogue, and the songs are sung by a single singer-piano player with a back-up band. The story centers on a group of Long Island youngsters growing up in the 1960s, their romances, and the impact on them of the Vietnam War. The show, with its twenty-nine musical numbers, was an international hit. It won nine Tony Awards.

Jersey Boys is a biographical musical based on the life and times of Frankie Valli and the Four Seasons, a singing group that had many hit songs in the 1960s. The show exclusively features the music sung by this group including the hits "Oh, What a Night," "My Eyes Adored You," "Sherry," and "Can't Take My Eyes Off You." In all, there are thirty-four musical numbers in *Jersey Boys*.

Joan Marcus

MAMMA MIA!

The film adaptation of *Mamma Mia!* in 2008 further burnished the international popularity of this jukebox musical. The stage version has been translated into eleven languages. It has long-running productions in dozens of cities around the world. Here, a moment from the 2001 Broadway production.

These three shows demonstrate that there are many approaches to cobbling together a jukebox musical: an original story into which the old songs can be slotted, an all danced-show where story is suggested by movement and pantomime, and a biographical "and then we sang ... " story. Not all jukebox musicals have been hits. Shows based on the music sung by Elvis Presley, Johnny Cash, and John Lennon were flops. One based on the music of Buddy Holly was successful in Toronto and London but not in New York.

Disney Recycles and Musical Revivals

Expensive and elaborate Disney productions appeared in the 1990s, beginning with *Beauty and the Beast* (1994), followed by *The Lion King* (1997) with music by Elton John, which used large puppets and symbolic rather than realistic scenery to achieve stunning visual effects. Again, the experimental theatre influenced a thoroughly commercial musical. Disney continued to produce on Broadway into the millennium, including *Aida* in 2000 with music by Elton John and Tim Rice, exemplifying a shift in commercial organization toward the corporate and the recycled; all the Disney stage shows had been Disney movies first, mostly animated movies.

But there is no simple formula for transferring a cartoon or film story to the musical stage. Among flops in recent years that tried to duplicate Disney's strategy are *Shrek the Musical* (2008), Disney's own *Tarzan* (2006), and *Jekyll & Hyde* (1997).

Spider-Man: Turn Off the Dark followed the Disney formula almost exactly: Julie Taymor directing as she did for *The Lion King* musical with music by rock music songwriters, in this case U2's Bono and the Edge. But *Spider-Man*'s producers were inexperienced in the Broadway theatre and allowed the production costs to grow to the incredible amount of $75 million, when an average Broadway musical cost $12 million to $15 million. *Spider-Man*'s weekly costs are relatively high as well, estimated to be close to $1 million. It played a record twenty-five weeks in previews. When finally opened, reviewers found it mediocre and boring but audiences bought tickets often worth more than $1.5 million a week.

By 2000, another trend was that much Broadway musical theatre was looking backward with revivals of hits from previous seasons: *Oklahoma!* (first staged 1944); *Cabaret* (1966); *Flower Drum Song* (1958); *The Pajama Game* (1954); *Grease* (1972) revived on Broadway in 1994 and 2007; *Chicago* (1975); *How To Succeed in Business* (1961) revived in 1995 and 2011; *Brigadoon* (1947); *South Pacific* (1947); and, from off-Broadway, *The Threepenny Opera* (1954, originally from the Berlin avant-garde of 1928). These examples seem to suggest that Broadway was, by intention or not, introducing new generations of audiences to the hits of the past.

As the new millennium began, long-running musicals continued to dominate Broadway and populate the road. Four shows running on Broadway in January 2000 were still playing in the winter of 2013: *The Phantom of the Opera, Mamma Mia!, Chicago,* and *The Lion King.* Other financially successful musicals opened during this period. None of these newer musicals had anything much in the way of stylistic breakthroughs, timely themes, or songs that anyone wanted to sing outside the theatre. Some of Broadway's successful musicals could be characterized as expensive carnival rides, colorful and fast-paced diversions that were quickly forgotten. Nevertheless, the successful ones made lots of money.

In short, it is easy to see the US musical as only a money machine, a triumph of commercial and marketing savvy over artistic achievement. For some artists, it has provided a genre for expression that is meaningful and lasting. If nothing else, the greatest musical theatre songs, the Great American Songbook, are a lasting treasure.

KEY TERMS

Key terms are boldface type in the text. Check your understanding against this list. Persons are page-references in the Index.

American musical, p. 258
book, p. 259
book musical, p. 261
burlesque, p. 257
Great American Songbook, p. 262
integrated musical, p. 262
jukebox musical, p. 274
librettist, p. 259

lyricist, p. 259
music hall, p. 257
operetta, p. 256
partitur, 267
recitative, p. 271
revue, p. 257
sung-through musical, p. 271
vaudeville, p. 257

Chapter 12 at a Glance

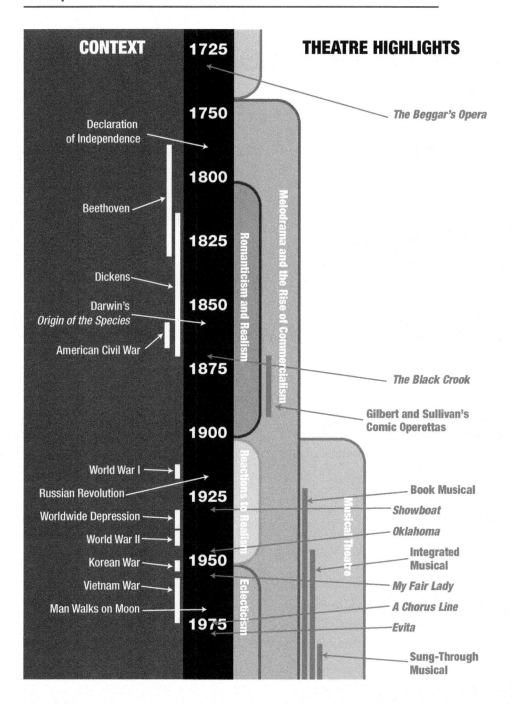

CONTEXT

1725

1750

Declaration
of Independence

1800

Beethoven

1825

Dickens

Darwin's
Origin of the Species   1850

American Civil War

1875

1900

World War I

Russian Revolution   1925

Worldwide Depression

World War II

Korean War   1950

Vietnam War

Man Walks on Moon

1975

THEATRE HIGHLIGHTS

The Beggar's Opera

Melodrama and the Rise of Commercialism

Romanticism and Realism

The Black Crook

Gilbert and Sullivan's
Comic Operettas

Reactions to Realism

Musical Theatre

Book Musical

Showboat

Oklahoma

Integrated
Musical

Eclecticism

My Fair Lady

A Chorus Line

Evita

Sung-Through
Musical

Eclecticism: US Theatre from 1950

When you have completed this chapter, you should be able to:

- Distinguish between the professional commercial theatre and not-for-profit theatre.
- Identify and discuss the principal theatre trends of this period.
- Identify and discuss three political theatre movements of this period.
- Define and discuss absurdism.
- Cite examples of eclecticism in US theatre.
- Describe identity theatre.
- Identify and discuss two avant-garde theatres of this period.
- Discuss how modernism and postmodernism differ.
- List some ways in which theatre responded to the 9/11 attacks.
- Describe the nature and advantages of limited-run nonmusical commercial productions.

Context

The Age of Anxiety

The period following the Second World War has often been termed the "Age of Anxiety." People were anxious for a number of reasons:

- The Nazi government of Germany had perpetrated the Holocaust: the systematic, industrialized killing of six million European Jews.

- The United States dropped atomic bombs on two Japanese cities, Hiroshima and Nagasaki, killing an estimated 150,000 to 240,000 people with just two devices.

- Antagonism renewed between the countries of the West and the Soviet Union and its dependencies, known as the Cold War.

Real wars broke out within and between client states of the Soviet Union and the United States and Europe. These conflicts included the Korean War and the Vietnam War, to name the two with the greatest cost of US lives.

In the 1960s, the emerging medium of television gave the country immediate news of a shocking series of assassinations of prominent Americans:

- President John F. Kennedy, 1963, followed in days by the on-air murder of his accused killer, Lee Harvey Oswald.

- Malcolm X, a leader of the militant side of the African American civil rights movement, 1965.

- Reverend Martin Luther King Jr., a leader of the civil disobedience side of the civil rights movement, 1968

- Senator Robert Kennedy, President Kennedy's brother and at the time a candidate for the presidency, 1968.

Richard Nixon was forced to leave the presidency in 1974 facing impeachment for his involvement in covering up a political burglary. Shortly after his inauguration in 1981, Ronald Reagan was shot by a would-be assassin and lived. Some asked whether the United States was really a mature, safe, and stable democracy, capable of political change through the voting booth.

Societal Changes

Thousands of soldiers brought back new ideas and expectations from World War II. The simple pieties of "hot dogs and apple pie" would not be enough for an increasingly sophisticated and anxious populace. The GI Bill allowed thousands of veterans—mostly men—to enter college for the first time. Later the government poured money into expanding postsecondary education, as a bulwark in the competition with Communism.

African American soldiers were changed by living and fighting in a Europe where Jim Crow laws and expectations did not exist. Women worked in factories and offices during the war and could see the possibility of life beyond the suburban front door. In the experience of African Americans and women in the war are the starts of the civil rights movement and women's movement.

In the late 1950s and 1960s, African Americans began to demand equal treatment in public accommodation and voting. Many cities errupted into violent race riots, which were shown on television. About the same time, television showed the reality of the Vietnam War with an immediacy and graphic

A NEW SHAPE FOR AN ICONIC THEATRE

The Fichandler Arena Stage and the Kreeger proscenium theatre have been encased in a new building that adds a new theatre, The Kogod Cradle, a small black box space. A large central lobby, office spaces, rehearsal rooms, and a restaurant were also added. The entire complex, completed in 2010, is now known as the Mead Center for American Theatre.

violence not seen during war before. It also gave coverage to a growing anti-war movement in the country.

US and European popular culture was upturned. By the 1970s, television, advertising, and rock 'n' roll and much later hip-hop dominated US and world culture. History and authority faded as ways of knowing. The way was cleared for the eclectic approaches to art, including theatre, that characterize this era.

Technology

Technological developments changed the idea of theatre and its practice. By the late 1950s, television sets were commonplace in US homes. Personal computers appeared in the 1980s, and the Internet, widely accessible by the early 1990s, altered how people got news, personal messages, and entertainment. The new technologies increased the speed of communication and culture. The life cycle of innovation accelerated in technology and in art. If you knew instantly what was new and shocking, you quickly stopped being shocked. Andy Warhol, a quintessential US artist of the post-World War II era, was prescient when he said in 1968, "In the future, everyone will be world-famous for 15 minutes." The pace of change in fashion, culture, and politics greatly increased and is not slowing.

The Rise of Terrorism

The United States and much of Western Europe celebrated when the Soviet Union crumbled in 1991, but the triumphant feeling was short-lived. A minority of the largely Muslim peoples of the Middle East and Mediterranean

Africa promoted their drive for independence through "disproportionate means," which is to say, terrorism. Unable to match directly the West's money, armies, and technology, terrorists made symbolic and often deadly attacks on the property and citizens of countries they believed contributed to their powerlessness. The most gruesomely successful terrorist attack so far was the collapse of the twin World Trade Towers in Manhattan, caused by hijackers crashing two loaded passenger planes into the skyscrapers on September 11, 2001, now referred to as "9/11." The age of anxiety continues on modified terms.

Theatre Becomes Eclectic: An Overview

Given the stunning changes following World War II in society, science, and technology, it was inevitable that changes in art and in theatre would emerge. And in fact, the older conventions that had held theatre practice together grew weaker, under assault by many new alternatives. Thus, if anything can be said to characterize theatre from the 1950s to the present, both commercial and noncommercial, it has been its **eclecticism**. Eclecticism is the combination in a single work of a variety of stylistic influences. The generally conservative commercial theatre tolerated and exploited many styles and practices, coexisting with each other. Even new theatre buildings of this period were variously shaped and located. Theatrical productions were diversely conceived. Plays were of mixed forms, mixed media, and mixed theories with mixed audiences and critical reception.

ONE PARIS OPERA HOUSE
This 2,700-seat theatre opened in 1989. Note its late modern industrial touches, especially the gridded walls of glass that surround the main stage and auditorium and the exposed cast concrete.

Several theatrical-producing entities that we take for granted today became widespread during these years. Community theatres continued to increase in number. The numbers of educational theatres exploded during these years. It was during these boom years shortly after World War II that most colleges first established theatre departments and graduate and undergraduate degrees in theatre. With theatre departments and degrees came active producing programs on campus, a trend that quickly trickled down to high schools, middle schools, and elementary grades and established educational theatre as a major production venue in the United States.

Most important of all was Off-Broadway, usually dated from 1952, when Tennessee Williams's *Summer and Smoke* appeared there—the first major hit in thirty years in a theatre below Forty-Second Street in Manhattan. From then through the 1970s, Off-Broadway served as a showcase for new talent and "experimental" plays. By the twentieth century's end, however, Off-Broadway had moved toward commercialism.

Slowly after World War II and then with mounting speed in the 1960s, a new form of professional theatre seeded itself throughout the country. The **regional theatre**, a not-for-profit organization, was dependent on both ticket sales *and* donations to present plays and musicals. By the 1980s, the not-for-profit theatres would be essential engines for the development of new plays in the United States and, increasingly, the hatching of new musicals. The cap of this development was the colonization of Broadway by three important not-for-profit theatres.

Broadway theatre persisted almost exclusively as successful commerce. Theatre had once been an energetic alternative to the bland storytelling of film, but by the end of the millennium, commercial theatre borrowed stories and presold titles more and more from film and television. The techniques of eclectic theatre were aped by commercial theatre in an attempt to keep theatre relevant to the culture and to give theatre the appearance of being new and unique.

In essence, theatre since 1950 is characterized by:

- The growing importance of the not-for-profit theatre in new play development.

- Enormous profit potential of internationally successful Broadway musicals.

- Dwindling impact of experimental and politically-radical theatre and the absorption of some of its innovations into middle-of-the-road commercial theatre.

- An incremental growth in the mainstream production of works by new voices: African Americans, women, gays and lesbians, and Latinos/Latinas.

- New York remaining the center of professional theatre in the United States.

- Continued rise in Broadway ticket prices with the prices of the not-for-profit professional theatre following suit.

- Amateur community theatres continuing, with varying skill and increasing numbers, to present successful musicals and plays that had been proven on Broadway and Off-Broadway—mostly comedies—in many cities in the United States.

Professional Theatre

Professional theatre has two branches in the United States: Commercial theatre, which exists to make a profit for investors, and a growing number of professional not-for-profit theatres. New York City remains the center of US professional theatre by virtue of the sheer number of theatres, hefty budgets, and scale of productions staged there each year. In addition, many theatres from other communities hire actors, designers, and directors from New York City. In recent decades, New York was the home of Broadway's forty theatres, Off-Broadway's approximately eighty spaces, and the hundreds of small "studio" off-off-Broadway venues.

There are many more not-for-profit professional theatres than commercial ones. The distinction between the two types of legal organizations is first one of tax status. Each commercial production is a fully taxed, one-time venture, whereas not-for-profits are ongoing organizations that can accept charitable contributions that provide the donor tax incentives.

After World War II, it was typical for plays established on Broadway to be produced later in regional not-for-profit theatres. After the late 1960s, there emerged a different synergy between the commercial theatre and the not-for-profit theatre, with entire productions transferred from a not-for-profit for commercial Broadway runs. Transferring not-for-profit productions to Broadway began with Washington, D.C.'s Arena Stage, when its production of The Great White Hope moved to Broadway in 1967. It won a Tony Award, the New York Drama Critics Award, and the Pulitzer Prize for drama. By 2000, a connection between not-for-profit productions from around the country and the Broadway stage was commonplace.

Commercial Theatre

Except for a slump in attendance in the late 1980s, Broadway attendance trended upward throughout the period, but the number of new productions was significantly lower than before. About fifty-five shows opened on Broadway yearly between 1950 and 1960. In recent seasons, an average of forty new

Courtesy Mead Center for American Theatre

THE FIRST TRANSFER

The Arena Stage first produced *The Great White Hope*, a play by Howard Sackler starring James Earl Jones and Jane Alexander at its theatre in Washington, DC. The entire production then transferred to Broadway in 1968, becoming the first important transfer of a regional production to a commercial Broadway theatre. Now not-for-profit transfers to commercial venues are common. Both Jones and Alexander, seen here, won Tony Awards. They later stared in a film of the play.

productions has been staged yearly. Costs of production continued to rise. In 1964, the original production of *Fiddler on the Roof* cost $380,000, but its revival in 1976 cost almost double that. The musical *Rent* opened in 1994 at an estimated cost of $10 million. Investments for nonmusical plays on Broadway have also gone up. Playwright Edward Albee said, "We did *Who's Afraid of Virginia Woolf?* on Broadway, in 1962, for a total cost of $45,000. Now [2005], the revival is going to cost close to $2 million. We had ticket prices at seven dollars and now they're going to be $75."

The upper boundary of preopening production costs for musicals continues to be probed. Dreamworks, primarily a producer of film and television, is reported to have spent between $25 and $45 million bringing the stage version of the movie *Shrek* to the Broadway musical stage in 2008. Inexperienced theatre producers, working with director Julie Taymor and composer-lyricists Bono and The Edge from U2, invested about $75 million to bring *Spider-Man: Turn Off the Dark* to Broadway in 2011.

As production costs rose, long runs and higher ticket prices became important. The average Broadway ticket, including plays and musicals, cost about ten dollars in 1975, about thirty dollars by 1985, more than forty-five dollars by 1995, and about ninety dollars in 2011. One theatre businessman

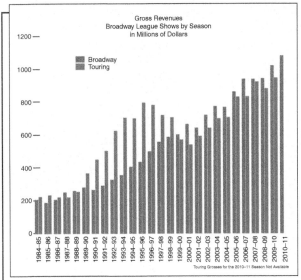
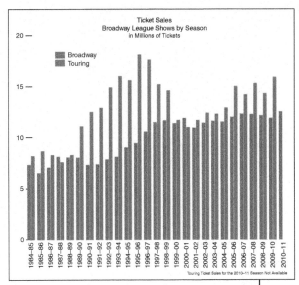

Gross ticket sales for Broadway and for Broadway League touring have fairly steadily increased since the mid-1980s.

estimated that a play that took ten weeks to earn back its initial investment in 1956 would have taken twenty weeks by the mid-1970s, and that a musical that took fifteen to twenty weeks to break even in 1956 would have taken a year or more by the mid-1970s.

As costs and prices rose, audiences and presenters got more conservative. By the late 1990s, **revivals** made up an increasing percentage of productions, more and more musicals were produced, and nonmusical plays grew rare on Broadway, appearing mostly Off-Broadway. For example, Broadway's 2010–2011 season had forty-three new shows staged.

- Six were concerts.
- Twelve were new musicals.
- Fourteen were revivals.
- Eleven were new plays.
- Five of the new plays were transfers from the London theatre.
- Another five of the new plays were staged by not-for-profit Broadway theatres.

The new millennium saw Broadway and Off-Broadway musicals open in Las Vegas hotel casinos, often with excellent financial results. Las Vegas is primarily a tourist town. Its population turns over every three days, on average, with visitors of all social classes from Europe and the Americas. Many English-speaking tourists are not regular theatergoers; non-English-speakers often find spoken drama too difficult. As a result, Las Vegas theatre

THE *PHANTOM* IN LAS VEGAS

The Phantom of the Opera opened in 1988 and is now the longest-running show on Broadway. It has been successfully produced around the world. Here, a marquee for the Las Vegas production that shortened both its running time and its title. Note the cab touting a magic act in another Las Vegas venue.

focuses on brand-name musicals that are presold because of long Broadway runs. The shows are often shortened because the casino owners, who house and bankroll the shows, want theatergoers to leave the auditorium and gamble.

The Phantom of the Opera was performed in a new theatre space specially designed to mirror the Paris opera house in which the story is set. Retitled *Phantom—The Las Vegas Spectacular*, it was shortened from the two-hour-plus playing time in New York to ninety-five minutes. The Las Vegas *Phantom* closed September 2, 2012, having played 2,691 performances.

Mamma Mia! was performed more than two thousand times in Las Vegas. *Hairspray* has also played there, as did *The Producers*, *Avenue Q*, and *Spamalot*. The original Broadway creative team for each musical—director and all designers—was involved in recreating these Broadway hits in Las Vegas.

Las Vegas is also home to a handful of Cirque du Soleil productions, each a paratheatrical hybrid of crowd-pleasing high-tech scenery, costumes, lights, clowning, a modest suggestion of a storyline, and traditional circus acts. Their look and feel is often otherworldly and dreamlike, resembling surrealism. Although not what is usually meant by drama, such productions are highly theatrical and financially successful.

Not-for-Profit Theatre

After a slow start in the late 1940s, professional **not-for-profit theatres** surged in the 1960s. In a departure from then-current New York practices, some of these theatres built spaces without proscenia, preferring theatres in the round, also called arena theatres or thrust stages. More than sixty such companies existed across the country by the mid-1970s and several hundred by the late 1990s. Theatre Communications Group, the trade organization for not-for-profit theatres in the United States, has seven hundred member theatres today.

An example of the strength and endurance of the not-for-profit theatre is the Guthrie Theater in Minneapolis. Inspired by the Stratford Shakespeare Festival in Ontario, Canada, the Guthrie began in 1963 with a production of Shakespeare's *Hamlet* as part of a four-play season. In June 2006, it opened a new three-stage building on the Mississippi River. It now employs more than nine hundred people and has a budget of more than $33 million a year. The theatre has an extensive education program for schools during the academic year.

Not-for-profit theatres also opened in New York City, offering an alternative to the commercial theatres there. Of these, arguably the most successful was the Roundabout Theatre Company. Opened in 1965, it went bankrupt

NOT-FOR-PROFIT REGIONAL THEATRE

Now among the oldest not-for-profits in the United States, Minneapolis's Guthrie Theatre was founded in 1963. It opened a new three-theatre complex in 2006 at a cost of more than $125 million. This distinctive structure features a postmodern "bridge to nowhere."

Amanda Ortland/Guthrie Theatre

in the 1970s but recovered and prospered in the 1980s. By the late 1980s, it had New York's largest subscription audience and regularly transferred shows to Broadway. During the 1990s, it moved to a permanent Broadway theatre (now called the American Airlines Theatre), soon added a second Broadway theatre (Studio 54), and in 2010 added a third Broadway theatre (now named the Stephen Sondheim Theatre). The Roundabout has earned many, many awards. And like the Guthrie, the Roundabout sponsors an important educational-outreach program.

In the new millennium, the nation's not-for-profit theatres continued to develop new plays and theatre artists. This trend, clear in the late twentieth century, became even more pronounced: Many new plays are now developed in workshops, readings, and initial productions in US regional theatres. From the 1999–2000 season through the 2007–2008 season, 341 productions opened on Broadway. Of these, 175—more than half—originated in not-for-profit theatres.

RENT IS COLLECTED EVERYWHERE

One of the most produced United States musicals, *Rent* is loosely based on the 1896 opera *La Boheme* by Giacomo Puccini. There is now a high school edition that avoids the seamier aspects of the original. Here, a production of the Broadway edition by Clemson University.

Tony Penna

Plays since 1950

Three of the most important and influential playwrights in the United States, writers of real challenge and bold expressivity, appeared first in the commercial theatre and dominated "serious" theatre for more than three decades.

Tennessee Williams

Tennessee Williams (1911–1983) won the Drama Critics Circle Award for his first major Broadway production, *The Glass Menagerie* (1945), a wistful memory play reminiscent of the symbolists and Anton Chekhov. *A Streetcar Named Desire* (1947) won both the Pulitzer Prize and the Drama Critics Circle Award and established Williams as a major playwright. These two plays, and five others that followed in the next fifteen years, became classics of US theatre. They include *Summer and Smoke* (1948), *The Rose Tattoo* (1950), *Cat on a Hot Tin Roof* (1954), *Sweet Bird of Youth* (1959), and *The Night of the Iguana* (1961). Williams wrote more than thirty produced plays, some that continue to be produced around the world.

Psychology and psychiatry had opened up study and discussion of the sexual subconscious of human life, and Williams built on this subject, giving sexuality poetic expression on the stage. Williams is famous for his portrayals of damaged women who are struggling to survive. However, he also wrote some powerful and unforgettable male roles, such as Big Daddy in *Cat on a Hot Tin Roof*, Stanley Kowalski in *A Streetcar Named Desire*, and the defrocked Reverend Shannon in *The Night of the Iguana*. Williams's

TENNESSEE WILLIAMS'S CLASSIC *STREETCAR*

This reimagined production of *A Streetcar Named Desire* by the Intiman Theatre in Seattle avoids the New Orleans French Quarter iconic décor, especially the intricate wrought iron balconies. Like many not-for-profit theatres across the country, the Intiman was hit hard by the recent recession and was forced to close in 2011. The company planned to return in 2012.

THE PLAY'S THE THING

Tennessee Williams's *A Streetcar Named Desire*, 1947

One of Tennessee Williams' twenty-five full-length plays, *A Streetcar Named Desire* is the largely realistic, domestic drama that cemented his stature as a great US dramatist. *Streetcar* portrays a universe shot through with violence: the descent into insanity, sexual and emotional abuse, suicide, torn families, and homophobia. There are also significant expressionistic devices in *Streetcar*: the use of polka music as well as jungle sounds that only Blanche seems to hear. There is even a strange crone who appears periodically hawking flowers for funerals, wailing, *"flores para los muertos."*

The Story of the Play Blanche Dubois arrives at her sister Stella's apartment in a New Orleans slum because she has nowhere else to live. Blanche is outwardly a Southern belle, ridiculously genteel; within, she is a wounded sufferer—of alcoholism, of loneliness, and of despair. She is appalled by Stella's surroundings and by her husband, Stanley Kowalski, who she calls "common."

Stanley, however, is much more than common. He is a patriarch (Stella is pregnant); he is also a brutal realist. He sees, correctly, that Blanche threatens his relationship with Stella (a mutually powerful sexual one) and his "possession" of Stella.

Stanley's friend Mitch is attracted to Blanche, and Blanche sees in him a last chance to find a protected place. She and Mitch seem headed toward marriage, but Stanley tells Mitch what he has learned from other men about Blanche's past: that she was fired from a teaching job because she seduced a seventeen-year-old and that she was notorious for one-night stands in cheap hotels. Blanche tells Stella more truths about herself: that she nursed their mother through a lingering death; that she lost the family home because she had no money; and that the "sensitive young man" she has often talked about so romantically was in fact her husband, whom she found in bed with another man and who, when she said he disgusted her, killed himself.

Mitch abandons her because of what Stanley told him. Stanley buys Blanche a bus ticket out of town. Then, when Stella is in the hospital having the baby, Stanley rapes Blanche. Some time later, Stella is home again. Blanche is disoriented, hallucinating that an old boyfriend is coming to save her. Instead, a doctor and nurse come to take her to a mental institution. She goes on the doctor's arm, murmuring, "I have always depended on the kindness of strangers."

Courtesy Triad Stage, North Carolina

---

stories were generally placed in the South, and he shaped southern US dialect into an evocative poetry.

Arthur Miller

Arthur Miller (1915–2005) was, like Williams, a realist of sorts, but whereas Williams's work tended toward the dreamlike and impressionistic, Miller's moved in harsher, more expressionistic ways. Williams's plays were about survival against the odds, and Miller focused on the overwhelming burden of guilt. *All My Sons* (1947) told of a US businessman who knowingly sold inferior products to the US military to turn a profit. In *Death of a Salesman* (1949), realistic scenes are interspersed with scenes remembered by the mentally muddled protagonist, Willy Loman. *Death of a Salesman* won both a Pulitzer Prize and the Drama Critics Circle Award. Miller was very much a moralist who saw himself as the successor to Henrik Ibsen. Sometimes he thought his plays to be like ancient Greek tragedies—about flawed protagonists destroyed by their moral choices.

Miller wrote more than thirty plays, including *The Crucible* (1953), *A View from the Bridge* (one-act, 1955; revised two-act, 1956), *After the Fall* (1964), and *The Price* (1968). Although these six plays continued to be revived around the world, his later work was less appreciated and seldom appeared on Broadway.

Both Williams and Miller told family stories, but Miller's plays evoked issues bigger than family dynamics and psychology. *Death of a Salesman*'s protagonist Willy Loman represents a class of men who worked for business and, in their old age, were set adrift. *The Crucible*'s story of the Salem witch trials had echoes with the Communist witch trials pursued by Congress in the era in which the play was first staged.

Williams and Miller lived long enough that their new scripts were no longer fashionable. The commercial theatre welcomed them at the end of World War II and then, as audiences wanted something else, left them largely unproduced on Broadway later in their lives.

Edward Albee

Beginning his career with a handful of brilliant one-act plays, including *The Zoo Story* (1958), *The Sandbox* (1959), and *The American Dream* (1960), Edward

ARTHUR MILLER'S *CRUCIBLE*
Based on the Salem witch trials of 1692, *The Crucible* also took a swipe at the House of Representatives Committee on Un-American Activities that wanted Miller and others to "name names" of US Communist sympathizers. Miller refused. *The Crucible* earned the 1953 Best Play Tony Award. Here, a production at the University of North Carolina–Charlotte.

Anita Tripathi Easterling

Albee (1928–) secured his position as a preeminent playwright with the production of *Who's Afraid of Virginia Woolf?* (1962), a hit on Broadway and around the world. The 1966 film adaptation won the Academy Award for best picture; Elizabeth Taylor, Richard Burton, George Segal, and Sandy Dennis won Academy Awards for acting; and the director Mike Nichols also won an Oscar.

Albee has written approximately thirty plays—so far—in a career that spanned much of the second half of the twentieth century. Albee has won three Pulitzer Prizes for Drama, a Tony award for Lifetime Achievement, and the National Medal of Arts in 1966. After *Virginia Woolf* few of Albee's plays were financial successes on Broadway. For a long while, his new works were staged Off-Broadway and in Europe.

His later plays were less commercially successful but were often critically well received. He remained a major force in US drama well past the end of the century, still winning top artistic awards. In 1994 he earned a Pulitzer Prize for *Three Tall Women*. In his seventy-fourth year, Albee saw the premiere on Broadway of *The Goat, or Who is Sylvia?* (2002), an unlikely comedy about a man who falls in love with and has sex with a goat. The play ends when the main character's wife drags the dead goat through the front door of their swank apartment. Successful on Broadway, *The Goat* has been staged across the United States. Albee continued to shock audiences, a quality evident in his first plays, staged in the late 1950s.

Albee is a late adherent of absurdism, reflecting its charge that communication is difficult or impossible and that life offers people little in the way of ultimate meaning.

Other US Plays and Playwrights

In the 1970s and 1980s, David Mamet (*Glengarry Glen Ross*, 1984) and Sam Shepard (*Buried Child*, 1978) both won major prizes, and each went on to write other important works. In the new millennium, however, successful and serious new US plays were rare on Broadway. David Auburn's *Proof* (2000) revolved about a mentally damaged but brilliant daughter of a recently deceased mathematics genius and tried to answer the question, did he leave important findings behind in his unpublished papers? *Doubt: A Parable* (2004) by John Patrick Shanley dramatized the standoff between a nun and a priest over whether a male student at their Catholic school had been or was being molested. Charles Busch, an Off-Broadway writer and performer known for his use of drag, had a Broadway success as the author of a conventional comedy, *The Tale of the Allergist's Wife* (2000), about an upper-middle-class woman's midlife crisis. All had long runs. In the 2010–2011 season, two new plays with star performers in **limited runs** paid back their investors: *The Mother****** with the Hat* (2011) written by Stephen Adly Guirgis, starring Bobby Cannavale and Chris Rock, and *Bengal Tiger in the Baghdad Zoo* (2011) written by Rajiv Joseph, featuring Robin Williams as the ghost of a dead tiger.

HOW WE KNOW

Theatre on Film and Tape Archive

Beginning in 1970, the New York Public Library Billy Rose Theatre Collection has been actively collecting an archive of live performances from Broadway, Off-Broadway, and other professional theatres in the United States as a research archive, called Theatre on Film and Tape (TOFT). Through this collection, theatre professionals and theatre historians can view a recording of a production and see the work of actors, directors, and designers as it appeared in a theatre with an audience. This is a collection of extraordinary historical value.

Theatre is ephemeral. How the parts of a production came together before TOFT was begun is hard or impossible to know: the movement, the timbre of voices, the physical business and blocking, and the audience response are all generally lost. It has been this way throughout theatre history.

The TOFT collection has more than 1,600 films and tapes of live performances, both hits and flops. It adds more than three hundred performances a year of which at least fifty are recorded by the library. Others are donated by the producers or not-for-profit theatres.

The TOFT archive was difficult to initiate because artists' unions were concerned about losing control and income from their members' creations. Now all the theatrical unions have consenting agreements with TOFT. Union members use the archive for essential research, especially for revivals. Viewers of TOFT recordings must be qualified professionals because of union concerns and the library's limited playback equipment. Recordings are restricted to students, theatre professionals, and researchers. About five thousand people yearly use the collections. Not every show is recorded because the library does not have the resources. Funding comes from the National Endowment for the Arts, the New York State Council on the Arts, and from individuals.

Patrick Hoffman, the Director of the Theatre on Film and Tape Archive, puts the archive's historical importance in a compelling manner, saying, "Imagine if I had a video tape of Sarah Bernhardt in *Hamlet*. How many actors wouldn't be interested in seeing that?" Actors, yes, and directors, historians, costumers, and others would be interested in seeing that. In the future, when information is needed on the US professional theatre after 1970, TOFT will be one of the main ways theatre historians will know.

This woodcut of William Kempe is the only known image of him to survive. Kempe was one of the share-holders in the Lord Chamberlain's Men. For some unknown reason, Kempe did a Morris dance from London to Norwich, a distance of more than one hundred miles. His book about the feat titled Nine Days Wonder *(1600) included this image, the only one of him that survives. (Color added to woodcut.)*

Imported Plays

The US commercial theatre would have been impoverished had it not been for imports. From the 1950s through the present, some of Broadway's best productions had already succeeded abroad. England's Harold Pinter (1930–2008) intrigued—and sometimes baffled—US audiences with his absurdist-influenced plays. The feminist British playwright Caryl Churchill (*Cloud Nine*, US Off-Broadway premiere 1981, *Top Girls*, Off-Broadway 1982, and others) became a major presence, as did Tom Stoppard with such plays as *Rosencrantz & Guildenstern Are Dead* (1966), *Jumpers* (1972), *Arcadia* (1993), and others. South African Athol Fugard's antiapartheid plays, such as *Master Harold and the Boys* (1982), also came to New York by way of London. As an example, the 2010–2011 season brought from London to Broadway *Brief Encounter, The Pitmen Painters, Elling, Arcadia, War Horse*, and *La Bête*. Two of these straight plays were revivals. London also supplied two new musicals in that season, *Sister Act,* based on the US film of 1992 with Whoopi Goldberg, and *Priscilla Queen of the Desert*, the stage musical that originated in Australia before London and was based on the Australian film of 1994.

Craig Schwartz

THE BENGAL TIGER AT THE BAGHDAD ZOO

Rajiv Joseph's play was first produced by the Center Theatre Group in Los Angeles. The ghost of a Bengal tiger leaves the Baghdad Zoo and roams the city observing the chaos caused by the 2003 invasion of Iraq and its effect on the citizens.

Comedy, Mostly Neil Simon

Commercial theatre also relied on comedy to ensure box office revenues. Neil Simon was the playwright most consistently successful—phenomenally successful—with audiences. Major plays from the 1960s and 1970s, such as *The Odd Couple*, established his reputation as the master gag writer of the theatre and were transferred to movies and television. And in 1991, Simon won the Pulitzer Prize for *Lost in Yonkers*. In all, Simon has had thirty-five Broadway premieres of comedies and musicals for which he wrote the book. He also worked as an uncredited "play doctor" on many other plays to help the creators clarify the plot and to add jokes to plays and musicals in preview. No other comic US writer shows either Simon's ability or his staying power.

Two of Wendy Wasserstein's plays cemented her reputation as a writer of commercial comedies. *The Heidi Chronicles* transferred from a not-for-profit Off-Broadway run to Broadway in 1989, winning a best play Tony Award, Drama Desk Awards, and New York Drama Critics Circle Award. *The Sisters Rosensweig* (1992) premiered on Broadway for a successful run. Wasserstein wrote five more well-received plays before her death in 2006 at age fifty-five.

Several British writers enriched comedy on Broadway. Michael Frayn was successful with *Noises Off* (1983), a masterly farce about the theatre itself. Alan Ayckbourn has written more than seventy-five plays, and nine appeared on Broadway between 1971 and 2005.

Jason Ayer

BURIED CHILD
Sam Shepard became one of the most important playwrights of the 1970s and 1980s. He won the 1979 Pulitzer Prize for his macabre exploration of the American dream. *Buried Child*, here in a production at Theatre South Carolina, was Shepard's first important success as a playwright.

The Decline of the Nonmusical Play on Broadway

Beginning roughly in the 1980s, nonmusical plays appeared less often on Broadway. In the new millennium, a growing number of star-studded, limited runs of comedies and serious plays have had impressive Broadway success. They were characterized by short playing periods and were loaded with familiar names from television, movies, and theatre including *Macbeth* with Patrick Stewart, *The Vertical Hour* with Julianne Moore, *A Moon for the Misbegotten* with Kevin Spacey, *Cyrano de Bergerac* with Kevin Kline and Jennifer Garner, *God of Carnage* with James Gandolfini, *The Country Girl* with Morgan Freeman, *Driving Miss Daisy* with James Earl Jones and Vanessa Redgrave, and *The Mountaintop* with Angela Bassett and Samuel L. Jackson. Salaries for the stars were expensive, but name recognition made sizable audiences more likely.

The Political Avant-Garde in Theatre

Although much of US and European theatre after 1950 continued to be commercial and crowd-pleasing diversions, there was also a non-commercial, avant-garde movement. ("Avant-garde" is French for "advanced guard" and is a term borrowed from military terminology to describe the most experimental arts.) The avant-garde groups—some focused on art, some on politics, and many concerned with both art and politics—remained vital for a while, getting new life from resistance to the Vietnam War, the civil rights battle, and the counterculture movement of the 1960s and 1970s. This new generation of arts reformers was again trying to make theatre important and serious—that is, to claim a place for it near the center of US culture. The political reformers were trying to use the theatre to carry vivid messages, to raise consciousness, to incite action. Both the artistic and the political avant-garde tried to rethink the relationship of theatre to life, of theatre to commerce, of actors to audience, and of text to performance. However, they did not become the mainstream any more than the avant-garde of 1890–1900 had done, although like their previous counterparts they influenced the mainstream. This theatrical counterculture began off-off-Broadway and elsewhere in the United States.

One noteworthy example of the political avant-garde starting early during the 1960s and 1970s was called street theatre or guerilla theatre. These were names given to political performances that went to the audience, first into the streets and second in hit-and-run "guerilla" raids on nontheatrical spaces wherever people could be found, including, for example, elevators and department stores. The reasoning behind this approach to staging was, if one only performed political acts in a theatre with pricey tickets and regular performance schedules, the audience would be made up of those who agreed with the theatre's political slant. One would preach to the choir. By interrupting an unsuspecting "audience" in the middle of its workday or shopping, political theatre might be more shocking and mind-altering.

The Political Avant-Garde in Miniature: The Living Theatre

The trajectory of the political avant-garde movement can be suggested by briefly tracking the history of one of its most important organizations, the **Living Theatre**. Founded in 1947 by Julian Beck and Judith Malina, The Living Theatre

GOING TO ST. IVES

Lee Blessing, the author of more than thirty-two plays, has seen his works performed in London, on Broadway, Off-Broadway, as well as in not for profit theatres around the country. Mainly though, his dramas are staples of Off-Broadway and regional companies because of their small casts and ease of production. *Going to St. Ives,* here staged at Ball State University, explores the lives of two extraordinary women, one a renowned eye specialist, the other the mother of a cruel dictator (think Idi Amin).

started as an art theatre in New York. Initially it looked back toward the previous avant-garde in Europe and did plays by such Europeans as García Lorca, Luigi Pirandello, and Bertolt Brecht. In the late 1950s, however, the group shifted toward new US works such as Jack Gelber's *The Connection*, a realistic look at the then little-known drug culture, and Kenneth Brown's *The Brig*, a harsh treatment of military prison. By the late 1960s, following a European tour, it became a political theatre, reorganizing into a commune to promote revolution through "benevolent anarchy." With a change in goals came a change in its approach to theatre. It quickly became famous for the direct participation of the audience, for performances that turned into protest marches, and for such shock tactics as nudity and obscenity. It had moved from modernism to postmodernism.

Probably its most famous production during this period was the group developed *Paradise Now,* which began with actors milling about the audience. Throughout the four or more hours of performance, actors verbally abused any spectators who seemed apathetic or hostile, shouting slogans and obscenities at them. Such confrontations, sometimes in the nude, were common in performance, and often, at the play's end, the group urged spectators to join it in taking the revolution out of the theatre and into the streets. When the performers did so, they were occasionally arrested and charged with things such as disturbing the peace, indecent exposure, and interfering with law enforcement.

Following another overseas tour, the group returned to the United States in the 1970s. With radicalism on the decline (from the drawdown of the Vietnam War and the muting of civil rights agitation), the Living Theatre entered a new phase, splitting itself into four "cells," each in a different city and each with a different emphasis: politics, the environment, the culture, and the spirit. Although the group remained active, by the 1980s its influence on US theatre and culture had abated—the victim of waning interest in revolution.

The Living Theatre, then, tracked the major shifts of the avant-garde, from its early roots in European practice, through a period of revolutionary politics, into expanding interests and locations, and finally into self-induced disappearance. It continued into the new millennium but almost invisibly. Its importance lies in its aftereffects and in the energy and innovativeness of its two founders. The Living Theatre embodied both major strands of twentieth-century US avant-gardism—politics and art.

The Living Theatre and Malina tried to reawaken the political avant-garde, only to provide a potent sign of the political avant-garde's eclipse. The Living Theatre had closed its New York theatre in 1993 but reopened under the leadership of its cofounder, Malina, in 2007. It reproduced then two of its signature hits, *The Connection* (1959) and *The Brig* (1963). Seen originally as seminal and groundbreaking avant-garde works presented in new and exciting ways, in revival these two plays were received as faded relics belonging to another age.

The Artistic Avant-Garde in Theatre

Unlike political theatres that sought to change society, some avant-garde theatres strove to change the art of the theatre. The division between the artistic and political was not always clearly differentiated. For example, the Living Theatre began as mostly artistic but quickly became mostly political. Artistic groups wanted to explore—either alone or in some combination—the nature of theatre, its relation to other kinds of performance and media, its arrangements for production, and the role of both script and audience in a performance. Probably closer to the previous European avant-garde than to the political theatres in their goals, these artistic theatres nonetheless differed profoundly from both the previous art theatres and the political theatres contemporary with them.

The Artistic Avant-Garde in Miniature: Joseph Chaikin and the Open Theatre

Among the most influential of the artistic avant-garde theatres was that of Joseph Chaikin, who proposed an "open" theatre to distinguish it from the "closed" theatres of Broadway, which he saw as rigid, text-bound, and uncreative. Believing that most theatres were overwhelmed by nonessentials, Chaikin sought a performance in which the primary focus was on the actor and groups of artists working together.

Thus, ensemble became the cornerstone of the **Open Theatre**, and actors were trained to work as a group rather than as individuals. To accomplish such an ensemble, Chaikin used a variety of theatre games and improvisations designed to develop sensitivity to group rhythms and dynamics, to increase mutual trust, and to replace competition for the audience's attention with cooperation among the group. The playwright, too, was considered a member of the ensemble and was encouraged to develop texts for the group out of the ideas of the group. Typically the writer would provide a scenario, an outline of the situation, and the group would improvise dialogue and action. The improvisations would be repeated several times, and the writer would select the best of them, add new materials as needed, rearrange sections, and finally develop "the text."

Although the plays varied enormously, they tended to share some combination of these characteristics:

- A unity achieved through exploring a central idea or theme rather than a story.
- A free and disconnected treatment of time and place.
- The use of *transformations*, a technique in which actors played first one character and then another without corresponding changes in costumes or makeup and without clear transitions provided by dialogue.

- A reliance on actors to provide their own environment by "becoming" the setting and sounds (e.g., an actor played a sheep in a field, another a snake on a tree; several became ambulance sirens).

Although the Open Theatre existed for only ten years, 1963–1973, its influence was lasting and profound. It focused attention on the centrality of the actor in performance; it demonstrated the willingness of audiences to substitute their imaginations for the usual setting, lights, and costumes; it popularized theatre games and improvisation as tools for training actors and as a source for group-inspired plays; and it showed that the usual theatrical hierarchy (a director leading a team of theatre specialists) was not the only way to organize theatrical production. Its techniques and theories are now part of the theatrical mainstream and contribute to theatre's eclecticism.

The Avant-Garde Fades

The political avant-garde remained vital only as long as political and social uneasiness were high. In the 1980s, however, the United States got over the most extreme divisions of the Vietnam War and became an apparently more optimistic and less questioning place. Society seemed not to want to probe or protest anymore. By the late 1980s, theorists were proclaiming avant-gardism dead. By the 1990s, the decade of e-commerce and big money, only local vestiges remained. (One significant vestige of the theatrical avant-garde can still be found in postsecondary educational theatre.)

Still, a limited avant-garde continued in a small number of troupes. For example, Mabou Mines toured a postmodern production of Ibsen's *A Doll's*

BLACK FEMINIST THEATRE

Playwright Ntozake Shange's *For Colored Girls Who Have Considered Suicide/When the Rainbow Is Enuf* began in California as a choreopoem—a series of some twenty monologues with movement. It moved to Broadway but remained controversial within the African American community because of its negative portrayal of African American men. Tyler Perry directed a film version in 2010 starring, among others, Phylicia Rashad and Janet Jackson. Here, *For Colored Girls* at the University of Missouri at Columbia.

House (1879) with a much-altered script, mock period music, an interpolated puppet opera, and most stunningly, all the male roles played by midgets and dwarfs. The tall female actors could barely sit on the tiny furniture made to accommodate the men. The casting and staging exaggerated outrageously the themes of the original play. In the script, the men are small-minded; here they were literally small. The setting was almost literally a doll house in which adult women could not fit.

Elements of much of the late twentieth-century avant-garde kept cropping up in otherwise mainstream productions, accepted by audiences with little note. A revival of Stephen Sondheim's opera-like musical *Sweeney Todd* was staged without a traditional orchestra; instead, the actors played the accompaniment on a variety of instruments when not actually singing or speaking. The female lead played the triangle and the tuba.

Frank Wedekind's play about teenage sexual tumult, *Spring's Awakening* (1891), was adapted into a musical of almost the same name, *Spring Awakening* (2007), with the dialogue scenes set in the original late Victorian period, but the songs styled as twenty-first-century rock. Both shows played on Broadway after initial productions at not-for-profit theatres.

In big ways and small, unity of tone and progression continued to be breached in twenty-first-century theatre—that is, eclecticism marked much of theatre in the new millennium. When the discontinuities served story and idea, the result seemed invigorating (*Spring Awakening*). At other times, the stylistic ruptures seemed like fashionable gambits, ineffective and cloying.

Identity Theatre Emerges

From the 1960s, a form of political theatre emerged that could be called **identity theatre**. In these groups, the creators expressed and proselytized for different peoples who by their identity—racial, gender, and sexual preference—were underrepresented in theatre: African Americans, women, gays, and lesbians. Later theatre for and by Spanish-speaking residents of the United States grew, referred to as Hispanic or Latino theatre. Beginning about 1990 and largely on the west coast, people of Asian origin began creating an identity theatre for Asian Americans. Identity theatre not only sought to change the medium of theatre and the social standing of underrepresented groups but also to serve as focuses of artistic expression for the slighted groups. Although the various kinds of identity theatre shared many basic assumptions, they differed in several ways.

Plays that might formerly have been identified primarily by race or gender were gradually assimilated into the mainstream over time. However, this assertion is not to claim that women artists, gay artists, African American artists, and Latino/Latina artists have reached equality in the US theatre.

Identity Theatre for African Americans

African American performers in the United States date from well before the Civil War, and **African American theatre** companies were firmly established within their own communities well before World War II. However, these performers were mostly unknown in mainstream theatre.

Two important plays seen by both white and African American audiences shortly after World War II, however, heralded a change. In 1959, Lorraine Hansberry's *A Raisin in the Sun* was produced on Broadway. This study of African American family life, in which the tensions between women and men were sympathetically and sensitively dramatized, won the Drama Critics Circle Award. The same year, French playwright Jean Genet's *The Blacks* was produced Off-Broadway; it reversed the traditions of the minstrel show and used African American actors in white makeup to reveal abuses of white power. Although many African Americans rejected the play's thesis—that blacks will come to power only by adopting the tactics of their white oppressors—few failed to realize that the play represented a turning point in the theatrical portrayal of African Americans. Note some essential differences between these two plays: Hansberry was African American and *Raisin* was a realistic, family drama; Genet was European—he was French, white, and appalled by the French government treatment of their African colony of Algeria in the late 1950s and early 1960s—and *The Blacks* was a postmodern work using masks and masklike makeup.

Revolutionary **black theatre** grew out of the racial turmoil of the 1950s and 1960s, when African Americans turned in large numbers to the arts as a way of demanding change and repairing their ruptured society. This theatre movement dates from 1964 and the Off-Broadway production of LeRoi Jones's *The Toilet* (1964) and *Dutchman* (1964), both of which presented chilling pictures of racial barriers, human hatred, and the suffering that results from racism. Thereafter, the stereotypical stage Negro was increasingly replaced by more honest, if often less ingratiating, black characters. Throughout the 1960s and early 1970s, Jones—now self-renamed Imamu Amiri Baraka—poet and playwright born in 1934, remained the most militant and best-known African American playwright.

In the same year—1964—Adrienne Kennedy first came to notice with her one-act play *Funnyhouse of a Negro*. Kennedy (1931–) grew up in an integrated neighborhood in Cleveland, her first experience of a play was Tennessee Williams's *The Glass Menagerie*, and she does not recall experiencing much racial prejudice before attending Ohio State University. She has written at least thirteen plays. The Signature Theatre, New York, named her playwright-in-residence in the 1996–1997 season where seven of her plays were staged. Kennedy's work is described as nonlinear, surrealistic, expressionistic, and poetic—in short, postmodern. The protagonist of *Funnyhouse* is Sarah, an African American obsessed with whiteness, who says, "I long to become even a more pallid Negro than I am." Her boyfriend is white. Her hobby is writing poetry

THE PLAY'S THE THING

August Wilson's Century of African American Life

August Wilson set out to write a series devoted to the African American experience with one play set in each decade of the twentieth century. Collectively known as the *Pittsburgh Cycle*, named for the city where they are set, the plays were produced in New York after development in not-for-profit theatres. The pattern of three or more regional productions allowed Wilson to hone the dramas for Broadway and Off-Broadway.

The first, *Ma Rainey's Black Bottom*, appeared in 1985, and the last, *Radio Golf*, in 2005. Within those twenty years, Wilson became one of the most important playwrights of his generation. His plays stand as a landmark in the history of African American culture, US literature, and Broadway theatre. Perhaps the most honored playwright in the past quarter century, Wilson was awarded two Tony Awards, seven New York Drama Critics Circle Awards, a Pulitzer Prize, and the Olivier Award (the British equivalent of the Tony), among many other prestigious awards.

The plays and the decade that they characterize are: *Gem of the Ocean* (1900s), *Joe Turner's Come and Gone* (1910s), *Ma Rainey's Black Bottom* (1920s), *The Piano Lesson* (1930s), *Seven Guitars* (1940s), *Fences* (1950s), *Two Trains Running* (1960s), *Jitney* (1970s), *King Hedley II* (1980s), and *Radio Golf* (1990s). They were not written or produced in this order, however.

These plays are connected by several shared traits. All but one play is set in the African American neighborhood of Pittsburgh's Hill District; characters from one play occasionally appear in others; the characters usually speak in the street dialect of the Hill, but Wilson manages to make the dialogue sound poetic and even musical; most are focused more on character than plot; and supernatural elements abound. The guiding spirit of the cycle seems to be Aunt Esther, a woman said to have lived for more than three centuries.

Quite soon after his death in 2005, a Broadway theatre was renamed in his honor—the August Wilson Theatre.

Ella Bromblin

GEM OF THE OCEAN

A moment from Gem of the Ocean, *a play in the ten-play cycle by August Wilson, produced on Broadway in 2004. Here, a production by Tisch Graduate School of the Arts.*

"filling white page after white page." She is haunted by Queen Victoria and the Duchess of Hapsburg, played by African American actresses in white face, who are expressionistic projections of Sarah's psyche. Together, Sarah and her other selves show a funhouse vision of Sarah's self-loathing and internalized racism.

Other African American plays studied the politics and economics of life within the African American community. Douglas Turner Ward's *Day of Absence* (1967) poked fun at whites as they were outwitted by African Americans, whose disappearance for a single day led to the collapse of the white social structure. Alice Childress's *Mojo* (1970) suggested that African American men and women could work out their differences and exist happily as equals if they loved and respected each other.

By the mid-1970s, African American authors could criticize their own community. Ntozake Shange's *For Colored Girls Who Have Considered Suicide/When the Rainbow Is Enuf* (1976) explored the double oppression of being African American and female. It was an unflattering portrait of some African American men brutalizing African American women as the men themselves had been brutalized by whites. Originally staged in an African American theatre, this powerful "choreopoem" (a postmodern form) eventually moved to Broadway, where it earned a Tony Award.

With the gradual improvement in the position of African American people and the increasing conservatism sweeping the United States by the mid-1980s, the energy of the black revolutionary theatre subsided. Although African American theatres and revolutionary playwrights and criticism persisted, African American playwrights increasingly moved into mainstream theatres, taking African American critics with them. An example of African American critics moving into the mainstream press is Hilton Als, theatre critic since 2002 for *New Yorker* magazine. Before 2002, Als wrote for the *Village Voice*, *The Nation*, and *Vibe* and collaborated on film scripts for *Swoon* and *Looking for Langston*. African American playwrights whose scripts moved into mainstream theatre included nearly all of the works of the late August Wilson and plays by Suzan-Lori Parks, Lynn Nottage, Stew, and Anna Deavere Smith. Both Parks and Nottage won the Pulitzer Prize for Drama.

A musical adaptation of Alice Walker's novel *The Color Purple* played Broadway from 2005 through 2008 and successfully toured the United States. Lorraine Hansberry's classic 1959 African American drama, *A Raisin in the Sun*, had a successful revival on Broadway in 2004 with a cast that included rap star Sean "Diddy" Combs. Broadway saw not only a revival of Tennessee Williams's *Cat on a Hot Tin Roof* with an all–African American cast but also a race-blind revival of William Inge's *Come Back, Little Sheba* starring African American television actress S. Epatha Merkerson as the lead in an otherwise white cast, both in 2008. African American audiences, however, have not generally grown much, except for the gospel plays of the chitlin' circuit.

African American plays and productions featuring African Americans appeared on Broadway in greater number in recent decades, including the

THE PLAY'S THE THING

Tyler Perry and the Chitlin' Circuit

The noted African American Harvard professor Henry Louis Gates Jr. borrowed the term *chitlin' circuit* to describe a contemporary touring theatre of plays made by, for, and about African Americans. The chitlin' circuit flourishes away from Broadway, Off-Broadway, and the not-for-profit theatre. It is professional in that everyone involved gets paid, but it is entirely nonunion. It has made loads of money for many involved.

The characters in chitlin' circuit plays are as standardized as those of commedia dell'arte. Typical roles include an outspoken fat woman, a beautiful woman of questionable morals, an over-the-top swishy gay man, and a handsome stud. The comedy is crude, full of insults and trash talk. At some point a gospel song is belted out. At stake in the plot is the loss of a family member or friend to drugs, gangs, prison, or prostitution. The happy ending often comes about from prayer and sometimes even from divine intervention in the form of angels or ghosts.

The audiences, as Gates noted, "are basically blue-collar and pink-collar, and not the type to attend traditional theatre." Gates continues, "However crude the script and the production, they're generating the kind of audience response that most playwrights can only dream of."

Some chitlin' circuit participants prefer to call their endeavors *urban theatre*, perhaps adapting the term from the music industry that uses "urban" to describe music intended to appeal mostly to an African American audience.

The crossover financial star of the chitlin' circuit is clearly Tyler Perry. In 1998, he staged his first play, *I Know I've Been Changed*, at Atlanta's House of Blues. He sold out eight nights at the House of Blues and two more nights at the 4,500-seat Fox Theatre. Soon Perry was doing two to three hundred performances a year, playing to thirty thousand people a week. Perry wrote, directed, produced, composed, did makeup and set design, all to keep the budget small.

Perry's innovation on the chitlin' circuit formula was to play the mother character himself, all six-foot-five of him, in drag. This character, Madea, takes the idea of the strong African American mother's holding the family together a gigantic step further. Madea carries two guns in her handbag and will whip them out if necessary. She smokes grass and is blunt-spoken.

In 2005 and 2006, Perry made his first two Madea films for a total budget of $11 million; each opened at number one in box office receipts, and together they grossed more than $110 million. His eleven stage plays have grossed more than $150 million, and DVDs of his movies and plays have sold more than 11 million copies. He even had a best-selling book in 2006, *Don't Make a Black Woman Take Off Her Earrings: Madea's Uninhibited Commentaries on Love and Life*.

---

musical *Passing Strange* and the historical monoplay *Thurgood*. Sarah Jones's one-woman show *Bridge & Tunnel* had a successful Broadway run.

"Bridge-and-tunnel" is a dismissive term for people who travel to Manhattan from the surrounding boroughs of New York. (Manhattan is an island mostly reached by bridges and tunnels.) The play, set at a public poetry reading, is a comic collage of people of many nationalities and both genders, getting by and searching for dignity and meaning while living in the outer parts of the city. With minimal costumes, Jones appeared as a Chinese American mother, a Russian Jewish father, a Nigerian political refugee, and Mitzi, an eighty-seven-year-old German immigrant.

Anna Deavere Smith   Like Sarah Jones, Anna Deavere Smith has developed one-person shows to wide acclaim. Smith interviews many people involved in a particular topic or event, edits the transcripts, then devises a multicharacter

Joan Marcus

ANNA DEAVERE SMITH'S *LET ME DOWN EASY*

This one-actor play that features twenty characters toured the country in 2010–2011 to strong reviews and full houses after a protracted development at several not-for-profit theatres.

play, which she then performs. Her recent *Let Me Down Easy* was developed at two not-for-profit theatres in 2008, then in 2009 after substantial revisions opened in New York City to strong reviews. A national tour followed. In *Let Me Down Easy*, Smith captures the essence of twenty characters—from a much-injured rodeo rider to champion cyclist Lance Armstrong to a musicologist—all united by the subject of medicine, health care, and mortality.

Smith's first nationally successful multicharacter, one-actor documentary-style play emerged in 1992. *Fires in the Mirror* was compiled from interviews with those involved in the days of rioting in the racially divided Crown Heights area in Brooklyn, New York. She performed twenty-nine characters reacting to the accidental killing of a seven-year-old African American child by a Hasidic Jewish driver. The next year, 1993, Smith presented *Twilight: Los Angeles 1992*, a series of monologues about the community's response to the beating of an African American by five California Highway Patrol officers. The brutal beating was caught on a widely distributed home video, but the police were acquitted by a jury of mostly white citizens. Six days of riots followed the acquittal.

Each of her one-actor plays is infused with Smith's brilliant impersonation of the character's vocal and speech patterns. The portrayals are clear and individual but not satirical so the characters emerge as real people, sometimes moving and sometimes funny.

Identity Theatre for Women

In recent years, women have been trying to address gender bias in the contemporary theatre. Evidence was provided by a 2009 Princeton economics PhD thesis—researched and written by a woman—that bias exists. The findings included:

- There are twice as many male as female playwrights, and the men write more plays.

- When a script was sent to artistic directors in not-for-profit theatres sometimes with a male author's name attached and sometimes with

TWILIGHT: LOS ANGELES 1992
Anna Deavere Smith originally conceived
Twilight: Los Angeles as a one-woman
performance piece, but it has been
performed as a multiactor vehicle. Here,
a production at Ball State University.

a female name, the same script received more positive responses when thought to have been written by a man.

- On Broadway, one in eight shows are written by women (12.5 percent) even though plays and musicals by women were 18 percent more profitable than those written by men.

- Plays with female protagonists are less likely to get produced.

As this history has documented, women have often been banned or limited in theatre work. It remained until the late twentieth century for gender inequity to be an openly discussed subject, and once discussed it was subjected to attempts to rectify the inequity, in the theatre and elsewhere. Whereas African American theatre and drama arose from the social upheavals of the late 1950s and 1960s, **women's theatre** was a phenomenon of the 1970s. Increasing numbers of people, mostly female, banded together into theatrical units that aimed to promote the goals of feminism, the careers of women artists, or both. By the mid-1970s, more than forty such groups were flourishing; by 1980, more than a hundred had formed. Unlike **African-American theatres**, which were usually found where there were high concentrations of African Americans in cities, women's theatres sprang up in places as diverse as New York City; Greenville, South Carolina; and Missoula, Montana.

The theatres ranged in size from those depending on one or two unpaid and inexperienced volunteers to organizations of professionals numbering in the hundreds. Budgets, too, varied widely, with some groups existing on a shoestring and the good wishes of friends, and others displaying a financial statement in the hundreds of thousands of dollars. Organization, repertory, working methods, and artistic excellence were highly diversified, but the groups all shared the conviction that women had been subjected to unfair discrimination based on gender and that theatre could serve in some way to correct the inequities.

Like the African American theatres, the women's theatres attempted to serve different audiences and to serve them in different ways. Some groups, like Women's Interart in New York City, existed primarily to provide employment for women artists. Such groups served as a showcase for the works of women playwrights, designers, and directors. Because their goal was to display women's art in the most favorable light, artistic excellence was a primary goal of each production. Critical acceptance by the theatrical mainstream was the ultimate measure of success. But other groups, like the now-defunct It's All Right to Be Woman Theatre (also in New York City), believed the problems of women to be so deeply rooted in society that only a major social upheaval could bring about their correction. Such groups were revolutionary and tended to adopt tactics designed to taunt, shock, or shame a lethargic society into corrective action. These groups cared not at all for the approval of established critics because they believed that traditional theatre was a male-dominated, and hence oppressive, institution.

Two techniques in particular came to be associated with revolutionary women's theatres: a preference for collective or communal organization and the use of improvised performance material, much of it uncommonly personal.

By 1990, however, leading feminist playwrights had moved to other matters, and women's theatres were in flux. Some had ceased producing, and some had moved away from feminism. Others moved in directions newly pointed to by feminism itself—emphasizing differences among women. Although hundreds of feminist plays were written, none became widely known. Their influence, however, is visible in works by female playwrights such as Wendy Wasserstein's *Uncommon Women* (1977), Marsha Norman's *Getting Out* (1979), and Beth Henley's *Crimes of the Heart* (1981).

Women have been increasingly accepted in recent decades as important playwrights and directors, including such playwriting talents as Claudia Shear (*Dirty Blonde*, 2000), Suzan-Lori Parks (*TopDog/Underdog*, 2002), Lynn Nottage (*Ruined*, 2009), Marsha Norman (adapting Alice Walker's novel for the musical *The Color Purple*, 2009), and Sarah Ruhl (*Eurydice* [2003], *The Clean House* [2004], *In the Next Room (or the Vibrator Play)* [2009]).

Peter Smith

UNCOMMON WOMEN AND OTHERS

Playwright Wendy Wasserstein drew on her experiences at Mount Holyoke College to write *Uncommon Women and Others*. It centers on a group of mature women who meet for lunch and discuss their college life together. There are many flashbacks to undergraduate events. The play was her graduate thesis at the Yale Drama School. Here, a production at the University of Michigan.

The plays by these and other women playwrights were mostly developed in the not-for-profit theatre and then staged on Broadway or Off-Broadway and throughout the United States. In the 1990s, Paula Vogel emerged as a major figure (*Baltimore Waltz*, 1992; *How I Learned to Drive*, 1997). Two women playwrights, both African American, won Pulitzer Prizes: Suzan-Lori Parks and Lynn Nottage.

Styles used by women playwrights were eclectic. In Sarah Ruhl's *The Clean House*, a Brazilian cleaning lady tells long jokes directly to the audience—in Portuguese. Suzan-Lori Park's *Topdog/Underdog* portrays two African American blood brothers named Lincoln and Booth. One is a card shark and Abe Lincoln impersonator in white makeup; the other has been a petty thief but wants to graduate to a more sophisticated con, three-card monte.

Female directors also guided major productions: Julie Taymor (*The Lion King*, 1994; *Spider-Man: Turn Off the Dark*, 2011), Susan Stroman (*Young Frankenstein*, 2009), Phyllida Lloyd (*Mamma Mia!*, 2001 and *Mary Stuart*, 2009), Emily Mann (*Anna in the Tropics*, 2003), Anna D. Shapiro (*August: Osage County*, 2007), and Diane Paulus (*Hair*, 2009 and *The Gershwins' Porgy and Bess*, 2012). The training of these directors was highly varied. Taymor, Shapiro, Paulus, and Mann come from the not-for-profit theatre. Lloyd learned the craft first at the British Broadcasting Corporation (BBC), followed by directing at government-subsidized regional theatres in England, at opera houses internationally, and in London's commercial theatre center, the West End. Stroman began as a choreographer of musical comedies and then moved to directing.

Identity Theatre for Gays and Lesbians

Many US cities had self-aware gay and lesbian communities long before the 1960s, but these were largely covert and "in the closet." Homosexual acts were illegal in most of the United States; public homosexual conduct, even language, was sometimes punishable under laws against indecency and obscenity. Therefore, plays about homosexual identity usually fell under the heading of prohibited speech. The exceptions were guarded, almost coded—for example, Lillian Hellman's *The Children's Hour* (1934). This situation

UNINTENDED INSPIRATION
Sarah Ruhl's comedy *The Clean House* was inspired by a casual remark overheard at a cocktail party. Here, a production at Tisch Graduate School of the Arts.

Ella Bromblin

THE PLAY'S THE THING

Paula Vogel's *The Baltimore Waltz*, 1992

The Baltimore Waltz was one of the early US theatrical responses to AIDS. It sees the AIDS crisis from the standpoint of family or friends, who are bewildered by the suffering of the ill, almost beyond the ability to make sense of what they hear and feel.

There are three actors: Anna, a second grade school teacher; her brother Carl, a librarian; and The Third Man, who also plays many other parts. Although Vogel specifies that the play takes place in a hospital in Baltimore, Maryland, it is a string of short, comic scenes, set in many places that often send up clichés from movies and folk tales. One repeated source is *The Third Man*, a suspense movie that took place in post-World War II Vienna.

The Story of the Play Anna tries to learn foreign languages in preparation for her European trip with her brother Carl. In the San Francisco Public Library, Carl leads his last "Reading Hour with Uncle Carl." He has been fired for wearing a pink triangle, a symbol from the Nazi concentration camps to identify homosexuals.

A doctor tells them that there is little time; there is nothing he can do; and medicine knows little about this fatal disease. Anna has Acquired Toilet Disease (ATD), caught—doctors think—from using toilets also used by young children. Anna and Carl decide that while she is healthy, they will take that European tour together. "Because," Anna says, "in whatever time this schoolteacher has left, I intend to fuck my brains out."

Carl learns there is an unorthodox Dr. Todesrocheln in Vienna who might help. Carl speaks to the Third Man on the phone, who says he can find Dr. Todesrocheln. Carl must bring the rabbit.

When Anna and Carl pass through security at the airport, Carl passes her a stuffed rabbit to take through security for him.

Carl and Anna are walking in Paris. Anna finds the Eiffel Tower phallic. They see the Third Man, holding a stuffed rabbit just like Carl's. Anna thinks he's following them. A waiter and Anna flirt and he offers her *la specialité de la maison*, meaning sex. In the hotel Anna and the waiter have noisy sex under the bed covers. Their words are parodies of a foreign language lesson.

Anna plays out the five emotional stages of dying, as defined by Dr. Elizabeth Kübler-Ross (a real person). With narration from the Third Man, she portrays denial and isolation, anger, bargaining, depression, and acceptance. Anna enacts a sixth stage not found in Kübler-Ross: hope. The Third Man offers a seventh stage as well: lust.

Going through customs on a train, again Carl gets Anna to hold the rabbit. She asks what's in the rabbit, drugs, jewels? Carl says she's better not knowing.

In Holland, Anna meets the Little Dutch Boy, the legendary figure that protected the Netherlands by holding his finger in a hole in the dykes. The little boy is fifty years old, but Anna has sex with him, too. Carl tells Anna about the rabbit. As a boy, he was not allowed to play with Anna's dolls, so their parents gave him a stuffed rabbit. Carl couldn't sleep without the rabbit. He takes it everywhere.

Carl and Anna show slides they took on their European trip. Carl describes European sights, but all but one of the slides are of Baltimore. In Munich, Anna seduces the bellhop, who is a virgin. In Berlin, she meets a radical student activist with the same result. In Vienna, as Anna waits for Dr. Todesrocheln in an examination room, Carl meets with the Third Man on a Ferris wheel. They fight over the rabbit to the movements of a waltz and the Third Man waltzes off with the rabbit.

Dr. Todesrocheln brings a urine sample in to Anna's examination room. His right hand wrestles his left hand over possession of the urine. He turns his back and drinks half of it. Dr. Todesrocheln suddenly starts insisting, *Wo ist dein Bruder*? ("Where is your brother?") Anna runs out of the examination room and finds her brother on a hospital bed with the sheet over his head. She removes the sheet and forces Carl out of bed. He is stiff-legged, dead-weight, but they move more-or-less in a waltz, until Carl falls back on the bed. The doctor—a real doctor, not Dr. Todesrocheln—tells Anna there was nothing they could do. He brings her the rabbit and the travel brochures from Carl's bedside table. Carl died of pneumonia, a relatively easy death for someone with AIDS.

THE MEANING OF "BENT"

Martin Sherman's 1979 play *Bent* focused on the persecution of homosexuals in Nazi Germany. The title was slang for homosexual in some European countries. The opposite of straight is bent. Here, a production at Frostburg State University.

changed in the 1960s, however, as court rulings extended free speech and concepts of privacy.

In 1968, Mart Crowley's *The Boys in the Band* was produced Off-Broadway and became the first homosexual hit comedy in a mainstream venue. Sympathetic to the lives and problems of gay men, Crowley's play made a place in commercial theatre for plays in which homosexuality was acceptable and nonthreatening—and funny. Self-deprecating and sometimes self-destructive wit positioned homosexuals as victims, however, and thus ran the risk of sentimentality.

The gay rights movement dates itself generally from 1969, with the Stonewall Riot, when police raided the gay bar called the Stonewall Inn in New York City and were resisted by those they came to arrest. **Gay and lesbian theatre** is usually dated from 1976, when John Glines opened his theatre in New York City. The Glines theatre was dedicated to producing plays by and about gay people, including lesbians. Specifically lesbian theatre companies surfaced in the 1980s (e.g., Split Britches). Also by the 1980s, sympathetic gay plays grew common in mainstream theatre, the more so when the AIDS epidemic became national news, and "AIDS plays" became a subgenre (e.g., *As Is*, 1984).

The rapid acceptance of gay and lesbian plays in the commercial theatre probably came in part from the longstanding acceptance of homosexuality within the theatre community. In gay and lesbian theatre, coherent theory was elusive because of real problems of definition. What is a gay play—a play about gay men? By a gay man? Does a play by a gay or lesbian author but with a different subject fit? Is a play that is critical of gay people a gay play? What of those plays of the past by homosexual authors (e.g., Oscar Wilde, Tennessee Williams) that have no ostensibly homosexual content? Or, as one gay playwright jokingly put it, is a gay play a play that sleeps with other plays? Partly to deal with such theoretical problems, the idea of queer theatre and queer studies evolved, in which *queer* is both an umbrella and a political term, a weapon seized from "the enemy" and turned around. Queer theatre announces itself and has pride in itself, that is, it does not speak in code and it is not apologetic.

Plays with stories of special interest to gay people continued to cross over from not-for-profit theatres to commercial Broadway houses in recent decades.

Doug Wright's *I Am My Own Wife* (2004), for example, is a biographical one-person show about the German transvestite Charlotte von Mahlsdorf. She survived life under both the Nazi and East German socialist regimes. The question: Was she a gay hero for living an open life as a cross-dresser in these repressive regimes or a gay villain because of unsavory acts she undertook to survive? Another Broadway critical and financial success, Richard Greenburg's comedy *Take Me Out* (2002), concerns a star baseball player—handsome, well spoken, well paid, and masculine—who announces he is gay. Banter among the players in the locker and shower rooms is never the same.

Tom Stoppard's historical drama about the closeted homosexual poet A. E. Housman, *The Invention of Love* (1997), also played on Broadway. Meanwhile, plays with gay themes, including the musical *Rent* (1994, Broadway 1996) and *The Laramie Project* (2000), were being produced at churches and regional, community, and college theatres.

The Tectonic Theatre Project conducted interviews with inhabitants of Laramie, Wyoming, in the aftermath of the brutal killing of Matthew Shepard. An openly gay college student, Shepard was enticed from a bar by two men and then robbed and beaten to death, his body left by the side of a rural road. In the resulting documentary play, *The Laramie Project*, eight actors portrayed more than sixty characters in a series of short scenes.

The outstanding serious drama of the 1990s was *Angels in America* by Tony Kushner, which won prestigious prizes in both 1993 and 1994. The play's subtitle is *A Gay Fantasia on National Themes*. The play's principal subjects were homosexual life, only recently real to most Americans; AIDS, an epidemic little more than a decade old when the play was written; love and personal loyalty; and, through the real historical figure Roy Cohn, political and moral corruption.

Identity Theatre for Latinos/Latinas

Playwrights of Latino/Latina identity including Maria Irene Fornes, Nilo Cruz, Eduardo Machado, Sylvia Bofill, Ricardo Bracho, Ed Cardona Jr., and others gradually moved toward the mainstream in recent years. Many of the plays by these authors and others were developed at

TONY KUSHNER'S ICONIC PLAY

Angels in America: A Gay Fantasia on National Themes was first produced on Broadway in 1993. The first part, *Millennium Approaches*, appeared in May followed by the second part, *Perestroika*, in November. Each part is a full evening's play. Here, a production at Ball State University.

IN THE HISPANIC NEIGHBORHOOD

Lin-Manuel Miranda conceived, wrote the music and lyrics, and starred in this invigorating look at Latino life *In the Heights*. The book was by Auiara Alegria Hudes. The musical ran for more than a thousand performances on Broadway, winning four Tony Awards, including one for Best Musical.

Joan Marcus

INTAR, a New York City not-for-profit **Latino/ Latina theatre** producing in English.

Nilo Cruz won the Pulitzer Prize (2003) for *Anna in the Tropics*. Set at the start of the Great Depression of the 1930s, the play takes place in a cigar factory in Tampa's Spanish-Cuban area. During work, a reader or *lector* reads Tolstoy's *Anna Karenina* aloud to the employees. First staged in a not-for-profit theatre in Miami, the play won the Pulitzer Prize and received a Broadway production in 2001. Cruz's plays are produced at many leading not-for-profits.

Maria Irene Fornes (1930–), a writer and director, was Cruz's playwriting mentor. Fornes helped ignite the Off-Broadway movement when her first of forty plays, translations, and adaptations was staged in 1963, *Tango Palace*. Cuban born, Fornes has been awarded nine Obie Awards, including one in 1982 for sustained achievement in theatre. (Obie awards are given by the New York City weekly, the *Village Voice*, mostly for Off- and off-off-Broadway shows and artists.) Her plays are characterized by a nonlinear, unconventional structure. She has been nicknamed "Mother Avant Garde" by her admirers. Many of her productions have been staged by women's theatre groups. Signature Theatre in New York City devoted a full season in 1999 to the plays of Fornes.

Latino/Latina artists are now sometimes produced in the commercial theatres. The energetic musical *In the Heights*, by Lin-Manuel Miranda and Quiara Alegría Hudes, about a mixed Hispanic New York City neighborhood, graduated from an Off-Broadway commercial production to a Broadway commercial production and quickly turned a profit, and led to a touring production. It is slated to become a film.

Identity Theatre into the Mainstream: Two Examples

Perhaps two productions will serve to highlight the transition of identity theatre into the broader theatrical culture. Tony Kushner, working with composer Jeanine Tesori, wrote the musical *Caroline, or Change* (1999, Broadway 2004). Caroline, an African American maid working for a middle-class Jewish family in Louisiana in 1963, is instructed to keep any loose change she finds in the

son's pockets during laundry as a way of teaching the boy to be more careful. The bits of money mean little to the boy's family but become significant
for Caroline's poor household. A crisis develops when a twenty-dollar bill is
found in the laundry. Kushner, author of *Angels in America*, is a gay man; both
he and Tesori are Jewish. The musical was directed by George C. Wolfe, a gay
African American. Significantly, almost no commentator noted any conflict
in a white man's and woman's telling an African American story.

Assimilation of African American playwrights into the mainstream
was not always without controversy. In 2009, a revival of August Wilson's
Joe Turner's Come and Gone was staged on Broadway. The play's setting is a
Pittsburgh boardinghouse that serves as a makeshift home for a changing
mix of African Americans during the "great migration," the first decade of
the twentieth century when descendants of former slaves moved toward
the industrial cities of the North seeking jobs and new starts in life. Some
active in African American theatre, however, bemoaned that the $1.7 million
production was directed by a white man, Bartlett Sher. In his lifetime,
August Wilson would not approve a white director for any of his plays; this
insistence is, in part, why no films have been made of his stories. His reason
for demanding African American directors was to get work for them in what
is a largely white, male profession. But the playwright's widow, Constanza
Romero, personally approved this production and director, saying, "My work
is to get these stories out there and to help ensure that audiences walk out of
the plays with a deeper understanding for these American stories and for the
ways our cultures intertwine."

Romero's work—getting the stories out there—has been at the heart of
identity theatre's goals. But both the commercial and not-for-profit professional theatres increasingly acknowledge and showcase the unity of the human
experience in people of many races and both genders.

Absurdism, Performance Art, and Postmodernism

Art movements are sometimes started with intent—surrealism even had a
manifesto!—but more often are recognized after the fact. **Absurdism** and
performance art, two late-twentieth century theatre genres, are now generally
characterized as forms of **postmodernism**, a genre and philosophy of art
that extends beyond the theatre.

Absurdism

Plays called "absurdist" by critics—not by their authors—appeared just after
World War II in Europe, when several new playwrights were so grouped by

critics. Absurdism (flourishing 1950s–1960s) was itself a blend of *Dadaism* (flourishing 1920s), with which it shared an emphasis on life's meaningless-ness and art's irrelevancy; surrealism, with which it shared an emphasis on the subconscious; and existentialism, a philosophy of existence and behavior. Absurdism's commitment to irrationality and nihilism was a response to a world that had just experienced the Holocaust, the wartime destruction of Europe, and the atomic attack on Hiroshima and Nagasaki. *Absurd* meant not "ridiculous" but "without meaning." Absurdists abandoned story and dramatic unity based on causality. The plays were often constructed as a circle (ending just where they had begun, after displaying a series of unre-lated incidents) or as the intensification of a single event (ending just where they had begun but in the midst of more people or more objects). Usually, the puzzling quality of the plays came from the devaluation of language as a carrier of meaning. In the plays, what *happened* on stage often transcended and contradicted what was *said* there. Absurdists included Samuel Beckett, Eugene Ionesco, Edward Albee, and Arthur Kopit, and they influenced later playwrights including Harold Pinter.

Performance Art

Performance art probably began in European art circles early in the twen-tieth century among the Dadaists, and it found echoes in the *happenings* of the 1960s. (Happenings were one-off and not to be repeated, nonlinear, and deliberately meaningless events that tried to redefine what was meant by theatre.) The resurgence of performance art in the 1980s made it the last energetic expression of the avant-garde. It is a form that defies traditional categories like theatre or dance or painting and the form varies widely among its practitioners. As its name suggests, it depends on both performance and art, and despite its diversity it tends to share certain traits:

- Preference for a nonlinear structure, one unified more often by images and ideas than by plots.

- Emphasis on visual and aural rather than literary elements.

- Tendency to mix elements of several arts, especially music, dance, painting, and theatre.

Some performance art seems clearly to meet the strict definition of theatre whereas other pieces are paratheatrical.

Performance art involves a combination of time, space, the performers' bodies, and a relationship with an audience. It produces no lasting object like painting or music. Although performance art includes many group works, a large proportion are conceived and performed by individual artists working alone.

Performance art probes the boundaries between life and art and among the several arts. Its frank experimentation has made it controversial not

DESIRE UNDER THE ELMS

A shortened version of Eugene O'Neill's 1920s drama *Desire under the Elms* transferred to Broadway in 2009 after an initial production at the Goodman Theatre, Chicago. The unforgiving New England landscape where the play is set is here rendered with post-modern images. The play first opened in 1924 Off-Broadway and then transferred for a successful run on Broadway.

Liz Lauren

only among those who resist blurring the boundaries of arts but also among those who resent its often graphic portrayal of repugnant ideas or activities. Performance art is rarely realistic, but many of its devices—the solo performer, the confessional mode, and the lack of deliberate technique—seek to authenticate its reality.

Postmodernism

Both absurdism and performance art are probably expressions of the bigger artistic movement called *postmodernism*. Postmodernism is a still-evolving term for another set of changes in the arts and culture that was indentified in the 1960s and 1970s. Once named, examples of postmodernism were found by critics dating from the 1950s and arguably before that time.

To define postmodernism, it is important to characterize **modernism**, the artistic movement that has dominated much of art and architecture for the past one hundred years or more. Modernism was a reaction against the comfortable, insular world of Victorian Europe and the United States. In the theatre, the reaction was largely against realistic melodrama. Modernism largely rejected the pieties of religion and country and it was both suspicious of science and technology and reveled in them. Modernist theatre opened up to more nonrepresentational styles of design. In theatre, modernism was reflected by an embrace of different storytelling approaches and with exposing social problems.

By contrast, the assumptions underlying postmodernism include:

• Doubt of the concepts of objectivity and truth.

• Doubt of the concept of absolute meaning.

• Belief in bottom-up participation rather than top-down dictation.

- Belief in differences and shades of meaning rather than black/white opposites.

- Suspicion of ideas of progress, objectivity, reason, certainty, and personal identity.

- Belief that the closest one can get to the truth is via exposing cultural bias and exploring myth, cliché, and metaphor.

Some postmodern theatre came to be characterized by parody, satire, self-reference, irony, and wit. Other postmodern works emphasized the impossibility of communication or political or social improvement—a general nihilism.

As an idea, postmodernism coalesced from writings by French theorists. One branch argued that literature is not about reality but about previous literature. At the extreme case, this branch argued that language is so separated from reality that it has no meaning and can be deconstructed by clever critics to reveal its meaninglessness. The other branch posited that language is a tool of the dominant parts of society to control others by defining the denotation and connotation of words. The control is such that some things cannot even be said without inventing new language. This discussion of French postmodern theorists is highly simplified. Scholars of postmodernism do not always agree about its meaning.

THE GLASS MENAGERIE ON GLASS
Here, in a production from Triad Stage, is a postmodern version of Tennessee Williams's memory play set in 1930s St. Louis, *The Glass Menagerie*.

Postmodern plays, as they evolved after the 1960s, were mostly not unified in tone, time, or style. Instead of linear actions organized by psychology and causality, postmodern theatre created unity through image, allusion, and metaphor; it often appropriated the images and stories of popular culture and used them in subversive ways.

Theatrical Responses to 9/11 and New Wars

Commercial theatre, not-for-profit theatre, and grassroots political theatre attempted to help audiences come to terms with this 2001 terrorist atrocity. Although political avant-garde theatre had waned, the theatre clearly reflected the impact of terrorism and the Iraq and Afghanistan wars that followed. Five productions may stand for the theatre's responses to 9/11 and the actions of the United States thereafter.

METAMORPHOSES

The play, first staged at Northwestern University, moved to the not-for-profit Lookingglass Theatre in Chicago under the title *Six Myths*. When it was staged in New York, it was renamed *Metamorphoses*. Here, a scene from a later production at Virginia Commonwealth University.

Metamorphoses: New York

Mary Zimmerman had worked for some years in Chicago on a stage adaptation of tales by the Roman writer Ovid called *Metamorphoses*. The result was a gentle, humorous, often moving short evening of tales. Many dealt in magical ways with love that lasts past death. The production came to New York City's Second Stage Theatre, a not-for-profit, in October 2001. The *New York Times* reviewer Ben Brantley wrote, "It was then less than a month after the terrorist attacks of Sept. 11, and the show's ritualistic portrayal of love, death and transformation somehow seemed to flow directly from the collective unconscious of a stunned city."

Guantánamo: British

Guantánamo: "Honor Bound to Defend Freedom" was a documentary play, originating in Britain, that was also produced in New York by the Culture Project in August 2004. The play is made of crisscrossing monologues, sometimes surprisingly witty, from the actual words of five British detainees released from the US military prison at Guantánamo, Cuba, along with letters of other captives and testimony from family members, lawyers, and public officials. Since the New York production, the play has been staged across the United States.

The Lysistrata Project: International

As a peace action, Kathryn Blume and Sharon Bower organized "The Lysistrata Project: The First-Ever Worldwide Theatrical Act of Dissent." Thus, March 3, 2003, saw 1,029 performances of the ancient Greek satirical play *Lysistrata* staged in fifty-nine countries and all fifty US states. "The Lysistrata Project" saw readings and stagings of varied accomplishment, some with amateur performers and some with a few of the best-known actors in the world.

Black Watch: Scotland

Out of the National Theatre of Scotland in 2006 came *Black Watch*, a view of the Iraq War as experienced by soldiers in a Scottish regiment. The play moves between postwar interviews in pubs and reenacted deployment scenes depicting the crushing boredom of war spiked by moments of terror, all spiced by the music of regimental folk songs and bagpipes. The production toured Scotland, the United States, Australia, Scotland, and the United States again, and then played London, where it won four 2009 Olivier Awards, the London equivalent of the Tony Awards. It returned to New York City in 2011.

All My Sons: New York

In 2008, a commercial revival of Arthur Miller's 1947 play *All My Sons* opened on Broadway. Shortly after World War II, a Midwestern family comes apart as a long-held secret is revealed: The father, who became wealthy as a supplier to the military, had knowingly shipped defective airplane engine parts, causing the deaths of twenty pilots. One of the pilots may have been the family's eldest son, a pilot who is missing and presumed dead. The shame of one man's profiting by death in war was not lost on an audience in the era of the Iraq War and the government's granting no-bid contracts for rebuilding.

STAR POWER

Crowds flocked to see *All My Sons* in a strong production with a theme that struck audiences as timely. The fact that the Arthur Miller play had four star actors helped to draw audiences.

The Cultural Displacement of Theatre

Despite its commercial successes, US theatre in the last half of the twentieth century was giving out warning signals. The avant-garde of the 1960s through 1980s was all but dead by the 1990s. Dinner theatre—the avant-garde's near opposite—also was in decline. On the bright side, not-for-profit theatres, educational theatres, and community theatres remain vigorous. But the Broadway theatre—the theatre most US people think of when they think of theatre—was struggling against rising costs, rising ticket prices, and stagnant audiences.

The worldwide recession that began in 2008 bankrupted some not-for-profit theatres and other not-for-profit arts endeavors, including orchestras, art museums, and dance companies. Educational theatre, too, was seriously undermined by significant cuts in funding. Many public school districts, under the stresses of lowered budgets and federally mandated testing, eliminated arts training, including theatre. Colleges and universities also suffered: some educational programs were reduced or eliminated.

Some of theatre's problems came simply from increasing competition for the entertainment dollar. Just as radio and moving pictures competed with theatre for audiences before World War II, television, DVDs, computers, and cell phones all competed for attention after the war—and mostly, technology won. Television, not commercially available until the late 1940s, had a set in nine of ten US households by the late 1960s. Although cable television had only about 15,000 subscribers in the 1950s, it had 103 million by the 2010. Computers enabled e-mail and Internet communication by the 1990s, when DVDs and cell phones also became widespread. Such technologies could bring movies, sports, and spectacles into a living room—some could bring them into a car or up to the top of a mountain—and for less money than a legitimate theatre ticket.

Changing technologies seemed to lead a change in the needs and desires of people—or maybe the technologies simply reflected changes already under way. The desire to participate with a group brought together for a single event—such as a theatre audience—seemed to give way to individual enjoyment in front of a machine or even interacting with that faceless machine. People increasingly want to experience media on their own schedules, in their own environment. Theatre from the start has been a social experience as well as an artistic one, a chance for a people in a community to see and be seen together in one space. Theatre, a product of an oral culture, seemed increasingly out of place in a world dominated by an electronic culture. Yet perhaps this will be theatre's saving grace: as film, television, and even books, are mediated through electronics, theatre can remain a hand-made, human-scaled art.

KEY TERMS

Key terms are boldface type in the text. Check your understanding against this list. Persons are page-referenced in the index.

absurdism, p. 312
African-American theatre, p. 305
black theatre, p. 300
eclecticism, p. 281
gay and lesbian theatre, p. 309
Latino/Latina theatre, p. 311
limited run, p. 291
Living Theatre, p. 295
identity theatre, p. 299

modernism, p. 314
not-for-profit theatres, p. 286
Open Theatre, p. 297
performance art, p. 313
postmodernism, p. 312
regional theatre, p. 282
revivals, p. 285
women's theatre, p. 305

European Theatre after 1950

Context

Most of Europe was destroyed at the end of World War II. Although theatre is not essential to eating or heating homes, most countries began early on to restore theatres. For most European countries, theatre had a long tradition of being central to cultural life.

Theatre in non-Communist European countries generally divided into public and private parts. The private theatres were commercial enterprises for the most part. Public theatres were largely supported from government funds, with the government share being fifty percent or more of budgets.

The worldwide recession that began in 2008, however, is threatening government support for many European theatre and other arts programs, with government officials recommending that theatre imitate the US model for not-for-profit theatre: a mix of box office sales; charitable donations from corporations, foundations, and individuals; and a smaller percentage of government support.

In the United States today, federal government money accounts for less than 1.5 percent of not-for-profit theatre budgets; state and local governments on average contribute less than 5 percent.

Although the countries of Western Europe had been engaged in an all-out war, sharing of the arts between countries quickly surmounted barriers including those of language. As these countries moved to a European Economic Union, travel of people and goods became even easier, and theatre traveled among the countries as well. Audience tastes, especially in the commercial theatre, never became uniform, but the best of the non-commercial theatre influenced all of Europe and the United States. This history focuses on a small number of European theatre artists, especially those who have had an international impact.

After the war, many countries on the border of the Soviet Union came under the dominion of that country. In these countries—Eastern Europe—and in the Union of Soviet Socialist Republics, theatre was seen as the property of the government like all other institutions and was managed by elaborate bureaucratic structures to meet government goals. In these countries, government supplied almost all theatre budgets with the small remainder coming from ticket sales. Ticket prices were kept low compared with theatre prices in Western European countries to encourage attendance by all social classes. Still, the content of theatre was strictly censored and controlled. The collapse of the Soviet Union in 1991 brought freedom to most Eastern Bloc countries, on varying time frames and to varying extents.

One exception to the destruction of Europe by World War II was Spain, which was not a participant in the war. Spain underwent a Civil War from 1936 to 1939. The fascists won and General Francisco Franco became dictator. The Spanish government censored the arts, including theatre, until Franco's death in 1975. It approved a new constitution and became a democracy in 1978.

Today there are subsidized national theatres in Romania, Greece, Slovakia, Serbia, Spain, Norway, Austria, Bulgaria, Romania, Hungary, Poland, Finland, Great Britain, France, and Croatia among others. Some of these theatres trace their origins back more than one hundred years. One notable exception is Italy, which for centuries was more interested in opera than theatre. Italy has no subsidized theatre.

Germany

As a defeated, occupied country, divided into four parts occupied by France, England, the United States, and the Soviet Union, theatre in Germany was controlled and censored immediately after the war. The Western occupiers

THE GOOD PERSON OF SETZUAN
Bertolt Brecht completed this moral parable in
1943 while he was living in the United States.
It recounts the struggles of a young prostitute
to live a "good" life as dictated by her gods.
Her neighbors are so venal that she must
invent a male cousin to protect herself. Here, a
production by Butler University Theatre.

published approved lists of plays for production and paid for the translation of
certain plays for German audiences. Occupation of Western Germany ended in
1949, but the Russian-occupied area remained apart. Germany was effectively
two countries, democratic West Germany and socialist East Germany.

From 1950 through 1966, West Germany repaired and rebuilt theatre
buildings damaged in the war and erected new theatres. The playwrights
produced were French (Jean Giraudoux and Jean-Paul Sartre), Swiss (Max
Frisch and Friedrich Dürrenmatt), and US and English (T. S. Eliot, Thornton
Wilder, and Eugene O'Neill).

In Eastern Germany after the war, theatre was centralized in Berlin
with most West German plays forbidden. The main repertoire at first was
translated Russian plays. The government supported training and facilities,
but the selection of scripts was limited.

The two Germanys were reunited in 1990. In 1991, there were about
35,000 performances in Germany's public theatres, about 28,000 in private
theatres, and about 7,700 performances by touring companies. Today
Germany has two national theatres devoted mainly to plays. They are located
in Mannheim and Munich.

Important German Playwrights

Bertolt Brecht   As a communist, the German poet and playwright Bertolt
Brecht (1898–1956) fled Nazi Germany, eventually living a few years in
the United States. When offered a theatre and theatre company by the East
German government, he immigrated there to found and direct the Berliner
Ensemble which became a world-famous interpreter of Brechtian theatre
of alienation. However, he maintained his Austrian passport, foreign bank
accounts, and copyrights to his work. Perhaps he did not trust the Soviet-East

THE THREEPENNY OPERA

Perhaps Bertolt Brecht's most often performed work is an adaptation of John Gay's *The Beggars Opera* with a score by Kurt Weill. Here, a production at Wake Forest University.

German regime, or perhaps he had been chased about Europe and the United States long enough to be wary of any regime.

It is difficult to overstate the extent of Brecht's impact on politically engaged theatre almost everywhere in the world. His theory of the alienation effect (see discussion in Chapter 11) combined with his play scripts and the impact of the Berliner Ensemble when it toured had a tremendous and lasting effect. Plays such as *Mother Courage and Her Children* (1939), *Life of Galileo* (1939), *Caucasian Chalk Circle* (1945), and *The Good Person of Setzuan* (1942) continue to be played throughout the world, although in the United States mostly at educational theatres. Settings of his lyrics to music by Kurt Weill from the 1920s are staples of the world song repertory. Bits and pieces of Brecht's theatrical effects show up in other peoples' plays or directors' conceptions: the use of projections and title cards, actors who are not in a scene remaining at the edges of the stage, nonillusionistic lighting, and the use of song that interrupts and comments on the story instead of heightening the emotional effect of a scene, etc.

Peter Weiss Peter Weiss (1916–1982), a German playwright, novelist, and painter, moved to Sweden to escape the Nazis, motivated in part because his father was Jewish. Of his many plays, the most widely translated and performed is *The Persecution and Assassination of Jean-Paul Marat as Performed by the Inmates of the Asylum of Charenton Under the Direction of the Marquis de Sade*, usually referred to as *Marat/Sade* (1964). Weiss was influenced by Antonin Artaud and Brecht, and the play is interrupted by song. It takes place in a lunatic asylum shortly after the French Revolution of the 1790s. The writer and later namesake for a form of sexual perversion, the Marquis de

MARAT/SADE
Peter Weiss's *The Persecution and Assassination of Jean-Paul Marat as Performed by the Inmates of the Asylum of Charenton under the Direction of the Marquis de Sade* was first performed in West Germany in 1964. That same year Peter Brook directed a world-famous production for the Royal Shakespeare Company. Weiss was born in Germany but adopted a Swedish nationality. Here, a production staged at Purdue University.

Sade, directs the inmates in a play about the murder of Jean-Paul Marat, one of the leaders of the French Revolution. The idea is inspired by history: de Sade was an inmate and directed plays in the institution in this time period. In Weiss's script, the hospital director tries to censor the production so that the inmates will not get too excited and so that the script supports the then-current government under Napoleon. De Sade and the patient playing Marat engage in political discussions: Marat supporting a ruthless revolutionary ideal and de Sade presenting something like individualist existentialism. Does meaning in life come from dedication to a cause or from inner growth? The inmates get caught up in the ideas of revolution and act out their own individual pathologies. The asylum breaks into chaos. First performed in Berlin in 1964, *Marat/Sade* in an English translation played at England's Royal Shakespeare Company that same year and was brought to Broadway the next year, running for 145 performances and garnering several Tony awards.

German-Speaking Swiss Playwrights: Dürrenmatt and Frisch Friedrich Dürrenmatt (1921–1990) and Max Frisch (1911–1991) were German-speaking Swiss authors and playwrights. Dürrenmatt adopted the techniques of Brechtian theatre. He is best known in the United States for the plays *The Visit* (1956) and *The Physicist* (1962). In *The Visit*, an extravagantly rich old woman, Claire, returns to the poor village where she grew up. She comes with two bodyguards and a butler, her husband, two blind eunuchs, a black panther, luggage, and a coffin. She offers the town one billion pieces of money—the currency is not specified and does not matter—on the condition that someone kill Alfred, an old man of the town who had sexually betrayed the woman when they both were young. The townspeople are aghast, but soon they are buying new things, living beyond their means, with credit they will never be able to re-pay without Claire's money. This extravagance is visualized in part by the whole town wearing new yellow shoes. Alfred seeks help from many individuals—a policeman, the mayor, and the priest—who offer none. The individuals are reflective of society's institutions, such as law, government, and religion. In a town meeting, Alfred is killed by a mob. The mayor tells reporters Alfred died of a heart attack. The reporters cry out that Alfred died of joy. The money is paid and Claire's visit ends with her taking Alfred's body away in the coffin she brought for that purpose.

In the United States, *Biedermann and the Firebugs* (1958) is Max Frisch's most often produced play. In a town troubled by arsonists, Biedermann reads about them in his newspaper but believes he could not be taken in. A man named Schmitz appears and using bullying and persuasion, he gets Biedermann to let him spend the night in his attic. Schmitz is soon joined by another stranger, Eisenring. Shortly later Biedermann finds the attic is full of barrels of gasoline. He even gives the two strangers some matches. In the final scene Biedermann and his wife are in hell where they meet Schmitz and Eisenring again and discover that the two are really Beelzebub and the Devil.

Great Britain

Theatre in England is vital, in both subsidized and commercial theatres. Public theatres in England rarely receive as much as one-half of their budgets from the government. Thus, ticket prices are higher than in many other European countries and public theatres are alert to audience response. Just as the not-for-profit theatres in the United States serve as a research-and-development arm of the commercial theatre, public theatres in England regularly move productions from their subsidized theatres to commercial theatres, especially those on the West End—London's equivalent of New York's Broadway theatre district. As of 2000, there were about five hundred theatres in the United Kingdom. About three hundred other performance venues are visited regularly by touring theatre productions.

And despite being a long-standing democracy, England censored theatre until 1968. Censorship was not supposed to be political rather it was supposed to protect religion, the monarchy, the family, and the British way of life. After precensoring was halted, it was still possible to be prosecuted for obscenity unless "the performance in question was justified as being for the public good on the ground that it was in the interests of drama, opera, ballet or any other art, or of literature or learning." There have been few successful obscenity prosecutions.

Stephen Cummisky

The Royal Shakespeare Company and the Royal National Theatre

Attempts to produce Shakespeare's plays in the town of his birth, Stratford-on-Avon, were made repeatedly before and after World War II. In 1961, the Royal Shakespeare Company (RSC) was established in Stratford. Originally an independent, not-for-profit group, it began to receive government subsidies in 1963. The founding of the RSC can be seen as a sign that Britain was finally emerging from the deprivations brought about by the war. Today, it employs about seven hundred people, producing twenty productions a year of Shakespeare's corpus, plays by Shakespeare's contemporaries, supplemented with new plays, and traveling regularly to London and about Britain and sometimes to the United States. It has two theatres, one seating a little more than one thousand people and the other slightly less than five hundred people. The RSC has been an artistic home for a great number of Britain's greatest actors, directors, and designers of the postwar period, including actors such as Kenneth Branagh, Tim Curry, Judi Dench, Michael Gambon, John Gielgud, Nigel Hawthorne, Jeremy Irons, Derek Jacobi, Ben Kingsley, Jude Law, Alec McCowen, Ian McKellen, Ian McDiarmid, Helen Mirren, Gary Oldman, Peter O'Toole, Vanessa Redgrave, Alan Rickman, Patrick Stewart, and David Tennant and directors including Peter Brook, Trevor Nunn, Peter Hall, and Matthew Warchus. These artists have enriched theatre, especially English-language theatre, around the world.

In some ways the RSC's main counterpart, at least in prestige and government support, is the Royal National Theatre (NT) in London. In 2010, the RSC received £19.3 million of government support, about 30 percent of its budget; the NT got £15.6 million or about 56 percent of its smaller budget. (In US dollars, the government support is about $30 million for the RSC and $25 million for the NT. For comparison, the National Endowment for the Arts [NEA] in 2011 granted less than $4.5 million for *all* theatre in the United States.) Founded in 1963, the NT operated out of the Old Vic theatre building before moving into its colossal concrete facility on the south side of the Thames in

Ludo des Cognets

1976. It offers a mixed program that includes Shakespeare and other classic dramas and new plays. NT shows sometimes transfer to commercial runs in London's West End and to Broadway runs or international tours. Its most recent productions to move to the West End and New York include Alan Bennett's play *The History Boys* and *War Horse*, adapted by playwright Nick Stafford from a children's novel. The list of artistic directors of the NT since its founding contains many major British theatre directors of the last fifty years or so: Peter Hall, Richard Eyre, Trevor Nunn, and Nicholas Hytner, plus its found-ing director, the late actor Lawrence Olivier. As with the RSC, the NT's artists have had a profound influence on English-language theatre wherever it occurs.

Scotland established a national theatre in 2006; it has no permanent home theatre building but performs in venues around the country.

British Playwrights

John Osborne Britain has spawned a number of playwrights that have been important for both British and US theatre. In the period after World War II, the first to emerge was John Osborne (1929–1994), with his play *Look Back in Anger* (1956). It is difficult today to recover how shocking *Look Back* was originally, in part because Osborne's harsh sarcasm and irony and his questioning of long-standing traditions have become part of our common mind-set. And his play's one-set, quotidian family drama has become routine in the theatre. But compared to the polite world of British theatre before Osborne, the cruelty and sexual content of the play was scandalous.

In the play, Jimmy is working class; his wife Alison's family is upper-middle class. Jimmy is incessantly angry, belittling Alison to his friend Cliff. Alison loves

Jimmy because she is in a rebellion against her upbringing and she admires his leftist views. She is pregnant and Jimmy does not know.

Alison's father, Colonel Redfern, comes to take her back to the family home. Referring to British society following the war, Alison tells her father, "You're hurt because everything's changed, and Jimmy's hurt because everything's stayed the same." Helena stays on, and when Jimmy returns, they fight and then they kiss and fall into bed.

Months pass. Jimmy is kinder to Helena than he was to Alison. Jimmy finds Alison at the apartment door, looking ill. Alison tells Helena that she lost the baby. Helena leaves and, left alone, Jimmy and Alison play a game they used to play and seem to reconcile.

Harold Pinter The plays of Harold Pinter (1930–2008) often seem to be family dramas, but there is always something off, something unsaid, menacing, and unsettling. Audiences cannot say clearly after the curtain falls exactly what happened nor can they describe the characters without ambiguity. Pinter is considered one of the absurdists according to many critics. His first professionally produced play, *The Birthday Party* (1958) along with *The Homecoming* (1964) are perhaps his most well-known scripts. *The Birthday Party*'s first production was not well reviewed, but one critic championed it, writing that Pinter "possesses the most original, disturbing and arresting talent in theatrical London."

In *The Birthday Party*, Stanley Webber, an unsuccessful piano player in his thirties, lives in a rundown boarding house, run by Meg and Petey. Two sinister strangers, Goldberg and McCann, arrive on Stanley's birthday looking for him. Stanley avoids meeting the two whose conversation is made up of vague and clichéd bureaucratic discussion of some job they are to do. Later, Stanley denies that it is his birthday although Meg is planning a party. McCann confronts Stanley, with questions like, "Why did you leave the organization?" and "Why did you betray us?" Still the birthday party begins. Everyone quickly becomes drunk except for Stanley. In the next scene, McCann brings on Stanley, his glasses broken, unable to speak. McCann and Goldberg take Stanley out of the house to a car waiting to take him to "Monty," whoever that person is. Meg enters and Petey does not tell her that Stanley is gone.

Alan Bennett and Michael Frayn Born within two years of each other, in 1935 and 1933, respectively, Alan Bennett and Michael Frayn came to playwriting from different paths. Born of middle-class parents, both studied at Cambridge University; Bennett also studied at Oxford University. Frayn's university subjects were Russian and moral philosophy yet out of university he became first a journalist where he was known for satire. Bennett also studied Russian and history and first came to notice as part of a four-man comedy group that included Dudley Moore (later a famous comic actor in

AN INTERNATIONAL HIT

Alan Bennett's *The History Boys* opened at the National Theatre and from there toured to Hong Kong; Wellington, New Zealand; Sydney, Australia; and New York City where it earned a Tony Award as Best Play. *History Boys* returned to London for another run. Here, Richard Griffiths as Hector with one of his pupils.

movies), Jonathan Miller (later a famous director especially of opera), and Peter Cook (who stuck with comedy as a writer and performer on stage, film, and television).

Alan Bennett writes books and scripts for television, film, radio, and the stage. His plays are generally light entertainments with surprising story matter. *The Lady in the Van* (1990) was based on a true story of a homeless, probably crazy, woman who lived for years in a trailer in Bennett's driveway. *The Madness of George III* (1991) was about the British king who "lost the colonies" in the US Revolutionary War and who suffered from a mental illness late in life; his court does not know what to do with a nutty monarch.

The History Boys (2004) takes place in a lower-class grammar school in the 1980s during an attempt by the head master to prepare the boys for entry exams for the Cambridge or Oxford universities, together called "Oxbridge." Two teachers are highly contrasted in style: Irwin, a young man focused on techniques to win the exams and Hector, an older, homosexual teacher who teaches challenging, entertaining, wide-ranging classes. The eight boys all get in, and we learn in an epilogue that all but one had some success in life given their lower-class starting points. They remember Hector as the most important person in their lives, although Irwin probably had more to do with them getting into school. *The History Boys* toured internationally, played an extended time on Broadway where it won six Tony Awards, returned to play again in London's West End, and, in the meanwhile, was made into a successful film using the stage cast.

Michael Frayn first garnered worldwide theatrical success with a fast-paced, silly farce called *Noises Off* (1982) and followed that some years later with two serious, intellectual dramas, *Copenhagen* (1998) and *Democracy* (2003). In *Noises Off*, a not-very-talented regional theatre company in Britain is presenting a farce, called "Noises On," and there are back stories and back stabbing among the players. The first act is a discouraging rehearsal, the second act is the first performance seen from backstage, and the third act is the play seen from the front-of-house near the end of the troupe's run when everyone is tired and antagonistic and can *just* finish the performance.

Copenhagen is based on a true incident about which no details are firmly known. The physicists Niels Bohr of Denmark and Werner Heisenberg of Germany met during World War II. Frayn imagines their discussion in this fraught time. *Democracy* dramatized another true story, this time from the Cold War of the late 1960s and early 1970s. West German Chancellor Willy Brandt's assistant Günter Guillaume turned out to be an East German spy. Dauntingly intellectual, these two plays were nonetheless international successes. Frayn has also written ten novels.

Tom Stoppard Tom Stoppard (1937–) was also a journalist before becoming a playwright. Born in Czechoslovakia to Jewish parents, when Stoppard was young the family moved to Singapore to escape the Nazis. When Japan threatened Singapore, the family moved to Australia except for Stoppard's father, who later died in a Japanese prisoner of war camp. At the age of five, his family moved to India and his mother married an Englishman who adopted Stoppard and moved the family to England after the war. Stoppard says his background gave him a sense of being always an outsider, which is reflected in his plays. His first important success was the absurdist *Rosencrantz & Guildenstern Are Dead* (1966). Rosencrantz and Guildenstern are two minor characters in Shakespeare's *Hamlet*. In Stoppard's play, they joke and vamp to waste time as, now and then, a bit of Shakespeare's play happens behind them. Here are several postmodern tropes: classics of another era evoked in ironic ways and characters whose life is random and not meaningful, the opposite of heroic or tragic protagonists.

Inspired by and deconstructing history or biography with erudite wit while exploring themes of identity and purpose and sometimes politics continued in many of Stoppard's works. Some of the plays pose puzzles for the viewer. *Travesties* (1974), set in Zürich during the First World War, imagines that the modernist author James Joyce when writing *Ulysses*, the artist Tristan Tzara while instrumental in the artistic movement called Dada, and Lenin as he worked for the Russian Revolution, all interacted. (Historically, all were in Zürich at the time but there is no record that they ever met.) *Arcadia* (1993) takes place in a room of a grand English country house in the early years of the 1800s and in 1993. In the present, scholars are investigating and arguing about what happened in the house in the 1800s; in past scenes, the audience sees what happened. Meanwhile, scientific ideas are bruited about in both

MAD FOREST

Like some of Caryl Churchill's plays, *Mad Forest* was a collaboration with the performers, in this case among English and Romanian drama students, the play's director, and the playwright. Churchill and her group spent about two months in Romania, and shortly thereafter Churchill fashioned a play from this research. Although the play is written in English, the cast is required to speak some Romanian and sing the Romanian National Anthem.

periods: recursion and its cousin chaos theory, entropy, esthetics—especially of gardens—and Fermat's last theorem, which, at the time Stoppard first presented the play, was neither proven nor disproven.

Caryl Churchill Born in England around the same time (1938), Caryl Churchill spent much of her youth in Canada, returning to England to attend Oxford from which she graduated in 1960 with a degree in literature. She started writing plays while at Oxford. As a dramatist, she was affected by Brecht and Artaud and mixed them with a postmodern freedom of form and tone. Her first international success was *Cloud Nine* (1979), which might be termed a serious sex farce. The first act takes place in British colonial Africa in Victorian times. The second act moves the same characters forward to London in 1979, but the characters are only twenty-five years older. To add to the fun or the puzzle, actors take different roles in each act. A male actor plays the mother in the first act but plays her son, a homosexual tough, in the second. A child is played by a very large man in one act and by a doll in the other. A black servant in the first act is played by a white man. There are no servants for the family in 1979. Sexual and racial oppression are implicitly conjoined. Although society and its expectations changed much over the century or so between the acts, children, women, and minorities seem to have made little real progress.

Churchill has also been fond of developing plays through improvisation with an acting company from which she finalizes a script. For example, both *Mad Forest* (about the Romanian revolution of 1989) and *Fen* (about lower-class life in the Fens area of England) were created through the improvisational approach.

France

Theatre in Paris continued through the Nazi occupation with sometimes effective censorship—Hitler loved Paris. After the war, the urgent question was who, in all domains, including theatre, had collaborated with the Nazis and who was a good, loyal French person. Books are still being written today trying to scout out the villains of occupied France. Like much of the rest of Europe, theatre in France split between the serious, state-supported theatre

THE PLAY'S THE THING

Caryl Churchill's *Top Girls*, 1982

Caryl Churchill has two seemingly contradictory qualities as a playwright: She is freely creative and theatrical in her imagination and fully rigorous in her political and social themes. One recurring larger issue in her plays is feminism, the subject of *Top Girls*. However, *Top Girls* is far from a polemic; instead it offers a disquieting dialectic, an exchange of ideas, which does not try to make one position prevail.

The play has an unusual structure—not unusual for Churchill who is a fully postmodern writer—but unusual for most plays. The first scene is biggest in number of characters on stage, flamboyance in costuming, and opportunities for humor, and subsequent scenes march regularly downward in scale. The last act is dominated by two sisters talking and drinking as the night comes on.

The Story of the Play The first act takes place in the early 1980s in a restaurant. Marlene is celebrating her work promotion with an extraordinary group of guests, some historical and some mythical, including

- Isabella Bird (1831–1904) who lived in Edinburgh and was noteworthy for her adventurous travels around the world and her travel writings.
- Lady Nijo (1258–?), a courtesan of the Japanese Emperor who traveled on foot throughout Japan, writing an autobiography.
- Dull Gret, a subject in a Brueghel painting of 1562. In the painting, Gret leads an army of peasant women on a rampage in hell.
- Pope Joan, a legendary woman who lived disguised as a man and became Pope in the Middle Ages.
- Patient Griselda, the obedient wife from Chaucer's *The Canterbury Tales* (late fourteenth century).

The women describe their lives. Their tales overlap in theme:

- difficult but joyful travel
- the loss of children often through the action of men

- a level of ambition and accomplishment that was unwomanly in their eras

The next scene is in the Top Girls employment agency, a business that finds jobs exclusively for women, where Marlene has recently been promoted. Staff interview job seekers who are vague about what they seek and what they offer. In the next scene, in Marlene's sister, Joyce's, back yard, Joyce's daughter Angie, sixteen, is playing with her only friend, twelve-year-old Kit. Angie is a little socially and intellectually backward for her age, so the two girls get along. Angie talks about her aunt, Marlene, whom she reveres; Angie imagines she is her aunt's child. Angie is wearing a dress that is too small for her. She tells Kit that she put on the dress to kill her mother with a brick.

Back at the Top Girls offices, Mrs. Kidd, the wife of an unseen male staff member, comes to upbraid Marlene for taking the promotion that her husband thought was rightfully his. Marlene and Mrs. Kidd have an unsatisfying confrontation. The office later hears that Mr. Kidd is in hospital for a heart attack.

The next scene is a year earlier. Marlene visits her sister, Joyce, bringing several gifts for Angie, including a dress—the one Angie wears in the prior scene. As Angie is sent to bed, the two sisters drink and have a rambling, disputative talk. It is revealed that Joyce adopted Marlene's child, Angie. Marlene says she has had many lovers—and more than one abortion—but none of the men were satisfactory. Joyce sees Marlene as coldly ambitious and unhappy. Marlene contends she could not stay in their small town where there was no opportunity. She is "going up up up" in her work. Joyce says Marlene is one of "them," the conservative, money-motivated people, supporters of Margaret Thatcher (then Prime Minister). Marlene counters ironically that Joyce and their miserable poor parents must therefore be "us, wonderful us." After Joyce retires and Marlene lies down to sleep on the sofa, Angie comes down to be comforted by Marlene from a bad dream that was "Frightening....Frightening."

and commercial "boulevard" theatres presenting light entertainment for a well-to-do audience. By the 1990s, the government provided about 50 percent of the budget for supported theatres. At the same time, forty-seven commercial theatres existed in Paris alone with more than four thousand amateur groups spread about the country. There came to be independent avant-garde theatres, too. And in the group of independent producers, the *Vieux Colombier* and the *Theatre Antoine* continued.

French Playwrights

Jean Anouilh Jean Anouilh (1910–1987) began writing plays before World War II and continued afterward. His stories were often adapted from mythical and historical sources. His best known works in the United States are *Antigone* (1944), *Ring 'Round the Moon* (1947), *The Lark* (1952), *Beckett* (1959); dates are all for the French premieres. *Antigone* is an adaptation of the classical Greek play. *The Lark* and *Beckett* concern historical characters, albeit ones that have taken on aspects of myth: Joan of Arc and Thomas Beckett and his conflict with England's Henry II. *Ring 'Round the Moon*—called in French, *Invitation to the Castle*—is a different thing totally, a witty period romance about the upper classes, character and morality, and love and marriage.

Eugene Ionesco Eugene Ionesco's (1909–1994) first play, *The Bald Soprano*, premiered in 1940. It is said to be the most often performed play in France. He was born in Romania, grew up in France, attended university in Romania, and returned to live in France in the late 1930s. In *The Bald Soprano*, two couples plus a maid and the maid's lover talk in non-sequiturs. Ionesco

Joan Marcus

RING 'ROUND THE MOON

Christopher Fry, the noted English poet and playwright, was commissioned to adapt Jean Anouilh's *Invitation to the Castle* (1947), which he retitled *Ring 'Round the Moon*. Peter Brook directed the retitled play in 1950. Here, a production by Lincoln Center Theatre starring Marion Seldes, seated.

says he was inspired by the dialogue in books he studied attempting to learn English. As the lover leaves, he mentions in passing a bald soprano, to which, one of the women replies, "She always wears her hair in the same style." Even though the dialogue is meaningless, the two couples become irate and the lights go out on their shouting. When the lights come up again, the play begins again, with the same lines but this time said by different characters, until the lights slowly die. Ionesco's plays often parade the impossibility of communication, making him one of the absurdists.

Samuel Beckett Samuel Beckett (1906–1989) was an Irishman who studied French in university and lived in France beginning in the 1930s. Early in life, he was a prolific novelist of dour, difficult, and esteemed works, much admired and influential. During World War II, he worked with the French resistance. Only after the war did he start writing plays. He said that he wrote his plays in French—hence his inclusion in this section of the book—before translating them into English because French was the only language one could write in "without a style." This observation may have been meant as a dry joke. He continued to write plays all his life and many were well received, but nothing matched the international impact of his first produced play, *Waiting for Godot* (1953). It provoked argument, laughter, and intrigue, in roughly equal measures.

The play's two acts portray two days in the lives of two men in a desolate landscape, Vladimir and Estragon, whiling away the time as they wait for someone named Godot to come. They discuss weighty matters frivolously, sing, tell jokes for which they can not remember the punch lines, argue, and nap. At one point, the self-important Pozzo and his abject slave Lucky pass through. Vladimir and Estragon are stricken by Lucky's ill treatment but make only meager complaint. Before leaving, Pozzo has Lucky do his song and dance, a pathetic and disjointed thing. At the end of the first act, a boy appears to tell the pair that Godot will not be coming this evening but certainly tomorrow. The second act repeats the action of the first—waiting, clowning, the passing through of Pozzo and Lucky, the boy who says "not today but certainly tomorrow"—but with a sense of waning energy, of things running down, of entropy. Vladimir and Estragon decide to find a better place to wait for Godot, but they do not leave.

Much critical energy has been spent speculating who or what Godot could be. Beckett refused to answer,

Joan Marcus

WAITING FOR GODOT

A 2009 Broadway revival of Samuel Beckett's play, starring Nathan Lane (*left*) and Bill Irwin, received rave reviews. The production was nominated for three Tony Awards. One reviewer called it a "transcendent" production performed by two of the great clowns of the United States.

although he was adamant that Godot is not God, however it might sound in English. (In the United States, Godot is pronounced "guh-DOE"; in Britain, "GOD-oe." Beckett wrote the play first in French, where the word for God is "*Dieu*.") Does it matter? Vladimir and Estragon wait for something outside of themselves to change their meaningless lives and thus reflect in exaggerated and absurdist manner the predicament of many people in the period after the Second World War.

Beckett continued to write plays after *Godot*, and they tended to be increasingly shorter and more taciturn, reflecting perhaps the absurdist belief that communication is impossible. He received the Nobel Prize in Literature in 1969.

Italy

Italian critics generally acknowledge that after the war theatre has never become central to Italian culture. It has been swamped by film and television, for both audiences and artists. From the end of World War II until 1963, theatre was strictly censored and no social ills could be presented on stage. The result was to further defang the stage as an important art. Beginning in the 1960s, musicals became a large chunk of the commercial theatre, largely imports of US and English musicals but some homegrown Italian ones, too. In the 1991–1992 season, there were 64,000 performances in Italy, given in 615 theatres and in a number of summer arts festivals about the country. This number includes opera, a much more popular performance genre in Italy than plays or musicals.

Like other European avant-garde theatres, the politically and artistically engaged theatre in Italy was heavily influenced by Brecht and the touring Berliner Ensemble, the Living Theatre tours, the theories of Jerzy Grotowski, and the experiments of the English-emigrant-in-France, Peter Brook.

Playwright, Performer, Provocateur: Dario Fo One internationally important theatre maker in Italy after World War II has been Dario Fo (1936–). Satirist, performer, composer, playwright, Fo took inspiration from the Italian commedia dell'arte. His works often lampoon topics of political and social importance in Italy—organized crime, government inefficiency, the Catholic Church hierarchy, and the Middle East fighting, which is just half the Mediterranean Sea away. When performed elsewhere, they are often adapted to include local issues. His acting troupe is run with his wife, the actress Franca Rame. Between 1955 and 1959, the two worked in film. Since 1960, the work of his company has received enthusiastic support from audiences in Italy and elsewhere. They have also been threatened, variously, by the Mafia, the right-wing, and the Catholic Church. Although the Communist party in Italy initially supported Fo and Rame against attacks from the right, eventually it too turned against them.

His plays have been performed in at least fifty-seven countries and translated into more than thirty languages. Perhaps his best known play is *Mistero Buffo* (*Comic Mysteries*), an episodic fractured retelling of passion and mystery plays from the Middle Ages overlaid with com-media lazzi and political commentary. The Vatican declared the play to be blas-phemous. Performed by Fo, *Mistero Buffo* is a one-person show. Most other com-panies presenting the play use multiple actors and sometimes puppets. Although a playwright, Fo trusts the improvisa-tory nature of the commedia and so encourages script changes to be made when his works are performed by oth-ers. In 1997 he was awarded the Nobel

DARIO FO'S ODD MYSTERY
Here, a performance in Italy. Dario Fo's connection to commedia dell'arte techniques is evident in this seemingly temporary stage with a curtain backdrop.

Prize in Literature, the prize honoring a writer "who emulates the jesters of the Middle Ages in scourging authority and upholding the dignity of the downtrodden."

Poland

Although theatre in Poland was totally destroyed by Nazi occupation, by May 1945 a dozen theatres were performing again, often within dilapidated buildings. Soon after the war, as in other Communist states, the government became the owner and financial supporter of theatre in Poland. Realism was favored; art should be for the masses. Directors in this period favored classical works of Polish romanticism or works by the ancient Greeks or by Shakespeare. But new plays were produced that were often set in factories, shipyards, farming cooperatives, and such. Political control of theatre eased after Joseph Stalin's death in 1953. Only then were important European and US plays from the previous twenty years performed. Brecht's work was also staged and was highly influential. In this period, physical design grew in importance, in a style that was antirealistic, spectacular, and expensive—and used for plays of all eras.

Communism in Poland collapsed in 1989, resulting in contradictory changes for the theatre. The stage was free to pursue all topics and playwrights but suddenly without much government subsidy. Before, theatres on average received 80 to 90 percent of their budgets from the Communist state. By 1991, government money went primarily to a handful of national theatres. In 1992, there were sixty-nine theatres in Poland. For many companies, comedies and farces were typical repertoire, in an attempt to attract more paying customers. The extravagant and expensive physical productions of the Communist era could no longer be afforded.

Today, the National Theatre of Poland, founded in 1765, is located in Warsaw. It has traditionally housed opera, theatre, and ballet performances.

Theorist and Experimenter: Jerzy Grotowski and "Poor Theatre"

Jerzy Grotowski (1933–1999) was an experimental theatre director who followed his development of new ideas, his "research," in several directions. In doing so, he influenced non-commercial theatre throughout the Western world. Beginning with typical dramatic texts often treated with great freedom, he moved to theatre based on nondramatic texts, often not from European sources. An early production in 1960 was based on the Sanskrit drama *Shakuntala* (for more about the original play, see page 59). One milestone production was *Akropolis* (1964), loosely built on a play of 1904 by Stanisław Wyspiański. The actors build a crematorium around the audience while incongruously acting out stories from the Bible and Greek mythology. *Akropolis* was filmed and later revived in international touring to enormous effect.

Grotowski's concept of **poor theatre** had wide-ranging impact, although his writings about the poor theatre can be difficult to clearly explicate. "Poor" does not refer to money but to effects. Theatre cannot compete with film, Grotowski argued, so rather than piling on scenery and lighting, it should be "poor" and focus on actors and audiences. He believed that those two things were the essence of theatre and everything else was additional, distracting. His acting training was opposed to any layering of "tricks" on the actor, such as vocal training, the Stanislavski method, and such. Rather, he saw actor training as a psychic and emotional stripping down. "The actor makes a gift of himself," Grotowski wrote, "This is the technique of the 'trance' and the integration of the actor's psychic and bodily powers…"

Grotowski's later research took him away from the play script even further. Dubbed his "paratheatrical period," Grotowski attempted in later years to develop ritual-like performances, through communal rites involving performers and audience members. He later traveled to Third World countries, including Mexico, India, Haiti, and elsewhere, to learn about theatre there, again in an attempt to return theatre to elemental roots. He tried to develop something he called "objective drama," looking for songs or movements that could have an effect on the doer without reference to meaning or culture. Later he worked on theatre as a vehicle to lead to other levels of perception. Some might say his later research went beyond theatre as it has been generally defined.

Grotowski influenced many directors and theatre makers internationally. Peter Brook (1925–), an English director who early in his career worked with the RSC, became a disciple and propagandist. At the RSC, Brook directed the first English-language production of Peter Weiss's *Marat/Sade.* Just before moving to France in the 1970s to start the International Center for Theatre Research, Brook directed an acclaimed production of *A Midsummer Night's Dream* (1970). Eschewing previous scenic conventions, the stage set was the interior of a white box. The fairies entered on trapeze bars; Puck's love potion was a red plate spinning on a stick; Bottom's transformation into an ass was signified by the actor donning a red clown nose. From his French Center, one of his important works was a production (1985) of the epic Hindu text, the *Mahabharata,* that was nine hours long.

European Theatre after World War II Had Wide Impact

European theatre after the end of the Second World War rebuilt quickly. At first, it largely staged revivals and classics, but gradually new playwrights of stature emerged. The theories of Bertolt Brecht and Antonin Artaud deeply influenced politically-engaged theatres in Europe throughout this era. Somewhat later, the experiments of Jerzy Grotowski deeply influenced the artistic avant-garde around the world. Theatre in many European countries in this period has been supported by government grants although the recession that began in 2008 is whittling away state money for all the arts, including drama. Without government support, theatre companies tend to program comedies and musicals to attract a wider, paying audience.

KEY TERM

Key term is boldface type in the text. Check your understanding against this list. Persons are page-referenced in the index.

poor theatre, p. 336

Theatre in Asia from 1800

Context

Western countries had traded with Asia for centuries but almost always by the land routes called the Silk Road with many middlemen taking a share of the value of the goods. With ship building, navigation, and business organization greatly improved in the eighteenth and nineteenth centuries, European powers sought direct trade with the east. In some cases, European and North American countries only wanted trade, often enforced with gunships. In other cases, they sought colonies in India, China, and Japan.

India

British influence on India begins with the East India Company in the seventeenth century, and the East India Company had essential trade monopoly by 1763. Operating for more than two centuries, the East India Company traded in cotton, silk, indigo, saltpeter, tea, and opium. It came to command large areas of India through the use of a company-owned military from 1757 until 1858 when the British Crown took over direct administration of India. Modern India and Pakistan became independent in 1947. After independence for India, the culture became dominated by the local film industry and professional live theatre dwindled.

China

When the Chinese authorities tried to stop the British trade in opium, which had addicted many of its citizens, England declared war, the so-called Opium Wars of 1839–1842 and 1856–1860, which resulted in a treaty giving first England, then many other European powers, special trading and legal rights in China. England needed to trade opium it raised and processed in India to maintain a favorable balance of trade. Because China had so many goods England wanted, such as tea and silk, without opium sales the balance of trade was bad for England.

China overthrew the emperor in 1912 and briefly founded a republic, which quickly fell apart in factional fighting. That fighting continued up to the founding of the Chinese Communist government under Mao Tse-Tung in 1949. Communist China had fateful effects on everything in the region, including theatre. Since about the turn of the millennium, China's economic growth has marked it as a future world power.

HINDU PARATHEATRICAL RITUAL CELEBRATION

Theyyam, a Hindu ritual performed for at least a thousand years but whose roots are probably even older, continues in the Kerala state in southern India. The colorfully dressed lower caste celebrants are considered incarnations of the deities of the shrine and thus are worshiped by the crowd.

Japan

In 1854, Commodore Matthew Perry of the United States took gun boats to Japan to forcefully open that country to trade with the United States. Other Western powers soon followed. In part as a result of this foreign embarrassment, a revolution in Japan restored the emperor to the throne, and Japan launched a modernization initiative, essentially an effort to absorb the technology and governance styles of the West, resulting eventually in Japan's aggressive approach to its Asian neighbors and, during World War II, to fighting Western powers.

The two world wars—especially the second—further integrated Asia with the West. Defeated Japan, occupied by the US armed forces, became focused on Western culture, incorporating parts of it while remaining Japanese as well. In the postwar period, Asia remained a focus of the two superpowers, the United States and the Soviet Union, in their struggle for world dominance.

Theatre in India since ca. 1800

Before Western economic and political dominance on the Indian subcontinent, folk theatre was performed everywhere. It varied in scale and style by locale but expressed some of the visual extravagance of Sanskrit drama. Although Sanskrit drama was gone by the conquest of the Moghul Empire of the ninth century, an indigenous dance-drama called **Kathakali** continued in the southernmost area, and it is now believed to be the most direct descendant of Sanskrit drama in India. Kathakali is a classical dance-drama with highly stylized makeup and costumes, using prescribed gestures and body movements, drawing from a large but limited range of traditional stories. It is performed in a mix of the local language and Sanskrit. As such, it shares many elements with other of the regional, indigenous theatre forms in India.

Western-Style Theatre Emerges

When India was declared a British dominion in 1858, many Western traditions were brought to India. Colonists from England built universities that resulted in English being the second language of educated locals. The British established three large cities—Calcutta, Bombay (now Mumbai), and Madras—to focus on the efficient financial exploitation of Indian materials to Western markets and as stopping points in the movement of goods from farther east to Europe. To those cities, Britain brought its love of theatre, presenting English plays with English actors in proscenium theatres modeled on those in London. Modern dramas styled after English plays but written in Indian languages and performed by Indian actors emerged in the late nineteenth century. These were essentially realistic dramas, comedies, and melodramas, resembling in style the plays of Britain. Some producers used the theatre as a forum for social and political ideas. After a production of an inflammatory play in a northern Indian city resulted in a small riot by Europeans—the play depicted a white planter raping a native woman—the English enacted the Dramatic Performances Act of 1879. That act gave the English authorities the power to censor the Indian theatre.

Rabindranath Tagore Poet, novelist, musician, painter, and playwright Rabindranath Tagore (1861–1941) is India's best-known modern writer for the stage. Perhaps his most often performed play in the West is *Dak Ghar* or *The Post Office* of 1912.

Tagore's *The Post Office*, 1912

Tagore's *The Post Office* was hailed throughout Europe. Irish poet and playwright W. B. Yeats produced an English-language version. It was translated into Spanish and French, the later version read on the radio the night before Paris fell to the Nazis during World War II. A Polish version was performed by orphans in the Warsaw ghetto.

The story of *The Post Office* is appealing in its symbolism and simplicity. The protagonist's quiet death resonated with European readers and audiences living through the murderous twentieth century. As Tagore put it, death in *The Post Office* is "spiritual freedom" from "the world of hoarded wealth and certified creeds."

The Story of the Play An adopted child, Amal, stays in the family's courtyard, asking passers-by about where they are going. He cannot leave because of illness. A new post office nearby leads Amal to fantasize about receiving a letter from the king or that he could be the king's postman. The village chief mocks the illiterate Amal, leading him on with a made-up tale that he has received a letter from the king writing that he is sending the royal physician to Amal. Strangely, the royal physician really does come, with a herald announcing the king's impending arrival. Amal's guardian whispers to him, "My child, the King loves you. He is coming himself. Beg for a gift from him. You know our humble circumstances." Amal replies, "I shall ask him to make me one of his postmen that I may wander far and wide, delivering his message from door to door." In peace and with visions of a starry sky, Amal falls asleep—or does he die?

Tagore grew up in a literate and literary family and was educated at home. For example, his elder brother Jyotirindranath wrote plays and adaptations of Molière, which were performed in the family home, and later founded a theatre group. Rabindranath Tagore was not primarily a playwright: he wrote novels, stories, songs, and political and personal essays. He was awarded the Nobel Prize for Literature in 1913. He was knighted by Britain in 1915 but later returned the honor in protest of British rule of India. He did not live to see India's independence.

"Bollywood" Undermines Western-style Theatre The rise of Indian cinema in the twentieth century—universally referred to by the half-joking name of *Bollywood*—had an adverse impact on commercial theatre. (The term is based on *Hollywood* with the "h" replaced by the "b" in Bombay [now Mumbai], then the center of the Indian film industry.) **Bollywood** films are usually musical love stories with much singing and dancing. The rise of Indian films decimated live theatre. The impact was in part financial: performers, writers, and designers could make more money in film than they could in theatre. Bollywood films, with an emphasis on color and movement, transcend the many local languages, which touring theatre would have to find a means to bridge.

Today, India has relatively few commercial theatres given the size of the population. These are concentrated in the large cities, with the greatest group in Calcutta. Most of India's theatre today is amateur, with groups ranging widely in size and quality. Calcutta alone has roughly three thousand registered, not-for-profit theatres and Mumbai has about five hundred. Play scripts are written in the local language of the area in which the theatre exists and sometimes in English or even a mix of languages. And the local folk dramas and dance-dramas continue to be performed throughout the country.

Chinese Theatre after 1790

China had a strong and popular theatrical convention in the *Kunqu* opera, whose romantic stories dominated the stage for more than one hundred years, beginning in the mid-1500s.

Beijing Opera

Kunqu set the stage for the development of *Jingqi*, the so-called Peking Opera or **Beijing Opera**, once the European transliteration of the city's name was changed. A more accurate translation of Jingqi would be "opera of the capital." Developed in the 1790s, it was highly conventionalized, with performers, all male, using strictly prescribed movements. Violent action was often shown through acrobatic displays. Makeup and costuming were extravagant, but scenery and properties were minimal. Scenery was changed in full view of the audience, and performers often stood at the side of the stage in view when not performing. Singing and dancing would be interrupted with spoken narration. Beijing Opera was staged on square platforms with the audience on three sides. Musicians were visible on the front stage area. The stage generally had a table and chair, which was used to represent a wall, a bed, even a mountain. Peking Opera is still performed today, although the companies now incorporate female performers.

Mei Lanfang, a famous performer of female roles in the Beijing Opera and Kunqu, was instrumental in bringing the opera to western audiences, touring the United States in 1930 and Europe in 1935. It is said that the performances of Lanfang's troupe influenced Bertolt Brecht as he developed epic theatre. After the revolution in 1949, Lanfang directed the China Beijing Opera Theater and the Chinese Opera Research Institute.

A CHINESE AMBASSADOR
Mei Lanfang, a great Chinese actor, toured Bejing Opera and Kunqu to the United States and Europe.

BEIJING OPERA CONTINUES TODAY

Beijing Opera is often performed today for tourists. Colorful costumes with dramatic sword fights, music, dance, and stylized gestures are the hallmarks of Beijing Opera.

Spoken Drama

Spoken language theatre, called **huaju**, was first performed in Chinese in 1907. The first proscenium style theatre in China was built in 1908. Spoken theatre in China was clearly looking to the West. It was also politically and socially engaged. The first play was *The Black Slave's Cry to Heaven*, a Chinese adaptation of Harriet Beecher Stowe's antislavery novel, *Uncle Tom's Cabin*. *The Main Event of One's Life* from 1919 was inspired by Henrik Ibsen's *A Doll's House*. Spoken theatre remained a minority art form until the mid-twentieth century.

Even the Peking Opera was influenced by the West. The proscenium theatre slowly came to predominate in China—actors separated from the audience by a raised stage fronted with a frame, the proscenium, and the audience seated in rows in the dark—whether for spoken plays or for opera performances. A new form of song theatre developed in the early twentieth century, the **geju** or "song drama," inspired by Western opera. *Geju*, meaning "sung plays," are either political dramas incorporating folk songs and new tunes in the style of folk songs, accompanied by European instruments or Chinese versions of European light opera, mixing spoken passages, and decorative and delicate singing.

Theatre in Communist China

The totalitarian leader of Communist China, Mao Tse-Tung (1893–1976), wrote, "All culture, all literature and art belong to definite classes and are geared to definite political lines. There is in fact no such thing as art for art's sake,...Proletarian literature and art are part of the whole proletarian revolutionary cause; they are...cogs and wheels in the whole revolutionary machine." With that directive, it was inevitable that the Communist government that unified China in 1949 would govern the arts, including theatre. Over time, theatres were nationalized—their assets becoming the property of the government—as part of the nationalization of all businesses.

Whereas the Soviet Union under Joseph Stalin had a fairly clear and abiding concept of what proletarian art should be—socialist realism—Communist China kept changing its mind as to what kind of theatre was considered appropriate. This was not just an intellectual debate; government support or censorship, an artist's lionization or dismissal, changed with every stance the government's culture ministry took. With the country's alliance with the Soviet Union, Western style theatre was encouraged. Then, no, the people love the indigenous opera forms so they were allowed to return. But after a time it was noticed that many of the old operas supported feudalism and so could not be performed in a Communist country. Other operas could be performed if edited for the correct political message. New operas were written that followed the government line. Yes, but even the old feudal operas could be performed for special occasions and holidays. Finally, during the chaotic Cultural Revolution (1966-1976), traditional Chinese theatre was condemned.

Today, some say that theatre is unimportant to culture. Theatre in totalitarian countries is the evidence that refutes that claim. At least in tightly controlled countries, theatre is seen as *very* important, worthy of close censorship or total suppression. The Communist government in the early decades saw theatre was a vital tool of propaganda. Wanting all peoples to be able to see politically correct theatre, the government made tickets cheap enough that even the poorest citizen could attend.

One popular new opera of 1960 was based on a historical story. The Communist government encouraged the work, *Women Generals of the Yang*

COMMUNIST CHINESE DANCE DRAMA
This is a moment from the production of *The Red Detachment of Women,* a communist-era dance drama performed for President Nixon's unprecedented visit to China in 1972.

Family, as a means of encouraging equality for women in Chinese society. China was invaded in the eleventh century, the story of the opera goes. The Yang family men were all killed in battles. The widow She Taijun, at the age of one hundred, convinced the Emperor to allow her to lead troops with her granddaughter-in-law. Under their leadership, the army routed the enemy. After defeat, the opposing army retreated but took the only remaining male heir of the Yang family. The widow and her granddaughter-in-law demolished the invaders' camp and enabled the continuance of their family name by rescuing the last male heir.

After Mao, Western influence on Chinese theatre greatly increased. One totemic incident marking this change is that the US playwright Arthur Miller was invited in 1983 to spend several months in Beijing directing a Chinese language version of his *Death of a Salesman*. It is unclear whether the Miller-directed *Salesman* did much to accelerate China's interest in Western-style spoken language theatre, but the production received wide international attention.

Today, Chinese theatre professionals and researchers debate whether their theatre should be realistic in the Stanislavski mode, be epic like the theatre of Brecht, or use nonrealistic storytelling, such as absurdism. The audience for spoken drama is said to be younger, wealthier, and better educated than that for the traditional forms.

In October 2011, the Chengdu International Theater Festival was inaugurated presenting nine plays, including a production of Harold Pinter's *Betrayal* and a new play from Taiwan. The Chengdu festival of spoken-language plays follows existing festivals in Shanghai and Beijing. Playwright Liao Yimei said,

EASTERN ELEMENTS IN WESTERN THEATRE

This production of John Fletcher's *The Woman's Prize* or *The Tamer Tamed*, originally set in Italy, has been given an Asian interpretation by Butler University. Note the use of masks in both images.

"The Chinese government is rich and really wants to promote culture.... After the economy develops, a nation wants culture. That's natural."

Most visitors to China, however, see a traditional-seeming Peking Opera-styled production, such as *Havoc in Heaven*, which is staged in a specially constructed theatre seating about one thousand in the Qianmen Hotel in Beijing. *Havoc* is based on an ancient fairy tale: The Empire of Heaven planned a peach banquet but did not invite the Monkey King. (Many stories exist of the Monkey King and some have been adapted for the stage; he is a mischievous but powerful demigod of Chinese legend.) This angered the Monkey King, so before the banquet he ate the peaches and the Pills of Immortality meant for the banquet. Then he wrecked many of Heaven's palaces. Because the staging is vigorous, using a great deal of stylized martial arts, this is one of China's most popular operas for tourists.

Outside the theatre after the hour-and-three-quarter show, the audience exits through a shop with products for sale related to the traditional Chinese theatre, expensive goods aimed solely at tourists.

Later Japanese Theatre

Although Kabuki and Noh continued in Japan, the theatre began in the twentieth century to be influenced by Western techniques. The first totally spoken language theatre, **shingeki** meaning "modern theatre," was performed in the early years of the twentieth century. The first permanent theatre building for Western drama opened in 1924; its first season included plays by a German, a Russian, and a Frenchman. Over time, Japanese authors wrote in the new styles, with a particular emphasis on historical dramas. Women appeared on stage in shingeki for the first time in centuries.

Japanese modern theatre tended to be socially reformist and leftist in politics. Thus, when the country veered to the political right in the lead up to World War II, the government suppressed shingeki, sometimes arresting its key organizers or artists. But after the war with the country occupied by the Allied Powers, shingeki came to dominate Japanese theatre. At first, Stanislavski-style realism dominated, but theatre styles expanded in the late twentieth century to include epic and absurdist styles.

One popular play of the Japanese absurd is Betsuyaku's *The Elephant* from the early 1960s. It takes place in a hospital for victims of radiation sickness. A character titled Invalid, now bedridden, once showed his scars publicly in Hiroshima, which brought him public attention and personal satisfaction. He is visited by Man, his argumentative young nephew. Invalid wants to leave the hospital and have public attention again. Man believes that his uncle should remain peaceful, accepting his fate. Eventually the nephew reveals signs of radiation sickness as well and is hospitalized in the same room. By the end of the play, Invalid is dead and Man, the nephew, is left alone. The play explores how Japan should feel about Hiroshima: proudly defiant or indifferent and future-focused. By extension, perhaps, the play is concerned with how Japan should absorb the whole crushing defeat of World War II. The play's ending shows that for the proud or the apathetic, the wounds remain.

Butoh: Dance, Theatre, or What?

Another new performance style—said by many critics to be impossible to define but clearly more dance than legitimate theatre—emerged in the postwar era starting in 1959. **Butoh** is dance, performance, or movement with playful and bizarre imagery, covering unmentionable topics in extreme or illogical settings. Traditionally *Butoh* is performed in white body makeup. It is said to be a reaction both to the country's mad rush into war and to the dance scene in Japan at the time, which either imitated Western dance or imitated the Noh. Like many surreal or postmodern forms in the later decades of the twentieth century, Butoh has gathered an international, if small, audience.

Kabuki Continues

The immediate post-World War II era was difficult for Kabuki, but it has gradually become the most popular of the traditional styles of Japanese theatre. "Most popular of the traditional styles"

BUTOH PERFORMANCE IN NEW YORK CITY

Butoh performances are vivid and dreamlike as usually the performers are covered in white body makeup. Here, the late Kazuo Ohno (*left*), one of the founders of *Butoh*, performs with his son Yoshito in 1999 for the Japan Society in New York City.

should not be read for widely popular with Japanese audiences. There are several Kabuki companies in Tokyo, Kyoto, and Osaka and many smaller groups throughout the country. Female actors now sometimes appear in Kabuki. There have been several Kabuki-style stagings of Western plays, including Shakespeare. But Kabuki tickets are very expensive. Now with descriptions in English and other languages on headphones, much of the audience is made up of tourists.

Why Asian Theatre Is Often Western-Focused

India, China, and Japan have traveled in different ways toward similar destinations. Each maintains its unique and indigenous theatre styles, sometimes as regional phenomenon and other times as primarily tourist-attracting ventures. Meanwhile, each has also incorporated theatre styles of the West. These societies often identified Western theatre with other desirable things from the West, sometimes called in shorthand "modernity." It is tempting to see the reason for the adoption of Western theatre styles as colonialism of varying kinds: India and Britain, Communist China and Soviet Russia, and Japan and the western Allied powers occupying it after World War II.

Meanwhile, too, first film and then television spread all about the globe powerful storytelling based on psychological realism. Film is not theatre but much of twentieth-century theatre depends on psychological realism, too. In the modern era, Asian societies have also been, at varying speeds and to differing extents, drifting away from feudalism toward capitalism and from general illiteracy to widespread literacy. Both changes affect the arts as well, moving them away from a focus on the elite and toward the personal and individual and away from an ideal or heroic subject to the muddled conflicts of middle-class and blue-collar life. Whatever the causes of the hegemony of Western style theatre, the galloping wave of globalization affects most all parts of world culture.

KEY TERMS

Key terms are boldface type in the text. Check your understanding against this list. Persons are page-referenced in the index.

Beijing Opera, p. 342

Bollywood, p. 341

Butoh, p. 347

geju (gyou), p. 343

hauju (HOW-you), p. 343

Kathakali (kah-thah-KAH-li), p. 340

shingeki (shin-AY-key), p. 346

Globalization of Theatre

When you have completed this chapter, you should be able to:

- Describe the proliferation of Western musicals around the world by giving a few examples.
- Explain how Western artists are incorporating world theatre techniques by giving a few examples.
- Discuss evidence that supports the contention that Shakespeare has become a worldwide phenomenon.
- Characterize how Western theatre artists have encouraged political theatre in totalitarian societies.

Context

Globalization is a term for the increasingly interconnected economic systems of the world. Since World War II, the world's economies have become ever more interlinked, for good and bad. The theatre is also increasingly interconnected internationally, financially, culturally, and politically. This chapter looks briefly at four examples of the globalization of theatre, but it is far from exhaustive:

- The internationalization of the musical.
- Western artists learning about and borrowing from world theatre techniques.
- Shakespeare as a worldwide inspiration.
- Support for political theatre in totalitarian societies by artists in the democratic west.

AN ECONOMIC ENGINE
When companies expand, the economies of the global market expand. A French company makes tires in the United States for the US market. A Belgian company makes small arms for the US military in South Carolina. McDonald's is everywhere.

US brand names such as Coca-Cola, McDonald's, and KFC can be found almost everywhere in the world. US entertainment products also dominate internationally: pop music, movies, and television. For some time, English theatre has moved easily among the English-speaking countries. But elsewhere, theatre trailed this trend until the last thirty years or so. Now theatre is becoming globalized as well. At least in part, theatre's internationalization is driven by economics, as is all globalization.

Broadway shows, for example, are of interest to travelers from other countries, especially musicals, which do not demand highly developed English-language skills. The Broadway League, the trade association of Broadway and professional tour presenters in the United States, claims that 540,000 people from other countries each year come to New York, at least in part to see Broadway shows, spending more than $2 billion during their stays in New York City.

Not every one in every country thinks globalization is a good idea. In McDonald's early years in France, a farmer-turned-activist protested by driving his tractor into the side of a McDonald's restaurant. That was in 1991. In 2011, France had more than eight hundred of the restaurants the French call McDo—pronounced "mac-dough"—and France was the second-highest-grossing country in the McDonald's chain. It has embraced the international market, but as strong as its brand name is, McDonald's does not ignore local tastes. Beginning in fall 2011, French McDonald's offered fresh baked baguettes in the morning. And in India, for another example, McDonald's does not sell beef hamburgers. Hindus revere cows. Instead, McDonald's in India offers chicken, fish, vegetable, and cheese sandwiches.

The money in worldwide brands may be attractive, but culture is often another matter. For example, France's *Académie Française* regulates what words should be said in French and rejects many foreign words, recently excluding *e-mail*, *blog*, and *wifi*. And the Académie does not restrict itself to technology terms, recently banning *supermodel*, *fast food*, and *low-cost airline*. Canada requires that at least 50 percent of the content in television broadcasts during primetime to have been originated in Canada. Other examples could be cited of countries attempting to protect the culture from foreign dominance.

Other than in Canada, US television is largely unrestricted, and many US hit shows are international hits as well, often dubbed into the local language. US pop music is everywhere in the world with no translation necessary.

In culture and art, at least, there is an exchange in the other direction as well, albeit less lucrative. English-speaking countries are interested in foreign art, dance, music, cinema, and to some extent, theatre. Some Western theatre artists are borrowing storytelling practices from Asia and Africa to enhance and expand their repertoire of techniques.

Musicals in Asia

"*Mamma Mia!*, The Global Smash Hit" was the title of the musical production's Web site in early 2013. This marketing hype is actually true. In July 2011, *Mamma Mia!* became the first Western musical to be performed in mainland China. *Mamma Mia!* had played in Singapore four years before in English, but for the Shanghai production, the script was translated into Mandarin Chinese, with a sprinkling of Shanghai slang that reportedly got big laughs from the audience. The material was racy for the Chinese audience because mild physical intimacy and the open confession of homosexuality have not been common on Chinese stages. The acting, too, was discomforting for Chinese audiences at least at first. The company played in a broad, Western style, nothing like the restrained and conventionalized style of Chinese opera. But according to London's *The Telegraph* newspaper, by the curtain, the audience was on its feet, dancing and clapping to the tunes "Dancing Queen," "Mamma Mia," and "Waterloo." Following Shanghai, the production was scheduled to tour Chinese cities and, eventually, Chinese-speaking areas outside the mainland, such as, Hong Kong, Macao, Taiwan, and Singapore. Because China is a government-controlled economy, the production comes with the government's blessing, part of a five-year plan to grow culture industries in China to account for 5 percent of its gross domestic product.

GIRLS DREAMING IN SEOUL
A joint US-Korean production of a revival of the musical *Dreamgirls* played first in Seoul in 2009.

From the start *Mamma Mia!* was an international product, at least to some extent: a jukebox musical, devised in London, built around the music of the Swedish disco group ABBA, and set largely on a Greek island. It opened in London in 1999 and in New York in 2001 and was still playing in both cities in January 2013. It played in Toronto, Canada, for five years and in Las Vegas for six years. It has been translated into seventeen languages and has appeared in more than thirty countries. It was made into a movie in 2008 that received mixed reviews but still grossed $602 million dollars, making it the fifth-highest grossing film of the year.

The Swedish singing group ABBA was active from 1972 through 1982 and was the first group from a non-English speaking country to see consistent pop music successes in the United States, Britain, Canada, and Australia. ABBA has sold more than 375 million records worldwide and continues to sell two to three million albums a year although they disbanded in 1983.

The lead producer of *Mamma Mia!*, Judy Craymer, spent fifteen years pulling the show together, first getting rights from the ABBA songwriters and then hiring a playwright to write the book. She had to remortgage her home to finance the production. It paid off. According to a 2011 estimate she is worth £62 million, about US$98 million.

This focus on money is relevant because the musical has no compelling reason to exist except to make money by pleasing audiences. The story is a silly trifle, a farcical manikin on which to array ABBA's infectious pop music. As a young girl is planning her wedding, she yearns to find out who her father is. Her mother had been a free spirit, sleeping with three different men around the time of the girl's conception. The girl invites all three to her wedding on a Greek isle, and hilarity is supposed to ensue as she finds out which is her dad.

GREASE IN BARCELONA
US musicals are produced around the world. Here, a Spanish-language production of *Grease* mobbed by teens.

Mamma Mia! will not be the last Chinese musical based on Western properties. British producer Cameron Mackintosh's production company has signed a deal with the China Art and Entertainment Group to bring to China musicals translated into Mandarin: first up, it is reported, will be *Les Misérables*. The US theatre owner and producing group the Nederlander Company has created a US-Chinese company dubbed "Nederlander New Century" with unspecified plans to move stage productions in both directions, from the United States to China and from China to English-speaking countries.

This growing collaboration with Asian countries and the English-language musical theatre can work in different ways as well. A US producer developed a 2009 revival of the 1981 musical *Dreamgirls* with South Korean partners. The revival was first mounted in Seoul with an all-Korean cast to enthusiastic reviews. The financial incentives of first producing in South Korea were significant: the stage set of moving LED panels was made there, and the South Korean partner paid most of the Korean costs, including wages and expenses for twenty Americans on the creative staff to live in the country for periods of weeks or months while developing the revival. The US tour of the production, with US actors in costumes remade for the US company, opened in New York's Apollo Theatre and set off on a planned thirteen-city, seven-month tour of the United States, which was successful enough to be extended through the end of 2010.

The US-style musical is so popular that other countries are developing their own indigenous musicals. For one example, a South Korean-originated musical, *Hero: The Musical*, had a sold-out run in Seoul in 2009 and embarked in 2011 on an international tour, playing ten days at New York City's Koch Theater in Lincoln Center, presented in Korean with English supertitles.

Other International Musical Successes

Mamma Mia! was not the first global musical, although it was the first to be performed in Mandarin. Prior to about 1980, a successful musical would play in the United States, England, Canada, and Australia and only rarely elsewhere. Now it is unusual if a successful West End or Broadway show does not have an international tour. *The Phantom of the Opera* (Broadway 1988–) has played in at least twenty-three countries. *Cats* (Broadway 1982–2000) played in at least thirty. *Les Misérables* (Broadway 1978–1990) has played in forty-two countries and is the subject of sixty-five official cast recordings. The revival of *Chicago* (Broadway 1996–) played professionally in at least thirty-two countries with amateur productions in at least twelve others. Disney's stage musical of *The Lion King* (Broadway 1997–) has been staged in at least fourteen countries, *Beauty and the Beast* (Broadway 1994–2004) at least nine, and *Aida* (Broadway 2000–2004) at least fifteen.

STILL STORMING THE BARRICADES

Les Misérables opened in London in 1985. The musical has been produced in dozens of languages around the world. A movie is now in the works with important film stars. Here, a climactic moment from the original Broadway production.

Joan Marcus

These mega-musicals play in all continents except for Antarctica. Musicals are financially successful only in large cities, however. In South America, tours stop in Buenos Aires, Argentina, and Rio de Janeiro, Brazil. In Africa, they play in Johannesburg, Pretoria, Durbin, and Cape Town, South Africa, large cities where many citizens speak English. In Mexico, the venue is Mexico City, a metropolis of nearly 9 million people.

Successful US shows do not always travel well. For example, *Jersey Boys* (2005–) has been an enormous success in the United States, to a lesser extent in other English-speaking countries, but it has not had international tours. One presumes the subject matter, a jukebox musical based on the career of US pop singers Frankie Valli and the Four Seasons of the 1960s, is specifically of interest to English-speaking audiences.

Cultural critics sometimes bewail the dominance of English-language, largely US, cultural output covering the world. They fear that US music, television, and film soak up time and money that would otherwise go for local entertainment and culture. Given technology advances, the fear about US music inhibiting the growth of local music is probably misplaced. Both the creation of first-rate recordings, audio and visual, and their distribution over the Internet are increasingly affordable. Talent is always in short supply everywhere, however.

Those concerned about mega-musicals' world dominance often see English-language musical theatre as a kind of colonialism. They fear that these highly marketed musicals will drain money from the local theatre, inhibiting its growth and maturity.

The alternative view—that sees nothing wrong and everything right in cultural globalization—is expressed in at least two forms. There's the laissez faire capitalism argument: people have a limited supply of expendable cash and spend it on things they find rewarding. If the money is spent on English-language imports, they must be worthwhile for the audience. There is also an argument that citizens of the United States may overestimate the depth and quality of media from other countries because only the rare—often superlative—examples are brought to our shores. An undefined amount of capital investment is necessary to develop superior entertainment products and, at least for now, that capital is in the United States primarily. Some go even further, arguing that the globalization of culture will inhibit war.

Techniques and Styles Travel the World

In February 2011, the *Comédie Française* of Paris opened its first staging in its 330-year history of a foreign play, *Un tramway nommé désir* (*A Streetcar Named Desire*, the 1941 play by Tennessee Williams). To direct it, they hired an American, Lee Breuer, one of the founders of the avant-garde troupe Mabou Mines. (For a discussion of Mabou Mines's postmodern production of Henrik Ibsen's 1879 *A Doll's House*, see pages 298–299. For a *precis* of *A Streetcar Named Desire*, see page 289.)

The stage works of Lee Breuer (1937–), writer, filmmaker, and stage director, have stunned audiences and reviewers, in both the positive and negative meanings of the word *stun*. Politically engaged with a wide-ranging intellect, Breuer believes that theatre happens half on stage and half in each audience member's head. He wants to disturb what the audience expects to see so that what happens in the viewers' head is dialectic, an internal argument leading to a new position or insight termed a synthesis. In focusing on the dialectic, Breuer's work might be compared with that of Brecht, but Breuer is much more disruptive and postmodern. Many of Breuer's works have toured avant-garde theatre festivals for years. Breuer's deconstructed *A Doll's House* played in New York in 2001, and his puppet and human adaptation of the Peter Pan stories, *Peter and Wendy*, premiered in the Spoleto Festival in Charleston, South Carolina, in 1996 and both are still touring. His work has been solely in the not-for-profit theatre, and Breuer wants to continue to work in the noncommercial theatre. He said, "I want to work bigger, wider, more flamboyantly

OLD TECHNOLOGY SUPPORTING
NEW VISIONS
A chariot-and-pole system for scenery changes like
the one shown here still exists at the Comédie
Française. It took a postmodernist like Lee Breuer
to incorporate this 17th century technology into a 21st
century production.

than I could ever do as a 'blacker' and I don't want to wait." By "blacker," he means someone who makes money, who is "in the black."

By hiring a lifelong theatre provocateur, a postmodernist, like Lee Breuer, the Comédie did not intend to mount a traditional production of *Streetcar*. Breuer said of the artistic director of the Comédie, "She wanted something a little crazy." She got her wish. Working with the US puppeteer and designer Basil Twist, Breuer developed a physical design that often borrowed from Japanese staging ideas. A series of painted panels slide in, up, out, and fold, offering different visual effects, sometimes even exaggerated painted perspective, a style called *dogugaeshi* borrowed from an extinct form of Japanese puppet theatre. For example, during the poker playing scene in *Streetcar*, each card played appeared on a painted screen. For some transitions, the screens changed using the Comédie's ancient substage tracks and pulleys, a technique the Comédie learned from Italian renaissance scenery. This old technology for scene changing is almost never used today because it can make a loud, ratchety noise. Twist says he and Breuer loved the sound, exclaiming, "Great! Streetcar tracks!"

The production also used black dressed stage assistants, a Japanese theatre convention called *kuroko*. Breuer thought they helped keep the staging minimal, saying as an example, "When Blanche wants to smoke, they bring on a cigarette, lighter, and ashtray; when she's done, they take them off." Breuer also used the kuroko in non-Japanese ways. As Stanley threatened Blanche in the climactic rape scene, the kuroko donned green fright wings— Stanley had played with such a wig early in the production—and purple silk pajamas that match what Stanley was wearing. Stanley's menace was visually multiplied by four.

Why this US, French, Japanese theatrical stew? Breuer said he wanted to break out of the psychological realism of the play's original staging and the famous film based on it that made Marlon Brando an international film star. He sees a sharing between the US Deep South and Japan, both having a sense of formalism and hidden violence. The French, he continued, have had a long fascination with Japanese-like things, what is called "Japonism."

Critical reception was mixed. *Le Monde* headline read, "A Streetcar Stopped at the Boredom Station," but *Le Figaro*'s reviewer called the production "powerful, profound, grand and unique." The run of the play sold out. The production received international media attention, and that may have been the venerable theatre's aim. The Comédie Française needs new revenue because the government cut cultural spending in response to the 2008 recession. Muriel Mayette, the troupe's administrator, said, "Our future is international, and it's necessary to enrich our repertoire." At least in this example, globalism has a financial tinge even in the not-for-profit theatre.

The Comédie Française production received unwanted attention, too. The holders of Tennessee Williams's literary estate, Sewanee: The University of the South, had its lawyers send cease-and-desist letters for the Paris production as they have for many other productions about the world that have not staged the plays "as written," which the licensing contract requires. In fact, Sewanee added a rider to the usual contract that, in the case of Williams's work, the characters would be cast by actors of the gender described for the character. Forward-looking theatre groups are upset with Sewanee's limiting, protective stance. Traditionalists are happy they will not have to see Blanche DuBois performed by a man in drag.

Other non-European techniques have been used by Western theatre makers. One of lasting influence is the use of puppets for which the human operators are not concealed. Julie Taymor (1952–), a playwright, director, and designer, has studied many non-European theatres and used what she learned first in the noncommercial and then the commercial theatre and opera. She became interested in theatre as a child growing up in Massachusetts. She spent time abroad while still in high school, in Sri Lanka and India, and studied in *L'École Internationale de Théâtre*, Paris, which emphasized mime. When an undergraduate, she left college for a while to work with Joseph Chaikin's Open Theatre and attended a summer program of the American Society for Eastern Arts in Seattle that focused on Indonesian masked dance-drama and shadow puppetry. Later she received a grant to study puppetry in Japan. Her work in the not-for-profit theatre, largely using puppetry and masks to tell mythical or mythlike stories, included an adaptation of a Carlo Gozzi fairy tale, *The King Stag*, which toured to sixty-six countries. In 1991 she was awarded a MacArthur Fellowship, the so-called "genius grant."

Then the Disney theatre production group, looking for a way to stage a musical based on the animated film *The Lion King*, engaged Julie Taymor to direct and codesign the production. When it opened on Broadway in 1997, she received a Tony Award for costume design and became the first woman to win a Tony Award for directing. The show has been an international hit

THE *LION* ROARS WORLDWIDE
The director and costume designer for the stage version of *The Lion King*, Julie Taymor is a Phi Beta Kappa graduate from Oberlin College in Ohio. After graduation she studied theatre in Indonesia and puppetry in Japan. Here, an example of her nonrealistic work based on Asian styles using puppets and masks in *The Lion King*.

for its mixture of the music of singer and songwriter Elton John with lyrics by Tim Rice (*Evita, Jesus Christ Superstar*), the pure and clear storytelling and jokes of Disney, and the imagination-stoking wonder of Taymor's puppetry and masks. In addition to the United States and London, *The Lion King* has played in at least thirteen countries.

Since *The Lion King*, Taymor has directed opera—including *The Magic Flute* for the Metropolitan Opera in New York City, again using puppets—and movies, most of which have been less realistic than the usual Hollywood product. She was one of several creators of the stage musical *Spider-Man: Turn Off the Dark* (2011), a show using masks, puppets, expressionistic staging, and flying, which is reputed to have had the largest budget in Broadway musical history. She was fired from that assignment before the show officially opened, but much of her input in the show's visual style remained.

Puppets received a somewhat different outing in *War Horse*, developed at Britain's National Theatre in 2007. The production then moved to the commercial West End in London and also opened in New York in 2011. Based on a children's book about a boy and his horse in the First World War, *War Horse* used life-sized horse puppets made of metal, leather, and bent wood. The operators are seen inside and sometimes beside the puppets. Under the control of handlers dressed in period costumes, the life-size horses snort, feed, gallop, rise on their hindlegs and, most importantly, breathe. Audience members receptive to their charms are torn between the truth—they are just puppets—and the thrilling suspension of disbelief that allows the horses to seem alive.

The puppets were developed by a South African theatre company, Handspring Puppet Company. Handspring began doing children's television but starting in 1985 became fascinated by the potential to use puppetry for adult audiences. The founders received moral support by what they saw at the annual World Festival of Puppet Theatre, held in Charleville-Mezieres, France. The World Festival has been held since 1961 and now hosts presenters from more than thirty countries. Even puppet theatre is global.

Non-European Theatre in Western Countries

At one time, the only way to learn about non-European theatre was to travel and live in the countries of origin. Increasingly, globalization is bringing authentic, indigenous theatre arts to Western countries, generally as part of not-for-profit theatre festivals. For example, *The Peony Pavilion*, an adaptation of a fourteenth-century Chinese *Kunqu* opera, was staged at the Lincoln Center for the Performing Arts Festival in 1999. A twenty-hour performance that played over several nights, it toured to nine cities internationally. (For a description of the play for *The Peony Pavilion*, see page 64.) Not as authentic, *Monkey: Journey to the West*, a modern Chinese-British adaptation of a four-hundred-year-old Buddhist myth in a production that incorporated dance and martial arts, opened in 2007 at the Manchester International Festival, England, and then played Paris; the Spoleto Festival, Charleston, South Carolina; and London.

Kennedy Center, Washington, D.C., hosted a "Maximum India" festival in 2011 that included an Indian company performing an adaptation of Henrik Ibsen's *When We Dead Awaken* (1899) in Manipuri, a northern Indian language, incorporating stylized movement of the indigenous Indian theatre. Another company from India performed in reader's theatre style three twentieth-century short stories written in Urdu. Both shows had supertitles. The Ishara Puppet Theatre Trust performed *Images of Truth* using marionettes, hand puppets, and giant puppets to present the life and philosophy of Mahatma Gandhi. The festival also featured dance, music, film, and food. The theatre at the festival reflected current Indian theatre influenced by folk traditions.

The not-for-profit festivals sometimes bring in other hybrids. One example is *One Thousand and One Nights*, a staging of some of the collection of Middle Eastern and South Asian tales from before the eighteenth century known by the same name. Produced and directed by Tim Supple, a British Jew, the cast was made up of performers from many countries in the Middle East. Supple visited Damascus and Aleppo in Syria; Alexandria, Egypt; Amman, Jordan; Ramallah in the Palestinian West Bank; and elsewhere to gather a company of twenty-four actors and musicians and began workshops in Cairo in 2006. The improvised result, refined by a Lebanese playwright, was a two-night, six-hour show. The production first played at the Toronto Festival of Arts and Creativity, Canada, and then the Edinburgh Festival, Scotland, in 2011. Whatever its artistic merits, it is a wonder the show could be produced at all, given the revolutionary events in the Arab world in 2011.

Global Shakespeare

Shakespeare has been a truly global playwright since the romantics adopted Shakespeare as one of their own in the eighteenth century. A 2011 study by the Royal Shakespeare Company (RSC) and the British Council found that one-half of world schoolchildren study Shakespeare in school, about 64 million children. In 2001 the Ninth World Shakespeare Congress took place not in London or Stratford-upon-Avon but in Prague, Czech Republic. As part of the cultural events surrounding the Summer Olympics in London in 2012, a "World Shakespeare" festival was organized. The New Globe Theatre in London, a more-or-less accurate reproduction of Shakespeare's Globe Theatre, presented thirty-seven Shakespearean plays performed by thirty-seven different international theatre companies, in the companies' native languages. Productions included a Portuguese *Two Roses for Richard III* from Brazil, a Russian *A Midsummer Night's Dream*, and an Arabic version of *Macbeth* called *Leila and Ben—A Bloody History*.

The reasons for Shakespeare's international reputation are arguable. Many critics consider his plays to be the best written in English. Certainly more criticism and biography has been written about Shakespeare than about any other secular writer. Others demure that Shakespeare's prominence is an accident of timing, economics, and the cultural dominance of the English-speaking countries. The mixed style of many Shakespearean plays—comedy, poetry, romance, pathos, and tragedy—suited the romantics and some say it suits our postmodern era, where unified, well-made stories are often considered boring. It is also true that Shakespeare's stories are vivid, compelling, and extreme but at root human. Shakespeare's plays invite statements on things that matter: loyalty, betrayal, love, evil, retribution, forgiveness, balancing conflicting values, and fighting despair.

Shakespeare may be easier for audiences when performed in translation. For modern English-speakers, understanding Shakespeare's language, the English of four centuries ago, can be trying. In translation perhaps the dialogue can be more easily understood. Shakespeare's scripts become strong structures on which artists and audiences can project their own metaphors, comparisons, and meaning.

A *Kathakali King Lear* was developed by an Australian playwright and a French actor-director with the Kerala State Arts Academy. It was performed by

A RECONSTRUCTED GLOBE
This view of the New Globe Theatre displays the significant features of the structure, which opened in 1966 near the site of the original theatre. Note the three stacked galleries, the covered stage supported by two columns, the three entrances on stage level, as well as the open gallery above and at the rear of the stage. The "fish-eye" photo makes the theatre look bigger than it truly is.

a mixed Indian and European cast in India, Italy, the Netherlands, France, and Spain in 1989 and in Singapore and at the Edinburgh Theatre Festival in 1990. The story was truncated—the typed script amounted to about twenty pages—and Indian Kathakali techniques were applied including gesture, singing, makeup, and costuming. Some Indian actors could not accept the character of Lear: it was unbelievable, within Indian culture, that an eighty-year-old king would be so childish and naïve. One English critic said the resulting production had little to do with *King Lear*. The script had cut all the subplots, leaving just Lear and his three daughters. Other attempts to adapt European stories, especially those of Shakespeare, have continued in other Asian and African genres, with mixed success.

A Safe Way to Dissent

In countries where the theatre is under government censorship, Shakespeare's international reputation can open a crack for a theatre company to enlarge the social and political discussion. So *Hamlet* includes the killing of a usurping king: "It's not about our country; it's Shakespeare; it's a classic known the world over." Shakespeare's plays have served this subtly subversive role repeatedly in the countries of the Soviet bloc and still serve that function in repressive societies in Europe, Asia, and the Middle East.

As a modest example, a British theatre group, Jericho House, took a production of *The Tempest* to the Middle East in 2011, performing in East Jerusalem, Bethlehem, Nablus, and Haifa, including an open-air performance in a Palestinian refugee camp. Director Jonathan Holmes said of *The Tempest* that the play "becomes a contest for territory between people of different cultures, and people of the same culture. Shakespeare uses this dynamic to explore different systems and ideas of political resistance....We're not trying to make it overtly about the situation here. We're offering a neutral production and we'll see if the resonances are heard."

Similarly, in 2008, a Shakespeare play inspired a film *In Fair Palestine: A Story of Romeo and Juliet*. Produced by Palestinian students at a Quaker-run school, it retells the Shakespearean story set in modern-day Ramallah. The film follows the Shakespeare story with a few changes. Romeo does not hear

Karl Hugh

of Juliet's faked death because the messenger is stopped at an Israeli checkpoint. The student playing Mercutio said, "We thought we would use a play that has values and principles that are shared by people all over the world."

Theme-Park Shakespeare

Unquestionably, Shakespeare is also seen in many countries as good business. The near reproduction of the Globe, the many-sided theatre on the South bank of the Thames River in London near where many of Shakespeare's plays premiered, was completed in 1997. The New Globe's budget in 2010 was £14.3 million, roughly US$22.5 million. The New Globe, built close to the location of the original Elizabethan theatre, is listed as one of the top ten entertainment attractions in London. But there are reproductions of the Elizabethan theatres around the world.

The largest number of Globe theatres are in the United States, including the Oregon Shakespearean Festival in Ashland; The Old Globe Theatre in San Diego, California; Adams Shakespearean Theatre in Cedar City, Utah; and the Globe Theatre of the Great Southwest in Odessa, Texas, another in Dallas, and in Busch Gardens Williamsburg in Virginia. In Germany, there is the Globe Neuss, in Neuss on the Rhine; the Rust Globe, built in an amusement park in Baden; and the Globe Theatre in Schwabisch Hall in Baden-Württemberg. A Globe theatre is planned for Berlin and one for Gdansk, Poland. Among trees in Rome's Villa Borghese park is a Globe theatre reproduction. Japan has a Globe theatre, built of pink concrete and with a roof. The first production was a touring production from Sweden of *Hamlet* directed by the internationally renowned film and stage director Ingmar Bergman. The pink Tokyo Globe is now more often used for rock concerts than for the bard. For six weeks during the summer of 2011, the RSC performed in New York City, in a portable theatre structure it brought from England and assembled inside the huge Park Avenue Armory. Although not a reconstruction of the Globe theatre, per se, it was a reproduction of the RSC's theatre in Stratford, England, a thrust stage à la the Elizabethan theatre. The Blackfriars Theatre, an enclosed London venue where some of Shakespeare's plays were performed is also copied at the American Shakespeare Center in Staunton, Virginia.

And in winter 2003, a reproduction of the Globe Theatre was made of ice, in Sweden near the famous Ice Hotel. It did not have balconies; the ice would not support them. Among other things, they performed an abridged *Hamlet* there, translated into *saami*, the language of the native Laplanders.

Belarus Free Theatre

The Belarus Free Theatre was due to appear in New York City in January 2011 as part of the Under the Radar festival, which focuses on international theatre that is "exciting, independent, and experimental." Two members of the troupe had been arrested in their home country during December protests of a presidential election in Belarus that international observers declared to be rigged in favor of the ruling party. The rest of the troupe went underground. Eventually, they left Belarus in small groups, concealed in trucks and cars, changing vehicles regularly to confuse the government security forces. Once out of Belarus, it was unclear if they would ever be able to return. The international theatre community embraced the troupe, and they have performed at the Under the Radar festival, in a benefit at New York's Public Theatre and at the PEN American Center, in Chicago, in Los Angeles, later at the Edinburgh Festival in Scotland and in London, and elsewhere in Britain, in Hong Kong, and back in New York for a run at LaMaMa Theatre. Their performances have received powerful and positive critical notice, for their art as well as their politics.

Belarus is called the last dictatorship in Europe. A small landlocked country bordering Russia and Poland, Belarus was freed when the Soviet Union dissolved in 1991, but since 1994 the country's president, Alexander Lukashenko, has usurped legislative and court powers, held rigged elections, and violently suppressed political opponents. Radio, television, film, and newspapers are government controlled. There is evidence that as many as 1,500 people a year in Belarus disappear, presumably because of the security force's actions.

The Belarus Free Theatre was not acceptable to the state. Some actors were fired from their day jobs whereas others had their relatives threatened. The troupe performed in cafes, restaurants, apartments, even in the woods, sometimes disguising the gatherings as weddings, birthdays, or Christmas

Courtesy Andrew Caldwell

THE GLOBE ON ICE

Shakespeare is an international brand, not unlike Coca-Cola and McDonald's. Here, a reproduction in Sweden of the Globe theatre made of ice. It only lasted one winter.

parties. Still, British playwright Tom Stoppard saw their work and was moved to help. Film and stage actor Jude Law has worked on the troupe's behalf. Amnesty International, a global movement against the restriction of human rights, has taken on the troupe's cause.

The history of theatre shows that if it changes societies and politics at all, it does so in small increments and over large spans of time. In the case of the Belarus Free Theater, at least the global theatre community is reaching out to help its members in their exile.

Is Globalization Theatre's Destiny?

In the Introduction to this history, we described a 2009 production in a modern London theatre of a 1677 French neoclassical play based on an Ancient Greek tragedy. This production was also performed in the fourth century BCE Greek theatre of Epidaurus and broadcast live to movie theatres around the globe. This was one unusual, technology-mediated example of globalization in the theatre.

In the time of Alexander the Great, the fourth century BCE, theatres were built in many places Alexander ruled about the Mediterranean. The ancient Romans up to the time of the fall of the Western empire in 476 CE built theatres in much of the Mediterranean and up into the more northern parts of Europe. Some scholars believe that theatre in ancient India influenced theatre throughout Asia over the course of centuries, following the trade routes. Starting with the Renaissance in the fourteenth century CE, theatre techniques and stories moved about Western countries, slowly at first but with mounting speed. In the twentieth century, many cultures outside of Europe identified Western-style theatre with modernization and adopted that style, for good or ill.

It is only a slight exaggeration to maintain that theatre has always been moving to a global activity, although the capabilities for theatre to be shared among peoples of different geographical areas, with different languages and cultural practices, have changed radically over time. Now is an era of extensive theatre globalization, in pursuit of money, of art, of novelty, and of understanding.

Glossary

What follows is a compilation of *Key Terms* found at the end of each chapter. Numbers at the end of each entry refer to the page(s) where a fuller discussion can be found.

absurdism A style of drama originating in France after World War II that viewed human existence as meaningless and treated language as an inadequate means of communication. Major authors include Samuel Beckett and Eugène Ionesco. (232, 312)

actor-manager A starring actor who is head and nominal artistic director of a company; for example, Sir Henry Irving in the late nineteenth century in England. (173)

A-effect See *alienation effect.* (233)

African-American theatre A theatre movement of the 1960s and after, primarily for African-American audiences, actors, and playwrights, originally connected with the black power movement, a political ideology. (300)

afterpiece A short play that followed the main attraction. (161)

Alarinjo The name of traveling theatre groups of the Yoruba people, largely in Nigeria, Africa. Their style grew out of ritual observances for the dead. (219)

alienation effect Customary, but perhaps misleading, translation of the German *Verfremdungseffekt* ("to make strange"). Term now almost always associated with Bertolt Brecht's epic theatre, which aims to distance the spectator from the play's action to force conscious consideration of the political and social issues raised by the play. Shortened often to A-effect. (233)

alienation theatre Plays or production styles associated with the alienation effect. (232)

American Method Term for the dominant twentieth-century acting style and actor training approach, inspired by readings and misreadings of the works of the Russian teacher/director Constantin Stanislavsky. It emphasizes psychological realism and the performance of subtext. (239)

American musical A stage production that uses story, song, and dance, to create a satisfying entertainment. (258)

amphitheatre In Ancient Roman territories, a large public space for paratheatrical entertainments, such as animal and gladiator fights, resembling today's football stadiums. (48)

art theatre movement A theatrical movement of the late nineteenth and early twentieth centuries that tried to separate itself from commercial theatre and the reliance on box office. (241)

Atellan farce A brassy comic indigenous style of theatre before and maybe during the Roman era. Perhaps related to Greek middle comedy, Roman comedy, or *commedia dell'arte.* (46)

autos sacramentales Spanish plays from the sixteenth and seventeenth centuries about the mysteries of the Eucharist, usually allegorical. (135)

avant-garde Art thought ahead of the mainstream, experimental, literally meaning "vanguard."

backdrop Painted two-dimensional hanging, usually as part of a scenic background. (108)

Beijing opera Traditional Chinese theatrical form, spectacular, and nonrealistic; formerly termed "Peking opera." (342)

biomechanics The concept and the complex of techniques devised by Vsevolod Meyerhold to train actors so that their bodies could be as responsive as a machine. (242)

Bollywood An informal name for the Indian film industry centered in Mumbai, formerly called Bombay. (341)

book For this history, the spoken text of a play or musical. (259)

book musical An entertainment with song, dance, and comedy and just enough of a story to hold the event together. (261)

border Curtain, or less often flats or cutouts, suspended at intervals behind the proscenium arch to mask the overhead rigging, particularly important in Italianate settings. (108)

box set Interior setting represented by flats forming three sides (the invisible fourth wall being the proscenium line); first used around 1830 and common after 1850. (180)

burlesque In eighteenth- and nineteenth-century theatre, a form of "minor" drama popular in England and featuring satire and parody. In the United States of the late nineteenth century and the twentieth century, a kind of entertainment originally dependent on a series of variety acts but later including elements of female display (including striptease) in its major offerings. After moving to the fringes of respectability by the 1940s, burlesque disappeared in the United States by the late 1950s. (257)

Butoh A contemporary dance-performance style, originating in Japan after the Second World War, traditionally performed in white body makeup with exaggeratedly slow movement. (347)

chariot-and-pole system An elaborate system for changing elements of the scenery simultaneously. Devised by Giacomo Torelli in the seventeenth century, the system involved scenery attached to poles that rose through slits in the stage floor from chariots that ran on tracks in the basement and depended on an intricate system of interlocking ropes, pulleys, wheels, and windlasses for their simultaneous movement. (109)

chorus In Greek drama of the fifth century BCE, a group of men (number uncertain) who sang, chanted, spoke, and moved, usually in unison, and who with the actors performed the plays. In the Renaissance, a single character named Chorus who provided information and commentary about the action in some tragedies. In modern times, the groups that sing or dance in musical comedies, operettas, ballets, and operas. (17)

circus In ancient Rome, a circular space for performances, especially for horse racing. (50)

closet drama Plays written to be read, not performed. (44, 197)

combination company A theatre company that performed only one play and toured to a new venue when the audience waned. Compare to *repertory company*. (174)

comedy A form (genre) of drama variously discussed in terms of its having a happy ending; dealing with the material, mundane world; dealing with the low and middle classes; dealing with myths of rebirth and social regeneration; and so on. (99)

comedy of manners Refers most often to seventeenth- and eighteenth-century comedies whose focus is the proper social behavior of a single class. (156)

comic opera A "minor" form of musical drama popular first in the eighteenth century and characterized then by sentimental stories set to original music. Later used to mean an opera in which some parts were spoken, in contrast to "grand opera," where everything was sung.

commedia Short for *commedia dell'arte.*

commedia dell'arte Italian popular comedy of the fifteenth through seventeenth centuries. Featured performances improvised from scenarios by a set of stock characters. See also *lazzi*. (110)

commercial theatre A movement after about 1760 that saw the financing of theatre move from the state, a wealthy individual, or the church to companies or individuals that wished to make a profit through the sale of tickets. (169)

confidant(e) In drama, a character to whom another leading character gives private information. (98)

confraternity In France, a religious brotherhood, many of which sponsored or produced plays during the Middle Ages. One, the Confraternity of the Passion, held a monopoly on play production in Paris into the 1570s. (83)

constructivism A nonrealistic style of scenic design associated with Vsevolod Meyerhold and marked by the view that a good set is a machine for doing plays, not a representation of familiar locales. Incorporated simple machines on stage and often revealed the method of their own construction. (232)

continental seating First devised by Richard Wagner in the late nineteenth century for his theatre at Bayreuth; eschews a central aisle in favor of entrances and exits at the end of each aisle and does not generally have boxes for seating elevated above the orchestra. (199)

Corpus Christi plays Medieval cycle plays and cosmic dramas often performed during a spring festival established in the fourteenth century in honor of the Christian Eucharist. (79)

corral Spanish theatre of the late Middle Ages, sited in open courtyards among houses. (136)

Corral del Principe The name of the second corral to open in Madrid; it was used for performances from 1583 to 1744. (136)

cosmic drama Long dramatic presentations popular in the Middle Ages that depicted religious events from the creation to the Last Judgment. Short plays were combined until the total presentation could last several days or weeks and occasionally a month or more. See also *cycle play*. (81)

cothurnus High boot with platform sole for tragic actor, Hellenistic Greece. (32)

court theatre A theatre located at the court of a nobleman. After the Renaissance, Italianate theatre, whose perspective was drawn with the vanishing points established from the chair of the theatre where the ruler sat, making his the best seat in the house. (136)

cubism A twentieth-century art style pioneered by Pablo Picasso and George Braque that broke up the flat plane of conventional realistic painting, presenting objects that were fractured and reassembled in abstracted form. In the theatre of the 1920s and 1930s, primarily used in scenic and costume design. (232)

cycle play Medieval dramas covering the "cycle" of history from the creation of the world to doomsday, mostly found in England. See also *cosmic drama*. (81)

decorum In neoclassical theory, the behavior of a dramatic character in keeping with his or her social status, age, sex, and occupation; based on the requirements of verisimilitude. (98)

denouement From old French for "untie," the last part of a play or story, after the climax, when remaining issues are resolved. (33)

director-manager A type of theatre organization in which it is the director who is responsible for all financial and artistic aspects of the performance. Contrast with *actor-manager* and *producer*. (173)

discovery space Permanent or temporary space in the Elizabethan (Shakespearean) playhouse that permitted actors and locales to be hidden from view and then "discovered" (or revealed) when needed. Location, appearance, and even invariable existence of the space are disputed. (121)

domestic tragedy A serious play dealing with domestic problems of the middle or lower classes. In the eighteenth century, a reaction against "regular" or neoclassical tragedy. (161)

eccyclema In classical Greece, a machine used to thrust objects or people (often dead) from inside the skene into view of the audience. Probably some sort of wheeled platform that rolled or rotated through the skene's central door. (26)

eclecticism Gathering of materials from many sources; popularly, a mixture of styles and methods. In twentieth-century theatre, the idea that each play calls forth its own production style. (281)

elements of drama The six elements of drama that distinguish drama from other literature identified in Aristotle's *Poetics*. They are generally translated as plot, character, thought, diction, melody, and spectacle. (33)

emblematic staging An emblem was a device (usually an object or picture of an object) used as an identifying mark; something that stands for something else. In the Middle Ages, a key stood for St. Peter, a crooked staff for a bishop, and such. Emblematic staging used these devices rather than realistic or illusionistic costuming. (76)

environmental Theatre performed in a space found for it instead of a space made for theatre, especially during the medieval period. (76)

epic theatre Term originated by Erwin Piscator and popularized by Bertolt Brecht to describe a theatre in which the audience response is objective, not subjective, and in which such narrative devices as film projections, titles, and storytelling are used. See also *alienation effect*. (232)

expressionism A style of theatre originating in Europe after World War I and typified by presentation of meaning as viewed from the standpoint of the main character who is undergoing mental pressures. As a result, there are distortions of time, space, and proportion. (232)

facade stage A stage that puts the actors in front of a nonrepresentational background. (25)

false perspective A style of set design that exaggerates the real depth of the stage by building elements smaller than life size that are supposed to be farther from the audience. (103)

fair theatre Theatre in France and England performed at large, periodic fairs rather than in established theatre spaces or licensed theatres. (163)

fourth wall In a box set, the fourth wall of the set is invisible to the audience. It runs along the proscenium opening. (204)

galleries Areas for seating that are above the pit or orchestra, usually at a higher ticket price. (120)

gay and lesbian theatre Theatre of, by, and often for a gay and lesbian community. (309)

geju "Song drama," a form of opera developed in China in the twentieth century, inspired by Western opera. (343)

gentlemanly melodrama Later melodrama for middle-class audiences with upper-middle-class subjects and settings. Also called realistic melodrama. (180)

gesamtkunstwerk (master artwork) Both term and concept popularized by Richard Wagner, who argued that such a work would be the artistic fusion of all major artistic elements, including music, into a single work under the artistic supervision of a single master artist. (198)

glories In medieval and Renaissance art, a cloud or sunburst in which divinities appeared. In the theatre of those periods, a flown platform made to look like a cloud or sunburst. (89)

Golden Age The great age of any culture. In Spain, the period c. 1550–1650, the greatest age of Spanish drama; in France, the age of Louis XIV 1638–1715; and in England, the age of Elizabeth and Shakespeare c. 1558–1603. (118)

Graeco-Roman period That period in Greece and Greek lands when Roman domination had arrived, usually dated from c. 100 BCE to the fall of the Western Roman Empire, c. 550 CE. In theatre architecture, those Greek theatres that were remodeled to bring them in closer accord with the Roman ideals (not to be confused with Roman theatres built in Greek lands.) (35)

Great American Songbook The body of enduring popular songs written from the late nineteenth century through the late twentieth century, performed and recorded regularly still by many singers, many of which originated as songs in US musicals. (262)

Great Dionysia The yearly festival in ancient Athens where Greek drama originated. (18)

griot West African storyteller. (218)

groove system A way of changing scenery using a shallow channel in the stage floor in which a scenic flat rode; a bank of several grooves would allow one flat to be pulled aside while another was pushed on in its place, seemingly in the same plane. (109)

guild Religious and, sometimes, trade or professional organization in the Middle Ages that became the producer of civic medieval theatre. (83)

hanamichi In the Japanese *Kabuki* theatre, a walkway through the audience used by actors to get to and from the stage.

hashigakari In the Japanese Noh theatre, a walkway at the side of the stage for the actors' entrances and exits. (66)

hauju "Word drama," spoken language theatre in China developed in the early years of the twentieth century. (343)

heavens 1. Area above the stage; in the Elizabethan theatre, the underside of the roof that extended over the stage. 2. In the nineteenth century, the highest gallery. (120)

Hellenistic period 1. That period of Greek history dating from the coming of Alexander the Great to his death and sometime after, and the rise of Roman dominance over Greece (c. 336 BCE–c. 146 BCE). 2. In theatre architecture, those Greek theatres built during the Hellenistic period. (29)

hikinuki In Japanese Kabuki performance, the sudden transformation of a costume into a completely different one. (68)

hireling In professional companies of the Renaissance and after, an actor or technician hired by the shareholders to work for a set wage at a set task. (126)

householder Member of an acting company who owns a share of the theatre building itself. (125)

humanism A philosophy that believes that people should be at the center of their own deepest concerns. (95, 127)

hut In Elizabethan public theatre, small space below roof, probably for machinery. (121)

identity theatre Political theatre identified by race, gender, or ethnic origin. (299)

illusionism Scenic practice (with analogs in acting, directing, and other theatre arts) that imitates the real world on stage. (97)

independent theatre movement In nineteenth-century Europe, the appearance of non-commercial theatres in several countries more or less simultaneously, most of them amateur or nontraditional and able to operate outside the usual censorship, "independent" of commercial demands. (205)

integrated musical Musical with songs and dances that are organic parts of story and character. (262)

interlude A short simple play or dramatic entertainment between portions of a larger entertainment, such as a banquet, a drama, a ballet, an opera, and so on. (90)

intermezzi Italian entertainments usually given at courts and presented between other forms of entertainment. (110)

Italianate staging A kind of staging developed during the Renaissance in Italy and marked by a proscenium arch and perspective scenery arranged in wing and shutter. (107)

jukebox musical A musical built around songs written by one composer or lyricist or made popular by one performer. (274)

Kabuki Traditional Japanese theatre beginning in the early 1600s of great spectacle and powerful stories, often heroic and chivalric or military. (67)

Kathakali Traditional dance-drama form of southern India, believed by some to be a direct descendant of *Sanskrit drama*. (340)

Kunqu opera A national genre of China beginning in the mid-1500s and lasting for about one hundred years; romantic and literate with sentimental music. (61)

kyogen Japanese theatre form: comic interludes between parts of a Noh performance. (65)

Latin music drama Medieval dramas performed inside churches by clergy. The dramas unfolded in Latin rather than the vernacular and were sung rather than spoken, thus the name. Also called *liturgical drama*. (76)

Latino/Latina theatre Theatre of, by, and for Latinos/Latinas. (311)

lazzi Stock bits of business designed to provoke a particular response, usually laughter, from the audience. Associated particularly with the commedia dell'arte and the French farce of the seventeenth century. (112)

librettist The author of the book portion of a musical, the spoken parts, which is called the libretto. (259)

limited run Short, predetermined playing period usually with well-known performers. (294)

lines of business A range of roles in which an actor would specialize for the major part of his or her acting career (e.g., young lover, walking gentlewoman, or comic servant), particularly important during the seventeenth and eighteenth centuries. (152)

liturgical drama Plays that were done inside churches as part of the religious services and thus were performed in Latin, by the clergy, and were usually chanted or sung rather than spoken. Liturgical drama is also called *Latin music drama*. (76)

liturgy The rites of worship of the church. (74)

living newspaper A theatrical presentation based on current events, which was created by the Federal Theatre Project of the US Government's Work Projects Administration during the Great Depression. Living newspapers often urged social action. (240)

Living Theatre A highly influential US avant-garde theatre formed in 1947 by Julian Beck and Judith Malina. (295)

lords' room Expansive space close to the tiring house in Elizabethan theatre. (120)

ludi 1. In Rome, festivals given for public worship of a variety of gods and on various public occasions like military victories and the funerals of government officials. As drama was often included as a part of the festivals, they are important in a history of Roman theatre. 2. Early medieval term for plays. (39)

lyricist Author of the words to songs, the lyrics. (259)

machine play Any play written especially to show off the special effects and movable scenery in a theatre. Especially popular during the Neoclassical period, when regular plays obeyed "unity of place" and so had few opportunities for elaborate scenic changes. (146)

mansion The particularized setting in the medieval theatre that, together with the *platea*, or generalized playing space, constituted the major staging elements of the theatre. Several mansions were placed around or adjacent to the platea at once—thus "simultaneous staging." (76)

masque Spectacular theatrical form, especially of the Renaissance and the Neoclassical periods, usually associated with court theatres or special events. Emphasis was put on costumes and effects, with much music and dancing; amateur actors frequently performed. For example, Ben Jonson's many court masques. (132)

masters of secrets That craftsman/artist of the medieval theatre charged with the execution of special effects in the dramas. (89)

mechane Machine, or *machina*. In classical Greece, a crane by which actors and objects could be flown into the playing area. (27)

medieval That period of world history dating roughly from the fall of the Western Roman Empire (c. 550 CE) to the fall of Constantinople and the beginning of the Renaissance (c. 1450). In drama, the period between 975, the first record of drama, and c. 1550, when religious drama was outlawed in many countries throughout Europe. (73)

melodrama Literally "music drama." A kind of drama associated with a simplified moral universe, a set of stock characters (hero, heroine, villain, and comic relief), rapid turns in the dramatic action, and story driven by the villain threatening the hero/heroine. Leading form of drama throughout the nineteenth century. (178)

Middle Ages An early name for the Medieval period. (73)

middle comedy That transitional kind of Greek comedy dating from c. 404 BCE, the defeat of Athens by Sparta, to 336 BCE, the beginning of the Hellenistic period. Less topical than Greek old comedy, middle comedy dealt more with domestic issues and everyday life of the Athenian middle class. (29)

mime 1. A kind of drama in which unmasked actors of both sexes portrayed often bawdy and obscene stories. In Rome, it became the most popular kind of drama after the first century CE. 2. Form of silent modern theatre. (33)

miracle play Medieval play treating the lives of saints. (79)

modernism Name for art of a period (roughly 1890–1950 and maybe beyond) identified by radical experimentation with form and nonrealism. (230, 314)

morality play Allegorical medieval play, like *Everyman*, that depicts the eternal struggle between good and evil that transpires in this world, using characters like Vice, Virtue, Wisdom, and so on. (79)

multipoint perspective Perspective creates the impression of three dimensions in a flat work and in multipoint perspective, there are multiple vanishing points to which the lines in depth meet. (152)

music hall From about 1850, a form of entertainment in England that included song, comedy, dance, novelty acts, and so on. (257)

musicians' gallery A space about stage level suitable for musicians in the theatre of Elizabethan England. (121)

mystery plays Usually drawn from biblical stories, these medieval plays were often staged in cycles, treating events from the creation to the Last Judgment. Often staged in connection with Christian festivals, some mysteries were quite elaborate and took days or even weeks to perform. (79)

naturalism A style of theatre and drama most popular from c. 1880 to 1900 that dealt with the sordid problems of the middle and lower classes in settings remarkable for the number and accuracy of details. Practitioners included Émile Zola, André Antoine, and Maxim Gorky. (200)

Natyasastra Ancient Indian work written in Sanskrit on theatre aesthetics. (57)

neoclassicism A style of drama and theatre from the Italian Renaissance based loosely on interpretations of Aristotle and Horace. Major tenets were verisimilitude, decorum, purity of genres, the five-act form, and the twofold purpose of drama: to teach and to please. (97)

new comedy That form of Greek comedy dating from the Hellenistic and Graeco-Roman periods and treating the domestic complications of the Athenian middle class. A major source for Roman comedy. (30)

new stagecraft A movement in stage design in the United States that favored simplified, often abstract, settings. It was, in effect, a reaction to overly realistic settings. Lighting played an important part in the design. Designers of the new stagecraft often sought alternatives to the proscenium stage like the arena or thrust configurations. (243)

Noh Austere, poetic drama of medieval Japan, based in Zen Buddhism. (65)

not-for-profit theatres Professional theatres whose income comes only partly from ticket sales, the rest from donations and grants; given federal tax breaks. (286)

old comedy That form of Greek comedy written during the classical period and featuring topical political and social commentary set in highly predictable structural and metrical patterns. (23)

onkos The high headdress of the Roman, and perhaps Hellenistic Greek, actor. (32)

Open Theatre A highly influential US avant-garde theatre founded by Joseph Chaikin, operating from 1963–1973. (297)

operetta A usually comic, usually short opera with some spoken dialogue. (256)

orchestra 1. That area of the Greek and Roman theatre that lay between the audience area and the scene house. 2. Originally the circular space where actors and chorus danced and performed plays; later a half-circle that was used as a seating space for important people and only occasionally as a performance area. 3. In modern times, the prized seating area on the ground level of a theatre and adjacent to the stage. (24)

pageant In the medieval period, a movable stage, a wagon on which plays were mounted and performed in parts of England, Spain, and occasionally continental Europe. By extension, the plays performed on such wagons. (86)

pageant wagon See *pageant*. (86)

pantomime In the Roman theatre, a dance/ story performed by a single actor with the accompaniment of a small group of musicians, particularly during the Christian era. In the eighteenth and nineteenth centuries, a "minor" form of entertainment marked by elaborate spectacle and often featuring commedia-like characters and scenes of magical transformation. This later form of pantomime, often called "panto," is still performed in Britain at the Christmas holidays as a family entertainment. (46, 161)

passion play A dramatic presentation of the passion of Jesus Christ, that is, his trial, suffering, and death. (79)

Peking Opera Older English term for *Beijing Opera*.

periaktoi Stage machines in use by the Hellenistic period in Greece. An early method of scene changing that consisted of a triangle extended in space and mounted on a central pivot so that when the pivot was rotated, three different scenes could be shown to an audience. (45)

perspective Simulation of visual distance by the manipulation of the apparent size of objects. (102)

pinake In the Greek theatre, a frame covered with stretched fabric that could be painted with scenic elements. (26)

pit 1. Area of the audience on the ground floor and adjacent to the stage. Historically an inexpensive area because originally no seats were provided there and later only backless benches were used. By the end of the nineteenth century, a preferred seating area (now called the orchestra section). 2. Now refers often to the area reserved

for members of the orchestra playing for opera, ballet, and musical comedy. (119)

platea The unlocalized playing area in the medieval theatre. See also *mansion*. (76)

Poetics A book by Aristotle in 335 BCE that describes the qualities of ancient Greek tragedies and that was highly influential on European drama after its rediscovery in the 1500s. (32)

poor theatre The twentieth-century theory of Jerzy Grotowski that as theatre cannot compete with the spectacle of film it should make itself "poor," which is, to focus on actors creating theatre together with the audience. (336)

possession of parts During the seventeenth and especially the eighteenth centuries, the practice of leaving a role with an actor throughout a career. Under the system, a sixty-year-old woman playing Juliet in Shakespeare's tragedy was not unheard of. (152)

postmodernism A critical approach that denies the possibility of social or cultural progress and doubts the possibility of objectivity and that favors, consequently, the open acknowledgement of socially constructed meanings and investigates the implications of those meanings. Postmodernism remains a term of controversy. (233, 312)

private theatre In Elizabethan and Stuart England, indoor theatres that were open to the public but were expensive because of their relatively limited seating capacity. Located on monastic lands, these theatres were outside the jurisdiction of the city of London. Initially they housed children's troupes, but later the regular adult troupes used them as a winter home. (124)

problem play Beginning in the nineteenth century, problem plays were well-made plays, melodramas, with a focus on a social problem. (186)

producer Executive who arranges financing and who oversees a commercial production. (169)

proscenium (theatre, arch) Theatre building in which the audience area is set off from the acting area by a proscenium arch that frames the stage. The audience views the onstage action from one side only. (106)

protagonist In Greek theatre, the first (or major) actor, the one who competed for the prize in acting. Later, the leading character in any play (the "hero"). (26)

public theatre In Elizabethan and Stuart England, outdoor theatres like the Globe. Because larger than the indoor theatres, public theatres tended to be relatively inexpensive and so attract a general audience. (119)

purity of genres Neoclassical tenet that elements of tragedy and those of comedy could not be mixed. The injunction was not merely against including funny scenes in tragedy but also against treating domestic issues or writing in prose, these elements being of the nature of comedy. (99)

Quem Quaeritis A liturgical trope that opens, "Whom do you seek?" and that has early connection to drama, most especially in Ethelwold's *Regularis Concordia* of the tenth century, in which the trope was accompanied by directions for staging. (76)

raked stage Stage slanted up from front to back to enhance the perspective. Stages began their rakes either at the front of the apron or at the proscenium line. (108)

rasa Important element of Sanskrit aesthetic theory—the inducing of an appropriate emotion in the audience. (57)

realism The style of drama and theatre dating from the late nineteenth and early twentieth centuries that strove to reproduce on stage the details of everyday life. (199)

realistic melodrama Developing about 1850, a form of melodrama that took place in realistic settings and where the conflict between good and evil was less flamboyant than in full-blown melodrama. (180)

recitative Speech set to music; it differs from song by the musical lines not being repeated. Although sung, it resembles speech more than song. (271)

Renaissance Literally, "rebirth"; refers to a renewed interest in the learning and culture of ancient Greece and Rome and the start of the growth of humanism and secularism. Beginning in Italy, the Renaissance spread throughout Western Europe from c. 1450 to c. 1650. (94)

repertory Group of performance pieces done by a company. Also, the practice in such a company of alternating pieces so that they are done in repertory. Loosely, a resident professional theatre company in the United States; a repertory theatre. (174)

Restoration comedy English comedies written after the restoration of the monarchy in 1660 and lasting to c. 1710, characterized by a new explicitness about sexual behavior in the upper classes. (160)

revival A new production of a play after its initial run. (285)

revue A show combining comedy, song, dance, and skits, without a story, sometimes lampooning current events. (257)

romanticism A style of theatre and drama dating from c. 1790 to c. 1850 and marked by an interest in the exotic, the subjective, the emotional, and the individual. Began in part as a reaction against the strictures of neoclassicism; grew out of the eighteenth century's sentimentalism. (191)

royalties Payments made to playwrights and other theatre artists that are a percentage of ticket sales. Prior to royalties, playwrights were paid a lump sum for their plays and had no financial interest in their success. (183)

Sanskrit drama Drama of ancient India, performed in the language of Hinduism, Sanskrit. (56)

sarugaku A Japanese circus-like entertainment beginning in twelfth century, the literal translation: "monkey music." (63)

satyr play A short, rustic, and often obscene play included in the Dionysian festivals of Greece at the conclusion of the tragedies. In neoclassicism, this description was misread and that misreading led to the pastoral play, a play concerned with rustic, country people. (18)

scaffold In medieval staging in England, the localizing structure in or near the platea. See also *mansion*. (85)

scenario In general, the prose description of a play's story. In the commedia dell'arte, the written outline of plot and characters from which the actors improvised the particular actions of a given performance. (112)

secularism Belief in the validity and importance of life and things on earth. Often contrasted with spiritualism, otherworldliness, or religiosity. The Renaissance period was marked by a rising secularism. (95)

selective realism A stage design style of the mid-twentieth century that used some real items—one's that were important to the story—but did not show realistic depictions of all elements of the design. (239)

sentimental comedy A kind of comedy particularly popular during the eighteenth century in which people's virtues rather than their foibles were stressed. The audience was expected to experience something "too exquisite for laughter." Virtuous characters expressed themselves in pious "sentiments." (161)

sentimentalism Prevalent during the eighteenth century, sentimentalism assumed the innate goodness of humanity and attributed evil to faulty instruction or bad example. A precursor of the romanticism of the nineteenth century. (151)

sentimentality The arousing of feelings out of proportion to their cause. (177)

sharing company One made up of shareholders. A member of a sharing company owned a part of the company's stocks of costumes, scenery, properties, and so on. Sharing companies were the usual organization of troupes from the Renaissance until the eighteenth century and beyond, when some actors began to prefer fixed salaries to shares. (125)

shingeki "Modern theatre," Western style theatre in Japan, developed in the early twentieth century. (346)

shutter Large flat, paired with another of the same kind, to close off the back of the scene in Italianate staging; an alternative to a backdrop; sometimes used for units at the sides. When pierced with a cutout, it became a "relieve" and showed a diorama. (108)

signature music Music associated with certain characters or certain types of characters, particularly in the melodramas of the nineteenth century. Stage directions indicate "Mary's music," "Jim's music," and so on. (178)

simultaneous staging The practice, particularly during the Middle Ages, of representing several locations on the stage at one time. In medieval staging, several mansions, representing particular places, were arranged around a *platea*, or generalized playing space. (76)

single-point perspective A technique for achieving a sense of depth by establishing a single vanishing point and painting or building all objects to diminish to it. (108)

skene The scene house in the Greek theatre. Its appearance can first be documented with the first performance of the *Oresteia* in 458 BCE. Its exact appearance from that time until the first stone theatre came into existence is uncertain. (24)

socialist realism A style resulting from the position of the Stalinist Soviet Union that art, literature, and music should reflect and promote socialist ideals, typically in a manner that working people could appreciate. (252)

star system Company organization in which minor characters are played by actors for the season, whereas central roles are taken by well-known actors—stars—brought in for one production; still common in opera, sometimes seen in summer theatres. (174)

stock types Characters who are drawn from cliche and stereotype, not custom-made but "pulled from stock." (179)

stock company Theatre company in which actors play standardized roles and (originally) owned shares of stock in the company.

Sturm und Drang (storm and stress) A theatrical movement in Germany during the 1770s and 1780s that was marked by its militant experimentation with dramatic form, theatrical style, and social statement. (195)

sung-through musical A type of musical, dominant in the 1980s and 1990s, that used no or almost no dialogue. Also called pop opera. (271)

surrealism A style popular immediately following World War I that rejected everyday logic in favor of a free expression of the subconscious or dream state. (231)

symbolism A style of theatre and drama popular during the 1890s and the early twentieth century that stressed the importance of subjectivity and spirituality and sought its effects through the use of symbol, legend, myth, and mood. (231)

theatre for development Use of theatrical techniques for both community involvement and community instruction. (224)

theatre of cruelty Phrase popularized by Antonin Artaud to describe a kind of theatre that touched the basic precivilized elements of people through disrupting normal "civilized" expectations about appearance, practice, sound, and so forth. (236)

Theatrical Syndicate A syndicate or monopoly that controlled nearly all touring theatres in the United States from 1896 to 1908. (175)

three unities In neoclassical dramatic theory, the unities of time, place, and action. (99)

tiring house The building from which the Elizabethan platform, or thrust, stage extended; a place where the actors attired themselves. (120)

tragedy In popular parlance, any serious play, usually including an unhappy ending. According to Aristotle, "an imitation of a worthy or illustrious and perfect action, possessing magnitude, in pleasing language, using separately the several species of imitation in its parts, by men acting, and not through narration, through pity and fear effecting a catharsis of such passion." (99)

transformation 1. Technique popularized in the 1960s whereby an actor portrayed several characters without any changes in costume, makeup, or mask, relying instead on changing voice and body attitudes in full view of the audience. 2. In medieval and Renaissance theatre, seemingly magical changes of men into beasts, women into salt, and so on. 3. In English pantomime, magical changes made by Harlequin's wand. (161)

trap Unit in stage floor for appearances and disappearances; varies from a simple door to complex machines for raising and lowering while moving forward, backward, and sideways. (120)

trope An interpolation in a liturgical text. Some believe medieval drama to have been derived from medieval troping. (74)

utility player Actor hired to play a variety of small roles as needed. (152)

vaudeville 1. In the United States in the nineteenth and twentieth centuries, vaudeville was popular family entertainment featuring a collection of variety acts, skits, short plays, and song-and-dance routines. 2. In France in the eighteenth and nineteenth centuries, vaudeville referred to comédie-en-vaudeville, short satiric pieces, often topical, that were interspersed with new lyrics set to familiar tunes and sprinkled with rhyming couplets (vaudevilles). The form in France is roughly equivalent to the ballad opera in England. (257)

verisimilitude Central concept in neoclassical theory and criticism. Literal meaning is "truth-seemingness" but used in neoclassicism to refer to the general, typical, categorical truth. Not to be confused with realism. (98)

well-made play A play written by or in the manner of Eugène Scribe and marked by careful preparation, seeming cause-and-effect organization of action, announced entrances and exits, and heavy reliance on external objects or characters to provide apparent connections between diverse lines of action. Now often used as a term of derision. (186)

wings 1. Scenic pieces (flats) placed parallel to the stage front, or nearly so, on each side of the stage; combined with overhead units for "wing-and-border" settings. 2. The offstage area beyond the side units of scenery—"in the wings." (108)

women's theatre A theatre whose repertories and practices are devoted to the advancement of women. Such theatres offer some combination of theatre by women, for women, and about women. (305)

yard Another name for the pit in the Shakespearean theatre, where patrons stood on the ground in front of the stage. (119)

Yoruba A West-African ethnic and language group, largely centered in Nigeria. (219)

zanni In commedia dell'arte, the group of comic servants that includes Arlecchino, Trufaldino, and so on. (112)

Index

A

Abbey Theatre, 242
absurdism, 10, 232–233, 291, 312–313, 333, 334, 345, 346
Actor Prepares, An, 206
actor-manager, 170
Actors Studio, 239
Adams Shakespearean Theatre, 362
Adding Machine, The, 247, 248
Aeschylus, 15, 19, 20–21, 26, 97, 100
Africa, 5, 38, 46, 72, 212–227; sub-Saharan, 213–215, 217–224
African American theatre, 300–304
afterpieces, 162
Agamemnon, 15, 20, 26, 44
Ah, Wilderness!, 246
Aida (musical), 275, 353
Ajax, 22
Akropolis, 336
Aladdin and the Wonderful Lamp, 161
Alarinjo, 219–220
Albee, Edward, 284, 290–291, 313
Aldrich, Ira, 194
Aleotti, Grovanni Battista, 106
Alexander the Great, 29, 35, 38, 56–57, 101, 213, 216
al-Hakīm, Tawfig, 217
alienation. *See* epic theatre.
All My Sons, 289, 317
allegories, 79, 85, 135
Alleyn, Edward, 122–123, 126, 127
Als, Hilton, 302
American Dream, The, 290
American Method, 239
American musical. *See* musical theatre.
Aminta, 101
amphitheatre, 48
Amphitryon, 41
Andromache, 147
Andromède, 145
Angels in America, 310, 312
Anna Christie, 245
Anna in the Tropics, 307, 311
Annie Get Your Gun, 259, 260, 267
Anouilh, Jean, 252, 332
Antigone, 22; Anouilh's, 232, 252; Brecht's, 234
Antoine, André, 203–205
Antony and Cleopatra, 128, 158
Anything Goes, 259
apartheid, 215, 222, 223
Appia, Adolphe, 243
applied theatre or applied drama, 225, 227
Arcadia, 293, 329–330
Architectura, De, 43
Arena Stage Mead Center for American Theater, 265, 280, 293
arena stage, 241, 286
Aristophanes, 9, 18, 19, 23–24, 97, 100, 115, 147
Aristotle, 14, 29, 32–33, 43, 97
Ars Poetica, 43–44
art theatre movement, 241–242
Artaud, Antonin, 235–237, 322, 330
Artists of Dionysus, 30, 216
As You Like It, 128, 139, 184
Asian theatre, 5, 10, 54–70, 338–348
Astor Place Riots, 172
Atellan farce, 46, 49
August: Osage County, 307
auto sacramentales, 135
avant-garde, 294–299, 313
Awake and Sing!, 239

B

Bacchae, The, 13, 22, 23, 222
backdrop, 108
Bakhīl, Al-, 217
Bald Soprano, The, 332
ballad opera, 12
ballad, 266
Baltimore Waltz, 307, 308
Bath House, The, 243
Bayreuth, 198
Beaumont, Francis, 127, 131
Beauty and the Beast, 275, 354
Beck, Julian, 295–296
Beckett, Samuel, 313, 333–334
Beggar's Opera, The, 222, 256
Behn, Aphra, 157
Beijing Opera, 342–343
Bel Geddes, Norman, 244
Belarus Free Theatre, 363–364
Belasco, David, 182, 187
benefit performances, 158–159
Bennett, Alan, 326, 327–328
Berlin, Irving, 259, 260, 261
Berliner Ensemble, 234, 321–322
Bernhardt, Sarah, 175
Betterton, Thomas, 159
Biedermann and the Firebugs, 334
Biejer, Agne, 153
biomechanics, 242
Birds, The, 23
Birthday Party, The, 327
Black Crook, The, 258
black theatre. *See* African American theatre.
Black Watch, 316
blackface, 182, 261
Blackfriars Theatre, 118, 124, 127, 362
Blacks, The, 300
Blake, Eubie, 264–265
Blood Knot, The, 222
Boal, Augusto, 224
Bollywood, 341
Bono, 275, 284
book musical, 261–262
book of a musical, 259
borders, 108, 155
Boucicault, Dion, 178, 182–184
boulevard theatres, 154
Bourgeois Gentilhomme, Le, 151
box set, 180, 199
boy actors, 124
braggart soldier, 113
Braggart Warrior, The, 41
Brahma, 57
Brahmins, 58
Brecht, Bertolt, 222, 223, 232, 233–235, 237, 295, 321–322, 330, 335, 342, 345
breeches part, 159, 160
Breuer, Lee, 355–356
Brig, The, 295
Bring in Da Noise, Bring in Da Funk, 270
"British Blonds," 257
Broadway, 281, 282, 283–286, 317
Brook, Peter, 325, 332, 337
Buchel, Arend van, 120
Buddhism, 65
Buffalo Dance, 16
bugaku, 64–65
bunraku, 67
Burbage, Richard, 126, 127
Buried Child, 291, 294
burlesque, 253, 257
business, theatrical, 75
butoh, 346
Byzantine or Byzantium, 51, 71

C

Cabaret, 275
cabinet cards, 187
Cairo Codex, 31
Calderón de la Barca, Pedro, 135, 138, 139
cape-and-sword plays, 138
Capitano, 113
Captain's Tiger, The, 224
Caroline, or Change, 311–312
Carousel, 2, 238, 260, 262
cartes de visite, 187
Carthage, 39
Cat on a Hot Tin Roof, 288, 302
catharsis, 32
Cats, 271, 272, 273
Caucasian Chalk Circle, The, 234, 322
censorship, 169, 203, 251, 320–321, 324, 335, 340, 343–344, 363–364
Chaikin, Joseph, 297–298, 357
Chalk Circle, 62
character, 33
chariot-and-pole, 109–110, 145, 153, 356
Charles II, 154, 158, 159
Charles VI, 143
Chekhov, Anton, 201, 207–208, 288
Cherry Orchard, The, 207
Chicago, 275, 276, 353
Children's Hour, The, 307
Childress, Alice, 302
China Art and Entertainment Group, 353
China, 12, 55, 60–64
chitlin' circuit, 302, 303
chorus girl, 258
Chorus Line, A, 267, 269
chorus, 17
Christian church, 72; opposition to theatre, 47–48; orthodox, 51; Roman Catholic, 92
Chronegk, Ludwig, 202
Church of England, 118
Churchill, Caryl, 293, 330, 331
Cid, Le, 144
Circus Maximus, 48
circus, 48
Cirque du Soleil, 286
civil rights movement, 279–280
Civil War (English), 135
claqueurs, 196
Clorindy; or, The Origin of the Cakewalk, 264

closet dramas, 40, 44, 178, 197
cloud machines, 134
Cloud Nine, 293, 330, 331
Clouds, The, 27
Coliseum, 48
colonialism, 355
Color Purple, The, 302, 306
combination companies, 174
Comden, Betty, 264
Come Back, Little Sheba, 302
Comédie Française, 150, 152, 186, 196–197, 355–357
comedy of intrigue, 157
comedy of manners, 156–157, 160
comedy, 99; middle, 29; new, 30; old, 23; Roman, 40, 148; sentimental, 160; situation, 216
comic song, 266
commedia dell'arte, 97, 100, 110–115, 145, 148, 152, 303, 334–335
commedia erudita, 100
commedia, 138
commercial theatre, 117, 165–187, 229–230, 283–286
Communist China, 339
community development theatre. See theatre for development.
community theatres, 244–245, 282, 283, 317
Company, 268, 270
composer, 259
concept musicals, 269–270
confidant, 65, 98
confraternities, 83, 136
Confraternity of the Passion, 143
Congreve, William, 156–157
Connection, The, 295
Conservatoire, Paris, 203
Constantine, Emperor, 48, 50
Constantinople, 50, 71; fall of, 96–97
constructivism, 231, 232, 242, 243
continental seating, 198
contract system, 158
Contrast, The, 169
Cook, Will Marion, 264
"coon shows," 261
Copeau, Jacques, 241, 242
copyright, 184
Corneille, Pierre, 145–146
Corpus Christi plays, 79
Corral del Cruz, 136
Corral del Príncipe, 136–137
cosmic dramas, 81
cothurnus, 32
Country Wife, The, 156
court masques. See masques
court theatres, 136
Coward, Noel, 250–251
Crabtree, Lotta, 182
Craig, Edward Gordon, 172–173, 243, 244
Crawford, Cheryl, 239
Crazy for You, 263
Crimes of the Heart, 306
Cromwell, Oliver, 135, 154
Crowley, Mart, 309
Crucible, The, 290
crusades, 51, 78
Cruz, Nilo, 310, 311
cubism, 232
Cultural Revolution, 344
Curtain, 122–123
curtain, 68
cycle plays, 81, 125
Cyrano de Bergerac, 294

D
Dadaism, 313
Dak Ghar, 340–341
Daly, Augustin, 176
dance theory, 15–16
Dante, Nicholas, 269
Darwin, Charles, 200
Davenant, William, 135, 154
Day of Absense, 302
De Mille, Agnes, 267
Death and the King's Horseman, 221
Death of a Salesman, 290, 345
decorum, 97, 98, 148
Dekker, Thomas, 127
Dell'Architectura, 103
Democracy, 329
denouement, 33
Design for Living, 250–251
Desire under the Elms, 2, 245, 314
deus ex machina, 27
Devonshire, Duke of, 134
DeWitt, Johnnas, 120
dinner theatre, 317
Dionysus, 13, 14, 38
Dionysus, Theatre of, 24
director-manager, 173
directors, 84
discovery space, 121, 136
Disney Productions, 275
dithyrambs, 14
Doll's House, A, 207, 208, 298–299, 343, 355
domestic tragedy, 161
Dottore, 112
Double Dealer, The, 156
Dr. Faustus, 127, 130
dream ballet, 267
Dreamgirls, 351
Dreamworks, 284
Drottningholm Theatre, 153
Drury Lane theatre, 154, 159, 160, 200
Dryden, John, 158, 159
Duchess of Malfi, The, 131; Brecht's, 234
Duke's Company, 160
Dürrenmatt, Friedrich, 321, 333–334
Dutchman, 300

E
East India Company, 338
ecclesial theatre, 74
eccyclema, 26
eclecticism, 241, 278–318
Edge, The, 275, 284
Edinburgh Theatre Festival, 361, 363
Edo, Japan, 68, 69
educational theatre, 282, 317
Edward II, 127, 130; Brecht's, 234
Egungun, 221
Egypt, 12, 29, 212, 226
Electra, 22, 23
elements of drama, 33
"eleven o'clock number," 266–267
Eliot, T. S., 272, 321
Elizabeth I, 118
emblematic staging or costumes, 66–67, 76, 85, 89–90, 117, 125, 143
English Stage Society, 241
entremeses, 138
entries, 90
environmental staging, 76, 117
epic theatre, 10, 207, 232, 233–235, 247–248, 321, 346
erudite drama, 100–101

Ethelwold, Bishop, 74–75
Etruscans, 37
Eumenides, 19, 20, 27
Euripides, 2, 13, 19, 22–23, 30, 49, 97, 100, 147, 222
Eurydice, 306
Everyman, 79, 82
Evita, 272
existentialism, 232, 313
expressionism, 231, 232, 247, 289

F
facade stage, 45
fairs, 78, 154
False Face Society of the Iroquois, 16
farce, 91, 148
Faust, 195
Feast of Fools, 76, 82
Feast of the Boy Bishops, 76
federal government support for arts, US, 320, 325
Federal Theatre Project, The, 239–240
Fen, 330
Fences, 301
festivals, 77; Athenian, 14, 17; Roman, 39
feudalism, 72, 73
Fiddler on the Roof, 267, 284
Fires in the Mirror, 304
Fiske, Minnie Maddern, 175
five-act form, 98, 99
flat, 109
Flavio's Good Fortune, 111
Fletcher, John, 127, 131
Flies, The, 252
flying, 134, 136, 137
Fo, Dario, 334–335
focus theatre, 224
folk drama, 207
For Colored Girls Who Have Considered Suicide/ When the Rainbow Is Enuf, 298, 302
Fornes, Maria Irene, 310, 311
Forrest, Edwin, 172
Fortune, The, 121, 122–123
Fouquet, Jean, 80
fourth wall, 204
France, 12, 73, 168, 330–334
Frankenstein, 190, 191
Franz, Ellen, 202
Frayn, Michael, 293, 327–328
Free Stage, The. See Die Freie Bühne.
Free Theatre. See Théâtre-Libre.
Freie Bühne, Die, 205
French Academy, 144, 188
Frisch, Max, 321, 333–334
Fry, Christopher, 332
Fuente Ovejuna, 138
Fugard, Athol, 222–224, 293
Funny Girl, 266, 268
Funny Thing Happened on the Way to the Forum, A, 41, 268, 271
Funnyhouse of a Negro, 300

G
galleries, 119; women's, 137
Garrick Gaities, 260
Garrick, David, 170–171, 200
Gates, Jr., Henry Louis, 303
gay and lesbian theatre, 307–310
Gay, John, 222, 256
geju, 343
Gelosi, I, 114
Gem of the Ocean, 301

Genet, Jean, 300
genre, 177
genre, purity of, 97, 99
gentlemanly melodrama. *See* realistic melodrama.
Georg II, Duke of Saxe-Meiningen, 201–203
Germany, 46, 73, 167–168, 320–324
Gershwin, George, 238, 260, 263, 267
Gershwin, Ira, 238, 263, 267
gesamtkunstwerk, 198
Ghosts, 205, 207
Gilbert, W. S., 257
Giraudoux, Jean, 321
Girl Crazy, 260, 263, 267
Glass Menagerie, The, 288, 300, 315
Glines Theatre, 309
globalization, 349–364
Globe, The, 121, 122–123, 127
gloire, 146
glories, 89
Goat, or Who Is Sylvia, The, 291
Goethe, Johann Wolfgang von, 195
Going to St. Ives, 295
golden age; Athenian theatre, 13; English theatre, 117–135; German theatre, 197; Spanish theatre, 135–140
Goldoni, Carlo, 114
Goldsmith, Oliver, 185
Good Person of Setzuan, The, 234, 321, 322
Goodman Theatre, 251, 314
Gorky, Maxim, 206, 209
gothic melodrama, 180
Gottshed, Johann, 167
Gozzi, Carlo, 114, 357
Graeco-Roman, 35
Grease, 275, 352
Great American Songbook, 262, 276
Great Depression, 229, 245, 250, 253
Great Dionysia, 18, 23
great man theory, 14–15
Great White Hope, The, 283, 284
Greek comedy, ancient, 9
Greek theatre or culture, 11–36, 37, 49, 95
Grein, Jakob T., 205
griot, 218
groove system, 109, 134
grooves, 155
Grotowski, Jerzy, 336–337
Grouch, The, 30
group protagonist, 209
Group Theatre, The, 238–239
guerilla theatre, 295
guilds, 83
Guthrie Theatre, 20, 286, 287
Guthrie, Tyrone, 15
Guys and Dolls, 266
Gwynn, Eleanor "Nell," 159
Gypsy, 268, 271

H

ha, 65
Hair, 269, 307
Hairy Ape, The, 247
Hall, Peter, 325, 326
Hallam, William and Lewis, 168–169
hamartia, 33
Hamburg Dramaturgy, 194
Hamlet, 126, 127, 128, 130, 139, 159, 245, 286, 329, 362, 363
Hammerstein II, Oscar, 261, 262
Han dynasty, 60
Handspring Puppet Company, 359
Hansberry, Lorraine, 300, 302

happy idea, 23
Hardy, Aléxandre, 143
Hart, Lorenz, 261
Hart, Moss, 250
hashigakari, 67
Hauptman, Gerhart, 203, 209
Heartbreak House, 251
heavens, 120
Hedda Gabler, 207
Heidi Chronicles, The, 293
Hellenistic period, 38
Hellenistic theatre or culture, 23, 26, 28–34, 37, 39, 45, 49, 215
Hellman, Lillian, 184, 307
Hello, Dolly!, 266, 267, 268
Hell's mouth or Hellmouth, 87, 89
Henley, Beth, 306
Henry IV, 142
Henry IV, 63, 114, 123, 128; Pirandello's; 248
Henry V, 128
Henry VI, 128
Henry VII, 132
Henry VIII, 128, 131
Henslowe, Philip, 122–123, 127; inventory, 126
Herbert, Victor, 259, 260
Herman, Jerry, 266, 268
Hernani, 196–197
hikinuki, 68
Hinduism, 56, 57
Hippolytus, 2, 147
hirelings, 126
History Boys, The, 2, 326, 328
histriones, 73
Holly, Buddy, 273–274, 275
Homecoming, The, 327
Horace, 43–44, 100
horn butting game, 61
Hôtel de Bourgogne, 143, 144, 145
House of Atreus, The, 15, 20
householders, 125–126, 150
Howard, Sidney, 238
Hroswitha, 74
huaju, 343
Hudes, Auiara Alegria, 311
Hugo, Victor, 196–197
humanism, 95, 127
Huruma, 224–225
hut, 120
Hytner, Nicholas, 2, 326

I

I Am My Own Wife, 310
"I song," 266
Ibsen, Henrik, 173, 185, 203, 205, 207, 208, 250, 290, 298–299, 343
Iceman Cometh, The, 245
identity theatre, 299–312
idolatry, 55, 216
Ikhernofret stele, 216
illegitimate theatres, 154
illusionism, 68, 97, 101–102, 134
Imaginary Invalid, The, 150
impersonation, 75
Importance of Being Earnest, The, 174, 181, 186–187
improvisation, 297, 330
In the Heights, 311
independent theatre movement, 204–205
Independent Theatre, The, 205
India, 12, 29, 55, 56–60, 61, 96, 340–342
Indian Folk Theatre, 58–60
Inge, William, 302

innamorati, 112
integrated musical, 262, 264
interlude, 90
intermezzi, 110
Into the Woods, 271
ioculatores, 73
Ionesco, Eugene, 313, 332–333
Iron Curtain, 52
Ishara Puppet Theatre Trust, 359
Isis, 48
Islam, 51, 55, 72, 216
Italianate staging, 107–108, 134, 136, 144, 146, 154, 155
Italy, 12, 73, 101, 334–335
It's All Right to Be Woman Theatre, 306

J

Jacobean, 130
James I, 134
Japan, 55, 64–69, 346–348
Jericho House, 361
Jersey Boys, 274, 353
Jesus Christ Superstar, 272
Jet of Blood, 235–236
Jew of Malta, The, 127, 130
Jingqi, 342–343
Jitney, 301
jo, 65
Joe Turner's Come and Gone, 301, 312
John, Elton, 275, 358
Jones, Inigo, 133, 134
Jones, LeRoy, 300
Jones, Robert Edmond, 244, 245, 246
Jones, Sir William, 60
Jonson, Ben, 126, 127, 130
Joseph, Rajiv, 291
Judaism, 48
jukebox musicals, 273–275
Julius Caesar, 128, 202

K

Kabuki, 67–69, 347
Kaifeng, 61
Kalidasa, 59
Kanami, 65
Kathakali King Lear, 360
Kathakali, 58, 340
Kaufman, George, S., 250
Kazan, Elia, 239
Kean, Charles, 173
Kean, Edmund, 171, 173
Kempe, Will, 126, 127, 292
Kennedy, Adrienne, 300
Kern, Jerome, 259, 260, 261, 262
Killigrew, Thomas, 154, 158
King Hedley II, 301
King Lear, 127, 128, 139, 156, 171
King Stag, The, 357
King's Men, 123, 126–127
Kirkwood, Jr., James, 269
Kiss Me, Kate, 259
Kizingo Arts Troupe, 224–225
Knights, The, 24
Korea, 64
koruko, 356
krater, 12
Krishna, 58
Kunqu opera, 61–64
Kushner, Tony, 310, 311–312
Kyd, Thomas, 127, 130
kyogen, 65
kyu, 65

L

LaMaMa Theatre, 363
Laramie Project, The, 310
Latin music drama, 76, 135
Latino/Latina theatre, 310–311
lazzo/lazzi, 112, 115, 150
Lenaia, 18, 23
Lerner, Alan J., 268
Lessing, Gotthold, 194
Let Me Down Easy, 304
Li Xingdao, 62
librettists, 259
Libya, 46, 212, 215
Life is a Dream, 138, 139
Lillo, George, 161
limited runs, 291, 294
Lincoln's Inn Fields, 160
lines of business, 152, 155
Lion King, The, 275, 276, 307, 353, 357–358
Little Night Music, A, 268
little theatres, 244
liturgical drama, 76
liturgy, 74
living newspaper, 240
Living Theatre, The, 295–296
Lloyd, Phyllida, 307
Loesser, Frank, 261, 266
Loewe, Frederick, 268
London Assurance, 182–183
London Merchant or the History of George Barnwell, The, 161
Long Day's Journey into Night, 245–246
Look Back in Anger, 326–327
Lord Admiral's Men, 123, 127
Lord Chamberlain, 205
Lord Chamberlain's Men, 123, 126–127
lord, 72
lords' rooms, 119
"losers' stories," 177
Louis XIII, 143
Louis XIV, 143, 146, 147, 151
Loutherbourg, Phillippe-Jacques, 170, 171, 199, 200
Love's Labour's Lost, 114, 128
Lower Depths, The, 206, 209
ludi, 39
Lugné-Poë, Aurélien-François, 241
Lully, Jean-Baptiste, 150
Luther, Martin, 76, 91, 95
lyricist, 259, 261
Lysistrata Project, The, 18, 316
Lysistrata, 18, 316

M

Ma Rainey's Black Bottom, 301
Mabou Mines, 298–299, 355
Macbeth, 128, 172, 240, 294
MacDermot, Galt, 269
Machado, Eduardo, 310
Machiavelli, Niccolò, 101
machine plays, 146
Mackintosh, Cameron, 273, 353
Macready, William Charles, 132, 171–172
Madea, 303
Madmen and Specialists, 220
Madness of George III, The, 328
Mahabharata, 59
Major Barbara, 250
malaprop, 185
Malina, Judith, 295–296
Mamet, David, 291
Mamma Mia!, 274, 276, 286, 307, 351–353

Man Who Came to Dinner, The, 250
Mandela, Nelson, 215
Mandrake, The, 101
mansions, 76, 85, 87
Mao Tse-Tung, 339
Marat/Sade. See The Persecution and Assassination of Jean-Paul Marat as Performed by the Inmates of the Asylum of Charenton under the Direction of the Marquis de Sade.
Marlowe, Christopher, 126, 127, 130
Martyrdom of St. Appolonia, The, 80
Mary Stuart, 307
masks, 13, 27–28, 32, 45, 49, 60, 90, 125
masques, 132–135
master artwork. *See* gesamtkunstwerk.
Master Harold...and the Boys, 222, 293
master of secrets, 80, 89
Master of the Revels, 215
Mazarin, Cardinal, 143, 145
Measure for Measure, 128, 139, 184
mechane, 27
Medea, 23, 27, 44
medieval. *See* Middle Ages
Mei Lanfang, 342
Meisner, Sanford, 239
melodrama, 23, 30, 165–187, 314
Menaechmi, The, 41–42
Menander, 23, 30, 31, 49, 115
Merchant of Venice, The, 169, 184
Merry Wives of Windsor, The, 114
Metamorphoses, 316
Meyerhold Theatre, 241
Meyerhold, Vsevolod, 234, 241
Middle Ages, 51, 71–93, 117
Middle East, 38–39, 55
Middleton, Thomas, 126
Midsummer Night's Dream, A, 128, 337
Mikado, The, 257
Miller, Arthur, 289–290, 345
mime, 33–34, 39, 46, 47–48, 49, 52, 143, 216, 218
mimi, 73
Ming dynasty, 61
minstrel show, 261
miracle plays, 79
Miranda, Lin-Manuel, 311
Mirren, Helen, 2, 325
Misalliance, 250
Misanthrope, The, 150
Miser, The, 114, 150, 217
Misérables, Les, 271, 272, 273, 353
Miss Saigon, 2, 271, 272–273
Mistero Buffo, 335
modernism, 314
Mojo, 302
Molière, 41, 114, 145, 147–150, 151, 154, 166, 217, 341
monkey music, 65
Monkey: Journey to the West, 359
monopoly, 150, 152, 168, 175
Moon for the Misbegotten, A, 245, 294
morality plays, 79, 91, 135
Moscow Art Theatre, 201, 205–207, 244
Mother Courage and Her Children, 234–235, 322
*Mother******* with the Hat, The*, 291
Mountaintop, The, 294
Mourning Becomes Electra, 245
Movin' Out, 274
Much Ado about Nothing, 63, 127, 128, 184
music hall, 257
musical theatre, 256–277, 282; in Asia, 351–353
musicians' gallery, 121

Muslim, 51, 96, 216
My Fair Lady, 250, 268
mystery plays, 79, 143; York, 78

N

Nathan the Wise, 194
National Centre for Early Music, 78
National Endowment for the Arts, 325
National Theatre of Scotland, 316
national theatres, 320
nationalism, 79
naturalism, 231
nature, 192
Natyasastra, 57–58
Nazi Germany, 252
Nederlander Company and Nederlander New Century, 353
Nemirovich-Danchenko, Vladimir, 205–207
neoclassicism, 2, 97–110, 144–146, 151, 152, 158, 178
Neuber, Carolina, 167
New Globe Theatre, 360
new stagecraft, 243–244
New York Public Library Billy Rose Theatre Collection, 292
Nigeria, 219–220
Nigerian Popular Theatre Alliance, 224
Ninth World Shakespeare Congress, 360
Noah and the Flood, 78
Noh, 65–66, 346
Noises Off, 293, 328
not-for-profit theatre, 282, 286–287, 317
Nottage, Lynn, 302, 306, 307

O

Oberammergau Passion Play, 85–86
Octoroon or Life in Louisiana, The, 183, 184
Odets, Clifford, 239
Oedipus at Colonus, 22
Oedipus Rex, 19, 21, 44, 104, 129
Of Thee I Sing, 260
Off-Broadway, 282
Ogunde, Hubert, 220
Oklahoma!, 238, 260, 262, 265, 267, 275
Oldfield, Anne, 160
One Thousand and One Nights, 217, 359–360
O'Neill, Eugene, 2, 19, 244, 245–247, 314, 321
onkos, 32, 45
Open Theatre, The, 297–298, 357
Opera Wonyosi, 222
opera, 4, 97, 110, 115, 135, 146, 153, 196; comic, 150
operetta, 256, 257
Opium Wars, 339
orchestra, 24, 31
Oresteia, 15
Orestes, 245, 252
Osborne, John, 326–327
Osiris, 16, 226
Othello, 127, 128
Our Town, 247–248

P

pageant wagons, 86–87, 88
pageants, 86–87, 90
Pakistan, 29, 59
Pal Joey, 260, 262
palimpsest manuscripts, 31
Palladio, Andrea, 103
Pantalone, 112
pantomime, 39, 46, 49, 161, 162, 216

Paradise Now, 296
paratheatrical, 4, 7, 8, 43, 46–47, 49, 61, 64–65, 73, 313, 336
Parks, Suzan-Lori, 302, 306, 307
parodoi, 24
partitur, 267
pasos, 138
Passing Strange, 303
passion plays, 79
pastoral, 100
patio, 137
peasants, 73
Peony Pavilion, The, 63–64, 359
performance art, 312, 313–314
periaktoi, 45
Pericles, 13
Perry, Tyler, 303
Persecution and Assassination of Jean-Paul Marat as Performed by the Inmates of the Asylum of Charenton under the Direction of the Marquis de Sade, The, 322–323, 337
Persians, The, 20
perspective, 102–103; false, 103, 104, 134; linear, 102; multi-point, 152; one-point, 102, 108, 134
Phaedra, 2, 44, 245
phallus, 28, 34
Phantom of the Opera, The, 271, 273, 276, 286, 353
Phantom—The Las Vegas Spectacular, 286
Phèdre, 1, 148
Philocetes, 22
photography, early theatre, 187
Piano Lesson, The, 301
pinake, 26
Pinter, Harold, 313, 327, 345
Pirandello, Luigi, 248, 295
Piranesi, Giovanni Battista, 152
Pirates of Penzance, The, 257
Piscator, Erwin, 234
pit, 119
Pittsburgh Cycle, 301
platea, 76, 85, 125
Plautus, 40, 41–42, 49, 100, 115
play doctor, 293
plot, 33
Poel, William, 241
Poetics, 14, 32–33, 43
point of attack, 129
Poland, 139, 335–336
polis or poleis, 12, 28
pomo. *See* postmodernism.
Pompeii, 46, 48–49
poor theatre, 336–337
pop opera, 271–273
popular songs from musicals, 271
Poquelin, Jean-Baptiste. *See* Molière.
Porgy and Bess, 238, 260, 165
Porter, Cole, 259, 260, 261
possession of parts, 152, 155
Post Office, The, 340–341
postmodernism, 233, 248, 300, 302, 312, 314–315, 329, 331, 347, 355, 360
printing press, 95
private theatres, 124
problem play, 186, 199, 207
producer, 169, 173–174
professional theatre, 283–286
Prohibition, 229
Prometheus, 20
prompters, 84
property players, 84
proscenium, 101, 106, 108, 146, 241, 242, 286

protagonist, 24, 65
Provincetown Players or Provincetown Playhouse, 244, 245
psychological realism, 206, 207, 345, 346
Public Theatre (NYC), 269, 363
Public Theatres; England, 119–123; Spain, 136–137
puppets or puppet theatre, 8, 216, 357
Pygmalion, 250

Q
Qing dynasty, 61, 63
queer theatre or queer plays, 309
Quem Queritis, 74–75
Qur'ān, 55, 217

R
Racine, Jean, 1, 19, 147, 148
Radio Golf, 301
raked stage, 108
Rama, 58
Rame, Franca, 334–335
rasa, 57
realism, 199–211, 229–230
realistic melodrama, 176, 180–181
recitative, 271
Recovered Ring, The, 58
Red Detachment of Women, The, 344
reformation, 91, 92, 95
regional theatre, 282
Regularis Concordia, 74
Renaissance, 43, 45, 51–52, 73, 79, 117, 169; in Italy, 94–116
Rent, 287, 310
repertory, 174
Restoration, 154
revenge tragedy, 130
revivals, 285
revolving stage, 68
revue, 257
Rice, Elmer, 247
Rice, Tim, 272, 275, 358
Rich, John, 158
Richard II, 128
Richard III, 127, 128, 170
Richelieu, Cardinal, 143, 146, 188
ritual, 5, 6–7, 216; theory, 14
Rivals, The, 169, 185
"road, the," 174
Robbers, The, 196
Robeson, Paul, 238
Rodgers, Richard, 260, 261, 262
Roman theatre, 34, 37–52, 90, 95, 215
romanticism, 190–199
Romberg, Sigmund, 259, 260
Rome, 73
Romeo and Juliet, 123, 128, 139, 173
Romero, Constanza, 312
Rose Tattoo, The, 288
Rose theatre, The, 121, 122–123, 127
Rosencrantz &Guildenstern are Dead, 293, 329
Rosetta Stone, 226
Roundabout Theatre Company, 286–287
Rover, The, 157
Royal Court Theatre, 220
Royal National Theatre, 1, 325–326, 358
Royal Shakespeare Company, 325–326, 360, 362
royalties, 183–184
Rueda, Lope de, 138
Ruhl, Sarah, 306, 307

Ruined, 306
Russia, 52; Russian Revolution, 207
Rwanda, 225, 227

S
Sabbioneta Theatre, 105
Saint Mary's Abbey, 73, 83
Sanskrit drama, 56
Sartre, Jean-Paul, 204, 252, 321
sarugaku, 65
satyr play, 13, 18, 100
scaffolds, 85
Scala, Flaminio, 111
Scamozzi, Vincenzo, 104
scanae frons, 104
scenario, 111, 112
scene house, 24
Schiller, Friedrich von, 196
School for Scandal, The, 173, 185
School for Wives, The, 150
Scribe, Eugène, 186
Seagull, The, 207
Second Shepherd's Play, The, 79, 81
secular drama, 90–91
secularism, 95
selective realism, 239
Seneca, 2, 40, 44–45, 100
sententiae, 44
sentimentalism, 151, 160, 197
sentimentality, 177
sentiments, 161
Serlio, Sebastiano, 103, 107–108
Servant of Two Masters, The, 114
Seven against Thebes, 20
Seven Guitars, 301
shadow puppet, 56, 216
Shakespeare, William, 19, 41, 63, 84, 114, 118, 127–130, 143, 151, 154, 156, 158, 159, 166, 169, 172, 173, 184, 193–194, 196, 203, 219, 286, 360; German translations, 132; legacy, 131–132; theme park, 362–363
Shakuntala, 58, 59, 60, 64
Shange, Ntozake, 298, 302
sharing companies, 114, 125–126, 150
Shaw, George Bernard, 204, 219, 250
She Stoops To Conquer, 185
Shelley, Mary, 190, 191
Shepard, Sam, 291, 294
Sheridan, Richard Brinsley, 169, 185
Sherwood, Robert, 238
shingeki, 346
shite, 65
Show Boat, 259, 261, 262, 268
showboats, 174
Shrek the Musical, 275, 284
Shuffle Along, 264–265
Shun dynasty, 61
shutter, 108, 134, 155
signature music, 179
Signature Theatre, 300, 311
Silk Road, 60
Simon, Neil, 293
Simonson, Lee, 244, 248
simultaneous staging, 76, 117, 143
Sisters Rosensweig, The, 293
Six Characters in Search of an Author, 248
skene, 24, 31
Skin of Our Teeth, The, 248
slice of life, 201
Smith, Anna Deavere, 302, 303–304
socialist realism, 252, 344
Socrates, 22, 27

Sondheim, Stephen, 268, 270-271, 299
song forms, 266-267
Sophocles, 19, 21-22, 80, 95, 100
Sound of Music, The, 260
South Africa, 215, 222
South Pacific, 264, 266, 275
Soviet Union, 52, 320
Soyinka, Wole, 19, 220-222
Spain, 12, 72, 320; golden age of, 135-140
Spanish Tragedy, The, 130
Sparta, 12, 29
spectacle, 33, 100, 179
Spider-Man: Turn Off the Dark, 275, 284, 307, 358
Spring Awakening (musical), 299
stage directions, 75
staging, fixed or movable, 84-85
Stalin, Joseph, 242, 335
Stanislavski, Konstantin, 205-207, 239, 242, 345, 346
star system, 173-174
stereotype, 177
stock types, 179
Stoppard, Tom, 293, 310, 329-330, 364
storm and stress. *See* sturm und drang.
storytelling, 8; storytelling theory, 15
Stowe, Harriet Beecher, 181, 343
Strasberg, Lee, 239
Stratford Shakespeare Festival, 286
Stratford-upon-Avon, 127
street theatre, 295
Street, Peter, 122-123
Streetcar Named Desire, A, 288, 289, 355-356
Streets of New York, The, 178
Strindberg, August, 203
striptease, 257
Stroman, Susan, 307
Stuart kings and theatre, 130-131
Stuart, Mary, 118
Sturm und Drang, 194-195
Styne, Jule, 266, 268
subplots, 129
Sullivan, Arthur, 257
Summer and Smoke, 282, 288
Sun King, 143, 147
sung-through musical, 271-273
Suppliants, The, 20, 23
surrealism, 231-232, 313
Swan Theatre drawing, 120
Sweeney Todd, 268, 271. 299
symbolism, 207, 231, 241, 243

T

Tagore, Rabindranath, 340-341
Tairov, Alexander, 241
Talma, François Joseph, 171
Tamburlaine, 127, 130
Tango Palace, 311
Tarleton, Richard, 126
Tartuffe, 149, 150
Taylor, Royal, 169
Taymor, Julie, 275, 284, 307, 357-358
Teatro Farnese, 105-106
Teatro Olimpico, 103-104
Tectonic Theatre Project, 310
tennis courts, 144, 146, 154, 160
Terence, 40, 42-43, 49, 74, 100, 115
terrorism, 280-281
Terry, Ellen, 172-173
Theatre and Its Double, The, 236
Théâtre Antoine, 204
theatre as plague, 237
Theatre Communications Group, 286

Theatre d'Art, 241
Theatre de l'Oeuvre, 241
theatre for development, 224-227
Theatre Guild, The, 238, 245
theatre of cruelty, 235-237
Theatre on Film and Tape Archive, 292
Theatre Royal, Covent Garden, 166
Theatre Royal, Drury Lane. *See* Drury Lane theatre.
Theatre Tales for Performance, 111
Theatre, The, 118, 127
theatre; definition, 4-8
Théâtre-Libre, 203
theatrical syndicate, 175
theatron, 24
Thespis, 20
Thompson, Lydia, 257
Three Penny Opera, The, 222, 235, 275
Three Sisters, The, 201, 207
thrust stages, 119, 136, 241, 286
ticket prices, 284-285
Tidswell, Miss Charlotte, 171
tiring house, 120
Titus Andronicus, 194
Toilet, The, 300
Tolstoy, Leo, 203
tomming, 181
Top Girls, 293
TopDog/Underdog, 306, 307
Torelli, Giacomo, 109-110, 145
totalitarian countries and theatre, 132, 252
touring, 174
tragedy, 99, 157; domestic, 161; Greek, 52, 290; middle-class, 161; Roman, 39
transformation, 162, 297
trap door, 68, 89, 120, 136, 137
Trojan Women, The, 22, 23
trope, 74
trusts. *See* monopoly.
Turgenev, Ivan, 203
Twelfth Night, 128, 184
Twilight: Los Angeles, 304, 305
Twins, The. See The Menaechmi.
Two Noble Kinsmen, The, 131
Two Trains Running, 301
twofold purpose, 98, 99

U

Uncle Tom's Cabin, 181-183, 343
Uncle Vanya, 207
Uncommon Women and Others, 306
unconcious, 200
Under the Gaslight, 176
unions, 175, 253
United Company, 160
United States, theatre starts, 168
unities, three, 98, 99
University Wits, 127
urban theatre, 303
usury, 78
utility players, 152

V

Valenciennes, France, 87
Vampire, The, 183
vanishing point, 102
vaudeville, 253, 257
Vega, Lope de, 138
Verfremdungseffekt, 233
verisimilitude, 97, 98
Verona, Italy, 48
Versailles, 146

Vieux Colombier, 241, 242
View from the Bridge, The, 290
Virgil, 158
Visit, The, 333-334
Vitruvius, 43, 102-103
Vogel, Paula, 307, 308
Voltaire, 151
"Voodoo Macbeth," 240

W

Wagner, Richard, 198-199
Waiting for Godot, 333-334
Waiting for Lefty, 239
Wakefield Cycle, 81
waki, 65
Walker, Alice, 302
Walnut Street Theatre, 169
War Horse, 293, 326, 358-359
Ward, Douglas Turner, 302
Wasps, The, 147
Wasserstein, Wendy, 293, 306
Way of the World, The, 156, 160
Weavers, The, 209
Webber, Andrew Lloyd, 271-272
Webster, John, 130-131
Wedekind, Frank, 299
Weigle, Helene, 235
Weill, Kurt, 235, 322
Weiss, Peter, 322-323
Welles, Orson, 240
well-made play, 186
Werner, 196
West End, 334
West Side Story, 268
Who's Afraid of Virginia Woolf?, 238, 284, 291
Wild West Show, 182
Wilde, Oscar, 174, 181, 186-187, 204, 309
Wilder, Thornton, 247-248, 321
William Tell, 172, 196
Williams, Tennessee, 282, 286-287, 300, 302, 309, 315, 355
Wilson, August, 301, 302, 312
wings, 108, 155
Wolfe, George C., 312
Woman's Festival, The, 24
Women Generals of the Yang Family, 344-345
women performers, 34, 47, 58, 67, 83, 136, 150, 154, 158, 346
women playwrights, 74, 157
Women's Interart, 305
women's movement, 279-280
women's theatre, 304-307
Works Progress Administration, 240
Would-be Gentleman, The, 150, 151
Wycherley, William, 156

Y

yard, 119
York Mystery Plays, 83
Yoruba, 219-220

Z

zanni, 112, 113
Zeami, 65
Zen Buddhism, 65
Zeus, 38
Zhang Fei, 63
Ziegfeld Follies, 257, 264
Zimmerman, Mary, 316
Zoo Story, The, 290

Credits

Photo Credits

p. 2, © Geraint Lewis/Alamy; p. 5, © Goran Bogicevic/Fotolia; p. 15, courtesy Guthrie Theatre; p. 18, courtesy of Theatre South Carolina; p.20, Courtesy Guthrie Theatre; p. 46, Kev Harrison/Fotolia; p. 56, © Pavel_A/Fotolia; p. 64, CAMERA PRESS/James Veysey/Redux; p. 73, York Mystery Plays Archive, the National Centre for Early Music, St Margaret's, Off Walmgate, York, Yo1 9TK, UK; p. 78, York Mystery Plays Archive, the National Centre for Early Music, St Margaret's, Off Walmgate, York, Yo1 9TK, UK ;p. 83, York Mystery Plays Archive, the National Centre for Early Music, St Margaret's, Off Walmgate, York, Yo1 9TK, UK; p. 108, from the archives of the Duke of Devonshire; p. 124, photo by Tommy Thompson, John Hurrell in Shakespeare's *Henry V*, 2011), courtesy of the American Shakespeare Center; p. 128, courtesy Robert Reinecke; p. 133 (from the archives of the Duke of Devonshire); p. 137, from *The Reconstruction of a Spanish Global Playhouse*; p. 191, © Geraint Lewis/Alamy; p. 215, Igor Janicek/Shutterstock; p. 219, © tomalu/Fotolia; p. 263, Joan Marcus; p. 265, photography by Joan Marcus courtesy Mead Center for American Theatre; p. 296, PERRUCCI/Contrasto/Redux; p. 301, *Gem of the Ocean*, 2007–8 production in the Fifth Floor Theatre, directed by Benny Sato Ambush, scenery by Sara Walsh, costumes by Jennifer Nweke, Lighting by Zack Brown); p. 307, *Clean House*, a 2008–9 production in the Atlas Theatre, directed by Giovanna Sardelli, scenery by Jason Simms, Costumes by Malgosia Turzanska, lighting by Greg Goff); p. 335, Giorgio Lotti/contrasto/Redux; p. 339, Dorling Kindersley; p. 343, Colin Sinclair © Dorling Kindersley; p. 347, Japanese Society/William Irving; p. 350, Jonathan Smith/Rough Guides Dorling Kindersley; p. 353, Ruby Washington/New York Times/Redux Pictures; p. 361, A scene from the Utah Shakespeare Festival. (Photo by Karl Hugh. Copyright Utah Shakespeare Festival 2012.); p. 362, Utah Shakespeare Festival; p. 363, Photo courtesy of Andrew Caldwell.

The drawings on the following pages have been colored to enhance detail: 82, 89, 152, 162, 169, 174, 244, 292.